Taking Care of Today and Tomorrow

A Resource Guide for Health, Aging and Long-Term Care

By George J. Pfeiffer

Introduction by Donald M. Vickery, M.D., Co-author of the 4 million-copy bestseller, _Take Care of Yourself_

Here's the Book You've Been Waiting for:

- _Assess your LifeSkills. Find out how to become active, look better, live longer._

- _Learn about the prevention, diagnosis and treatment of adulthood's common, chronic ailments._

- _Identify resources to help care for an elderly parent or loved one._

Discover the Physical, Financial and Emotional Benefits of Taking Care of Today and Tomorrow

Taking Care of Today and Tomorrow

A Resource Guide For Health, Aging and Long-Term Care

by George J. Pfeiffer

Introduction
by Donald M. Vickery, M.D.

The Center for Corporate Health Promotion
Reston, Virginia

Copyright © 1989 by The Center for Corporate Health Promotion
1850 Centennial Park Drive
Suite 520
Reston, Virginia 22091

Cover design: Graphic Works
Text design: Chronicle Type and Design
Photography: Mitchell Booth, Jeff Yardis
Printing: R. R. Donnelly & Sons Company
Product Manager: Elin V. Silveous

Printed in the United States of America.
Library of Congress Catalog Card Number: 87-071285
ISBN 0-9616506-1-3
First Edition
Second Printing

Author's Note: The Center for Corporate Health Promotion, publisher of this book, continually strives to improve its products. Please help us by completing and returning the brief questionnaire in the back of this book. Many thanks for your time and interest.

To Our Readers

In planning this book, it was our design to provide our readers with a resource guide that would span four key content areas:

1. The processes of aging;
2. Lifestyle behaviors (LifeSkills) that contribute to health and longevity;
3. Chronic ailments that are common in older adults but, for some, are precipitated in early adulthood; and
4. The realities and complexities of long-term care.

Because of the book's comprehensive nature, it may at first seem overwhelming. However, *Taking Care of Today and Tomorrow* is not intended to be read from cover to cover. Rather, we encourage you to access the information that applies to your special needs and interests.

First, it's recommended that you read the general introduction, "Riding the Age Wave," and Section I, Chapter One, "Facts on Aging," in order to familiarize yourself with the basic issues and concepts. Next, Chapter Two, "How Are Your LifeSkills?" will help you evaluate your current knowledge and behaviors related to aging. Within the LifeSkills Inventory worksheet, a self-evaluation questionnaire, you will find a corresponding page number for each question. This quick reference feature will help you locate the information you need more easily within the text. For example, you may find that your level of physical activity is below par. The LifeSkills Inventory would advise you to reference Section II, Chapter One, "Stay Active," and Chapter Fifteen, "Use a Self-Management Plan," to learn the guiding principles of physical activity and how to incorporate exercise into your schedule.

There are other ways to use this book. For instance, if you had a relative unfortunately afflicted with Alzheimer's disease, and you wanted to understand more about this condition and its long-term care implications, you would refer to Section III, Chapter One, "Alzheimer's Disease," and Section IV, "Preparing for Long-Term Care," to be better prepared to deal with this catastrophic illness.

In closing, if *Taking Care of Today and Tomorrow* can help you or a family member become a little healthier, or help ease the burden of long-term care, then this book has met its objectives.   G.J.P.

Acknowledgments

Writing and producing a book can be a frustrating and humbling experience. After two false starts and almost two years of trying to find the right mix on such broad and complex subjects as aging and long-term care, I'm happy to present *Taking Care of Today and Tomorrow*. This book is the product of many dedicated people to whom I will be forever grateful.

First, I would like to thank Elin Silveous, who as project manager, had the patience of a saint, the motivation of a coach and a critical eye for detail.

I would like to thank our editorial team, which deciphered rough outlines and endless rewrites to help produce a manuscript that is readable and sensitive to the issues of aging: Jane Stein, Pat Warden, Con Dwyer and Lydia Schindler. Special gratitude goes to Catherine Reef who spearheaded the editorial effort and without whose research and writing a manuscript could not have been produced.

Next, I would like to salute Catalina McChesney, Joanne Bulka and Karen Misencik for document preparation. They tolerated endless drafts and sometimes needed the Rosetta Stone to translate my handwriting.

Finally, I would like to thank the following individuals who served as either content experts, final reviewers or sources of inspiration. I'm deeply indebted to: Donald M. Vickery, M.D., the Center for Corporate Health Promotion; Georgina Lucas and Joyce Ruddock, The Travelers Older Americans Program; Ken Dychtwald, Ph.D., Age Wave Inc.; Martha Holstein, American Society on Aging; Sara Harris and Raymond Harris, M.D., Center for the Study of Aging; William Baun; Alan Ryan, M.D.; Kenneth Pelletier, Ph.D.; Paul Brown, Loudoun County, VA, Area Agency on Aging; Judith Webster, R.N.; Diana Villalopos, R.N.; Carolyn Staub; Anne Fainsinger; Deborah Warren; Marc Michaelson; Terry Freedman; Joan Reynolds; Lois Reynolds; Barbara Skolnick; Robert Wilson; Lynn Schenck and Michael Manley of The Travelers Managed Care Program; Michael Pfeiffer, D.D.S.; George Sheehan, M.D.; Allen Douma, M.D.; James Otis, Thomas Golaszewski, Ed.D., Heather King, Drew Clearie, Charles Estey, Wendy Lynch, Ph.D., Cat Taylor, Craig Russell, and the rest of my colleagues and staff at the Center for Corporate Health Promotion.

Contents

Contents

INTRODUCTION

Riding the Age Wave

The 65-and-older age group is one of the fastest growing segments of our population, already accounting for 12 percent of American society. And as the 76 million "baby boomers" (those born between 1946 and 1964) grow older, we can project that by the middle of the 21st century, people over age 65 will constitute one-fourth of the population.

This is a book about aging and the aged.

It is about you and your parents.

It is about the triumphs and opportunities that are as inevitable as the challenges and problems of growing older.

When 76 million people leave the middle-adult ranks and join the already growing population over age 65, sweeping social changes will result. Our attitudes, social priorities, educational emphasis, careers, health care, retirement and legislation all will be affected. What psychologist and gerontologist Ken Dychtwald, Ph.D., has labeled the "age wave" is already touching shore.

Here are some of the trends we can look for:

- An increasing medical emphasis on geriatrics—the care of the elderly.
- Expanded options for home care.
- Healthier older people.
- New ways to finance health care.
- Research focused on the immune response.
- New treatments for debilitating diseases.
- New tools to diagnose the major "killers."
- Innovative housing options for older people.
- Increased political clout. Already a powerful force, the 65-plus population will exert even more influence as their numbers increase.

- A changed work force. As people live longer, careers will lengthen; second and even third careers will emerge. Already seniors are recruited for professions that are labor-short because of a limited youth pool.
- Expanded educational opportunities. Older people have returned to school, some to take courses, some to teach, some to learn new skills, and others to get degrees.

Despite these prospects, we may fear growing old. We may be watching a parent struggle with a chronic disease, or simply succumbing to fear of the unknown based on myths and stereotypes.

A decade ago, older people were rarely seen or heard on television. If the story line of a sit-com called for an older person, he or she was apt to be portrayed as an irascible old curmudgeon. But as their numbers have soared, the elderly have begun to catch the reluctant eye of the advertising industry. Now, attractive older models are beginning to show up in fashion spreads and cruise-ship commercials, although more can still be seen promoting arthritis medicines, false teeth, disposable adult undergarments or hearing aids—perhaps skewing our picture of aging.

Engineering Your Own Future

Aging is "inevitable," but scientific breakthroughs have taught us that we can influence the effect it will have—for good or for ill—upon us. You can make a difference in the way you age by taking responsibility for the area in your life that you have most control over, namely, your lifestyle. This book is designed to give working people, baby boomers and non-boomers alike, a basic understanding of the various processes of aging and to provide guidelines to help you remain vibrant and independent throughout life. This understanding is essential for you and for older individuals who may depend on you for care.

One important key to a healthy older life is applying knowledge and skills necessary for a responsible lifestyle. *Taking Care of Today and Tomorrow* provides that kind of knowledge. Each section of this book contains information you need if you are to make the best decisions and get the most out of your adult life.

- **Section I: Are You Aging Successfully?** This section provides an overview of the aging process, outlining common physical changes, social and psychological milestones, and the impact of the movement toward a more healthful lifestyle and appropriate medical self-care.

Successful aging is highly dependent upon a number of lifestyle factors that can either contribute to or detract from your chances of living a long and healthy life. The LifeSkills Inventory in this section will help you evaluate your current lifestyle practices, such as physical activity and nutrition, and your understanding of aging-related issues like chronic ailments and long-term care. Based on this quiz, you can gauge the knowledge and skills you may need to improve your chances of living a healthier, longer life.

• **Section II: Developing Your LifeSkills.** This section outlines strategies you can implement **at any age** to give you the best chance for a healthy middle and old age: exercise, attention to diet, stress management, social and mental activity, financial planning, medical consumerism and other appropriate Life-Skills.

• **Section III: Common Chronic Ailments of Older People.** Certain chronic diseases, such as coronary artery disease, occur more often in older people than in the young. Risk factors such as high blood cholesterol or high blood pressure, however, can start to show up as early as the 20s, when there's still time to check or moderate chronic disorders. This section explains the causes, symptoms, treatment and management of common ailments and outlines steps you can take now to prevent their occurrence.

• **Section IV: Preparing for Long-Term Care.** Overseeing the health of their parents or other family members is a responsibility that many adults are likely to face. A parent may require long-term care, so it is important to be prepared—to have some knowledge of the status of your parents' health and the financial, legal and practical concerns that may arise. This section is your primer for long-term care guidelines, so that you can help your parents remain as independent as possible.

It's a fact that more than 80 percent of caregivers are family members, most often women—wives, daughters or daughters-in-law. One of the realities of long-term care is that the caregiver may suffer emotional, physical, financial or social hardship as a result of caring for an aging relative. This section also contains strategies for coping and, equally important if you are the caregiver, taking care of yourself!

First, however, there are **feelings** that you should think about.

Will There Be a Way to Avoid Generational Tensions?

As a growing number of people grapple with such mixed feelings, tensions grow. It's crucial not to succumb to stereotypical images of the older generation. Moreover, it's important to avoid letting the myths become self-fulfilling prophecies.

Some grown children **will** resent parental encroachment on their leisure and retirement plans.

Their jobs may make full-time care impossible or even the most minimal care inconvenient. Much depends on the kind of relationship they have enjoyed with their parents throughout life. If there are tensions, they will increase. If not, then tension can come from concern. Some children may not be able to take care of their parents; others may not have to do so. Still others will expect the "system" to care for Mom and Dad. Many Americans believe that Medicare will cover the financial costs of long-term care, but unfortunately it does not now do so.

A generation gap, if it occurs, is apt to be rooted in misconceptions about aging, stereotypical images of older people, and conflicting expectations for older life. Do you consider yourself free from such misunderstanding? The following quiz, developed by the National Institute on Aging, allows you to compare your images of aging with reality.

What's Your Aging I.Q.?

TRUE OR FALSE

T	F	
☐	☐	1. Everyone becomes "senile" sooner or later, if he or she lives long enough.
☐	☐	2. American families have by and large abandoned their older members.
☐	☐	3. Depression is a serious problem for older people.
☐	☐	4. The numbers of older people are growing.
☐	☐	5. The vast majority of older people are self-sufficient.
☐	☐	6. Confusion is an inevitable, incurable consequence of old age.
☐	☐	7. Intelligence declines with age.
☐	☐	8. Sexual urges and activity normally cease around age 55 or 60.
☐	☐	9. If a person has been smoking for 30 or 40 years, it does no good to quit.
☐	☐	10. Older people should stop exercising.
☐	☐	11. As you grow older, you need more vitamins and minerals to stay healthy.
☐	☐	12. Only children need to be concerned about calcium for strong bones and teeth.
☐	☐	13. Extremes of heat and cold can be particularly dangerous to older people.
☐	☐	14. Many older people are hurt in accidents that could have been prevented.
☐	☐	15. More men than women survive to old age.
☐	☐	16. Deaths from stroke and heart disease are declining.

☐ ☐ 17. Older people, on the average, take more medications than younger people.

☐ ☐ 18. Snake-oil salesmen are as common today as they were on the frontier.

☐ ☐ 19. Personality changes with age, just like hair color and skin texture.

☐ ☐ 20. Sight declines with age.

ANSWERS:

1. **False.** Even among those who live to be 80 or older, only 20 percent to 25 percent develop Alzheimer's disease or some other incurable form of brain disease. "Senility" is a meaningless term that should be discarded.

2. **False.** The American family is still the number-one caregiver of older Americans. Most older people live close to their children and see them often; many live with their spouses. In all, eight out of 10 men and six out of 10 women live in family settings.

3. **True.** Depression, loss of self-esteem, loneliness and anxiety can become more common as older people face retirement, the deaths of relatives and friends, and other such crises—often at the same time. Fortunately, most depression is treatable.

4. **True.** Today, 12 percent of Americans are 65 or older. By the year 2030, one in five people will be over 65 years of age.

5. **True.** At any one time, only 5 percent of the older population live in nursing homes; the rest are basically healthy and self-sufficient.

6. **False.** Confusion and serious forgetfulness in old age can be caused by Alzheimer's disease or other conditions that irreparably damage the brain, but some 100 other problems can cause the same symptoms. A minor head injury, a high fever, poor nutrition, adverse reactions to medications and depression can all be treated, and the confusion they cause will be alleviated.

7. **False.** Intelligence *per se* does not decline without reason. Most people maintain their intellect or improve as they grow older.

8. **False.** Most older people can lead an active, satisfying sex life.

9. **False.** Stopping smoking at any age not only reduces the risk of cancer and heart disease, it also leads to healthier lungs.

10. **False.** Many older people enjoy—and benefit from—exercises such as walking, swimming and bicycle riding. Exercise at any age can help strengthen the heart and lungs, lower blood pressure, and increase muscle and bone mass.

11. **False.** Although certain requirements, such as that for "sunshine" vitamin D, may increase slightly with age, older people need the same amounts of most vitamins and minerals as younger people. Older people in particular should eat nutritious food and cut down on sweets, salty snack foods, high-calorie drinks, fats and alcohol.

12. **False.** Older people require fewer calories, but adequate intake of calcium for strong bones can become more important as you grow older. This is particularly true for women, whose risk of osteoporosis increases after menopause. Milk and cheese are rich in calcium, as are cooked dried beans, collards and broccoli. Some people need calcium supplements as well.

13. **True.** The body's thermostat tends to function less efficiently with age, and the older person's body may be less able to adapt to heat or cold.

14. **True.** A disproportionate number of older adults suffer accidents due primarily to falls and fires, which can be prevented in most cases.

15. **False.** Women tend to outlive men by an average of seven years. There are 150 women for every 100 men over age 65, and nearly 250 women for every 100 men over 85.

16. **True.** Fewer men and women are dying of stroke or heart disease. This has been a major factor in the increase in life expectancy.

17. **True.** The elderly consume 25 percent of all medications and, as a result, have many more problems with adverse drug reactions.

18. **True.** Medical quackery is a $10 billion business in the United States. People of all ages are commonly duped into "quick cures" for aging, arthritis and cancer.

19. **False.** Personality doesn't change with age. Therefore, all old people can't be described as rigid or cantankerous. You are what you are for as long as you live.

20. **False.** Serious vision problems, such as cataracts and glaucoma, are not natural aspects of aging. However, most older

adults will experience a decline in the ability to focus on close objects, which is called presbyopia.

Is It Right to Categorize Older People?

If you are like most Americans, this brief test made you aware of some misconceptions about aging. These misconceptions and the acceptance of inaccurate stereotypes do a disservice to you as well as the elderly.

According to Alan Pifer, president emeritus and senior consultant to the Carnegie Corporation of New York, "A person past 65 **may** be over the hill and **may** be poor. Some are. But for the great majority of this group, the stereotype is obsolete and inappropriate. The conferring of veteranship on them is patronizing and demeaning—and certainly unwarranted. They regard themselves—and are—little different from other Americans generally, except that they have more years of experience to their credit."

It's unfortunate that people who wouldn't think of prejudging others on the basis of race, ethnicity or religion hold strong preconceived notions about age—perhaps because aging is an unpleasant topic, one that they don't want to think about. However, prejudice can create a barrier.

The truth is that aging is not a curse. It is a natural process, and the older years can be a deeply rewarding time of life. Aging is something **you** are experiencing even if you are unaware of it.

Whether new generational tensions arise remains to be seen. But **you** can minimize problems in your own family and make the most of **your** older years by dealing with misconceptions. Here's how:

- Learn to understand the processes of aging—what they are, and what they are not.
- Adopt a lifestyle that decreases risks to your health, maintains vigor and helps you age successfully.
- Learn about chronic disorders, so that you can minimize your risk and feel comfortable and competent advising an afflicted relative.
- Become sensitive to the issues of the older generation, especially in the areas of long-term care. Aging is universal. What you learn from sharing your parents' or relatives' experience may very well affect your own future.

You don't have to live very long to realize that every age brings its own special joys. Experience and wisdom, both products of time, increase your capacity for enjoyment throughout life.

Growth is a lifelong process; it needn't stop at age 65 or even age 85. If you learn how to make the most of your older years, you're likely to find that life keeps getting better all the time.

Donald M. Vickery, M.D.
Reston, Virginia

Section I

Are You Aging Successfully?

INTRODUCTION

Are You Aging Successfully?

In 1900, the average life expectancy in the United States was 47 years of age. Today, the average life expectancy is 75. Men average 71.4 years, and women, 78.4 years.

This significant increase in average life expectancy—a gain of about three years per decade—is primarily attributed to reductions in infant mortality and premature death from infectious diseases and accidents. For example, the implementation of public health measures that cleaned our water and air, the introduction of vaccines and antibiotics, and healthier lifestyle practices have all contributed to increasing our life expectancy over this century.

Life expectancy, however, should not be confused with maximum life-span, or what some experts term maximum life potential. Life expectancy takes into consideration such factors as sex, infant mortality, disease, war, famine and accidents on the average survival of a specific group within a given population.

Maximum life-span, on the other hand, reflects the oldest age a **species** can attain if free of disease and accidents. The maximum life-span for the human species—unchanged for thousands of years—is estimated to be 115 years.

Many experts believe that a significant proportion of our society could move closer to our estimated life-span through specific "life-extension" strategies. For instance, within this century, 28 years have been added to our life expectancy. Yet there is still a 40-year difference between our average life expectancy of 75 years and our estimated human potential of 115 years. While we may not live to be 115, the numbers indicate that we have significant potential to extend our lives past our present average life expectancy. Testimony to this is the fact that the 85-and-older age group is the fastest growing segment of our population.

The Power of Lifestyle: Can We Live to Be 115?

To an extent, successful aging means postponing death for as long as possible while living life fully. Within this definition, not only is quantity important—total years lived—but **quality** as well—being active and alert, living a life filled with meaning rather than significantly disabled and dependent on others.

According to Donald M. Vickery, M.D., author of *LifePlan for Your Health* and an acknowledged expert on medical self-care, "Physicians like to say that the patient's objective is to live a long time—but die young."

Vickery continues, "Successful aging means living as long as possible, with vigor and independence, with minimal disability and loss of function. However, the patient needs to believe that it's not the miracles of modern medicine that will extend his life; rather, life extension lies in well-known lifestyle precepts: not smoking, exercising regularly, eating right and using alcohol in moderation. Though unspectacular and perhaps lacking the mystique of the 'magic pill'—the **power of lifestyle** is the best medicine for a long and productive life."

The power of lifestyle is further substantiated by the national Centers for Disease Control's identification of four key factors that influence an individual's chances of living to age 65.

As the following chart illustrates, lifestyle is the key factor influencing a person's survival, followed by environment, heredity and finally the medical care system.

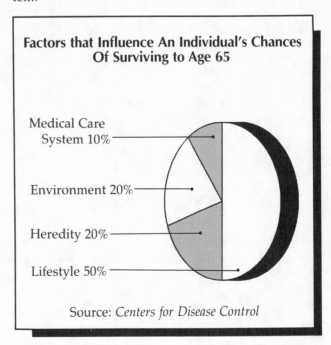

Factors that Influence An Individual's Chances Of Surviving to Age 65

Medical Care System 10%

Environment 20%

Heredity 20%

Lifestyle 50%

Source: *Centers for Disease Control*

It's interesting to note that the medical care system has a limited influence on survival. Yet our society is fixated on a discipline based on illness and disease rather than prevention. An inordinate amount of resources is spent "after the damage has been done." Though medicine has its definitive place in the continuum of care, there needs to be a realization that prevention is the best strategy for postponing the onset of chronic disease and other aging processes until much later in life. This allows people to be more active, more productive and less dependent upon the medical care system. In contrast, people who practice poor health habits, such as heavy smoking, are more likely to experience the onset of chronic diseases, such as emphysema, at a much earlier age. People who overlook lifestyle as a significant life-extender are far more likely, in their later years, to depend more on the medical care system and to have their quality of life severely affected.

This "pay me now or pay me later" scenario parallels what James Fries, M.D., and Lawrence Crapo, M.D., call the "compression of morbidity."

They have hypothesized that if, as a society, we were to embrace an aggressive prevention strategy, the onset of disease (morbidity) would be delayed to a later stage in the life-span. This compression would allow more people to be active, productive and less dependent upon the medical care system for an extended period. Finally, a greater percentage of people would survive past our current life expectancy and approach our estimated life-span.

Though this is only a theory, there are indications that the onset of some chronic disorders has been delayed or prevented. For instance, there have been significant decreases in mortality from heart disease and stroke over the past 20 years. Also, according to the National Center for Health Statistics, the average age at which first heart attacks occur has been extended by four years.

The bottom line is that successful aging has a lot to do with thoughtful lifestyle planning and management. Therefore, the sixty-four-thousand-dollar question is not: How long do you want to live? But rather: How long are you **planning** to live?

This section explores two areas essential for successful aging. Discussed first are common myths about the aging process—what aging really is and what it is not—and how they can be influenced. Secondly, you are given the opportunity to begin planning for successful aging by taking an inventory of your LifeSkills, those areas that have the greatest influence on improving your health and longevity.

CHAPTER ONE

Facts on Aging

Have you ever wondered what it's like to be "old"? You can find out how it feels to be a sedentary 75-year-old, regardless of your age. You only need to go to bed for a couple weeks.

- You'll lose both muscle tone and bone mass, and may develop anemia.
- You could become depressed and forgetful, or even have difficulty completing simple mental tasks.
- You'll lack endurance and be generally weak.

In short, you will display many of the characteristics we usually associate with inactive older people.

But are these characteristics natural and inevitable? Experts tell us they're not, that they are the byproducts of disuse. And although they are more common in older people, they can appear in younger, inactive adults as well. In the older population, they form what Robert N. Butler, M.D., labels a facade, masking aging's true attributes.

But if aging is not synonymous with decline, then how should it be defined? Butler, a specialist in geriatrics and adult development at Mt. Sinai Medical Center in New York, views aging as a "process or more precisely a series of processes of human development."

What Is "Natural" Aging?

As researchers learn more about older life, they are discovering that any physiological and mental deterioration that is a **natural** part of aging is minimal. The good news for adults of all ages is that even this minimal deterioration can be reduced and its timetable delayed through effective self-care. Moreover, as Butler reminds us, a positive component of aging is psy-

chological **growth**: development of "the capacities for sagacity, prudence, [and] wisdom, based on seasoning and experience."

One reason aging's negative facade has persisted is that many researchers on aging have approached their work with what may be a faulty assumption—that any decline observed in older people who were free of disease could be considered part of the natural aging process.

John W. Rowe, M.D., and Robert L. Kahn, M.D., have observed that this assumption ignores the effects of diet, exercise, personal habits and psychosocial factors. As a result, the role of age in decline has been overemphasized. Also, this assumption does not account for those individuals who show little or no decline, who, say Rowe and Kahn, exemplify what aging can and should be.

In an article in *Science*, Rowe and Kahn suggest that a distinction be made between **usual** aging and **successful** aging. What is considered "usual" or "average" in our culture might not be normal; and those who have aged "successfully," who demonstrate little, if any, decline in health and ability, are more likely to represent the normal aging process.

Rowe and Kahn cite a number of studies that demonstrate how lifestyle factors, rather than aging itself, contribute to decline. For example, a progressive loss of the body's ability to utilize glucose traditionally was considered a "normal" part of aging. But when researchers looked at the effects of exercise, diet and medication on glucose intolerance, aging's true role was found to be minimal.

Osteoporosis, the progressive loss of bone density that can result in fractures, is another condition attributed to aging. But now we know that there are a number of ways to prevent or reduce the risk—regular exercise, no cigarette smoking, moderate or no alcohol use, adequate calcium intake and estrogen replacement therapy.

Moreover, there are psychosocial factors that have been shown to contribute to successful aging, such things as:

- Feelings of autonomy and control—the ability to make decisions about how life will be lived. Lack of control and the stress that goes with it adversely affect a person's emotional state, physical well-being and performance. Therefore, it is healthier for the aging to make their own decisions than to let others take control.
- Social support. Being part of a network of family and friends helps people live longer.

In societies where successful aging is the norm, we find valuable clues. Kenneth R. Pelletier, Ph.D., a specialist in aging research, has identified seven "common denominators" among cultures with reported high populations of *centenarians*—persons age 100 or more. These include the Vilcambras of Ecuador, the Hunza people of the western Himalayas, and the Abkhazians of the Soviet Union. Though there has been much dispute within the scientific community that these "centenarian communities" truly exist, the fact remains that they do include large elder populations, which share some common traits:

1. **Hereditary or genetic influences.** How well we "select our parents" undoubtedly plays a significant role in influencing our susceptibility to chronic disease (i.e., heart disease) and therefore longevity. How much remains to be seen.

    Genetic research will continue to be in the forefront of unlocking the mysteries of aging. For example, Japanese scientists recently have isolated what they believe are "longevity genes."

2. **Dietary and nutritional factors.** The diet in these regions is often low in animal fat and high in vegetables and whole grains. Calorie consumption is far lower than the U.S. average.

3. **Moderate consumption of alcohol.** All of these societies consume alcohol in some form, yet for them, alcoholism doesn't exist. Whether this is due to strong social taboos or other factors is not known.

4. **Physical activity throughout life.** The "centenarians" studied are primarily farmers who labor by hand, walk a great deal across rugged terrain, ride horses and dance for recreation.

5. **Sexual activity prolonged into the advanced years.** Elders in these societies continue to be sexually active and feel free to express their sexuality.

6. **Social influences.** The older people remain active in community life. They are valued and respected for their wisdom and experience.

7. **Physical environment.** This factor needs more study, Pelletier notes, but wherever living to age 100 is common, the environment is conducive to exercise and relatively free of pollutants.

While these people differ greatly from Americans, these observations can show us how to age more successfully.

Here's what happens to most Americans as they age:

The average American male between the ages of 30 and 70 experiences a 20 percent decline in brain weight, a 20 percent decrease in blood flow to the brain, a 44 percent reduction in lung capacity, and a 40 percent decline in physical work capacity. Though these changes may seem significant, the human body is designed to have reserve capacity in its parts. For example, although we are capable of functioning well

on one kidney, we have two. Similarly, though we experience a loss of brain cells as we age, we don't necessarily lose our mental function. Where we do experience a decrease in function is in physical measures related to performance, such as speed of muscle contraction and muscle strength and endurance.

While we cannot expect to run as fast as we did 30 years ago, we can significantly slow down decline through ongoing conditioning. In fact, most experts believe that as they compare active individuals in their 50s, 60s and 70s to their sedentary counterparts, the majority of measured physical decline is a product of **disuse**, not what Americans think of as the "normal" aging process. Once again, the motto "use it or lose it" is the appropriate mind-set for today.

The following chart lists some changes associated with aging in men and women.

AVERAGE PHYSICAL CHANGES Ages 30 to 70	
Physical work (aerobic) capacity	-30% to -40%
Muscular strength	-25% to -30%
Muscle mass	-25% to -30%
Water in cells	-15% to -20%
Cardiac output*	-30%
Blood cholesterol	+10% to +25%
Systolic blood pressure	+10 mm Hg to +15 mm Hg
Diastolic blood pressure	+5 mm Hg to +10 mm Hg

Vital capacity (res-
  piratory func-
  tion)
	-40% to -50%

Bone density	-30% (in women)
Liver function	-40% to -50%

*Heart rate x stroke volume (blood pumped per heartbeat)
Adapted from: Maddox, et.al, *The Encyclopedia of Aging*, Springer Publishing Company, New York, 1987.

It is important to remember that in most instances, **experts believe that the majority of the decline in physical function can be attributed to disuse and poor lifestyle practices, not to the normal aging process.**

Some Changes Are Inevitable, We Think

Some physical changes cannot be avoided. Gray hair occurs naturally with age, as does a decreased tolerance for heat and cold. Reaction time slows because of changes within the central nervous system.

Wrinkling skin, though associated with aging, is to a great degree a reflection of decades of prolonged sun and wind exposure, as well as tobacco use.

Two important physical aspects of aging are sensory changes and menopause.

Sensory Changes. Older adults normally experience some diminishing of eyesight. *Presbyopia*, a decline in the ability to focus on close objects, occurs naturally. Increased sensitivity to light and, possibly, difficulty distinguishing certain colors may also occur. Other vision problems, such as cataracts and glaucoma, are **not** natural aspects of aging and can be treated. Only 7 percent of people between the ages of 65 and 74 experience serious loss of vision.

Hearing loss, in contrast, is a common physical impairment due to the aging process. It's not unusual for an older person to have difficulty hearing high pitches and discerning between certain sounds—someone's voice and the television, for instance. More extensive hearing loss can be caused by heredity, exposure to loud noises, illness, medication and a buildup of ear wax.

Menopause. Women and men alike experience hormonal changes with age. For women, these changes bring about a physiological milestone, the menopause.

The word "menopause" literally means the end of menstruation. Actually, the process by which levels of the hormone estrogen decrease and ova (egg) production ceases occurs gradually, over 15 to 20 years, and begins around age 40.

Low blood levels of estrogen during menopause cause some women to experience hot flashes, night sweats and loss of vaginal lubrication.

Most women experience only minor symptoms during menopause (contrary to the popular myth). Also, menopause does not necessitate a decline in sexual activity.

Three socially significant events that affect aging are widowhood, retirement and the hard realities of long-term care.

Widowhood. Five out of every six widowed people are women. Because women tend to live longer than men and to be younger than their spouses, most married women will face this trauma and spend many years alone.

Retirement. Retirement is a major life event and can be a potentially stressful transition that, if poorly planned, can have negative consequences on anyone's physical and mental health.

To ease the transition into retirement, it's wise to plan early to estimate financial needs and ways to meet them, to build a solid social network, and to develop interests outside of work that can easily be carried over into retirement.

Of course, not everyone has to retire. In 1984, 11 percent of men over age 70 and 4 percent of women in the same age group were employed. Some people simply never retire; they either continue working at their jobs, develop second careers after retiring, or decide that they prefer part-time work to total leisure.

Recognizing both a rapidly changing labor force and the value of older workers, corporations large and small offer various employment/retirement options as well as flextime and job sharing. The Travelers Companies, for instance, rehire retired workers on a daily basis. Retirees are registered at The Travelers' Job Bank to work as much as 40 hours a month without incurring pension penalties.

Long-Term Care. Though we are living longer, many older adults are living with chronic health conditions and are dependent upon formal and informal caregiving systems in order to remain as independent as possible. For many, however, especially the so-called "old-old" (those 85 years of age and older), institutionalized care within a nursing home is a sad fact of life. Long-term care is becoming a "predictable life event" that will have serious socioeconomic consequences for years to come. Not only are a significant number of working adults currently involved in the care of an older person and personally feeling its impact, but they are themselves questioning— How can I avoid the economic devastation that long-term care presents?—or simply—Who will take care of me? There are no easy answers, but it's imperative that we become aware of the issues surrounding long-term care and the resources available to assist us with this growing concern.

The Need for Prevention and Treatment

Findings published in 1963 by Butler and his research team at the National Institutes of Health are still relevant today: "If we can get behind the facade of chronological aging, we open up the possibility of modification through both prevention and treatment." In other words, although we cannot halt the aging process, we can prevent and treat much of the associated decline through proactive strategies.

Strength, stamina, mental agility—these are just some of the factors within our control. In fact, scientists have been able to measure and graph the effect of an active lifestyle on these and other characteristics as people grow older.

Called the Euro-American curve (it was derived from studies in Europe and the United States), the graph on page 8 demonstrates that for a wide variety of performance criteria, people's ability improves until about age 30. After that, it begins to decline slowly.

This is true for everyone, but as they age, active people continue to display the performance characteristics of sedentary people 30 years younger. If you look at the graph, you will see that beyond age 30, there is a 30-year gap between the ages of active and sedentary people at every performance level.

The Euro-American Curve

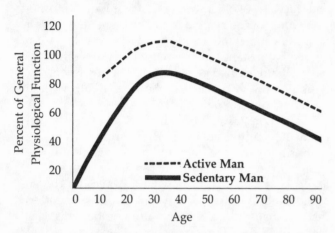

From *Exercise and Aging: The Scientific Basis* by Everett Smith and Robert Serfass. Copyright © 1981. By permission of Enslow Publishers.

The same 30-year gap was detected in the Alameda County, California study, one of the most publicized health studies of our time, which measured the impact of seven simple health habits on health status and life expectancy. These habits included not smoking, exercising, maintaining normal weight, consuming alcohol only in moderation, sleeping eight hours each night, eating breakfast daily and eating three meals a day.

One of the study's findings was that men who practiced six or seven of these good habits appeared to be as healthy as persons 30 years younger who did not practice these habits.

The most frequently cited finding was that a 45-year-old man who follows six to seven of the good health habits can expect to live 11.5 years longer than a man who practices only three. For a 45-year-old woman, the difference is seven years. This is no small increase, especially when you consider that if cancer were to be eliminated as a cause of death, life expectancy would only increase by about two years.

The Two A's: Attitude and Action

Put yourself in this picture: If you didn't know your age and had never seen your face, how old would you think you are, based on to your current activities? How old would you want to be?

Do you equate aging with illness and decreased performance, or with vigor and new opportunities? To a great degree you have the greatest say in how you choose to live and how you wish to age. Granted, there are areas in people's lives that do limit or serve as obstacles to successful aging, such as economic status, access to quality medical care and simply how well they "selected" their parents. But in the long run, successful aging relies heavily on the two A's: **attitude** and **action**. Together they allow you to direct your course. With a positive attitude and appropriate action, the likelihood of successful aging is increased. In contrast, a poor attitude and inappropriate or no action can lead to stagnation and an early death.

Perhaps the power of attitude and action is best exemplified by comedian George Burns, who at 92 in a *Time* magazine interview on aging said, "People practice to get old... the minute they get to be 65 or 70, they sit down slow, they get into a car with trouble. They start taking small steps."

Do you prefer to take small steps, or would you rather take great strides throughout your life? Section II of this book will give you the opportunity to learn and apply key LifeSkills that, no matter what your stage in life, can serve you well.

CHAPTER TWO

How Are Your LifeSkills?

In the previous chapter we talked about factors related to successful aging. We said that a large part of "normal aging" is really a matter of "disuse" and the lack of essential self-care skills. We emphasized that you are the best navigator to help steer aging's course. But what are the skills needed to fulfill your biological aging potential? Perhaps the best way to find out is by discovering which LifeSkills you currently use and which you don't.

The following LifeSkills Inventory is not presented as a definitive compilation of the skills that contribute to a long and healthy life. Rather, it serves as a starting point, a reference to the basic tools that can:

- Decrease your overall health risk.
- Increase your sense of well-being.
- Improve your financial health.
- Help you become an informed medical consumer.
- Assist you in developing a clearer understanding of the realities of aging and long-term care issues.

Tools are a means to an end. Use them to express your spirit, personality and vibrant health.

Completing the LifeSkills Inventory

Each of the following statements can be answered either "yes" or "no." Put a check in the "yes" column if a statement pretty well describes you. Put a check in the "no" column if the statement describes someone not like you. Be honest in your responses.

	Yes	No	Refer to page(s)
1. My daily activity level is equivalent to more than 45 minutes of formal activity, such as jogging, or informal activities, such as yard work, hiking or labor.	☐	☐	16
2. Part of my weekly activity is formal exercise—brisk walking, jogging, swimming, cycling—consisting of three to five sessions of 15 to 60 minutes in duration, at a moderate intensity.	☐	☐	17-23
3. I do exercises three days a week that maintain flexibility in my neck, shoulders, arms, hands, back, hips, knees and ankles.	☐	☐	23-24
4. I do exercises that help maintain strength in major muscle groups, those of the arms, shoulders, back, hips and legs.	☐	☐	27-32
5. I consider myself at ideal weight.	☐	☐	33-34
6. I limit my intake of fats—saturated and unsaturated—to less than 30 percent of my total calories per day.	☐	☐	36
7. My intake of dietary fiber is approximately one ounce per day and is in the form of cabbage, broccoli, carrots, grains or legumes.	☐	☐	36
8. I restrict my consumption of caffeine to fewer than five servings per day. (One serving equals one cup of coffee or tea or one can of soda.)	☐	☐	36
9. My protein sources are **primarily** fish, fowl, low-fat dairy products, lean beef, beans, rice, legumes and grains, rather than fatty meats.	☐	☐	38
10. My daily intake of carbohydrates is approximately 55 percent of my total calorie consumption.	☐	☐	38-39
11. I consume foods from the following food groups daily: fruits and vegetables, bread and cereals, meat and fish, and dairy products.	☐	☐	39-40
12. I consume 1,000 mg of calcium a day (men or women; post-menopausal women: 1,500 mg per day)	☐	☐	39

13. I can effectively deal with stress in my life; I'm in control. □ □ 42-49

14. I have developed a strong social network, balanced between work, family and friends. □ □ 50-54

15. I have a hobby that can be carried into retirement. □ □ 52

16. I have established short-term, mid-term and long-term financial goals for myself and/or my family. □ □ 56

17. My financial assets outweigh my liabilities; I have a positive net worth. □ □ 57

18. I'm able to save at least 5 percent of my annual take-home pay. □ □ 60

19. I have an emergency savings fund equivalent to three to six months of required expenses. □ □ 60

20. I have insurance appropriate to my stage in life, including health, life, disability and perhaps long-term care insurance. □ □ 64-65

21. I am an active participant and have the necessary knowledge and skills to make appropriate medical self-care decisions for myself or a family member. □ □ 68-70

22. I take an active role in decision-making for myself or a family member facing hospitalization. I question the cost-benefit ratio and the risks of recommended procedures. □ □ 70

23. I comply with recommended health screening schedules based upon my age, sex and relative risks. □ □ 73-77

24. I don't smoke. □ □ 78-81

25. I consume no more than two alcoholic drinks a day. □ □ 82-84

26. I never drive under the influence of alcohol. □ □ 82-84

27. I don't take drugs that alter my mood or personality. □ □ 85-87

28. I use my seat belt when driving or riding in a car. □ □ 88

29. I have conducted a safety audit of my household within the last three months. □ □ 88-94

30. When unsure of my partner's sexual history, I practice safe sex. □ □ 95-97

31. I sleep between seven and eight hours a day. □ □ 98

32. I avoid extreme exposure to the sun by using appropriate sunblocks and clothing. □ □ 99

33. I have sufficient knowledge of the ailments associated with older adults. □ □ 108-169

34. I understand what is needed for successfully developing an effective long-term care plan. □ □ 178-189

35. I feel I could assist my parents or another relative in making decisions about long-term care. □ □ 178-189

36. I know what resources are available in my community to meet long-term care needs. □ □ 190-215

37. I understand how long-term care is presently funded. □ □ 216-219

38. I have a general understanding of estate planning and legal matters regarding incapacity and long-term care. □ □ 220-223

39. I am aware of resources I may need to assist me, were I responsible for the long-term care of a loved one. □ □ 224-227

TOTAL: Yes _____ No _____

Self-Scoring the Inventory

Add up the number of checks in each column and match your inventory with the following standards.

all "yes" to 32 "yes"	Congratulations! You're a true artisan of aging.
31 "yes" to 27 "yes"	You're a good apprentice.
26 "yes" to 20 "yes"	You're skills are borderline; you need tutoring.
fewer than 20 "yes"	You're failing Aging 101. It's time to reassess your skills.

Are You an Artisan of Aging?

Any *yes* answer reflects a positive skill that is associated with improved health and well-being. The more affirmative statements that apply to you, the better.

If you answered *no* to any statement, refer to the appropriate section of the text; learn how to improve your skills and get on the road to a healthier, longer life!

Section II

Developing Your LifeSkills

INTRODUCTION

The Value of Other LifeSkills for a Long Life

Though the Center's study demonstrates the value of a few LifeSkills in enhancing health and longevity, it would be a gross oversimplification to say that this is all you need. The multiple stresses of contemporary life greatly influence the incidence of alcoholism, drug abuse, suicide and accidents, which lead to premature death and disability. It is imperative, now more than ever, to understand how to prevent or modify these conditions through informed self-care decision-making.

This section presents a variety of LifeSkills important to successful aging and suggests ways to incorporate them into your lifestyle through self-management planning.

Developing Your LifeSkills

In this section we will talk about specific behaviors and health practices—LifeSkills—and their importance in maintaining health and well-being. It would probably be safe to say that if an individual were to practice these LifeSkills, his or her chances of living a long and active life would be greatly improved.

In fact, our research at the Center for Corporate Health Promotion has shown that in a sample of approximately 100,000 working adults, those who exercised regularly, ate balanced meals low in cholesterol and fat, and practiced effective stress-management skills were also less likely to:

• Smoke.
• Use medications to alter their mood.
• Drink alcohol to excess.
• Feel a lack of control over their lives.

The Center also found that those who smoked, used mood-altering medications and/or had high levels of alcohol consumption were apt to be less physically active, practice poor eating habits and have a difficult time managing stress.

What this research has also shown is that changes in some lifestyle areas have the power to reduce the probability of negative health behaviors. Such changes help reduce overall health risk and promote prevention and longevity.

So what's the lesson to be learned? Convince smokers or substance abusers to jog, eat better and learn to relax, and they will drop their self-destructive habits? We wish it were that simple. But it is important to realize that these skills, coupled with others, such as social support and self-management planning, should be a primary strategy in helping individuals cope with the difficulty of **changing** negative health behaviors and **learning** new ones.

CHAPTER ONE

LifeSkill One: Stay Active

Suppose someone were to develop a "youth pill," one that would:

- Provide energy and vitality throughout life.
- Keep the heart and lungs functioning well.
- Lower blood pressure.
- Reduce excess body fat.
- Promote healthy blood cholesterol levels.
- Ward off such age-related ailments as arthritis, heart disease, diabetes, osteoporosis and some forms of cancer.
- Improve immune response.
- Reduce stress and tension.
- Ensure strength, flexibility and endurance.
- Reduce your overall health risks.
- Increase your chances of being mobile and independent in later life.

Wouldn't you rush right out and buy it, regardless of the cost?

Most people would respond to this question with a resounding "yes."

Even though no such pill exists, there **is** a **LifeSkill** that offers comparable benefits: **regular, physical activity.** Yet most of our population is reluctant to take advantage of it.

Though recent polls by Harris, Gallup and *American Health* magazine indicate that 60 percent to 70 percent of Americans say they exercise on a regular basis, a U.S. Public Health Service (PHS) report paints a different picture. The PHS report shows that less than 20 percent of adults really exercise enough to realize health benefits. Another 40 percent exercise only intermittently, and the remaining 40 percent are completely sedentary.

Another report, by the National Institute on Aging, showed that a high percentage of adults age 80 years and older were unable to perform simple, everyday tasks, such as stair climbing, heavy housework and using a toilet by themselves. This indicates that a significant number of older people lack adequate muscular strength, endurance and range of motion to function independently within their environment.

The Health Benefits of Regular Physical Activity

Proponents of regular physical activity may sound overzealous at times. However, there exists mounting evidence that in the proper "dosage," physical activity can effectively reduce such risk factors as high blood cholesterol, glucose intolerance and obesity, and therefore have a health benefit in such disorders as non-insulin-dependent diabetes, hypertension, and heart disease. The following is a brief summary of what research shows:

- Ralph Paffenbarger, M.D., of Stanford Medical School, traced the health histories of more than 17,000 Harvard alumni. He measured their activity level in terms of "calories burned," and divided the subjects into three groups: those who burned fewer than 500 calories in activity every week; those who burned between 500 and 2,000 calories; and those whose **total** weekly activity expenditure level was more than 2,000 calories. (It takes approximately 20 miles of brisk walking a week to burn 2,000 calories.)

  Paffenbarger found that those who were most active increased their life expectancy by an average of two years and significantly reduced their risk of heart disease and their death rate from all causes by 28 percent. This is the same increase in life expectancy that could be expected if all risk of cancer were eliminated.

- As reported in the *Journal of the American Medical Association*, Arthur S. Leon, M.D., and associates compared the activity levels of 12,138 middle-aged men who were at high risk for coronary heart disease. Leon found a 37 percent lower risk for coronary heart disease and sudden death, as well as a 30 percent reduction in overall mortality, in moderately active males, when compared with a group of less active males. The moderately active group was defined as those individuals who spent an average of 47 minutes a day in leisure activities, such as yard work, walking, golf and hunting; the least active group was active only 15 minutes a day.

- Another study cited in *The Physician and SportsMedicine* reported on middle-aged men who exercised regularly. Over 10 years, they showed no adverse changes in blood pressure, body weight or physical work capacity. The average decline in physical work capacity for sedentary males in this age group is 9 percent to 15 percent.

- Other studies have associated regular physical activity with the following benefits:

  —Reduced cancer risk.

  —Improved glucose tolerance for non-insulin-dependent diabetics.

  —Improved immune response.

  —Reductions in anxiety and mild depression.

  —Reduced risk of osteoporosis.

- Recently, scientists from the national Centers for Disease Control compared 43 studies suggesting that physical activity helped prevent heart disease. They found that regular exercise could do as much for heart health as quitting smoking, lowering blood cholesterol and controlling blood pressure.

Contrary to what you may have read, you don't need to join the "no pain, no gain" club or run marathons to realize the health benefits of regular physical activity.

As the cited research indicates, even moderate physical activity can provide significant protection from cardiovascular disease and other health risks. Though not a panacea, regular physical activity can and should be viewed as the cornerstone for any program designed to promote successful aging.

The remainder of this chapter will present the basic facts of the "active life," along with a recommended program that can be tailored to your particular needs and interests.

Guiding Principles to the Active Life

Before beginning any personal physical activity program, review the following guiding principles.

Principle One: Increase Your Overall Daily Activity Level

It is recommended that you increase your daily energy expenditure by 300 calories through informal and formal activities that not only increase your total caloric output, but raise and maintain your total fitness level (your ability to perform work).

How you increase your activity level is up to you. Activities such as walking after dinner, using stairs in the office, parking the car at the far end of the lot, gardening and heavy housework are examples of informal activities that can increase your caloric expenditure but don't necessarily improve your fitness level. However, formal activities, such as brisk walking, jogging, swimming, cycling, rowing, aerobic dance, and flexibility and weight training, are not only excellent calorie burners, but serve to improve overall fitness.

Use the chart on the following page to compare different activities and their relative caloric expenditure. This will help you achieve the 300-calorie equation.

Principle Two: Make Fitness Part of Your Schedule

Formally scheduled exercise sessions, if applied in the right "dosage" and used in conjunction with such other LifeSkills as nutrition and stress management, are one of the best ways to realize both health and fitness benefits. However, few people successfully incorporate formal exercise into their life. It's common for people to begin an exercise program with the best intentions but slowly lose their enthusiasm and motivation to continue. Research has shown that within six months, half of all new participants drop out, citing lack of time or being too busy as the primary reasons for stopping.

Before starting your exercise program, it's helpful to establish a self-management plan, a strategy that will get you off on the right foot and increase your chances of succeeding.

Your self-management plan helps clarify your general and intermediate goals, identifies the forces that help or hinder your progress, and helps you create a reward system for motivation. After reading this chapter you may wish to refer to Chapter Fifteen in this section to learn more about self-management planning.

The second step in your "preconditioning plan" is fitting your exercise sessions into your schedule. Your exercise program shouldn't be "catch-as-catch-can." Rather it should be scheduled for particular times, preferably the same time each day. The time-management skills outlined in Chapter Three of this section can help you plan for formal activity by identifying time wasters and ranking tasks.

Principle Three: Get the Proper F.I.T.T.

If your personal activity program is to be safe, effective and beneficial, it needs to comply with the F.I.T.T. Principle:

- **Frequency**: Research has shown that you need to exercise three to five times per week, preferably on alternate days, in order to realize a "training effect."

- **Intensity**: How hard you exercise is determined by your *exercise heart rate* (EHR), the point at which your pulse rate should be while exercising. You cannot have an effective workout unless your pulse is elevated and maintained within your *exercise heart rate zone* (EHRZ). If you exercise below the target zone, most likely you're not "working" the heart hard enough. (However, exercising near exhaustion is unnecessary and can even be harmful.)

  In order to find your EHRZ, use the following chart, keeping in mind your age and physical condition. For example, the chart shows that an individual 40 years old has an EHRZ of 126 to 153. This is

AVERAGE CALORIC EXPENDITURE
Per Hour By Activity

	Body Weight				Body Weight		
	110 lbs.	154 lbs.	198 lbs.		110 lbs.	154 lbs.	198 lbs.
Cleaning Windows	180	230	280	Baseball/Softball			
Chopping Wood	355	450	550	Infield/Outfield	220	280	340
Floor				Pitching	305	390	475
Mopping	195	275	355	Basketball			
Sweeping	160	225	290	Moderate	435	555	675
Gardening	155	215	280	Vigorous	585	750	910
Gardening and				Bicycling			
Weeding	250	315	380	(on level) 5.5 mph	190	245	295
Hoeing, Raking				13 mph	515	655	790
and Planting	205	285	370	Bowling (non-stop)	210	270	325
Housework	175	245	320	Canoeing (4 mph)	490	625	765
Mowing Grass				Golf			
Power, Self-				Twosome	295	380	460
Propelled	195	250	305	Foursome	210	270	325
Not Self-Propelled	210	270	325	Handball/			
Sawing Wood	180	230	280	Racquetball	610	775	945
Shoveling Snow	475	610	745	Rowing (20 strokes/			
Yard Work	155	215	275	min.)	515	655	795
Calisthenics	235	300	365	Running			
Dancing				5.5 mph	515	655	795
Moderate	350	445	540	7 mph	550	700	850
Vigorous	515	655	795	9 mph	720	920	1120
Fox Trot	195	250	305	Sailing (calm water)	120	155	190
Rhumba	215	300	365	Skating (ice)			
Square	330	420	510	Moderate	275	350	425
Waltz	195	250	305	Vigorous	485	620	755
Driving	130	180	235	Skiing			
Hill Climbing	470	600	730	Downhill	465	595	720
Motorcycling	165	205	250	Cross-Country			
Mountain Climbing	470	600	730	(5 mph)	550	700	950
Walking				Soccer	470	600	730
2 mph	145	185	225	Swimming			
4.5 mph	325	450	550	Backstroke			
Downstairs	355	450	550	(20 yards/min.)	165	235	305
Upstairs	720	920	1120	Breaststroke			
Brick Laying	160	205	250	(20 yards/min.)	210	295	380
Car Repair	180	230	280	Butterfly (per hr.)	490	630	760
Carpentry or Farm				Crawl (20 yards/			
Chores	180	230	280	min.)	235	300	365
House Painting	165	210	255	Sidestroke			
Office Work	115	145	175	(per hr.)	230	320	420
Pick and Shovel				Tennis			
Work	315	400	490	Moderate	335	425	520
Archery	245	315	380	Vigorous	470	600	730
Volleyball				Waterskiing	335	475	610
(Moderate)	275	350	425				

Adapted from *Diet Free* by Charles T. Kuntzleman: Arbor Press, Spring Arbor, MI.

based on 70 percent to 85 percent of his or her maximum attainable heart rate (182). Through aerobic exercise (e.g., cycling), this person should keep his or her heart rate within the zone for 15 to 60 minutes.

Individuals in poor to fair condition should exercise in the lower end of the EHRZ, those in good condition in the middle, and well conditioned individuals at the upper end. (Please note that as you age, your maximum heart rate decreases approximately one beat per year.)

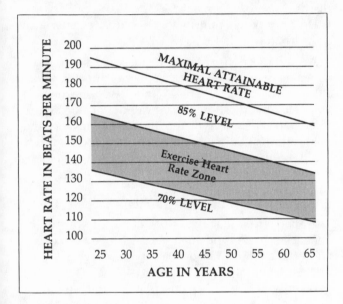

To determine whether you are in your proper heart rate zone, learn to count your pulse immediately upon finishing your exercise. Find your pulse with your first three fingers, either on the radial artery of the wrist or on the chest. Find the beat within a second and count for 10 seconds, counting the first beat as zero, then one, two, three, etc. Multiply by six to calculate your rate per minute.

If you are currently using any medications for your heart or for controlling blood pressure, consult your physician before starting.

Perceived Exertion

A second method of tuning into the right exercise intensity is rating your perceived exertion. Exercise physiologists have found that the following "Borg Scale" can help most individuals monitor their exercise intensity.

For most apparently healthy adults, a perceived exertion level of 3 (moderate) would be the thresh-

old for achieving a training effect. A rating between 4 and 5 (somewhat heavy to heavy) would signify the middle to upper levels of exertion for the average non-competitive adult. Please note that this chart does not apply to individuals who are under medical supervision for cardiovascular problems.

Perceived Exertion Chart
0 . . . . .Nothing at All
0.5 . . . . .Extremely Light
1 . . . . .Very Light
2 . . . . .Light
3 . . . . .Moderate
4 . . . . .Somewhat Heavy
5 . . . . .Heavy
6 . . . .
7 . . . . .Very Heavy
8 . . . .
9 . . . .
10 . . . . .Extremely Heavy
10+ . . . . .Maximal

From Borg's Category-Ratio Scale.

- **Time**: Each workout should be 15 to 60 minutes in duration. Your goal is to gradually work up to the point at which you can maintain a continuous, steady pace.
- **Type**: Not all exercises are alike; neither are their benefits. The core component in any adult fitness program is and should be aerobic exercise that trains the cardiovascular system to utilize oxygen more efficiently. Aerobic means **with oxygen.** Any activity that you are able to maintain for a sustained period, that moves large volumes of oxygen and uses large muscle groups, such as the legs and arms, is considered aerobic. This is in contrast to "short burst" activities, such as a 100-meter sprint or power lifting, which can only be maintained for a very short time before exhaustion sets in. These activities are considered *anaerobic*, meaning without oxygen. They use limited energy stores, which are quickly depleted, and have limited cardiovascular benefit.

The activities listed on the next page have been selected on the merit of their aerobic potential and their ability to burn calories, which makes them excellent exercises for weight control. (Remember, 3,500 calories must be expended to lose one pound of fat.)

Finally, to add variety and reduce boredom in your program, its recommended that you choose two or three activities that you can interchange at will. This is called cross-training and is discussed in Principle Ten.

Aerobic Activity	Average Calories Burned Per Hour (154-pound person)
Fitness Walking	450
Stationary Cycling	655
Bicycling	655 (13 mph)
Jogging	700 (7 mph)
Racquetball,	775
Squash,	775
Handball	775
Rowing	655
Cross-Country	
Skiing	700
Rope Skipping	654
Aerobic Dance	342
Swimming (crawl)	300
Stair-Climbing	
Machines	920
Basketball	555

Principle Four: Most People Don't Need an Exercise Stress Test to Begin Exercise

If you are in the 35-plus age group, you may have heard that you need a "stress test" or a medical check-up before starting to exercise, to uncover hidden heart problems.

Actually, if you accept this notion, you may let unfounded fears prevent you from enjoying activities that can benefit your health. Also, you may spend money on a test that probably won't uncover disease, has a good chance of yielding a false result, and may expose you to other diagnostic tests that are more expensive and pose greater risk.

The *graded exercise test* (GXT), sometimes called the stress test, is designed to measure the heart's response to physical exertion. In theory, it detects heart disease in people without symptoms. The test is usually performed on a treadmill or stationary bicycle, and is supervised by a physician. The individual exercises until fatigue or other symptoms inhibit further work, while the physician monitors his or her electrocardiogram and blood pressure.

In studies of people without symptoms, as many as 73 percent to 93 percent of those with "abnormal" stress-test results turned out **not** to have any heart disease, especially those who were younger than 45 years of age. A study of persons who **did** have heart disease found that as many as 62 percent had "normal" results. False positives and false negatives can always be expected in diagnostic tests, but with so many false results, the usefulness of the stress test as a **mass** screening protocol is severely limited, especially when you consider that the cost per test is $150 to $300.

However, there **are** people whose exercise should be medically supervised. These six questions can help you determine whether you should consult a physician before beginning an exercise program.

1. Do you ever have chest pain when you exert yourself (walking up stairs, doing yard work, engaging in formal exercise, etc.)?
2. Do you get short of breath with exertion?
3. Do you have pain in your legs when you walk that disappears when you rest?
4. Do you regularly have swelling of the ankles that is not associated with the menstrual cycle?
5. Has a doctor ever told you that you have heart disease?
6. Do you have a family history of cardiac events, such as heart attacks, before age 50?

A "yes" response to any of these questions from someone over age 35 is reason to see a doctor before starting to exercise. Those under 35 who answer "yes" to any question should call the doctor for advice. Some people will require further testing and medical consultation, but chances are good that they can develop an exercise program that accommodates their physical limitations.

Principle Five: Train, Don't Strain

Proper physical activity doesn't have to hurt to be beneficial. In fact, pushing yourself to levels of pain and exhaustion can lead to injury and decrease your interest and motivation.

When you begin, be conservative. You should always feel that you can do more when you finish your workout. Chronic muscular soreness, fatigue and lowered resistance to minor illnesses (e.g., colds) are indications of overuse. When these symptoms occur, it's advisable to reduce both the intensity and frequency of your training, take a few days off or exercise on alternate days.

Principle Six: Allow Adequate Time for Warm-Up and Cool-Down

A common mistake among exercisers is not allowing adequate periods of warm-up and cool-down before and after formal activity. Begin each exercise session with a *warm-up* period. Perform a low-level activity, such as walking or slow jogging, for several minutes, and then slowly stretch. Use the stretches beginning on page 23.

An adequate warm-up period allows the body to gradually adjust to an exercise stimulus by slowly increasing body temperature, oxygen consumption and the range of motion in major joints. Not only does warming up increase muscular efficiency, but it can help reduce soft-tissue injuries, such as muscle pulls, and, for some people, reduce the frequency of heart irregularities that can occur when they simply "plunge" into their activity.

An appropriate cool-down period allows the cardio-vascular system to slowly "downshift" to its pre-exercise state through a lower-level activity, such as walking for three to five minutes, followed by flexibility exercises.

Cool-down exercises are also intended to stretch muscles that are most likely shorter after your activity period (called contractures), to help speed recovery and to reduce post-exercise soreness.

One last word—it's not advisable to take a shower until you're adequately cooled down. Wait until your resting heart rate is within 20 to 30 beats of your average before you hit the showers. It's important that your shower be lukewarm rather than hot; hot showers can cause an opening up of the blood vessels in your legs (called *vasodilation*), leading to blood pooling and subsequent dizziness, fainting or a cardiac event in some people.

Principle Seven: When You Can, Exercise With a Friend

Don't make exercise a grim, solitary process. Participate with a friend or an associate who, if possible, is at your current fitness level. Companionship not only decreases boredom, but can provide peer support and encouragement that will help you adhere to your program.

Principle Eight: Wear the Right Footwear

Put your best foot forward! Match the proper footwear to the activity. With the fitness boom over the past decade, athletic shoe companies have capitalized on new markets, especially in aerobic dance and walking. This gives the consumer a variety of options that represent quality, comfort, protection and specialization.

When shopping for a jogging shoe, for example, look for a firm heel counter that cradles the heel, a soft midsole and insole that absorb road shock, good flexibility in the ball of the foot, and an inner liner that conforms to the contour of your foot.

When fitting shoes, be wary of any spots that are tight or rub; they'll create hot spots and blisters. Make sure to wear the right socks during the initial fitting, and allow approximately half a thumb nail's width at the big toe. Finally, it's advisable to buy your shoes in the afternoon rather than the morning, because people's feet tend to be swollen after sleeping.

Principle Nine: Take Your Time!

If you have been relatively inactive over the past few years, your body may remind you. Don't be discouraged or impatient. Gradually increase your dis-tance, speed and/or weight resistance when training. Remember the old Chinese saying: A thousand-mile journey begins with the first step. Refer to Chapter Fifteen on personal management planning for help in establishing realistic goals.

Principle Ten: Try Cross-Training

To reduce monotony and boredom, try cross-training, which has evolved from the triathlete movement. Its advocates have argued that by alternating activities such as swimming, cycling and running, important benefits can be realized:

• More specific muscle groups are trained, providing you with a more well-rounded conditioning program than you would realize from one activity.
• The frequency of overuse injuries, particularly to the knee and foot, are reported to be reduced.

To become a cross-trainer, select two or three **aerobic** activities that you can do year-round, that you enjoy, and that can easily fit into your schedule.

Principle Eleven: Exercise Caution in Hot or Cold Weather

Exercising in the Heat

Exercising in extreme heat and humidity can be a definite, even severe, hazard to your health. Heat stroke and heat exhaustion can only be avoided through proper preparation and awareness. High humidity with a relatively moderate temperature can be more harmful than a high temperature with low humidity. The reason is that for the body to cool, heat must be dissipated through the skin and into the air. If the air is saturated with moisture, perspiration stays on the skin, preventing heat loss, and body heat increases. Refer to the following chart to gauge your exertion level in hot and humid weather.

Temperature-Humidity Index

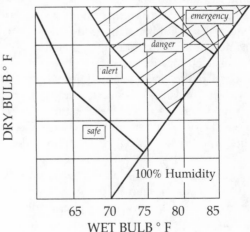

Source: National Weather Service Operations Manual

Symptoms and Treatment of Heat Exhaustion and Heat Stroke

Heat Exhaustion

Symptoms: Listlessness, apprehension, confusion, fatigue, semi-comatose state and normal body temperature

Cause: Loss of circulating blood volume due to dilation of blood vessels in skin and fluid loss through perspiration

Treatment: Take fluids (fruit juices and water) freely

Heat Stroke

Symptoms: Hot, dry skin; labored, rapid breathing; rapid pulse; nausea; blurred vision; irrational behavior; fainting

Cause: Uncontrolled rise in body temperature following prolonged exposure to heat

Treatment: Seek medical help immediately. Cover yourself or the victim with a blanket that you continually soak with cold water. Elevate the legs. Massage the skin in direction of the heart. If the victim is conscious, have him or her drink water or fruit juices.

Some Helpful Tips

• Condition and acclimatize yourself by slowly increasing your total workout time over two to four weeks.
• Avoid taking salt tablets or adding salt to your food; processed foods have enough. Take potassium instead. It's found in fruits, especially bananas.
• Take cool fluids at will while exercising. Drink two cups (8 fluid ounces each) of cold water within one hour of exercising. Commercial fluid-replacement drinks should be diluted to half strength, because their high glucose content may actually slow down fluid absorption.
• Wear light-colored clothing made of cotton or porous nylon mesh. On bright, sunny days, wear a light hat and an appropriate sunscreen.

Exercising in the Cold

• Active sports such as running and cross-country skiing require less clothing than stop-and-go activities such as downhill skiing, skating and sledding.
• Layer your clothing. Purchase underwear and socks made of a fabric, such as polypropylene, which "wicks away" moisture. Next, use a cotton turtleneck shirt to help insulate the body. For the outer layer, nylon shells or weather suits such as Gore-tex® "breathe" and prevent moisture retention in the inner layers.
• The head, hands and feet should be covered adequately, with down used in the gloves or mittens and wool for the head and feet. Twenty percent of body heat is lost through the head, so be sure to cover the head and ears.

• Exercising in extreme cold will not "frost the lungs." Cold air picks up moisture and heat before it reaches the lungs. Your throat may be a little raw during the first few days of exercise, but your body will soon adjust.
• Frostbite is a real danger, especially when the wind-chill factor increases. Warning signals of frostbite are redness of the skin and stinging, numbness and a lack of feeling or coordination in the fingers and feet. When skin turns a patchy white, frostbite has set in and immediate attention is required. You should warm the area with water that is about 108° F.

Principle Twelve: Keep an Exercise Diary

Maintain a daily record of your exercise activity. Record your morning resting pulse rate, body weight, activity, exercise pulse, distance covered, time, weight lifted by exercise (resistance) and how you felt.

Your diary can provide you with valuable feedback. For example, you may find that after weeks of training, your resting pulse rate will slowly decrease. This indicates improved cardiovascular efficiency: An appropriate training effect has taken place.

Getting into Motion: Putting Principles into Practice

The following personal activity program is designed to provide a balanced regimen of aerobic exercise, joint flexibility and resistance exercises that will:
• Improve and/or maintain your physical work capacity throughout life.
• Improve and maintain joint flexibility.
• Improve and maintain appropriate levels of muscular strength and endurance to meet the demands of daily living.
• Maintain optimum body weight and lean muscle mass.
• Reduce major health risks and improve health and longevity.

In designing your program, it's recommended that you develop a schedule for one week. Here is an example of a typical program for an adult who wishes to increase his or her general fitness level and is able to take part in five **formal** workout sessions per week. This doesn't take into account informal activities, such as gardening or housework, or leisure sports, such as golf or tennis.

Within this schedule, we assume a maximum of one hour per workout session, with aerobic conditioning scheduled three days a week and resistance training twice a week. However, flexibility is practiced six times a week, through warm-up and cool-down activities.

To modify this workout schedule, aerobic conditioning can be increased to five days a week and resistance training to three if time and interest allow. In turn, aerobic and resistance training can be combined in the same workout session, allowing alternate days of rest or leisure activities.

Sample Personal Activity Program

Monday:	Aerobic Conditioning (15 to 60 minutes)
Tuesday:	Resistance Training
Wednesday:	Aerobic Conditioning (15 to 60 minutes)
Thursday:	Resistance Training
Friday:	Rest
Saturday:	Aerobic Conditioning (15 to 60 minutes)
Sunday:	Leisure Activity

Each training session and leisure activity includes appropriate warm-up and cool-down exercises.

Whatever schedule you develop, it's important to keep in mind the principles outlined earlier and to be sensitive to such body cues as excessive muscle soreness, chronic fatigue and painful joints, which may indicate overuse.

The remainder of this chapter will discuss the three goals of a personal activity program: joint flexibility, aerobic conditioning, and muscular strength and endurance.

Goal One: Joint Flexibility

Your first objective is staying flexible. Flexibility refers to the range of motion within a joint, which is dependent upon the structure of the specific joint and the status of its connective tissues—the ligaments, tendons and muscles that support and move the joint. A common problem in older people is diminished flexibility due primarily to disuse. Limited flexibility decreases muscular efficiency, makes an older person more prone to injury, and can complicate such chronic ailments as arthritis and osteoporosis by further diminishing mobility and independence.

The exercises below can be used to promote general flexibility or as a warm-up and cool-down before and after your aerobic conditioning, resistance training or leisure activity.

Your Warm-Up and Cool-Down Program

Skipping warm-up and cool-down exercises is a common mistake. It can be a dangerous practice, especially if you're involved in rapid stop-and-go activities, such as racquetball or basketball, which require powerful movements that can easily stretch muscles beyond their normal range.

The following exercises can be used during your warm-up and cool-down periods and are designed to slowly stretch specific muscle groups: the shoulders, back, hips, thighs, calves and ankles.

All stretching exercises should be conducted in a slow, deliberate manner. Avoid bouncing and jerking movements. All stretches should be taken to a point of slight discomfort and held for 15 to 30 seconds. Be patient! In time you'll be able to increase your range of motion.

- *Preliminary Warm-Up: Walk Briskly, Cycle or Jog for Three to Five Minutes Before Stretching*
- *Preliminary Cool-Down: Walk Slowly for Three to Five Minutes Before Stretching*

1. **Shoulder Stretch**
   A. While standing, place your right hand over your head, reaching toward the middle of your back.
   B. Place your left hand on your right elbow.
   C. Push your right arm slowly down your back, to the point of tension.
   D. Hold for 15 to 30 seconds. Repeat twice.
   E. Repeat the exercise with your left arm.

2. **Yoga Side Stretch**
   A. While standing, place your feet wider apart than your shoulders.
   B. Turn your right foot out and your left foot slightly in.
   C. Slide your right hand down the back of your right leg, to the point of tension.
   D. Extend your left arm perpendicular to the floor.

E. Twist your head and look toward your left hand.

F. Hold this position for 15 to 30 seconds. Breathe rhythmically. Repeat twice.

G. Repeat on the left side.

3. Swimmer's Stretch

A. Stand with your feet shoulder-width apart.

B. Place your hands behind your back, right palm on the back of your left hand.

C. Bend slowly from the waist, with your legs slightly bent at the knees. Keep your head up.

D. Bring your arms up and forward.

E. Hold stretch for 15 to 30 seconds. Repeat twice.

4. Hip Flexor Stretch

A. Lie on your back, legs extended.

B. Bring your left knee up and grasp your leg under your knee.

C. Pull your knee toward your left shoulder. Keep your shoulder flat and your right leg extended.

D. Hold the stretch for 15 to 30 seconds.

E. Repeat with each leg twice.

5. Wall Stretch

A. Stand a little farther than arm's-length from a wall or tree.

B. Keep your heels flat, feet together, and your back and legs straight.

C. Slowly lean forward, using your hands for support.

D. Hold this position for 15 to 30 seconds. Repeat twice.

Goal Two: Aerobic Conditioning

Aerobic conditioning is at the core of your personal activity program, because of its broad health and fitness benefits. To realize these benefits, however, it's necessary to keep the F.I.T.T. Principle in mind, as well as the other guiding principles outlined earlier in this chapter.

Here are some guidelines for three popular aerobic activities: walking, jogging and aerobic dance. However, remember that there are many other aerobic activities, including cycling, rowing, swimming, rope skipping and cross-country skiing, that you can enjoy for life.

Walking Guidelines

Whether you want to break away from a sedentary lifestyle, lose weight, relax, gain the benefits of aerobic exercise, or simply enjoy a social activity, walking can help you achieve your goal.

"Almost anyone can walk; hardly anyone is too sick, too old or too fat," says Marsha Wallen of The WalkWays Center, a national non-profit organization that promotes walking. "Walking is particularly safe," Wallen adds. "It doesn't stress the joints or legs, it requires little investment or equipment, and it can be enjoyed almost anywhere."

With the aging of America and the search for activities that are less "traumatic," walking is becoming the aerobic activity of choice for many people.

Here are a few general guidelines for walking:

- **Aerobic, or "power" walking.** Aerobic or power walking is designed to raise your heart rate to your target level and, like any other activity, be performed three times a week for 15 to 60 minutes.

To minimize injury, start your walking program slowly; gradually increase the intensity and duration of your workouts. Exhaustion and pain are signs that you are going too fast or too far. Make

Sample Walking Program

Beginner Program

Week	Mileage	Pace (mph)	Heart Rate (% of maximum)	Frequency (times per week)
1	1.5	3.0	70	5
2	1.5	3.0	70	5
3	1.75	3.0	70	5
4	1.75	3.0	70	5
5	2.0	3.0	70	5
6	2.0	3.0	70	5
7	2.0	3.5	70	5
8	2.25	3.5	70	5
9	2.25	3.5	70	5
10	2.5	3.5	70	5
11	2.5	3.5	70	5
12	2.5	3.5	70	5
13	2.75	3.5	70	5
14	2.75	4.0	70-80	5
15	3.0	4.0	70-80	5
16	3.0	4.0	70-80	5
17	3.25	4.0	70-80	5
18	3.25	4.0	70-80	5
19	3.5	4.0	70-80	5
20	3.5	4.0	70-80	5

At the end of this 20-week fitness walking protocol you may either stay at this schedule or increase your pace and distance.

Adapted from: *Rockport's Fitness Walking* by Robert Sweetgall, The Putnam Publishing Group, New York, NY, 1985. Printed with permission.

sure to do appropriate warm-up and cool-down exercises.

When you reach a fitness level at which walking no longer raises your heart rate sufficiently, you can make your body work harder by wearing a weight belt, using hand weights, walking faster or uphill, or by trying the increasingly popular race walking. Refer to the beginner's walking schedule within this chapter.

- **Walking to win.** Race walking is the competitive form of walking, but you don't have to compete to enjoy it. Race walkers maintain a particular style and form, in which one foot is always in contact with the ground and the leg that is supporting the weight straightens momentarily as it passes under the body. To learn to race walk properly, work with a coach or qualified teacher, who may sponsor race walking clinics through your local recreation center or university.

- **Walking to lose.** By increasing the amount of walking you do, you can lose weight without decreasing your calorie intake. Recent studies have shown that 40 minutes of daily walking appears to be the threshold for significant weight loss in women. For example, someone weighing between 127 and 137 pounds would burn 4.50 calories per minute walking at three miles per hour, or 180 calories.

- **Walking to relax.** Walking may well be the best "all-natural tranquilizer." A recent report in the *Journal of the American Medical Association* stated that 40 minutes of vigorous walking can reduce anxiety and tension, and improve mood for two hours or more.

- **Walking for fun.** Many people have found that walking with a partner or joining a walking club is the ideal way to make exercise a social event.

Mall walking is an activity popular with older adults, but you don't have to be a senior to enjoy it. In the protected environment of a shopping mall, walkers may receive health screening (monitoring of blood pressure and heart rate) and encouragement from the group. A marked route tells them how far they have walked. There are approximately 1,100 mall-walking groups nationwide, including at least one in every state.

Proper Form for Fitness Walking

- Purchase fitness walking shoes that are designed to provide appropriate arch and heel support and optimal cushioning in the heel and ball of the foot.
- Walk erect, but stay relaxed.
- Foot contact should be heel to toe, with the supporting leg straight as you go into your next step.
- Arms should be at a 90-degree angle and swung vigorously forward and back to help maintain momentum. Avoid crossing your arms in front of your chest, especially when using hand weights.

Jogging Guidelines

If you are a beginning jogger, you can make the greatest progress by slowly increasing your work interval (jogging) while staying within your exercise heart rate zone.

For individuals graduating from a walking program, the first three weeks should be viewed as a preconditioning period that is designed to acclimate the joints and cardiovascular system to increased stress.

Obese individuals should not jog, but should embark on a regular walking program until there is a significant decrease in body fat.

By following this process, you can jog for progressively longer periods, ultimately working up to 15 to 30 minutes of continuous jogging, always staying within your exercise heart rate zone. At first, don't be concerned with speed, but with total time. Only when you are able to jog continuously and comfortably for at least 20 minutes should you increase your speed.

Proper Running Form

- Maintain an upright posture, so that an imaginary plumb line would pass through your earlobe, shoulder, hip, knee and ankle.
- Think of your torso as "going for a ride," as it sits on your hips. Let your legs propel you forward.

Sample Jogging Program			
Week	Workout Period	Recovery Period	Number of Repetitions
1-3	1 minute of jogging	1 minute of walking	20
4	2 minutes of jogging	2 minutes of walking	10
5	3 minutes of jogging	2 minutes of walking	7
6-7	5 minutes of jogging	2 minutes of walking	4
8-10	7 minutes of jogging	2 minutes of walking	3
11-12	10 minutes of jogging	2 minutes of walking	2

- Unless you are sprinting, use your arms for balance. Bend your arms at a 90-degree angle, and hold your hands at chest height. Touch your forefingers to your thumbs, and swing your arms gently back and forth—avoid a side-to-side motion.
- Your foot plant should be heel-to-toe. Touch the ground with the front of the heel, then roll to the toes.
- Also, plant your foot directly below the knee, not in front, which breaks your momentum. While running, choose a point on the horizon at eye level. If it appears to be bouncing, then you are overstriding. Shorten your stride until the bouncing diminishes.
- Breathe naturally, through your mouth. Some coaches recommend "belly breathing" to promote ventilation.

Aerobic Dance Guidelines

The number of people participating in aerobic dance classes is approximately 23 million—with injuries a major concern. Most of these injuries are not serious, and they can be avoided if aerobic dancers take certain precautions. It is important to exercise on proper surfaces, to wear appropriate shoes, and to avoid exercising too long and too hard.

Aerobic dance can be strenuous. Most injuries occur below the knee and result from the repeated impact of the feet on hard surfaces.

The shin is the most common site of injury, and shin splints are a frequent diagnosis. A shin splint is an inflammation of the membrane around the bone. Its symptoms are pain, tenderness and occasional swelling. Symptoms usually last a week to 10 days if the shin splint is treated with rest. Shin pain is a symptom of several conditions, including stress fractures, muscle sprain and tendinitis.

Sometimes aerobic dancers develop pain in the ankles, knees or back. This is often the result of old injuries being aggravated. Knee injuries include a variety of conditions, such as bursitis and damage to the joint capsule and surrounding ligaments.

● **Shock Absorption Is Important**. The ideal surface for aerobic dance should provide shock absorption and stability. This means it shouldn't be too hard or too soft. The safest surfaces for exercise are heavily padded carpeted floors, foam mats, and newly developed hardwood-over-airspace floors. The highest rates of injuries occur on carpet over concrete and tile-covered concrete.

Proper footwear is a must if aerobic dance injuries are to be minimized. Using running shoes for aerobic dance is a mistake—they are designed for forward movement, whereas aerobic dance involves many side-to-side movements. Aerobic dance shoes should provide ample flexibility in the ball of the foot, heel cushioning, lateral support and a slightly raised heel to take force off the achilles tendon.

● **Aerobic Dancers Shouldn't Overdo It**. As in any other aerobic activity, it takes time to build up cardiovascular endurance. Therefore, it's important to follow the F.I.T.T. Principle outlined earlier. People just getting into aerobic dance should be careful not to do too much too soon or to progress too rapidly in exercise programs. Also, insufficient or improper warm-up and cool-down exercises can result in injuries. It is important to stretch the key muscle groups in the legs, hips, thighs, hamstrings, calves and shins.

In addition, it's recommended that aerobic dancers cross-train by alternating their workouts with other aerobic activities or resistance exercises to avoid overuse injuries.

● **Know What to Look for in Aerobic Dance Instructors.** A qualified instructor will know about the factors contributing to safety in aerobic dance and will know how to screen people for contraindications to exercise. He or she is likely to be certified by a reputable professional organization. The American College of Sports Medicine (ACSM) certifies fitness instructors, as do the International Dance and Exercise Association (IDEA) and the Aerobics and Fitness Association of America (AFAA).

Most aerobic dance injuries do not need to be seen by a physician, and few people must stop exercising completely because of them. Bicycling or swimming can be substituted for aerobic dance when injury becomes apparent.

Aerobic dance has adapted to the injury issue by developing low-impact aerobic techniques. These movements eliminate the hard jumping, while still providing an appropriate training effect. To get the most benefit and minimize injuries, remember to:

- Exercise on appropriate surfaces.
- Wear shoes designed for aerobic dance.
- Perform adequate warm-up and cool-down exercises.
- Use low impact techniques if you have difficulty with more traditional movements.
- "Train, not strain." No one should exercise too much or too hard.
- Cross-train on alternate days.

Goal Three: Muscular Strength and Endurance

This section will show you how to integrate muscular strength and endurance into your personal activity program through resistance training. How much or how little you choose to do should be determined by your personal goals, such as improving muscular tone and appearance, or meeting the appropriate levels of muscular strength and endurance, especially in the upper body and back, to perform everyday tasks or leisure activities.

Maintaining appropriate levels of muscular strength and endurance is an often-neglected fitness component for adults.

Muscular strength can be defined as the maximum resistance or weight that a person can move or lift at one time. Muscular endurance, in contrast, is the maximum amount of repetitive work that can be performed before fatigue. For the average adult, developing muscular endurance rather then muscular strength is more desirable, because the activities of daily living—house cleaning, lifting, stair climbing, yard work—and most leisure sports require repetitive movements. Therefore, the following exercises are designed to develop localized muscular endurance rather than absolute strength, though strength will be improved as well. This is accomplished by emphasizing higher repetitions with a lower resistance.

Two resistance programs are provided. The first uses your own body weight as resistance and can be used just about anywhere. **This is especially attractive if you travel.**

The second resistance program uses dumbbells (hand weights) that can be purchased from any major sporting goods store. These exercises isolate more specific muscle groups and are excellent not only for increasing localized strength and endurance, but also for improving muscle definition and tone.

Basic Rules
• All exercises should take muscles through their full range of motion.
• All exercises should be performed slowly and rhythmically.
• Don't hold your breath; breathe rhythmically, exhaling on all contractions.
• Do 15 to 20 repetitions per set. A set is the number of repetitions per exercise.
• Allow two to three minutes of rest between sets.
• When using hand weights, such as dumbells, select a starting resistance (amount of weight) that is comfortable for you. As your endurance and strength increase, so should the amount of resistance and number of repetitions and sets.
• Remember, it's better to start at a lower resistance and adjust the weight gradually, rather than to attempt lifting a weight beyond your capacity.

Developmental Exercises
Utilizing Body Weight as Resistance

1. **Abdominal Curls**
   A. Begin with your arms crossed on your chest and chin tucked to your chest.
   B. The legs are to be bent, with heels flat on the floor. The feet should be six to 12 inches from the buttocks. The lower back should be flat on the floor.
   C. Sit up slowly, raising the shoulder blades six inches from the floor, but keeping the small of back on floor. Exhale as you come up. Don't hold your breath!
   D. Lower the upper body slowly to floor.
   E. Complete 15 to 20 repetitions for a set.
   F. Eventual goal: two to three sets.
   (If you have difficulty performing this exercise with your arms crossed on your chest, keep your hands on your thighs, and slide them to your kneecaps as you come up.)

2. **Trunk Extension**
   A. Lie on your stomach with your hands under your shoulders.
   B. Your feet should be six inches apart.
   C. Slowly extend your arms, raising your head and chest from the floor but keeping the hips, hands, legs and feet on the floor.
   D. Exhale as you come up.
   E. Slowly lower your body to floor.
   F. Complete 15 to 20 repetitions for a set.
   G. Eventual goal: two to three sets.

3. **Back Leg Lift**
   A. Assume a position on your hands and knees.
   B. Keep your head up and look ahead.
   C. Extend right leg back with toe on floor. Slowly lift leg to hip level, then lower almost to floor.
   D. Complete 15 to 20 repetitions for a set.
   E. Repeat on other leg.
   F. Eventual goal: two to three sets.

4. **Side Lift**
   A. Assume a position on your side.
   B. Slowly raise the top leg through its full range of motion.
   C. Slowly lower the leg to the floor, behind the bottom leg.
   D. Complete 15 to 20 repetitions for a set.
   E. Repeat on the other side.
   F. Eventual goal: two to three sets.

5. **Push-Ups (Modified)**
   A. Lean against counter top, arms extended.
   B. Keep head, back and legs straight.
   C. Lower chest to counter top, bending elbows.
   D. Extend arms, breathing out. Don't lock elbows.
   E. Complete 15 to 20 repetitions for a set.
   F. Eventual goal: two to three sets.

6. **Push-Ups (Advanced)**
   A. Lie chest to floor, with your hands under your shoulders.
   B. Keep your back and legs straight.
   C. Extend your arms, breathe out, and don't lock elbows.
   D. Return to the resting position.
   E. Complete 15 to 20 repetitions for a set.
   F. Eventual goal: two to three sets.

7. **Calf Rise**
   A. Stand with the balls of the feet on a stable block of wood or on a step. Keep the heels lower than the toes.
   B. Slowly raise the heels until you're up on your toes, keeping your arms at your side.
   C. Return slowly to the starting position.
   D. Complete 15 to 20 repetitions for a set.
   E. Eventual goal: two to three sets.

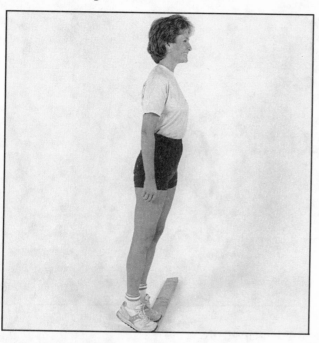

8. **Wall Sit**
   A. Assume a sitting position with your back flat against a wall.
   B. The thighs should be parallel to the floor. Hands are placed in your lap, on your kneecaps, or relaxed at your sides. **Don't hold your breath.**
   C. Hold this position initially for 20 seconds, gradually working up to a total of one minute.
   D. Eventual goal: two to three sets.

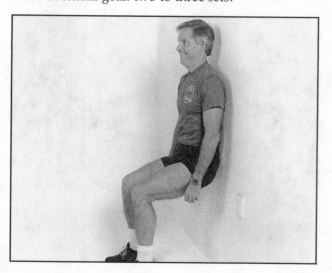

9. **Parallel Dips**
   A. Position yourself between two sturdy chairs.
   B. Body is in front lay-out position with one hand placed on each chair.
   C. With the legs kept straight, the body is lowered and arms are bent until the elbows are at shoulder height.
   D. Push up and extend the arms, keeping the body as straight as possible. Exhale as you come up.
   E. Complete 15 to 20 repetitions for a set.
   F. Eventual goal: two to three sets.

Dumbbell (Hand Weight) Exercises

1. **Chest Press**
   A. Lie on your back on an exercise bench, with your feet flat on the floor.
   B. Hold the dumbbells (hand weights) at your shoulders.
   C. Alternating arms, press the weights toward the ceiling; exhaling as you lift.
   D. Lower the weights with control and inhale.
   E. Complete 15 to 20 repetitions for a set.
   F. Eventual goal: two to three sets.

2. Shoulder Press

A. Sit on the bench with the dumbbells (hand weights) at your shoulders.

B. Alternating arms, lift each weight overhead to maximum extension. Exhale as you lift, keeping the back straight.

C. Lower the weights with control and exhale.

D. Complete 15 to 20 repetitions for a set.

E. Eventual goal: two to three sets.

3. Upright Rowing

A. Stand with your feet shoulder width apart.

B. Hold the dumbbells (hand weights) with your palms facing your body.

C. Keep your arms down at your sides, with the weights resting on top of your thighs.

D. Slowly raise both weights simultaneously, keeping elbows above hands, through the complete range of motion.

E. Raise the weights until they are even with your armpits. Breathe out when lifting.

F. Return to the starting position.

G. Complete 15 to 20 repetitions for a set.

H. Eventual goal: two to three sets.

4. Bicep Curl

A. Sit on a bench or chair. Keep your back straight.

B. Hold a dumbbell (hand weight) in each hand, with your arms hanging.

C. Bend your right elbow, slowly raising the weight to your shoulder; exhale.

D. Slowly lower the weight to the starting position; inhale.

E. Repeat with the left arm.

F. Alternate lifting with right and left arms.

G. Complete 15 to 20 repetitions for a set.

H. Eventual goal: two to three sets.

5. Tricep Extension

A. Sit on a bench or chair. Keep your back straight.

B. Grasp a dumbbell (hand weight) in your right hand. Place the weight behind your head, pointing the right elbow to the ceiling.

C. Stabilize your right arm with the left hand behind the right upper arm.

D. Slowly extend the right arm toward the ceiling. Exhale.

E. Slowly return to the starting position.

F. Complete 15 to 20 repetitions using the right arm.

G. Repeat for the left arm.

H. Complete two to three sets.

6. **Side Bend**
   A. Stand with your feet shoulder width apart.
   B. Grasp the dumbbell (hand weight) in your right hand, and place your left hand on your left hip.
   C. Keeping the right arm straight, slowly bend to the left.
   D. Feel the force pulling on your left side.
   E. Return to the upright position.
   F. Complete 15 to 20 repetitions for a set.
   G. Eventual goal: two to three sets.

7. **Double Leg Extension With Ankle Weights**
   A. Sit upright on a bench.
   B. Hold the bench with your hands.
   C. Slowly extend both legs until they are parallel to the floor.
   D. Lower your legs with control, and inhale.
   E. Complete 15 to 20 repetitions for a set.
   F. Eventual goal: two to three sets.

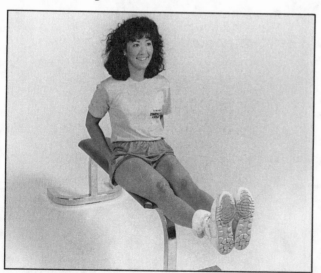

8. **Standing Leg Curl**
   A. Stand upright, holding the top of a chair for support.
   B. With an ankle weight on your right leg, slowly bring your heel to your buttocks.
   C. Slowly lower the heel to the floor.
   D. Complete 15 to 20 repetitions for a set.
   E. Repeat on the left leg.
   F. Eventual goal: two to three sets.

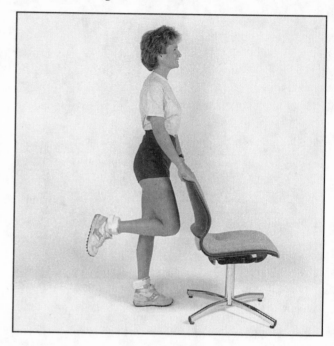

The Finish Line:
Is Physical Activity the Best Medicine?

In the preceding pages you have seen the many benefits that regular physical activity can provide, and you have been presented with useful strategies for putting more action in your life.

Though not a panacea, regular physical activity, when combined with other LifeSkills such as healthy eating and stress management, can be powerful medicine for reducing health risks, increasing longevity and adding quality to your life, no matter what your age. Perhaps cardiologist, author and runner George Sheehan, M.D., summed it up best when he said, "Physical activity is a generic drug. It's up to you to choose your name brand. Your brand may be running, cycling, or swimming. The important point is to be sure to take this drug on a regular basis, in the right dosage, and enjoy its effects!"

CHAPTER TWO

LifeSkill Two: Eat Healthy

"You are what you eat," Oscar Wilde once said. Now, a century later, scientists are affirming the validity of Wilde's observation. As data accumulate, it becomes clear that what we eat can have a direct impact on health, mood and longevity. This is not to say, however, that there's a special food or vitamin regimen for every ailment. But it does point to the fact that in most cases, the overconsumption of certain foods plays a major role in disease.

At the 1981 National Conference on Fitness and Aging, Dr. Myron Winick, director of Columbia University's Institute of Human Nutrition, said that food provides "the fuel for exercise" and "the raw materials for building a healthy body." In other words, for maximum performance and well-being, an adequate diet is a must. We are, indeed, the product of what we eat.

What's more, we can actually alter the aging process by eating wisely, according to Winick. Research has shown that diet plays a key role in such common health problems of aging as heart disease, cancer, stroke, diabetes and osteoporosis. Moreover, we can improve our appearance and energy levels by eating right.

Nutrition continues to make research headlines as scientists delve into the role of vitamins, fish oil and other dietary elements. Because of these exciting, pioneering efforts in nutrition, health science's new frontier, we can look forward to longer and more productive lives.

Despite the complexities of scientific theory, two simple words—balance and variety—describe nutrition at any age. Eating a balanced diet, one with the

Successful Weight Loss

Maintaining your ideal weight is more than a matter of appearance. Being overweight increases your risk of a number of health problems, including heart disease, high blood pressure and diabetes. Also, excess body fat can aggravate arthritis and other chronic conditions.

Losing weight and keeping it off require permanent lifestyle changes—sensible eating habits combined with regular physical activity.

Exercise increases your metabolism, the rate at which you burn calories. Even as little as 30 minutes of brisk walking or another continuous aerobic activity, performed three times a week, could cause an increase in metabolism sufficient to burn an extra 270 calories each day. You need to burn 3,500 calories to lose one pound of fat.

Caloric restriction alone doesn't work, because when you simply reduce the amount you eat, your metabolism drops to conserve energy—your body reacts to what seems like starvation. While you may lose weight, this is initially water weight, followed by lean body mass (muscle) and fat. When you stop dieting, much of the lost weight is regained (some experts theorize that each person has a biologically determined "set point" for body weight.)

With each diet, the body becomes more efficient at saving fat reserves. Weight comes off more slowly, and comes back more readily. This is called the "yo-yo" effect, and it works **against** most dieters.

A successful weight-loss plan involves several steps:

1. Begin by keeping an eating diary. For several days, list everything you eat, the

Weight Loss, continued

time, the place, the size of each portion, and the reason for eating. Study your diary to determine your cues for eating. Then, find ways to change your cues. For example, you might eat in only one place at home to minimize snacking, practice a relaxation technique when you're tense, or spend time at a hobby when you are bored.

2. Increase your daily physical activity level through formal exercise. Not only do you burn calories during activity, but research has shown that your resting metabolism stays elevated up to 48 hours after you stop exercising, thus altering your set point.

Another major benefit of formal exercise is that the majority of your weight loss will be **fat** loss, with an increase in lean body mass. While strict caloric restriction leads to some fat loss, an inordinate amount of muscle mass is lost as well.

3. Learn to replace high-fat, high-calorie foods with items that contain less fat and therefore fewer calories. Here are some suggestions:

Instead of:	*Try:*	*Calories Saved:*
Coffee with cream and sugar	Black coffee	110
Pork sausage	Low-fat ham	205
Fried potatoes	One baked potato	380
Roasted peanuts (one cup)	Grapes (one cup)	1,310
Whole milk	Skim milk	80
Apple pie (one piece)	One tangerine	305
Baked beans	Green beans	290

right proportions of carbohydrates, proteins and fat, involves daily selections from the four food groups—fruits and vegetables, breads and cereals, meat and fish, and dairy products. By simply choosing a variety of foods within those groups, you will get your needed nutrients and probably won't require vitamin supplements.

Here's how you can eat to improve your long-term health and productivity.

The harvest of foods Americans choose from is a rich one—perhaps too rich. While our life expectancies and average body size indicate that, on the whole, our diets are adequate, common health problems are evidence that we often do not select wisely from this abundance.

The three leading causes of death in the nation—heart disease, cancer and stroke—can be linked in part to poor nutritional habits. Diet also contributes to such other diseases as *osteoporosis* (brittle-bone disease) and obesity, which increases the risk of diabetes and high blood pressure.

The right food choices and preparation methods

Changing Diet According to the Chart Below Reduces Risk of Diseases or Their Complications. **Change Diet:**	Reduce Risk of:				
	Heart Disease	Cancer	Stroke	Diabetes	Gastrointestinal Diseases [2]
Reduce Calories	▲	▲	▲	▲	▲
Reduce Fats	▲	▲	▲	▲	▲
Increase Fiber and Starch [1]		▲		▲	▲
Reduce Sodium	▲		▲		
Control Alcohol		▲	▲		▲

1) Starch refers to complex carbohydrates provided by fruits, vegetables, and whole grain products.
2) Primarily gall bladder disease (fat and energy), diverticular disease (fiber), and cirrhosis (alcohol).

Source: *The Surgeon General's Report on Nutrition and Health,* 1988.

can reduce health risks considerably. The first step is understanding the diet-disease connection. The second step is learning to sever it.

Heart Disease: *Saturated Fat's Deadly Legacy*. The most common form of heart disease in the United States is coronary artery disease, a condition that develops very slowly, as fatty deposits accumulate in the arteries and block the flow of blood.

The blood's major function is to carry nutrients to all body tissues, including the heart, which is the hardest working muscle in the body. If an artery supplying the heart becomes so clogged that the blood flow is cut off, a portion of the heart actually dies. This is called a myocardial infarction, or heart attack.

The accumulation of fatty deposits (called atherosclerosis) is related to a high blood level of one kind of cholesterol—low-density lipoprotein cholesterol, or LDL—and a low blood level of another—high-density lipoprotein cholesterol, or HDL. LDL and heart disease go hand in hand, while HDL seems to rid the body of harmful cholesterol.

Saturated fat, the kind that is hard at room temperatures, leads to harmful cholesterol levels. Saturated fat is found primarily in foods from animal sources—meat, particularly red meat, whole-milk dairy products, and the foods containing animal fat, including pastries and foods fried in lard or beef tallow. It is also found in coconut and palm oils.

Unsaturated fats, also called polyunsaturated or monounsaturated, do not contribute to elevated cholesterol. They are liquid at room temperature and include olive, peanut, sunflower, corn, cottonseed, soybean and safflower oils. Some fish oils are a newly popular source of unsaturated fat. Most margarine and vegetable oils contain primarily unsaturated fats. Some forms of monounsaturated fats may help to bring down LDL cholesterol levels.

Ten Leading Causes of Death
United States, 1987

Rank	Cause of Death	Number	Percent of Total Deaths
1(a)	Heart Diseases	759,400	35.7
2(a)	Cancers	476,700	22.4
3(a)	Strokes	148,700	7.0
4(b)	Unintentional injuries	92,500	4.4
5	Chronic obstructive lung diseases	78,000	3.7
6	Pneumonia and influenza	68,600	3.2
7(a)	Diabetes mellitus	37,800	1.8
8(b)	Suicide	29,600	1.4
9(b)	Chronic liver disease and cirrhosis	26,000	1.2
10(a)	Atherosclerosis	23,100	1.1

(a) Causes of death in which diet plays a part.

(b) Causes of death in which excessive alcohol consumption plays a part.

Source: *The Surgeon General's Report on Nutrition and Health*, 1988.

The Effects of Sugar, Alcohol and Caffeine

People who are concerned about nutrition frequently ask about their intake of sugar, alcohol and caffeine. While heavy consumption of these substances is not recommended, they usually don't cause problems in moderate amounts.

Sugar most directly affects the teeth, causing decay and, possibly, eventual tooth loss. Sugar also adds calories and little else to the diet. Eating too much sugar contributes to obesity and its complications—diabetes, heart disease and high blood pressure. The average American consumes more than 120 pounds of sugar per year!

If you eat a balanced diet and are not overweight, you probably don't eat too much sugar. But if your appetite has decreased with age, beware of sweets, which may take the place of nutrients you need.

A word about artificial sweeteners. Their risk clearly seems to be related to dosage, so using them occasionally should present little danger.

Alcohol supplies more calories than do proteins or carbohydrates—about seven per gram. So, like sugar, it can cause you to put on weight.

There is some evidence that moderate alcohol consumption—one or two drinks per day—may reduce the risk of heart disease. Alcohol abuse, however, can be very damaging to health. It is the primary cause of cirrhosis of the liver and vehicular accidents. Excessive drinking can destroy relationships between parent and child, between spouses and between associates. There is also evidence that the risk of some cancers is higher in individuals who combine alcohol use with cigarette smoking. Clearly, alcohol should be enjoyed in moderation, if at all. (See Chapter Nine.)

Caffeine from your first morning coffee or tea may help to get you started. Another cup or a can of cola at lunch might provide an afternoon pick-me-up. But consuming two or three caffeine-containing beverages within that many hours will only make you nervous. Drinking them in the evening may cost you extra hours counting sheep.

At least one study has shown a correlation between heavy coffee drinking—five or more cups a day—and an increased risk of heart attacks. Although more study is needed in this area before conclusions can be drawn, there clearly is no long-term benefit to heavy caffeine consumption.

Want to cut down on saturated fat? Here's how:
- Substitute margarine for butter.
- Trim all visible fat from meat before cooking.
- Eat more fish and poultry (skinless is best) and less red meat, including cold cuts.
- Use vegetable oil, not such animal fats as bacon grease or lard for cooking.
- Read labels carefully. "Made from 100 percent vegetable oil" does not always mean 100 percent polyunsaturated. The product may contain coconut oil or palm oil.

Cancer: *Reduce the Fat, Increase the Fiber.* Switching from saturated to unsaturated fat may ward off heart disease, but unless you decrease **total** fat consumption, you've done nothing to protect against cancer. Experts estimate that 35 percent of all cancer may be related to how people eat, particularly when they choose a diet that is high in fat **of all kinds** and low in fiber.

Conversely, a diet that is low in fat has been associated with a reduction in cancer of the colon, prostate and endometrium (the lining of the uterus). When that diet is also rich in fruits, vegetables and whole grains—all high-fiber foods—the cancer probability drops even further.

Here are suggestions for reducing **total** fat intake:

- Boil, bake or steam foods instead of frying.
- Eat more whole grain cereals, fruits and vegetables.
- Add less fat in food preparation. Salad dressings, mayonnaise, sauces and cream are potent fat sources.
- Use non-stick frying pans and vegetable oil sprays.
- Beware of hidden fat—its sources include hot dogs, "luncheon" and "variety" meats, such as sausages and salami, some breads and pastries.
- Substitute low-fat for high-fat food. Use yogurt to replace sour cream, for example. Substitute low-fat ground turkey for ground beef in tacos, casseroles and other favorite recipes.

Cutting down fat also reduces your weight. Fats are packed with calories—about nine calories per gram. A gram of protein or carbohydrate, in contrast, contains only four calories.

And while you're downplaying fat, start paying more attention to *fiber*—the part of plant cells that the digestive system can't break down. Fiber tends to pass through the intestines quickly, carrying along food and possible carcinogens (cancer-causing agents). High fiber diets have been associated with a lower risk of colorectal cancer.

A high-fiber diet has other benefits. It reduces the symptoms of chronic constipation, diverticular disease and some types of "irritable bowel."

Whole-wheat bread, oat bran, oatmeal, bran cereals, shredded wheat, all fruits and vegetables, dry peas and beans, and unbuttered popcorn are all high-fiber foods. Because there are several kinds of fiber with different chemical structures, it's wise to get your fiber from more than one source.

Recent research indicates that adequate levels of vitamins A, C and E may be associated with a lower cancer risk. But it's best not to increase your consumption of these vitamins by taking supplements. Instead, eat heartily from the foods that contain them: dark green and yellow-orange vegetables, such as spinach, carrots and leafy greens; members of the cabbage family, including broccoli, Brussels sprouts and cauliflower; and whole-grain breads. Nuts and peanut butter are rich in vitamin E, but they should be consumed in small amounts because of their high fat content.

Stroke: *When Diet Affects the Brain.* When atherosclerosis clogs the arteries leading to the brain and cuts off the cerebral oxygen supply, tissue dies, and part of the brain's functioning is lost. So lowered fat consumption offers triple protection—reduced chance of heart disease, some types of cancer **and** stroke.

But in some strokes, a blood vessel in the brain actually ruptures. This is called a cerebral hemorrhage, and there is evidence that hypertension, or high blood pressure, increases the risk.

High blood pressure is a disease with no symptoms and, frequently, no known cause. Although anyone can have hypertension, blood pressure tends to rise with age. This is more indicative of inactivity, being overweight, poor dietary habits and heredity than aging itself. Since being overweight increases the risk, it is important to exercise and eat sensibly, watching the consumption of three dietary minerals that influence blood pressure: sodium, calcium and potassium.

An estimated 25 percent of Americans are sodium sensitive, putting them at risk for hypertension. Most of the sodium consumed is sodium chloride, or common table salt. Only a tiny amount of sodium is needed every day. Most experts agree that sodium intake should be limited to 1,100 to 3,000 mg per day. But most people get several times that amount. One preliminary study on sodium consumption and hypertension indicated that sodium may have a greater effect on blood pressure when combined with chlorine than with other chemicals, as in monosodium glutamate (MSG).

People with high blood pressure are consequently advised to cut down on salt. And because there is no test to determine who is sodium sensitive, it's a good idea for everyone to do the same. A notable exception would be those advised by their doctors to take salt to counter medications which may take low blood pressure to dangerously lower levels.

Better Late Than Never

Healthy eating provides benefits at every age. Those age 55 and older who want to improve their diet should keep in mind some special concerns.

- Undernutrition—not consuming the proper nutrients, as opposed to not getting enough calories—can be a problem if you restrict yourself to certain foods. Be careful to eat a broad variety of foods every day, and stay away from those high in sugar and fat, which meet your calorie needs but provide little else.
- Living alone is no reason to skimp on nutrition. Learn how to shop wisely for one.
  —Decide which size of the item is best for you. Although it is cheaper to buy in quantity, a package isn't a bargain if you throw most of its contents away.
  —Share large packages with a friend.
  —Purchase frozen vegetables in large, economical bags. You can use small amounts and store the rest.
  —If a package at the meat or produce counter is too large for you, ask a supermarket employee to divide and rewrap the contents.
- As people grow older, their sensitivity to flavors and smells can decrease. If food tastes blander to you than it once did, don't try to compensate by adding salt. Try chewing more thoroughly, alternating bites of different foods, or experimenting with herbs and spices.
- Enliven your interest in eating by making mealtime a social occasion. Invite a friend for lunch or dinner, or join a "pot-luck" club, in which members contribute prepared dishes to assemble a dinner.
- Some people's diets decline in quality because of dental problems. If the condition of your teeth or dentures keeps you from chewing meat or biting into crisp vegetables, don't hesitate to see your dentist.
- The federal government provides food programs to help low-income older people. Consult your local Area Agency on Aging, church, synagogue or United Way for food programs within your community. Refer to Section IV, Chapter Three for information on congregate and home-delivered meals.

Fish Oil and Heart Health

The apparent link between a high-fish diet and a low rate of heart disease is a hot topic in nutritional research. The dietary components believed to help the heart are omega-3 polyunsaturated fatty acids, which are contained in cold-water fish. This finding was prompted by the low incidence of heart disease among Eskimos who consume large quantities of fish.

Omega-3 fatty acids seem to lower harmful blood levels of cholesterol and prevent blood from clotting. These effects may prevent the development of atherosclerosis.

Some people now take fish oil supplements in an effort to gain these alleged benefits. But more research is needed before this practice can be recommended. It hasn't been demonstrated, for instance, that it is fish oil, and not some **other** component of the Eskimos' diet, that helps the heart. Moreover, even if fish oil is beneficial, we don't know how much people should consume.

Fish oil supplements are not risk-free. A substance that can help prevent blood clotting could cause problems in the case of injuries. Therefore, fish oil taken in high doses or in combination with aspirin, which also interferes with blood clotting, could be dangerous.

There is one safe way to add fish oil to your diet: Eat more fish! Salmon, swordfish, mackerel, bluefish and fresh tuna provide protein and other nutrients as well as omega-3 fatty acids.

Try these suggestions for cutting down on salt consumption:

- Eat foods generally containing less sodium. Fresh meats and vegetables are low-sodium choices, as are fruits in most forms—fresh, frozen, canned or juice.
- Watch out for foods that have sodium added during processing: cold cuts, bacon, hot dogs and ham, canned vegetables and vegetable juices, sauces, and commercially prepared foods, such as frozen dinners and canned soups.
- Limit your intake of salty snack foods such as potato chips, corn chips, pretzels, popcorn and nuts.
- Read labels to learn the sodium content of foods. Many food manufacturers list the sodium content of their products on the labels. MSG, brine, baking soda, baking powder, sodium citrate and saccharin listed as ingredients all mean the product contains added sodium.
- Decrease the salt used in cooking. Lemon juice, pepper, herbs, spices, onion and garlic add flavor to food and pose no health risk.

Calcium and potassium, in adequate amounts, may help to prevent hypertension in those at low risk, or to lower blood pressure in those who already have the disease. Low-fat dairy products are a good source of calcium, as are tofu, salmon and dark green, leafy vegetables. Apricots, oranges, bananas and potatoes are excellent potassium sources, but all fruits and vegetables are good choices.

A Question of Balance

"OK," you're probably thinking. "I'll eat less fat and more fiber and cut down on salt. But how do I know which foods to choose? What **is** a good diet?"

Healthy eating is easier than you think. It doesn't require a detailed knowledge of the chemical composition of foods, just an awareness of how to get a balanced and varied diet.

The major nutrients are proteins, carbohydrates and fats. Each benefits the body in special ways.

Proteins contain the basic materials for growth and repair of all body cells—those that make up muscles, internal organs, skin, bones, blood and hair. Proteins aid in the formation of antibodies and thus help the body resist disease. Lean beef, skinless chicken, fish, dairy products, nuts and legumes are all sources of protein.

Carbohydrates are your best source of energy, particularly for strenuous activity. Carbohydrates come in two forms—complex and simple. Complex carbohydrates are the starches present in grains, cereals, legumes, potatoes and other vegetables, as well as the types of sugar contained in fruits and milk products.

Foods rich in complex carbohydrates are likely to supply other essential nutrients, such as vitamins and minerals.

Simple carbohydrates, also called "simple sugars," are found in sweet desserts, candy, honey, syrup and table sugar. They provide quick, unsustained energy—calories—but little else.

Fats in foods serve a variety of functions. Some dietary fat provides linoleic acid, needed for growth and healthy skin. Fats also aid in the absorption of the fat-soluble vitamins (vitamins A, D, E and K). But as stated previously, too much dietary fat can lead to serious health problems.

So how much of each major nutrient should people consume? The National Academy of Sciences has set some recommended guidelines. When you compare them with the typical American diet, you can see that most people need to cut down on saturated and unsaturated fat while eating more of the complex carbohydrates and less of the simple sugars.

	Recommended Diet	Typical American Diet
(percent of total daily calorie intake)		
Complex carbohydrates	40%	20%
Simple carbohydrates	15%	25%
Protein	15%	15%
Unsaturated fats	20%	25%
Saturated fats	10%	15%

Choosing Foods for Variety's Sake

Of course, trying to determine the exact percentages of carbohydrates, proteins and fats in your diet would be difficult. A good way to approach the recommended guidelines—and to ensure an adequate intake of vitamins and minerals—is to select a variety of foods every day from the major food groups: fruits and vegetables, breads and cereals, meat and fish, and dairy products.

Foods Rich in Calcium

A serving of any of the following foods provides at least 10 percent of the U.S. Recommended Daily Allowance (USRDA) of calcium. The USRDA is 1,000 milligrams for adult men and women, and 1,500 milligrams for postmenopausal women.

FOOD	SERVING SIZE	CALCIUM (mg)
Plain, low-fat yogurt	8 ounces	415
Canned sardines, with bones	3 ounces	371
Part skim-milk ricotta cheese	1/2 cup	334
Skim milk	1 cup	302-316
Two percent low-fat milk	1 cup	297-313
Swiss cheese	1 ounce	272
Soft-serve ice cream	1 cup	236
Non-fat dry milk	1/4 cup	209
Cheddar, muenster, or part skim-milk mozzarella cheese	1 ounce	203-207
Raw oysters	4-6 medium	226
Slivered almonds	1/2 cup	179
Cooked, chopped collards	1/2 cup	178
Pasteurized process American cheese	1 ounce	174
Canned salmon, with bones	3 ounces	167
Feta cheese	1 ounce	140
Cooked broccoli	3/4 cup	132
Tofu	1 piece (2½" x 2¾" x 1")	108

(Source: The U.S. Dept. of Agriculture's *Nutritive Value of Foods.* Home and Garden Bulletin Number 72)

Recommended Daily Servings

Fruits and Vegetables
3 to 5 (vegetables)   2 to 4 (fruits)

- Dark Green, Leafy Vegetables
  Vitamins A and C, Riboflavin, Folic Acid, Iron, Calcium, Potassium
- Deep Yellow and Orange Vegetables
  Vitamin A
- Starchy Vegetables
  Carbohydrates, Niacin, Vitamin B-6, Zinc, Potassium
- Citrus Fruits
  Vitamin C, Folic Acid, Potassium, Magnesium
- Deep Yellow Fruits
  Vitamin A, Folic Acid, Potassium, Magnesium

Meat and Fish
2 to 3 (5 to 7 ounces total)

- Meat, Fish and Eggs
  Protein, Niacin, Vitamins B-6 and B-12, Iron, Phosphorous, Zinc
- Dry Beans and Peas
  Thiamin, Folic Acid, Iron, Magnesium, Phosphorous, Zinc, Potassium, Protein, Carbohydrates

Breads and Cereals
6 to 11 (make sure several are whole grains)

- Whole-Grain Breads
  Carbohydrates, Fiber, Thiamin, Riboflavin, Niacin, Iron, Folic Acid, Magnesium, Zinc
- Enriched Breads and Cereals
  Carbohydrates, Thiamin, Riboflavin, Niacin, Iron

Dairy Products
2 to 4

- Milk, Cheese, Yogurt
  Calcium, Protein, Riboflavin, Thiamin, Vitamins B-12 and A (if fortified, Vitamin D)

Source: The U.S. Department of Agriculture. Home and Garden Bulletin Number 232-1.

Generally, the amount of food you need depends on your age, sex, physical condition and activity level. Almost everyone should have at least the minimum number of servings recommended from each food group every day. However, for people over 50, activity level is the only important variable for determining caloric needs.

In addition, The National Institutes of Health recommend that postmenopausal women consume 1,500 milligrams of calcium per day, or at least four servings of dairy products, to help prevent osteoporosis. (See Section III, Chapter Twelve.)

One Step at a Time

Changing long-established habits takes time. The best way to become a healthy eater is **gradually.** That way, you won't get discouraged and slip back into your old routine.

Begin by changing nothing: For several days, keep a food diary, noting everything you eat. Then, look it over to determine where changes can be made.

You may find, for example, that you consume fried foods almost every day, or that you usually snack on high-sugar foods. If so, try new preparation methods and reach for fruit when you feel hungry.

In time, you can make further changes by replacing fatty red meat with lean beef or skinless chicken, consuming more fresh vegetables or cutting down on salt. If you have a family, involve them in what you are doing—they may have good suggestions.

Some people are reluctant to change their eating style, because they can't bear the thought of parting forever from the foods they love. But those who eat wisely most of the time can enjoy an occasional steak or fancy dessert. The key is moderation. You may also find that as your body becomes accustomed to a healthy diet, you will have fewer cravings for "bad" food.

Above all, keep a positive attitude. As you develop new eating habits and cooking techniques, you'll acquire new tastes, lower your health risks, have fun and set yourself up to reap health dividends in years to come.

CHAPTER THREE

LifeSkill Three: Develop an Effective Stress Style

The adult years are a time for building careers, marriages, families, homes and savings. There are stresses involved in all of these tasks, but achieving success enhances personal growth and performance.

The same is true for a host of changes, or life events, that inevitably occur. Children grow up and move away. Retirement draws near. A family member requires long-term care.

Whether such events are exciting and challenging, or tragic and demanding, each carries a heavy load of stress. Because stress is inseparable from life events, no one is immune from its effects. However, some individuals handle change better than others.

According to Robert Wilson, M.S., manager of employee assistance programs for The Travelers Companies, "Too often the working adult attempts to juggle too many balls in the air, at the same time, making unrealistic demands and expectations of himself or herself and inevitably suffering the consequences of burnout and overload."

This chapter presents information and skills that can help you deal more effectively with your emotions and the demands of your life. It focuses on your "stress style" and how you can handle stressful situations more effectively. This chapter will help you:

- Gain a better understanding of stress.
- Identify your sources of stress and how you react to them.
- Take steps to control stress by developing positive coping skills.

Stress:
You Can't Live Without It

A certain amount of stress is beneficial; without it, life would have no excitement, no stimulation and no surprises. It's this good stress (called *eustress*) that adds spice to your life. But when stress becomes chronic, it can take its toll:

- Unchecked, chronic stress can result in such illnesses as headaches, high blood pressure, backaches, heart disease, ulcers and even cancer, and in such psychological disorders as anxiety and depression.
- It can weaken the immune system, making the individual vulnerable to disease.
- Because a high stress level is linked to such behaviors as smoking and drug and alcohol abuse, it indirectly causes additional health problems.
- Moreover, too much stress impairs a person's performance and ability to enjoy life.

Many Americans accept a heavy stress load as a way of life, and they pay a high price. It has been estimated that two-thirds of all illnesses and deaths occurring before age 65 are stress-related. The emerging understanding of stress and its relationship to disease has spawned a new, interdisciplinary approach to studying that relationship. Psychoneuroimmunology (PNI) involves collaboration between neuroscientists, psychologists and immunologists. Early PNI studies have shown a direct link between the mind and the body's ability to fight disease (the immune response).

In her book *Minding the Body, Mending the Mind*, Joan Borysenko, Ph.D., describes how this new field is helping to explain the body's inner workings. According to Borysenko:

"Much PNI research centers on a group of hormonal messengers called neuropeptides, which are secreted by the brain, by the immune system and by the nerve cells in various other organs. What scientists have found is that the areas of the brain that control emotion are particularly rich in receptors for these chemicals. At the same time, the brain also has receptor sites for molecules produced by the immune system alone—the lymphokines and interleukins. What we see, then, is a rich and intricate two-way communication system linking the mind, the immune system, and potentially all other systems, a pathway through which our emotions—our hopes and fears—can affect the body's ability to defend itself."

What this research so strongly suggests is that not only do negative emotions affect our well-being, because in a way we are psycho-physiologically "hardwired," but also that we have the capacity to help keep ourselves well, and possibly assist the healing process.

Many experts believe that as the field of PNI evolves, it will unlock some of the mysteries surrounding stress and disease. In turn, it will provide useful strategies and treatments for maintaining and/or boosting a healthy immune response.

The Stress Response:
We're Not in Bedrock With the Flintstones Anymore

Stress has been defined as "a non-specific response of the body to demands made upon it."

In simpler terms, the body prepares to defend itself against a perceived threat, either real or imagined, in a variety of ways. This perceived threat, or stress signal, is called a *stressor*.

The stressor could be an actual occurrence in the environment or an event that takes place only in the mind: something that hasn't happened but that the individual imagines **might** happen.

A threat doesn't have to be negative. Even good things, like getting married or receiving a pay raise, can cause stress, because they disrupt our *status quo*. They knock us out of our comfort zone and require us to adapt in some way, good or bad, to the change.

On the whole, stress is based upon our perceptions and experiences. For example, speaking before a group is stressful for some people while others relish the opportunity.

When an event is perceived as a threat, a signal is conveyed to the cerebral cortex, the portion of the brain that controls higher-level nervous functions, including memory. Here the event is compared to previous experiences and is judged to be either threatening or non-threatening. If the event is perceived as a threat, the brain alerts the body to prepare for action: The heart rate accelerates, blood flow to the arms and legs increases, muscles tense, the pupils dilate, and adrenaline and other hormones enter the system. This innate physiological arousal allows us to either confront the threat or run away from it. This *stress response*, also called the "fight-or-flight response," is our built-in emergency response system. It has been handed down from our prehistoric ancestors, whose survival was highly dependent upon their ability to react quickly to the physical threats of the day.

Though this response saved Fred and Wilma Flintstone and their neighbors of Bedrock, "fight-or-flight" is most often an ineffective and overblown response to what psychologist Earl Hipp calls the "imaginary tigers" of our day. Many times we react to deadlines, traffic jams and financial pressures as if we were looking down the throat of a saber-toothed tiger. Not only is this reaction inappropriate and counterproductive to the resolution of everyday problems, but as the field of PNI suggests, it can have serious effects on our health.

The Stress of Change

Many life events, significant or ordinary, welcomed or dreaded, are commonly perceived as threats to our *status quo*. This is because they represent change, and change in itself can bring stress.

Drs. Thomas Holmes and Richard Rahe, psychiatrists and researchers at the University of Washington, determined that when people fail to adapt successfully to change—whether good or bad—stress can create fertile ground for future illness. Holmes and Rahe ranked 43 life events and assigned a point value to each. They found that the more points scored in the past 12 months, the greater the probability of illness within the next two years. For example, a score of 200 points correlated with a 50 percent chance of becoming ill.

You can use the "Social Readjustment Scale" (see page 49) to gauge the amount of change that has taken place within your life over the past 12 months. However, this scale is not a sure-fire predictor of illness and certainly shouldn't generate any "self-fulfilling prophecies."

This scale can help you assess your current stressors and anticipate or plan for those over which you have control. You can use your results to devise coping strategies that either avoid, delay, modify, eliminate or redistribute the demands that stressors place on you. For example, if a parent has recently taken ill and you've just been offered a new position, it may be wise to postpone your job change until you feel comfortable that your parent's care needs are being met.

Personality-Driven Stress

There are people who claim that they never experience stress; but it's more likely that stress is so much a part of their lives that they no longer recognize it. They have forgotten how it feels not to be stressed. In fact, some individuals may have what Drs. Meyer Friedman and Ray Rosenman call a *Type A personality*. The research described in their book *Type A Behavior and Your Heart* showed that this personality type, when compared to its counterpart, the Type B personality (more relaxed, less competitive, more willing to "go with the flow"), had twice the rate of heart disease.

The Type A personality is categorized as exhibiting the following behaviors:

- A high sense of time urgency. They suffer from the "hurry sickness."
- Highly competitive.
- Impatient with others.
- Free-floating hostility or anger.
- Poor listener; interrupts in the middle of a conversation.
- Involved in too many activities; tries to juggle too many tasks at the same time.

Further research has shown that competitiveness, impatience and anger are more closely linked to the Type A's susceptibility to heart disease. However, in studies by Friedman, Type A's have been shown to modify their behavior through professional counseling and self-management techniques.

All of us fall somewhere along the Type A-Type B continuum. However, if Type A behavior reflects your common stress style, you may be over-reacting to life's demands and may suffer, in the long run, negative health consequences.

What's Your Stress Style?

How effective have you been in dealing with change? How does your personality influence your perceptions and ability to cope with life's pressures and challenges? What do you perceive as stressful? How do you react and respond to those events? What are the consequences of your actions? In other words, what's your stress style?

A common technique for helping individuals evaluate their stress style is conducting a personal stress audit. The following exercise is designed to help you identify and clarify those situations (stressors) that elicit feelings of stress (reactions) and how you respond (cope) in attempting to reduce their perceived threat. Take the time now to answer the following questions using the worksheet provided.

1. Which are the four most common stressors in your life?
2. How do you normally react to each stressful situation or event physically, psychologically and/or behaviorally?
3. How do you normally try to adapt or reduce the threat of each stressor? Do you use a tranquilizer to reduce anxiety, or do you practice a relaxation technique? Do you try to ignore the stressor and hope it goes away, or do you address it head on and try to remedy the problem?
4. What are the consequences of your action? Do you perceive your behavior as a positive adaptation or a maladaptive response? Maladaptive behavior provides temporary relief or escape but in the long run creates additional problems, such as substance or alcohol abuse and interpersonal conflict.
5. What new skills can be developed and applied to replace a maladaptive response?

DETERMINE YOUR STRESS STYLE

What are your major stressors?	How do you normally react: • physically? • psychologically? • behaviorally?	How do you normally respond to each stressor?	What are the consequences of your actions?	What new skills can be applied in the future?	What help do you need?
Stressor # 1					
Stressor # 2					
Stressor # 3					
Stressor # 4					

6. What support or help do you need to develop each new skill? For example, do you require professional assistance from a counselor, or do you only need an audiotape to learn to relax?
7. Finally, review your completed worksheet to become familiar with your current stress style. Next, mentally practice by applying the new skills that you identified to specific situations. Visualize executing your new stress style by imagining yourself experiencing each stressor in a more proactive fashion.

Developing a Positive Stress Style

Going for a jog in the middle of a heated business discussion is clearly not a suitable, or even logical, way to react to stress.

Thus, a key ingredient of an effective stress style is the development and use of appropriate coping strategies.

As you evaluate your present coping skills, you'll realize that negative reactions compound, rather than relieve, stress. For example, reaching for a tranquilizer every time you're anxious may bring short-term relief, but it ignores the source of your anxiety and can lead to dependence. Therefore, it's important that you develop and practice a repertoire of stress skills that are designed to:

- Build "immunity" by increasing your physical resistance to stress through proper LifeSkill practices.
- Help you avoid, eliminate or modify stressors when appropriate.
- Reduce the impact of stressors you cannot change.

How to Build Stress Immunity

As we've seen, chronic episodes of stress can compromise the immune system, increasing the risk of physical illness and leading to maladaptive behaviors, such as alcohol or drug abuse, overeating, and nicotine addiction, thus creating a vicious cycle that challenges and breaks down physical and psychological hardiness. It is essential, therefore, to replace maladaptive responses with coping methods that work. Here are a few key strategies:

Practice Appropriate LifeSkills

Through appropriate LifeSkills, you can build "stress immunity" by increasing your resilience against everyday pressures.

Regular physical activity, proper nutrition, not smoking, moderate alcohol consumption and adequate sleep are some of the basic LifeSkills that should be incorporated into your everyday routine. To learn more about specific LifeSkills and their value in building stress immunity, refer to the appropriate chapters in this section.

Learn to Relax

Controlled relaxation is a very effective method for reducing tension and anxiety. You can learn to reduce muscular tension systematically, through specific relaxation techniques that elicit the *relaxation response*. In contrast to the fight-or-flight response, the relaxation response "downshifts" the body, reducing muscular tension, respiration, heart rate and overall physiological arousal.

The "Sand Bag" and the "Calming Response," both presented in this chapter, are two effective relaxation techniques that you can practice. Additional techniques can be learned from books and tapes, or by enrolling in a stress-management workshop offered through a local university, hospital or private practitioner.

However, some people have great difficulty controlling muscular tension through traditional relaxation exercises and may need special therapy. Biofeedback can be a valuable option. Biofeedback uses sensitive instruments to monitor such physiological stress indicators as heart rate, skin temperature, muscle tension and brain waves. Through a system of signals, such as colored lights and/or audiotones, the practitioner receives instant feedback on the specific physiological function being monitored. By combining the feedback with mental imagery and other "autogenic techniques," the individual can quickly learn to control the signal and, therefore, the physical event (for example, muscle tension).

Licensed biofeedback professionals have been successful in treating such conditions as tension/migraine headaches, incontinence and impotence in patients who have been unsuccessful with other treatments.

Establishing Proactive Strategies

While the above strategies can help you become more resistant to life's slings and arrows, a chronic stressor can still eventually wear away your suit of armor. It's important to go directly to the source of your stress, to become proactive: to eliminate, avoid or modify the stressor whenever possible.

Review your list of stressors from your stress-style worksheet, and ask yourself the following questions:

- How much control do I have over each stressor?
- Am I able to eliminate or avoid the stressor entirely?
- If not, can I modify, or change, it to make it a minor nuisance?

Once you have identified stressors that you feel you can control, you need to determine what solutions are available.

For example, a common stressor for many people is rush-hour traffic. They could eliminate this stressor by changing their working hours, perhaps through flex-time, or by taking an alternate route.

The Sand Bag

Sit quietly in a chair, with your back straight and hands in your lap. Take one easy breath, then slowly exhale and feel all the tension leaving your chest.

Turn your attention to the rhythm of your breathing. It should be like a swinging door in a gentle breeze, swaying to an easy tempo.

Now, in your mind's eye, picture yourself as a large burlap bag filled with heavy sand, propped up in that chair. In fact, the sand is so heavy that the two corners of the bag that are your feet suddenly burst open . . . and now the sand is running out . . .

Feel the tension running out . . . no tension, no thinking . . . Feel the flow of that heavy sand running out of your feet . . . no resistance, just feel yourself empty all of that tension as the sand is running out.

Remain sitting erect, but visualize the top of the bag beginning to curl down as the sand empties . . . Feel the flow release all the tension and the sand.

Return to your breathing . . . return to the swinging door . . . no tension . . . no thinking.

Now, slowly sit back, keeping your eyes closed . . . Remain sitting for two minutes . . . with a feeling of recharged batteries . . . You will have a calm and alert disposition as you go about your business.

If either option is not practical, then it may be wise to make the best of a bad situation, perhaps by listening to self-development tapes or audio novels while driving.

Another proactive approach is finding ways to modify, or change, the stressor itself. For example, tactfully telling your supervisor that you would like to arrange a meeting to discuss how the workload can be better balanced allows you to address, directly, the perceived cause of your stress (a boss who is piling on the work). You may find that the workload is fairly distributed, and that you merely need help with ranking tasks and scheduling. Or, you both may agree on more realistic deadlines and a new, mutually acceptable schedule.

Going to the source of your stress is the most direct strategy. It puts the fire out, and it gives you a greater sense of self-control. Use it when you can.

Developing a Bag of Tricks

Every day can be a stress day, if you perceive it that way. Developing an effective stress style may very well mean changing the way you think about things.

We all have an inner voice that we listen and respond to. We call it "self-talk." Listen to yours. Is it negative? If it is, try to "accentuate the positive, eliminate the negative," as the song goes. Here are a few strategies:

Don't Make Horror Movies Out of Mental Snapshots

Many of the "threats" that cause us to experience stress are what psychologist Barbara Brown calls "products of the mind." Because we **perceive** a situation to be threatening, we can easily produce a "horror movie" from a mental snapshot. Here are some common examples of perceived threats:

- An upcoming dental appointment.
- Speaking before a group.
- A job interview.
- Taking a test.
- A new assignment at work.
- Interactions with other people.

These and similar events share a common denominator: They cause stress for some people but not for others. While one person worries and even loses sleep when the date for a presentation approaches, another barely gives the matter any thought and may even look upon public speaking as a positive experience.

Why? Because these threats are *perceived* rather than real. In most instances, it is possible to change your perception of the event through *cognitive restructuring*. What this simply means is that you first need to transform the snapshot, or negative image, into a pleasant movie rather than a horror film. It's also important that your self-talk conform to this new perception. For example, the person who fears making a speech probably thinks:

- "I'm going to fall off the podium."
- "I'll probably forget what to say."
- "People aren't really interested in what I have to say."
- "My boss will be in the audience and listening to every word."
- "People will laugh at me."
- "My speech is probably boring."

Already this individual is making a horror film from a number of mental snapshots and, in turn, creating more negative self-talk. The result: a self-fulfilling prophecy of more anxiety, more stress and poor performance.

All of these negative thoughts are signs of an imagination out of control. To get back in charge of the situation, this person needs to:

Freeze frame: Stop the thought, the image, the snapshot in mid-action.

Re-edit: Change the image and the dialogue into a positive script. For example, our anxious speaker could re-edit his or her movie script as follows:

- *Old script:* "I'm going to fall off the podium."
  Re-edit: "I'll get there 30 minutes early to get a feel for the stage and room."
- *Old script:* "I'll probably forget what to say."
  Re-edit: "After rehearsing three times I'll only need to refer to a brief outline."
- *Old script:* "People aren't really interested in what I have to say."
  Re-edit: "My topic must be interesting, because the audience chose mine from the four available presentations."
- *Old script:* "My boss will be in the audience and listening to every word."
  Re-edit: "After rehearsing three times, I'll be well prepared."
- *Old script:* "People will laugh at me."
  Re-edit: "People will be impressed with me."
- *Old script:* "My speech is probably boring."
  Re-edit: "My speech is well organized and topical."

Replay: Watch the new movie; reaffirm that this is the way it **will** happen!

Negative snapshots can represent inflated fears or expectations that seem enormous only until they are compared to reality. By freeze-framing the image, re-editing the perception and finally replaying the new ending, you can effectively learn to change perceived threats into positive images and significantly reduce your stress level.

Manage Your Time

Effective time management is another important skill, particularly for Type A personalities—those af-

The Calming Response

Most relaxation techiques take about 20 minutes to perform, so they can't be used in every situation. For this reason, it is important to have a technique that can be used anytime, anywhere. This technique requires you to produce positive mental pictures that are associated with a more optimistic outlook. Similar to the thought-stopping techniques outlined earlier, the calming response allows you to focus on the problem and cuts off runaway negative perceptions and the anger, tension or anxiety that they produce.

When you begin to feel tense, annoyed or upset:

1. *Freeze the thought*. Attempt to freeze-frame the thought or situation that is disturbing you.
2. *Think happy*. Quickly imagine a situation or thought that always makes you happy. Feel your face lighten up. Feel the tension leaving your forehead, jaw, neck and shoulders.
3. *Blow off the tension*. Inhale slowly. Fill up the lower part of your lungs by pushing out your belly as you inhale. Hold for a count of three, then slowly exhale through your nose. As you exhale, feel all the built-up tension leave your body. Feel cool, calm and collected.
4. *Return to focus*. Let the film roll once more. Focus on the problem in a calm, objective manner.

flicted with the hurry sickness.

In his book *The Time Trap*, author R. Alec Mackensie notes that effective time management begins with careful planning. He suggests:

1. Assessing your current situation.
2. Developing relevant assumptions about the conditions that are likely to exist within the time plan.
3. Establishing project objectives.
4. Developing alternative methods to reach those objectives.
5. Making and implementing the decision.
6. Establishing review and control procedures.

Too many of us spend 80 percent of our time on things that yield 20 percent of the results. That means we have only 20 percent of our time left over to gain 80 percent of our results! This equation demonstrates the need for better time management. Clearly, we should spend time on those things that produce the greatest benefit. This involves minimizing the time spent on such things as phone calls, memos, meetings and irrelevant reports whenever possible. Look for these ways to adjust the equation:

- Conduct a "time study." For three to five days, keep a log of your activities and the time they take.
- Categorize activities such as phone calls, projects, meetings, driving and eating, and list the total time spent on each one. Rank each task or activity as a #1 (high priority), #2 (mid-priority) or #3 (low priority).
- Identify those #3 items that consume an inordinate amount of time.
- Reduce the time spent on your #3 activities, or eliminate them altogether.
- Apply the same process to your #2 items as well.
- Use a calendar or log as a "time planner" to organize your schedule by days, weeks and months.
- Set realistic schedules on projects at work and home.
- Organize your work space in the office and at home. Know where things are: files, tools, equipment, etc.
- Set realistic goals.
- Rank your goals. What is really important?
- Learn to delegate non-essentials.
- Do it right the first time!
- Get away from your work, and schedule relaxation and leisure into your day.
- Save your phone messages whenever possible for a certain time of the day.
- Don't over-commit yourself. Learn to say no!

Learn to Communicate Effectively

Poor interpersonal communication is a common cause of stress. When messages are misintepreted, people can make wrong assumptions. This can lead to a great deal of worry, second-guessing, interpersonal conflict and, once again, negative self-talk.

To be an effective communicator, you must be a good sender and receiver of information. No matter how close the relationship is, other people can't know what you think or feel unless you let them know.

Here are a few tips:

- *Sending Skills.* Decide what your message really is. Phrase your message to get your point across. Choose the most specific words you can and follow-up on your message to make sure it was received correctly.
- *Receiving Skills.* "Active listening" means listening to understand and trying to avoid bias. Respond appropriately to others' messages and make sure that each person understands the other's expectations.
- *Feedback Skills.* Listening is not enough. Learn to respond to verbal and non-verbal cues so that you can help motivate the other person to achieve a desired end. When evaluating performance or providing constructive criticism, be direct and specific. Avoid involving personalities whenever possible.

Taking Control of Change

In this chapter, we have discussed the basic strategies you can use to develop an effective stress style. By following these recommendations you will be able to deal more effectively with change and transition.

To a great degree, stress can be viewed as either danger or opportunity. It's not only how you perceive stress, it's how well you adapt to its demands that influences your health and personal effectiveness. Major events such as divorce or caring for a dependent parent call for a specialized way of dealing with change. Therefore, it's important to have a stress style that has the flexibility to adapt to a specific demand, while producing the least resistance and loss of personal control.

Remember, life is change, and to a great extent, you choose how you wish to steer its course.

What Are the Changes in Your Life?

The following Social Readjustment Scale has been used extensively to help people become aware of one type of stressor. This scale measures the amount of stress due to change that an individual has experienced in the past 12 months. Note that a happy event, like marriage, can have a stress value as great as or even greater than a negative change, like the death of a close friend. Research has shown that the higher the score, the greater the chance of experiencing a stress-related illness within the next two years. For example, individuals who totaled more than 200 points in the previous year had a 50 percent chance of developing an illness. A score of more than 300 indicated an 80 percent chance of becoming ill.

Over the past 12 months, I have experienced the following changes in my life:

Social Readjustment Scale	
Life Events	Holmes Points
1. Death of spouse	100
2. Divorce	73
3. Marital separation	65
4. Jail term	63
5. Death of close family member	63
6. Personal injury or illness	53
7. Marriage	50
8. Fired from job	47
9. Marital reconciliation	45
10. Retirement	45
11. Change in health of family member	44
12. Pregnancy	40
13. Sex difficulties	39
14. Having a baby	39
15. Business readjustment	39
16. Change in financial state	38
17. Death of close friend	37
18. Change to different line of work	36
19. Change in number of arguments with spouse	35
20. Mortgage large in relation to income	31
21. Foreclosure of mortgage or loan	30
22. Change in responsibilities at work	29

Social Readjustment Scale	
Life Events	Holmes Points
23. Son or daughter leaving home	29
24. Trouble with in-laws	29
25. Outstanding personal achievement	28
26. Spouse begins or stops work	26
27. Begin or end school	26
28. Change in living conditions	25
29. Change in personal habits	24
30. Trouble with boss	23
31. Change in work hours or conditions	20
32. Change in residence	20
33. Change in schools	20
34. Change in church activities	19
35. Change in recreation	19
36. Change in social activities	18
37. Small mortgage in relation to income	17
38. Change in sleeping habits	16
39. Change in number of family get-togethers	15
40. Change in eating habits	13
41. Vacation	13
42. Christmas	12
43. Minor violations of the law	11

Reprinted with permission from the *Journal of Psychosomatic Research, II*; Thomas H. Holmes and Richard H. Rahe, "The Social Readjustment Rating Scale," 1967, Pergamon Press.

Life Events Worksheet

My score on the Social Readjustment Scale was _____

Over the next 12 months I can modify or control the following life events:

1. _____

2. _____

3. _____

4. _____

Refer to pages 45 to 46 for proactive strategies that can be used to directly influence each stressor.

Life events I feel I cannot control:

1. _____

2. _____

3. _____

4. _____

Refer to pages 46 to 48 for strategies that can be used to modify your **perception** of each stressor.

CHAPTER FOUR

LifeSkill Four:
Stay Interested in Life

Healthy people have a healthy interest in life, regardless of their age. They enjoy their families, friends, co-workers and neighbors. They keep up with current trends and events, pursuing interests and sharing ideas.

Staying in touch with our world gives our lives purpose and meaning. Gerontologist Alexander Leaf, who has observed cultures in which longevity is common, reports, "It is characteristic of each of the areas I visited that the old people continue to be contributing, productive members of their society. . . . People who no longer have a necessary role to play in the social and economic life of their society generally deteriorate rapidly."

Those who stay involved in life avoid loneliness, depression and possibly ill health. They generally have a better handle on stress and an easier time coping with change at all stages of life. They experience fewer health problems, and they may actually live longer. Certainly, they enjoy life more.

Do You Have a Purpose?

As a human being, you are capable of great things. You can learn and share knowledge, affection and understanding. You possess a mind that can tackle problems and comprehend abstract ideas. You experience creative urges and enjoy a wide range of activities.

But to a great extent, how you develop your potential as you grow older is up to you. According to some psychologists, this is your purpose, or mission, in life. Having purpose gives us a reason to feel that there is more to life than just getting up in the morning. Purpose means applying our talents and interests to goals that we believe in.

Describing the growth process that occurs in the adult years, Abraham Maslow, Ph.D., gave us his concept of *self-actualization*. Stated simply, self-actualization is an innate desire for fulfillment, common to all adults. Fulfillment means different things to different people, of course. It could be a desire to be a good parent or friend, to contribute to society, to develop artistic abilities, or to come up with new ideas. Maslow described self-actualized individuals as "doing the best that they are capable of doing."

Although everyone yearns for self-actualization, few people reach that goal. Many develop habits that discourage growth. Some are hindered by socioeconomic barriers. Others are "caught in a rut" but make little effort to change because they have no focus, no purpose, no plan.

Growth does not stop when we reach age 21, age 65 or any other age. We continue to learn, and we can contribute at any stage in life.

Who and What Make Up Your World?

Kenneth R. Pelletier, Ph.D., says, "An intact and stable social system may play a more important part in longevity than any nutritional, exercise, environmental or other factor." In fact, research from Alameda County, California has shown that adults who had social support through marriage, contacts with friends, church membership and informal and formal group associations had a lower likelihood of dying within the next nine years than individuals who had little or no involvement in those four areas.

There's some question about whether social contacts improve health, or whether health improves your social life. But we all know that social relationships are what life is all about. Building and maintaining social health is a crucial LifeSkill, one that provides us the opportunity to share interests and experiences with others. Social health gives us:

- A sense of identity with something greater than ourselves.
- A buffer against periods of stress.
- An informal care network during times of crisis.

How Wide Is Your Circle?

Your social circle will continue, throughout life, to include your family, friends, and associates from work and within the community. Each group meets unique needs and offers its own special rewards.

Start With Your Family

Your family is much more than a group of people to whom you are related. It helps define who you are, teaches basic values and provides role models, intimacy and support. A healthy family is a source of joy, confidence and inspiration.

Researchers have identified several qualities that healthy families share:

- **A clear understanding of each member's roles and responsibilities.** The members recognize distinctions between the generations. Parents fulfill the obligations of their role, and children engage in activities appropriate to their age.

- **An equal distribution of power.** Spouses share power and permit children certain choices. But power is not a big concern: The family's openness and acceptance nurture the desire to please.

- **Support and encouragement.** Children are guided and cared for, yet they are supported in their decision to live independently when the time is right. Adults anticipate and prepare for such eventualities as the "empty nest," retirement and possible widowhood.

- **Effective communication.** Members state what's on their minds and respond to one another honestly and constructively. If there's a problem, they work together creatively to find the solution that best meets everyone's needs. They share laughter and joy, disappointment and sorrow.

- **A shared system of values or beliefs.** This is a source of enjoyment and optimism for all family members, whether it's a shared belief in the goodness of people, an appreciation of nature or a belief in a supreme being.

The family, society's basic unit, is undergoing changes. Geography separates relatives, single-parent households grow, divorce rates soar. Is it any wonder that we need to work hard to keep family bonds strong?

If your relatives live far away, frequent letters and phone calls may be all that's possible. But those who are close, even in the same household, can plan more shared activities and develop new interests together.

Work with family members to develop those healthy qualities. Talk constructively about roles and mutual expectations. Share a funny story. Take pride in family members' accomplishments and spur them on to bigger and better things. Try creative problem solving the next time difficulties occur.

Families experiencing serious relationship problems should not hesitate to get help from a qualified professional. A child exhibiting negative or aggressive behavior, or changes in a marriage could signal family stress.

You can find a qualified family therapist by calling your county mental health agency, a licensed mental health clinic or a clinical social workers' association. The American Association for Marriage and Family

Rid Your Life of Loneliness

To cope with loneliness, you must face up to it. Dr. Miriam Stoppard offers these suggestions:

- For several weeks, keep a diary and note the times of day or night when you most miss the company of others. You may find, for example, that evenings or Sundays are your loneliest times.

- Plan activities to fill these hours **that involve other people**. You could take a course one evening each week and learn a craft on another day. On Sundays, invite friends for lunch or brunch.

- Make an effort to get out and meet people. Join a club that brings together men and women who share a common interest. Sign up for a travel-study program, or become a volunteer.

- If you are widowed, don't deny yourself the company of the opposite sex for fear of betraying your dead spouse. As Stoppard explains, "It is absolutely right that you should remember your partner, and feel loyal to him or her. It is also quite normal to want another to hold you, comfort you and make love to you."

Better Late Than Never

Even if you've never paid much attention to your social life or developed interests outside of work, it's not too late to start. But changing long-established living patterns takes time, so set modest goals. That way, you can experience a series of small successes and gradually change your life's course.

Plan one regular activity that will put you in contact with other people. Join a club or church group, begin an exercise program or take an adult education class in your community. Make an effort to get to know your co-workers outside the job.

Discover a new leisure pursuit. It may help to diverge from an activity you already enjoy, but about which there is little more to learn. For example, if you have sewn your own clothes for years, try quilting. If you enjoy caring for your lawn and shrubbery, put in a vegetable garden or begin tending indoor plants. Your new hobby could be your reason for enrolling in a class.

In a month or two, when your first small changes feel secure and comfortable, take on some new challenges. And remember that stress-management skills can ease you through these transitions.

Is A Hobby Worth Your Time?

Your spare time is valuable, so make sure you fill it wisely. Consider these guidelines when choosing new leisure activities.

- **Opt for lifelong enjoyment.** Parachuting and scuba diving are exciting, glamorous pursuits, but you probably won't be able to enjoy them frequently, now or in years to come. Instead, choose hobbies that will bring regular satisfaction through all stages of life and that can easily be carried over into retirement.
- **Seek out learning and growth.** Select activities that challenge your intellectual and creative faculties or that offer an opportunity to hone your skills. When you complete a project successfully, you'll increase your sense of self-worth!
- **Choose both outdoor and indoor activities.** You need at least one leisure interest that gets you out of the house to enjoy nature and the great outdoors. But you also need to occupy your spare hours productively in the evenings and when the weather turns foul.

Therapy, headquartered in Washington, D.C., can provide referrals.

Working Relationships

The workplace is a logical place for cultivating friendships. Putting in eight hours every day and not interacting with others can be a dreary existence and a stressful one as well. In contrast, people who work well together probably share similar work values, enjoy their work more and are apt to support each other on and off the job. This is not to say that every co-worker is or should be your "buddy," but your job can provide an opportunity to build lifelong friendships. Other work-related social activities can be as simple as having lunch or attending an after-work exercise class with a co-worker, or participating in team sports, theater outings or group vacations.

Reaching Out Into the Community

It's also important to cultivate friendships outside of the office to provide balance and help prepare for later life. Community involvement provides opportunities to meet people with whom you may share hobbies and interests. This kind of involvement can provide continuity and support through the various transitions of your life, such as becoming an "empty nester" or easing into retirement.

There are many opportunities within your community for interaction. Join a club or church group, sign up for a health club, take a class at a local college, or do volunteer work. By taking part, you are defining a purpose and contributing to the health of your community. And you'll make friends!

The Need for a Confidant

Acquiring and maintaining a broad social circle—family, co-workers and friends—is an important Life-Skill. But it's important also to be able to confide in another person, someone whose advice and opinions you respect and who is concerned for your best interests.

A confidant keeps you from feeling you have to bear your problems alone, and can be an excellent buffer during times of stress and transition.

Keep the Mental Wheels Turning

When social activities are also learning activities, they stimulate our brains. Classes, travel and museum visits can actually help prevent a decline in mental ability with age.

The idea that older people naturally lose some memory, alertness and even intelligence is a popular **fallacy.** Research points to the opposite conclusion: Most people over age 65 have not experienced significant memory loss or any other kind of mental dysfunction. They can remember, learn and solve problems as well as younger adults. In fact, people over 65, on average, have twice the vocabulary they did in their young adulthood.

But if "senility" is not a natural process, why do some older people deteriorate mentally? Explains Muriel Oberleder, Ph.D., in her book *Live Longer Live Better*, "Unless you are stimulated, which involves a kind of challenge to the status quo, the mind stagnates.. . If there is no stimulation and outlet for action, the brain will atrophy from disuse."

"It's very clear that in the absence of disease, those individuals who do not decline in their old age are typically individuals who have maintained a very high level of interaction with their environment," notes Warner K. Schaie, Ph.D., a psychologist at Pennsylvania State University.

In his long-term study of intellectual changes in older people, Schaie has demonstrated that a loss of mental ability can be reversed through problem-solving experiences. What's more, these same exercises can improve the performance of people who show no intellectual decline.

Clearly, "use it or lose it" applies to your brain as well as your muscles. Exercise your mind to get more enjoyment from life right now, to keep up with what's going on in the world, and to remain active and independent in your older years.

Head Back to School

If you look into a typical college classroom these days, you'll see a diverse group. Colleges and universities are urging adults to fill empty seats as the traditional college-age population declines.

The adults who occupy those classroom seats are there for several reasons:

• Some now have time to pursue interests they had to put aside when younger—anything from art to psychology, from photography to history, from literature to law. Others have returned to get the college degree that financial constraints or family demands made impossible years earlier.
• Some are making a career change and are taking the needed classes. Others are keeping up with the changing technologies in their professions.
• Finally, there are some people who simply enjoy learning for its own sake.

Many adults would like to resume their education but don't know how to begin, are afraid of failure, or of competing with younger students—even of looking silly! Those who have taken the plunge know that these fears are unfounded. A student's ability to learn, contribute and compete is not determined by his or her age. In reality, older students have the advantages of greater experience and self-knowledge. It's never

Sexual Activity in the Older Years

There is probably no aspect of aging so shrouded in myth as sexuality. It is commonly believed that people naturally lose interest in sex as they age; that in women, the menopause or a hysterectomy eliminates the sexual drive; and that sex among older people is unnatural or indecent.

Not so, say many studies. Sexuality remains an important part of adult life at all stages. In most people, the frequency of sexual intercourse does not decline significantly from early adulthood. In one study, 80 percent of the older people surveyed were still sexually active; half had intercourse once a week or more.

Research has confirmed that after a hysterectomy, a woman is just as likely to experience an increase in libido as a decline. Over-the-counter lubricants or hormone replacement therapy can put an end to discomfort during intercourse caused by menopausal changes.

The greatest problem men seem to face regarding sex in older life is fear of impotence, or of suffering a heart attack while engaged in sex. However, for many men, giving their bodies more time to respond to foreplay alleviates stress.

No older person should deny sexual feelings because of the mistaken notion that they are inappropriate. And if a medical problem inhibits sexual pleasure, the situation should be discussed with a physician or other health professional.

too late to earn your high school equivalency diploma or go back to college. Some institutions even offer college credit for life experience.

Most college registrars can assist you in selecting appropriate courses to ease the transition into school and meet your specific interests. Most colleges offer non-credit courses, which may be less expensive and do not require you to earn a grade or a degree. Courses are offered at night, to meet the needs of working adults, and during the day, for retired people.

If you would like to become a student once more, call a nearby university or community college to request a list of upcoming courses. Ask for special information for returning students. Or consult your newspaper or local school district to learn about adult education programs in your community.

Make Learning Fun

Students age 60 and over can take advantage of a program that combines learning with travel. Elderhostel offers low-cost, short-term academic programs and campus living for older adults. Programs are available at more than 1,000 colleges, cultural and other educational institutions in 50 states and 37 countries. More than 170,000 people were enrolled in 1988.

The Center for Creative Retirement at the Asheville campus of the University of North Carolina offers similar experiences. The National Council on the Aging also sponsors humanities programs which offer stimulating informal learning opportunities. Drawing on themes from literature, drama, history, folklore and philosophy, group discussions—augmented by tapes and texts—look at such things as "Life and Work," "The Search for Meaning" and "The Remembered Past."

Learning doesn't have to occur in a formal setting. In fact, many significant lessons are part of everyday life. People acknowledge this when they say, "Experience is the best teacher."

You have the ability to create your own learning experiences. Here are some ideas:

- **Do more reading**. You might make it your goal to read one book a month. If you're already a frequent reader, try different kinds of books—biographies, histories, travel, science or poetry. Join a book club, meet others and discuss what you read. Remember, if all the books you read are alike, you may be reading purely for entertainment, not for growth.

- **Follow current events.** Become aware of timely topics, and select one issue to follow in detail. The issue you choose could be national, international or regional, economic or social. Learn all you can about this topic by reading news stories and editorials, watching televised reports and discussing it with others. Then, express your educated opinion in a letter to the editor.

- **Visit museums and historical sites.** There's probably much you haven't seen in your city or region. Plan day trips and explore.

- **Develop your artistic side.** The creative process presents the artist with continual challenges and problems to solve. Your finished work will be a source of pride and self-esteem. Go to lectures at galleries—learn how others do it!

- **Volunteer for a position that teaches new skills.** For instance, you can learn to counsel others by staffing a hotline; to aid disaster victims by working with the American Red Cross; to assist the homeless; or to direct plays by joining a community theater group. Volunteering can open doors that are closed to you through paid employment. Sometimes it can lead to a new career.

Making Your Life More Meaningful

There's an old saying that "life is what you make it." Today, science is proving it's true. Enjoying the company of family and friends is a buffer against loneliness, a means of coping with stress, and a necessary ingredient for a long and productive life. Exercising your mind is the key to keeping it sharp throughout life: Remember, mental deterioration is **not** a natural part of aging.

To a great extent, it's up to you to reach your potential, to reach out to others and accept life's challenges. The rewards—satisfaction, learning and growth—are worth the effort, and they far outweigh the alternatives—depression, loneliness, a stagnant mind and diminished years.

CHAPTER FIVE

LifeSkill Five:
Plan for Financial Health

Money can't buy happiness, but good money management can bring you peace of mind. Perhaps nothing creates more stress than issues concerning money. Do you have enough? Where does the money go? How would your family fend if you were to die or become permanently disabled?

Good financial health involves careful planning to meet your personal needs and goals, and to reduce the risks that create fiscal anxiety and stress. Like physical health, financial health can improve the quality of your life. Financial health should not be confused with the ability to earn more money. Rather, it is a process that enables you to determine how much is enough for you and how to use your money more effectively.

Like other LifeSkills, planning for financial health is best begun in the early adult years. But regardless of your age, financial planning is a skill that can and must be developed if you are to enrich your life and reduce the impact of catastrophic illness or disability.

What Do You Want?

Which aspects of your life do you value most? Which give you the most satisfaction? To which areas would you like to devote more time?

Believe it or not, by answering these questions you've taken the first step toward becoming a competent financial planner.

Why? Because whether you value interacting with family and friends, derive satisfaction from intellectual interests or want more time for leisure activities, your ability to enjoy and devote time to these pursuits—now and in the future—is directly related to your financial health.

Only when you have defined your goals can you plan financially to achieve them and be assured of getting what you want from life at every age.

Many people shy away from talk of finances because they think it's tedious and unrelated to their interests. Maybe it simply scares them. They may think they don't have the expertise, much less the level of income, to make financial planning worthwhile. Some people may feel lucky simply to make ends meet. But those who feel controlled by their pocketbooks are the ones who most need to take charge and clarify their goals.

Where Are You Headed?

Some people have a clear direction in life; others get caught up in the flow of events and don't think about having a definite "plan." But most people have some notion of the kind of life they want now, in 10 years, in 20 years and in retirement. The chances are very good, though, that they have never put these goals down on paper.

Now is the time to do just that. Set aside a quiet block of time, and let your mind wander. Picture what you want your life to be like right now, and be realistic: You may dream of luxuries at first, but for most people these are not high-priority goals. Think about family activities, career and educational pursuits, hobbies, your home and things you would like to own. Be honest with yourself—it's the only way you'll benefit from this exercise.

Next, shift ahead five, 10 and 20 years, and visualize the changes that time will bring. Perhaps you hope to start a family or have another child. Will a son or daughter be in college? When will you need to replace your car, or buy or sell a home?

Finally, think ahead to retirement. Depending on your present age, it may or may not seem a long way off. But either way, it probably isn't too soon to plan. In fact, experts say that 35-year-olds are not too young to start planning for retirement. So think about where you might live, the interests you'll pursue and whether you or a loved one may require long-term care.

After you have completed this visualization exercise, get out a pencil and write down your short-term, mid-term and long-term goals on the worksheet that follows. Do you want to buy a new car next year or take a vacation? That would be a short-term goal. Buying a new house in 10 years or financing your children's education is an example of a mid-term goal. For some people, settling in a retirement home in the Sun Belt and being prepared for catastrophic illness would be long-term goals.

Next, estimate how much capital would be necessary to achieve each goal. Keep in mind the need to adjust for inflation when estimating your mid-term and long-term goals. For example, you might adjust your capital needs by 6 percent annually, a conservative inflation estimate. When estimating retirement resources, see your company's personnel manager for an explanation of your retirement benefits and assistance with planning.

Once you've clarified your goals, you can begin to develop a realistic financial plan that takes them into consideration. Planning will entail three phases: establishing your net worth, analyzing your budget, and developing investment strategies that give you **enough** capital to meet your needs.

Financial planning is a discovery process. As you evaluate your situation and possible options, you will uncover opportunities for cutting monthly expenses, increasing savings and putting your money to work.

Find Your Starting Point

While identifying your goals gives you a clear direction, determining your net worth establishes a starting point. Your net worth is a snapshot of your financial status and serves as your baseline for planning.

Think of your net worth as your financial "nitty-gritty." It's the amount that remains when you add up the value of everything you own and subtract everything you owe—your *assets* minus your *liabilities*. Your assets include bank accounts, stocks and bonds, real estate, personal property and other investments. Your liabilities comprise utility and medical bills, charge accounts, mortgages, consumer loans and any

personal obligations. Use the worksheet on page 57 to calculate your net worth.

Note that when completing the worksheet you should be concerned only with **current** assets and liabilities. Include the **present** value of bank accounts and possessions, and the **current** market value of real estate and securities. Don't include anticipated income, such as bonuses or an inheritance; the value of bonds when they mature; or debts that you have not yet shouldered, such as a planned consumer loan. Like a photograph, your net worth worksheet should capture the moment.

Where Does the Money Go?

Did your net worth surprise you?

If your liabilities exceed your assets—that is, if you have a negative net worth—you are probably living beyond your means. Consider whether your spending patterns are driving you into consumer debt, and whether you need to save more.

Perhaps you are worth more than you anticipated. Frequently, people who calculate their net worth ask, "If I'm worth so much, why am I always struggling to make ends meet?"

The only way to answer this question and improve your situation is to determine where your money goes and then establish a realistic budget. Though this implies austerity to many people, a good budget is a tool that helps you make the most of your monthly income and keeps you focused on your personal goals.

What are Your Goals and Estimated Expenses?
(List them in order of importance.)

Short-Term Goals   **Estimated Expenses**

1. _____   _____

2. _____   _____

3. _____   _____

Mid-Term Goals   **Estimated Expenses**

1. _____   _____

2. _____   _____

3. _____   _____

Long-Term Goals   **Estimated Expenses**

1. _____   _____

2. _____   _____

3. _____   _____

NET WORTH WORKSHEET

Assets
(Everything you own)

Bank Accounts:
Checking _____
Savings _____
Certificates of deposit _____

Securities:
Bonds _____
Stocks _____
Mutual funds _____
Money market funds _____
Treasury bills _____
Treasury notes _____

Real Estate:
Primary residence _____
Vacation home _____
Other properties _____

Other Investments:
Pension plan _____
Profit sharing _____
Payroll savings plan _____
Individual retirement
  account (IRA) _____
Insurance (cash value—
  not face value) _____
Other _____

Personal Property:
Automobile _____
Home furnishings/
  appliances _____
Jewelry _____
Antiques _____
Collections _____
Art _____
Home entertainment
  systems _____
Other _____

TOTAL ASSETS _____

Liabilities
(Everything you owe)

Mortgages:
Primary residence _____
Vacation home _____
Other properties _____

Installment Debt:
Automobile loan _____
Other consumer loans _____
Student loans _____
Credit cards _____
Other _____

Current Bills:
Utility bills _____
Medical/dental bills _____
Insurance _____
Other _____
Other liabilities (unpaid taxes, miscellaneous charge
accounts, etc.) _____

TOTAL LIABILITIES _____

TOTAL ASSETS _____
minus TOTAL LIABILITIES _____
equals your NET WORTH _____

The way to begin budgeting is not to set down rules and ultimatums, but to determine how your money is being spent. Use the worksheet below to calculate your monthly expenses. Add up your **fixed expenses**—those you have every month—and figure out how you're spending your **discretionary income**—the amount you have available for entertainment, consumer goods and other non-essentials. If you don't know where your discretionary income goes, keep a careful record for one month before completing this exercise.

Some of your fixed expenses, such as your mortgage and loan payments, remain the same every month; others fluctuate. For example, fuel bills may be high during winter months but remain low or non-existent in summer. Add up your yearly bills and divide by 12 so that you can pro-rate these costs. Telephone, food, clothing and other expenses also fluctuate. Therefore, you may want to use an average or a high estimate for some expenses when calculating your budget.

How Healthy Is Your Budget?

In the first column of the Budget Worksheet, list your monthly expenditure for each item listed. Then refer to the model budget that best matches your current situation. These models provide general spending guidelines based on age, marital status and income.

Compare your current allocations to the model budget's recommended range and determine which budget items need to be adjusted to meet your financial goals. For example, you may choose to reduce your out-of-pocket or entertainment expenses to help pay off your consumer loans or increase your savings. In the second column, adjust your budget accordingly.

Budget Worksheet

Your net monthly income (after taxes) is _____

Fixed Expenditures	Current Monthly Expenditures	Adjusted Monthly Expenditures
Mortgage or rent	_____	_____
Real estate taxes	_____	_____
Car loans	_____	_____
Student loans	_____	_____
Credit cards	_____	_____
Food*	_____	_____
Utilities*	_____	_____
Telephone*	_____	_____
Insurance (health, life, car, home, long-term care and disability)	_____	_____
Child care	_____	_____
Transportation including gasoline	_____	_____
Medical and dental bills	_____	_____
TOTAL FIXED EXPENSES	_____	_____
Discretionary Spending		
Savings	_____	_____
Entertainment	_____	_____
Household purchases	_____	_____
Clothing	_____	_____
Gifts and contributions	_____	_____
Vacations	_____	_____
Incidentals	_____	_____
TOTAL DISCRETIONARY SPENDING	_____	_____
NET MONTHLY INCOME	_____	
(minus) TOTAL MONTHLY EXPENSES	_____	
DIFFERENCE**	_____	

*Average monthly cost

**If your total monthly expenses exceed your net monthly income, go back to the columns and plan for the necessary adjustments. (Refer to page 60 on budget strategies.)

Is It Time to Reduce the Flab?

Your current budget may be an eye-opener. Are out-of-pocket expenses, credit and/or entertainment expenses in the stratosphere? Is most of your income used to pay fixed expenses? As a general rule, you should spend no more than 65 percent of your net monthly income—your take-home pay—on fixed expenses such as food, utilities, car loans and rent or mortgage payments.

The following model budgets, developed by the editors of *Money* magazine, set realistic ranges for different stages of life. The authors advise using the budget closest to your own situation as a guide in developing your spending and savings plan, and balancing your percentage allocations to equal 100 percent.

Model Budget #1

Single, age 25

Income: $25,000

Young singles are likely to go heavy on car payments and entertainment and fairly light on housing.

	Ideal range (%)
Housing	20-25
Loan payments	13-15
Food	10-15
Entertainment	7-14
Out-of-pocket expenses	8-12
Transportation	7-10
Clothing, personal care	4-8
Education	5-7
Utilities	4-7
Gifts, contributions	2-7
Savings	5-7
Insurance	1-3

Model Budget #2

Married couple in their mid-30s, childless

Two incomes: $40,000

Many two-income couples in this age group buy their first homes, whether or not they have children.

	Ideal range (%)
Housing	25-30
Loan payments	15-17
Food	10-15
Clothing, personal care	8-10
Out-of-pocket expenses	7-10
Transportation	7-10
Utilities	7-9
Savings	5-7
Vacations	3-7
Insurance	3-5
Hobbies, entertainment	2-4
Gifts, contributions	1-3

Model Budget #3

Married couple in their 40s, two children

Two incomes: $60,000

Budgeting gets stricter for working couples with children to raise and educate. Saving takes discipline.

	Ideal range (%)
Housing	30
Loan payments	13-15
Food	10-15
Child care	8-10
Out-of-pocket expenses	5-8
Education	5-7
Savings	5-7
Clothing, personal care	4-10
Utilities	4-7
Vacations	3-7
Hobbies, entertainment	3-7
Insurance	3-5
Gifts, contributions	2-5

Model Budget #4

Married couple in their 60s

Retirement income: $35,000

Retirees may have paid off their mortgage, easing that expense. Chances are they will now spend more on recreation and medical care.

	Ideal range (%)
Housing	10-15
Food	15-20
Utilities	15-18
Clothing, personal care	1-5
Transportation	10-12
Insurance	1-5
Vacations	10-15
Gifts, contributions	1-7
Out-of-pocket expenses	7-10
Hobbies, entertainment	2-4
Savings	1-5
Medical expenses	15-20

From *The Money Book of Money: Your Personal Financial Planner* by Robert J. Klein and the editors of *Money Magazine*, Copyright (c) 1987 by Time, Inc. by permission of Little, Brown and Company.

Getting Your Budget Under Control

The last step in winning the war of the balanced budget is developing a plan that you and your family, if you have one, can live with.

If your budget is to work, you must not feel that you are sacrificing too much. Be realistic when you plan to cut your spending. Analyze your fixed budget first and see which areas can be trimmed. Can you cut back on certain foods or reduce your utility costs?

Next, analyze your discretionary expenses and see how those funds can be used to pay off excess debt and increase your savings. Watch out for credit-card purchases, which start out as discretionary spending. They can quickly become a fixed expense to a tune of up to 22 percent interest a year!

Here are a few strategies to help increase your savings and manage your expenses:

- **Pay and protect yourself first.** Financial Planner Carolyn Staub recommends that you pay and **protect** yourself through two strategies:
  1. Establish a savings plan that first builds an emergency fund containing the equivalent of three to six months' expenses.
  2. Protect what you currently have and your family's future in case of accidents, disability or death. Consider adequate health, life, disability, personal property and perhaps long-term care insurance.

  Beyond that, your short-term, mid-term and long-term goals will help determine how much you should save, with investments based on your goals and time frames. Most Americans save less than 5 percent of their paycheck. (In comparison, the average Japanese saves 16 percent.) Saving 5 percent to 7 percent would be a better strategy to meet long-term financial goals, experts say. To make saving easier, take advantage of payroll savings plans such as 401(k) plans and automatic deposit services. Try to bank pay increases, bonuses and monetary gifts.

- **Explore refinancing your home mortgage.** It usually doesn't make sense to refinance unless your mortgage interest rate is reduced at least two or three points and you plan to stay in your home for two years or more.

- **Limit your credit cards to one, unless you travel extensively.** VISA or MasterCard credit cards are the most widely used. But before you acquire a card, do some comparison shopping. Credit-card interest rates can vary from 14 percent to 22 percent.

- **Reduce your long-distance phone expenses** by calling during non-peak hours and shopping for the best rates among the various phone services.

- **Look at your transportation expenses**. Are you paying excessive insurance, personal property taxes, maintenance, fuel costs and loan payments to keep that expensive luxury car in the garage? Consider a less expensive model, or look into leasing options.

- *Money* **magazine recommends that each member of the family be allotted some "mad money."** This reduces the likelihood of arguments over discretionary expenses.

- **Talk to a financial planner**, tax advisor or certified public accountant about ways to **cut taxes.**

- **Keep in mind, as the months pass, that your budget is not carved in stone.** If it doesn't work, adjust it to your current situation.

Finally, take time every six months to re-assess your budget needs in relation to your goals.

Investment Strategies: Working Toward Your Goals

For most people, having money available for investment means opening a savings account. Savings accounts are secure, pay a fixed interest rate and are federally insured.

But other types of investments, although they may involve varying degrees of risk, can yield a higher return. How you decide to invest your money depends upon your savings goals, when you need the money, your total savings, the degree of risk you are willing to take and your stage of life.

Here are some popular investment possibilities. One or more could help you meet your goals.

- **Certificates of Deposit.** By purchasing a certificate of deposit (CD), you agree to keep your money deposited in the bank for a specific period, perhaps six months, a year or longer. In return, you receive a higher rate of interest than you would for an ordinary savings account. However, you must pay a penalty if you withdraw your money early. Before you buy a CD, shop around to compare interest rates and the penalties for early withdrawal.

Government Securities

- **U.S. Treasury Bonds.** Treasury bonds represent a "risk-free" return, due to the U.S. government's full faith and credit. Not only is your investment safe, because it's unlikely that the government will ever go broke, but your interest is exempt from state and local taxes.

- **U.S. Savings Bonds.** United States savings bonds are a good, safe investment that offers some tax advantages. Series EE savings bonds are purchased at less than discount face value; interest is paid after five years, when the bonds are mature. There is no federal tax owed until the bonds are cashed in.

  Once series EE bonds have been held for five years, their interest rate fluctuates according to the market interest rate. However, a minimum return of

6 percent is guaranteed, to protect investors against a market drop.

Mature series EE bonds can be traded in for series HH bonds, which pay 6 percent interest in twice-yearly payments. By making the trade you can protect the interest earned on your series EE bonds from taxation.

- **Treasury Bills and Treasury Notes.** The federal government offers the safest short-term investment opportunities. Treasury bills mature in as little time as 13 weeks, and the interest they pay is exempt from local taxes. They require a minimum investment of $9,000. Treasury notes are similar to treasury bills, but they require a smaller initial investment ($1,000 is their smallest denomination) and they take longer to mature—from one to 10 years.

Municipal and Corporate Bonds

- **Bonds.** A bond is a long-term promissory note. When you buy a bond from a corporation, city or state, you are actually lending money to that organization for a specific length of time. Most bonds pay a fixed rate of interest, which you receive at regular intervals. The interest rate is based upon its credit rating, with AAA representing the highest rating and lowest risk. When the bond matures, you cash it in and receive the original face value of the bond.

  Bonds are not without risk. For example, because interest rates fluctuate, a bond whose rate of return seems attractive now could become less appealing as interest rates rise. And because such a bond would not interest other investors, you could not sell it for the price of your initial investment. Of course, should interest rates fall, your bond would continue to pay its high rate.

  By owning certain bonds, you can avoid paying taxes on your interest income. Municipal bonds, those issued by state and local governments, are free from federal income tax.

- **Stocks.** Stocks are actually shares of ownership in corporations. While stocks tend to perform better than most other investments, profits are not guaranteed. Stocks can pay dividends or increase in value, but their worth can also decrease. Investing in the stock market requires research and careful planning to minimize your risk. Your greatest risk is that the company you invest in won't be profitable. If the company goes bankrupt, its shareholders are the last in line to receive any compensation from liquidation of assets. Your stockbroker can advise you on investment strategies, and Standard & Poor's *Stock Guide* can provide detailed information on various issues.

  Once you have narrowed the field to a group of possible stock investments, use your newspaper's stock tables to chart their progress, and read each company's annual report.

  To minimize the effects of stock-market fluctuations, it's a good strategy to diversify your holdings. Although you may invest initially in only one or two corporations, you may consider a varied portfolio of stock in five to 10 companies to spread your risk.

- **Mutual Funds.** As one of a group of investors in a mutual fund, you share in the purchase of a group of carefully selected stocks and/or bonds that is professionally managed. Mutual funds provide diversification with the goals of minimizing the effects of wide fluctuations and providing the investor with long-term growth in relation to the stock market. Those looking for long-term capital growth should explore *growth funds*, which invest in the stocks of growing but well-established companies. *Growth-and-income funds* add to your capital and pay cash at regular intervals. And because bonds pay an unusually high and guaranteed interest rate, investing in a *bond fund* is a good way to augment current income.

  Mutual-fund plans are referred to as "load" or "no-load." You pay a commission to a broker or salesman (e.g., 8 1/2 percent) to buy into a load fund, whereas a no-load fund charges no sales commission. Research has shown that over time, load and no-load funds perform about equally. However, no-load funds are usually better for investments of less than a year's duration, because a load fund will have to compensate for the commission charged.

- **Money Market Funds.** Like mutual funds, money market funds allow a group of investors to diversify their holdings. However, money in these funds is invested in high-quality, short-term government and corporate bonds. Although money market funds generally are considered safe, they are not risk-free. So before investing in a money market fund, do your homework: Make sure the group sponsoring the fund has a reputation for fiscal responsibility; study the fund's performance over the past 10 years; and look for investments with a short average maturity—60 days at most—so that your money is not tied up in unprofitable investments. Finally, be wary of "hot" trends, which may promise high returns but be very risky ventures.

- **Hard Assets.** A good hedge against inflation is investing in hard assets, such as real estate and precious metals. Investing in your home is one of the best ways to increase your equity and therefore your net worth. In turn, your primary residence allows you to reduce your tax holding by deducting monthly interest; after age 55 you are allowed to take a one-time capital gains tax exemption of $125,000. A second strategy is investing in precious metals such as gold or silver. This can be done by purchasing gold coins or by investing in a mutual fund that speculates in precious metals.

Investing for Retirement

• **Individual Retirement Account (IRA).** Everyone younger than 70 1/2 years of age who earns money from employment can deposit $2,000 per year in an IRA, with two-income couples able to contribute up to $4,000 per year. IRAs can be invested in such instruments as mutual funds, stock, money market funds, bonds and U.S. Treasury securities.

The 1986 tax law no longer allows individuals to deduct every dollar invested in an IRA from their income tax. To qualify for such deductions, an individual must be ineligible for a company pension plan or earn less than $25,000 if single, or $40,000 if married or head of a household. A single person with an adjusted salary of up to $35,000 and a married person or head of household with an adjusted salary up to $50,000 can deduct a relative proportion of his or her IRA contribution.

But even if your income or pension plan prohibits you from taking advantage of the immediate tax savings, your IRA is still a good investment strategy for meeting long-term goals. Your contributions, interest, dividends and capital gains are deferred until you make withdrawals, usually after retirement.

Should you decide to use IRA funds before you reach age 59 1/2, you will be charged a 10 percent penalty and be required to pay taxes on the money withdrawn.

• **401(k) Salary Reduction Plan.** Because of the recent IRA limitations, this relatively new plan is popular among employees. It is one of the fastest-growing investment options. Up to 10 percent of your gross monthly income (but no more than $7,313 was allowed in 1988) is invested in company stock, equity or income funds selected by your employer. You determine how your money is to be distributed or transferred among the funds.

A major advantage of a 401(k) plan is that it reduces your taxable income but has a minor impact on your take-home pay. In turn, your taxes are deferred on principal, interest and/or dividends until retirement.

There is a 10 percent penalty and tax exposure on any amount withdrawn before age 59 1/2. Therefore, this plan should be viewed as part of your long-term investment strategy for retirement.

• **Keogh Plan.** A Keogh plan is a tax-deductible retirement fund for someone who is self-employed. It permits an individual to shelter more income than an IRA does—up to 20 percent of earnings from employment, but not more than $30,000 per year. One person can maintain both an IRA and a Keogh plan.

• **Annuity.** An annuity is a savings plan offered by an insurance company that allows you to put away money for long-term investments. Your investment earns interest, which is not taxed until it is withdrawn.

When you withdraw your annuity during retirement, you receive your principal and interest as specified in your agreement with the insurance company, either as a lump sum or as regular payments, disbursed for a fixed period or for the rest of your life.

Your annuity agreement will permit you to withdraw some of your investment before you retire, but not without a penalty.

How Safe Is Your Money?

Unless you're willing to gamble in a high-risk, potentially high-profit venture, you'll want to know that your money is secure. Your savings account, certificate of deposit, IRA or Keogh account is safest if federally insured. Accounts in most banks are covered for up to $100,000 by the Federal Deposit Insurance Corporation. The Federal Savings and Loan Insurance Corporation and the National Credit Union Insurance Fund provide the same guarantee for their member institutions.

Investment Strategies for Your Stage of Life

Once you have developed your emergency fund, you can begin to explore investment options. Investing in certificates of deposit, mutual funds, conservative stocks and a high-yield money market fund are all options, but must be balanced with your assumption of risk, the *liquidity* of your money, (how easily money can be withdrawn and possible penalties) and how they meet your investment goals. And be sure to take advantage of any savings plan offered by your employer.

Do You Need a Financial Planner?

If, after taking a hard look at your financial situation, you still need help with budgeting, taxes or investments, you might want to seek advice from a professional financial planner.

But be forewarned: This service could cost you an initial $500 to $5,000, depending on your income and net worth, the planner's experience and expertise, and whether the planner charges a commission.

Because people with all kinds of backgrounds can call themselves financial planners, make sure the one you choose is certified. The initials CFP (for certified financial planner) following the individual's name indicate that he or she is certified by the College for Financial Planning in Denver, CO. ChFC, for chartered financial consultant, ensures certification by the American College in Bryn Mawr, PA.

Other affiliations attest to particular expertise. A chartered life underwriter (CLU) will be knowledgeable about insurance needs. A certified public accountant (CPA) will provide expert advice on taxes. (Not all accountants are CPAs and may not be qualified to give you well-rounded advice.)

Before you engage a financial planner, ask him or her: Do you earn your money strictly from fees, or do you receive a commission on insurance policies, mutual funds or other products that you sell? How much commission do you earn?

While there is nothing wrong with a financial planner charging a commission, you want to be sure that the advice you receive benefits you more than it does the financial planner. A good financial planner will channel your money into a variety of investments to ensure stability.

Retirement Planning

Most financial planners agree that, married or single, with children or without, people should begin retirement planning in their 30s. However, many adults don't start preparing until retirement is almost around the corner. While starting late may limit your options and capital growth, you can still take steps to make the most of what you have.

Retirement planning sounds like an awesome task, but if you have performed the visualization exercises—looking into your future—and calculated your net worth as outlined previously, you have already done a significant part of the work. You know where you would like to be and where you stand right now.

Planning for retirement involves a three-prong strategy for accumulating income: personal investments, a company pension plan or Keogh account, and Social Security. Many people plan on their monthly pension and Social Security checks to maintain their standard of living. Unfortunately they are in for a rude awakening when they realize the limitations of this strategy during times of inflation and when unexpected expenses occur. Pension and Social Security income should be viewed as supplemental to your personal savings plan. Therefore, "financial independence" in your retirement years should be based on a sound savings/investment strategy that meets the majority of your financial obligations.

Understanding Social Security: A Supplement, Not a Support

It's a common misconception that Social Security is meant to provide full support for people in their later years. In actuality, the related federal programs that are managed by the Social Security Administration are intended to replace some—but not all—earned income. This point is crucial to bear in mind as you plan for retirement. You need to look at the total financial picture, with Social Security as only one part of a diversified income.

Not all workers can draw Social Security benefits. Those eligible include people age 62 or older, the disabled and the surviving spouses of some workers. Those not covered include federal employees—except members of the armed services and non-military workers hired after 1983—and some state and local government workers.

Social Security is financed through taxes on wages. Employers and workers pay equal amounts; the self-employed are taxed at a higher rate. Social Security pools the collected money and distributes monthly checks to about 17 percent of all Americans.

The program serves as a major source of income for about 40 percent of those age 65 and older. Yet the amounts they receive constitute a sobering set of statistics:

- The **average** monthly benefit for each Social Security recipient is roughly $450—about $5,400 per year.
- The **average** monthly benefit for a retired couple in 1987 was $833—less than $10,000 per year.
- The **maximum** monthly benefit for a retired couple in 1987 was $1,183—about $14,200 for the year.

In addition, individuals who qualify for several of Social Security's plans are only permitted to draw from one. For instance, someone who is disabled and over age 65 may draw either a disability or old-age benefit, but not both. The exception is an eligibility gained through someone else, such as a spouse.

To be fully insured, you must have earned a certain amount of income over the years. In each year, the level of income necessary to qualify for post-retirement benefits is divided into "quarters," for which "work credits" are earned. A worker can earn a maximum of four credits annually.

If you stop working, you don't lose the credits you've earned. They remain on your record and begin accumulating again when you return to work. Generally, anyone who has worked steadily for 10 years has earned the necessary quarter-credits to get full benefits.

The size of your benefit depends on how much money you contributed to the Social Security Trust Fund during your working years. It can also be affected by congressional action and the age at which you retire.

Although automatic cost of living adjustments have been part of Social Security since 1972, Congress can routinely amend the regulations governing Social Security benefits. For instance, in 1987 Congress re-

Choosing the Right Kind of Life Insurance

Life insurance protects your family by protecting your income. Your policy ensures that if you were to die, your family would not experience financial hardship. For that reason alone, it's an important investment and should be viewed as a "pay yourself first" strategy.

But not all life insurance is alike. The kind to choose depends on your **present** needs:

- **Term insurance** is life insurance that you buy for a specific term, or period, normally one to five years. It's one advantage is that it is inexpensive. It offers good, cheap protection for those who are young and whose expenses are high.
- **Whole life, or straight, insurance** provides protection and builds your savings. As you pay your premiums, the insurance company credits your account, and your savings accumulate. You have the option of borrowing against your savings; thus, you can make use of the policy while you are still alive. However, if you die before the loan is repaid, the balance you owe will be deducted from the amount your beneficiary receives.
- **Universal life insurance** combines term insurance with a tax-deferred savings account at a competitive interest rate. Not only is a universal life policy an excellent way to build a cash reserve, but you can borrow from it and change your amount of protection.

Term, whole life or universal life insurance—which is right for you? Before you buy, investigate the insurance benefits that your employer offers. Many employers provide generous insurance benefits at no cost or at a reasonable cost. Once you have explored what is covered, you may wish to augment certain policies, such as life and disability, through personal purchases.

If you are newly married or have young children, term insurance may be your best choice. It is inexpensive and provides the protection you need, and it can be converted to whole life insurance later on.

For those who can afford it, the savings potential of whole life insurance makes it a good buy. Borrowing against a whole life policy can make a major expense like college tuition easier to bear.

Universal life insurance could be right for you if you require $50,000 or more in coverage.

duced Social Security's regular cost-of-living increment from 3 percent to 1.3 percent.

Retiring early will shrink your Social Security benefit. The reason is logical: You will voluntarily cut short your working years and contribute less to the Social Security pot. Also, because Social Security must pay you benefits over a longer period, the size of each payment will be smaller. As a result, someone who would have received $700 per month by retiring at age 65 would only get $560 per month by leaving work three years earlier.

Not surprisingly, the system works the other way around, giving greater benefits to those who delay retirement. For example, workers turning 65 between 1986 and 1989 can reap an added 3 percent for each continued year of employment.

Investment Strategies for Retirement

To maintain a comfortable lifestyle, many older people find that they need the income from well-planned investments. As discussed earlier, most experts agree that IRA, Keogh and 401(k) accounts are the best ways to begin saving for retirement. Other investment strategies are recommended according to your age and circumstances:

- Those in their 30s might be willing to take some risks in the hopes of a high return, perhaps by investing in common stock or high-yield mutual funds.
- By the mid-40s, it may be more prudent to transfer your retirement investments to something that yields less interest but is more secure, such as U.S. Treasury securities.
- If you are an "empty nester" and have never opened a 401(k) account, IRA or Keogh account (if you are self-employed), now is the time to explore these options. One strategy is to invest what was previously spent on child rearing and educational expenses in high-quality stocks and bonds that are relatively secure and pay high dividends or interest.

Retiring on Your Home

The inflation of recent decades has provided numerous older people with a source of retirement income that is literally under their feet. The increases in real estate values that have occurred in many areas have made selling a home a workable option for increasing income and lowering expenses.

According to an article in the Spring 1988 issue of *Money* magazine's *Family Wealth*, as many as 75 percent of people over age 65 own their own homes, with an average of $50,000 in equity. Because they are over age 55, these people are allowed a one-time exemption on capital gains tax on up to $125,000 if they have occupied the home for three of the five years preceding the sale.

Therefore, selling a house and either buying a less expensive home or renting would provide capital for income-generating investments, such as tax-free bonds and mutual funds; it would also reduce property taxes, insurance premiums and maintenance costs.

Another way for a retired homeowner to collect monthly income while still living in his or her residence is through a "reverse mortgage." The lender contracts to make a loan of up to 60 percent to 80 percent of the appraised value of the home at an interest rate on the outstanding balance usually about two points above the prime rate. Each month, for seven to 10 years, the owner draws upon the loan in a fixed amount, which is regarded as a return of capital by the Internal Revenue Service and thus is not subject to income tax. At the end of the time, however, the owner must either pay off the loan, including the compounded interest, or negotiate a new one. New ways of making such loans are being developed, including one that increases the monthly payment at regular intervals to allow for expected increases in the cost of living.

The major drawback to a reverse mortgage is the chance that the owner might have to sell the home if he or she outlives the original term and has no means to pay it off. Of course, normal inflation might have increased the home's value sufficiently to make refinancing fairly easy.

Guide Yourself to Financial Health

The goal of this chapter was to provide you with some basic skills to improve financial decision-making and, as a consequence, achieve financial health. Like other LifeSkills, these principles can only be beneficial if they are practiced regularly.

Financial health and the sense of security it brings not only contribute to successful aging, but help to reduce fiscal anxiety, especially in the areas of retirement planning and meeting the cost of long-term care.

Other Insurance

Those whose children have grown, who have reached retirement age, and who have saved and invested wisely may no longer need life insurance.

You may also want to consider insurance coverage for disability and long-term care:

- **Disability insurance** provides benefits in the event that you are unable to work for several weeks or longer following a serious illness or accident.

  While it is true that Social Security provides a disability benefit, Social Security was never intended to support people, but to replace **part** of their lost income. Therefore, those who qualify may discover that the benefits don't meet their expenses.

  The cost of a disability policy can range from several hundred dollars to more than $1,000, depending on the size of benefit payments, the length of time benefits are paid, and the amount of time you must wait to begin receiving benefits.

  In general, experts recommend purchasing an individual policy that will pay 50 percent to 60 percent of your present pre-tax salary. You will not need to replace your full salary, because your benefits will not be taxed. However, you will be required to pay taxes if your disability policy is paid for by your employer. It is also advisable to look for a policy with *guaranteed renewability*, so that the insurance company cannot discontinue your coverage.

- **Long-term care insurance.** Just as it is unwise to expect Social Security to meet your expenses in the event of disability, it is unrealistic to think that Medicare, the Social Security System's health insurance plan, will fund long-term care. Medicare is designed to cover the costs of acute illness; long-term care for most chronic conditions is beyond its scope.

  A new option for protection against the devastating cost of long-term care is long-term care insurance, which protects your assets in the event such care is required. Long-term care insurance can be purchased through independent agents or through major insurance carriers. Currently, employers are beginning to offer long-term care policies to employees (and their families) through voluntary contributions at competitive prices. For a more detailed discussion of long-term care insurance, Refer to Section IV, Chapter Five.

CHAPTER SIX

LifeSkill Six:
Be a Good Medical Consumer

Now more than ever, using the medical care system well requires skill—being able to determine the need for professional care, choosing the appropriate physician, weighing treatment options, and playing an active role in making decisions throughout the care process.

Not only have medical advances made greater choice possible, but physicians are learning that having an informed, participating patient helps them to provide better care.

People are demanding greater involvement, too. Medical consumers are more informed about health issues today than in years past. And as the population ages and interaction with health professionals becomes more frequent, people are insisting on quality and appropriateness in their care.

The changing role of the health care consumer has led Tom Ferguson, M.D., editor-in-chief of *Medical SelfCare*, to borrow the term "prosumer" from writer Alvin Toffler to describe the engaged, knowledgeable individual who interacts positively and effectively with the health care system. In his book *The Third Wave*, Toffler maintains that as our economy shifts from one based on manufacturing to one emphasizing information and services, the distinction between producers and consumers will blur.

According to Ferguson, that distinction is already disappearing in health care. Speaking at the July 1988 National Wellness Conference in Stevens Point, Wisconsin, Ferguson identified 10 "megatrends" in medical care that encourage prosumerism. He calls them:

1. **Befriending the wizard.** There has been a shift away from depending on health professionals and standing in awe of their knowledge toward taking personal responsibility for health.

2. **Healing knowledge.** At one time, health information was communicated almost exclusively to physicians. Now, such data are widely distributed through the popular media, thus contributing to overall health and well-being.

3. **The invisible health care system.** It was once commonplace for people experiencing illness or surgery to feel isolated. Not so any more; there is a strong support network available, consisting of self-help groups, books and other literature, therapists, and counselors.

4. **The new medical consumer.** Today's prosumers play an active role in managing their health.

5. **The patient as partner.** Health professionals have evolved from authorities who dictated treatment regimens to facilitators who help their patients practice preventive behaviors and maintain maximum autonomy. Because of this trend, many physicians have had to become knowledgeable about nutrition, exercise and other LifeSkills.

6. **Out of the hospital, into the home.** Home-care options and technological advances have made it possible for many patients to get out of the hospital sooner and receive the care they need at home.

7. **Beyond "one ill, one pill."** Today's patients often face not one course of treatment, but a choice between several options.

8. **Health as fulfillment.** The focus of health care is shifting from treating illness to helping people stay well; from concentrating solely on physical symptoms to caring for body and mind.

9. **The doctor in the schoolroom.** It is no longer enough for physicians to give patients instructions, advising them to comply with "doctor's orders." The doctor must now act as health educator, leading patients to a higher level of health literacy.

10. **Why empowerment works.** Ferguson labels the passive approach to medical care, common in the past, "pathological." He calls patient responsibility a "healing" trend, because it results in better health, greater independence and higher levels of personal fulfillment.

It is evident that prosumerism requires skill—or, more accurately, a variety of skills. Specifically, it demands the ability to:

• Understand the health care continuum, or the alternatives for medical intervention.

- Decide when to seek medical care and when to treat problems at home.
- Select a physician.
- Provide an accurate medical history.
- Effectively question your doctor about treatment alternatives.
- Determine whether an outside consultation would be helpful.
- Make wise decisions about hospitalization.
- Use medications responsibly.

Considered as a group, these skills may appear formidable. Yet most require not a vast accumulation of medical knowledge, but a good understanding of your own health and an awareness of your rights and responsibilities, alternatives and resources. This chapter's purpose is to give you that understanding. It can also serve as a reference later on, as questions or problems occur.

The Continuum of Care

One way to think of our health care system is to imagine it as a continuum, or progression, from those services that promote health and well-being to those that resolve a physical problem. At each transition, the number of people providing care increases, as do the variety, complexity and cost of the treatments they administer.

The top of the continuum represents a stable and functional health status. Here, individuals manage their health through appropriate LifeSkills, including medical self-care—treating minor complaints at home and having recommended screening tests. At this level, interaction with the medical system is minimal, perhaps limited to telephone calls to the physician's office, screening at health fairs or clinics, and regular dental checkups.

However, when an illness or injury that cannot be treated at home occurs, the individual begins to use the formal system, usually at the ambulatory, or outpatient, level. The patient visits the physician, nurse-practitioner or other health professional at his or her office, a clinic or free-standing surgical center, and returns home following diagnosis or treatment. Professional care is limited to those procedures that can safely be performed in these settings.

Hospitals, with their larger, more diversified staff and sophisticated equipment, appear next on the continuum. Depending on the medical problem, the hospitalized patient may be cared for by one or more physicians, nurses, social workers, counselors, medical technicians, dietitians, or physical, occupational or speech therapists. The hospital setting allows the patient to be monitored round-the-clock.

At a still more invasive level is the hospital's intensive care unit (ICU), where the patient receives so-

The Health Care Continuum

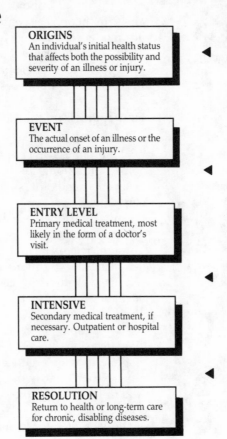

ORIGINS
An individual's initial health status that affects both the possibility and severity of an illness or injury.

EVENT
The actual onset of an illness or the occurrence of an injury.

ENTRY LEVEL
Primary medical treatment, most likely in the form of a doctor's visit.

INTENSIVE
Secondary medical treatment, if necessary. Outpatient or hospital care.

RESOLUTION
Return to health or long-term care for chronic, disabling diseases.

Prevention
- How can I lower my blood pressure?
- Is it too late to quit smoking?
- What's my cholesterol level and what does it mean?
- What can I do to reduce the effects of stress in my life?

Initial Response (I)
- Can I call the doctor with my questions, or do I need to make an appointment?
- Do I need a prescription drug, or will over-the-counter medicine work?
- How long do these symptoms usually last?
- Are my child's symptoms serious, or can I treat them myself?

Hospitalization
- How do I choose the right doctor and hospital?
- Are these tests necessary?
- Should I get a second opinion?
- Can I have this treatment done as an outpatient?

Rehabilitation
- What can I expect during the recovery process?
- When can I begin exercising again?
- How will my surgery affect my diet?
- What recurring symptoms do I need to be aware of?

Your Rights and Responsibilities as a Patient

In his book *Taking Part: The Consumer's Guide to the Hospital*, Donald M. Vickery, M.D., outlines the rights and responsibilities of a patient as follows.

You have the right to:

- Be informed as to the problem, alternative approaches, and the expected benefits and risks of each approach.
- Make choices when appropriate.
- Have health professionals accept the fact that the patient is entitled to take part in the decision-making involved in his or her own health care.

Your responsibilities include:

- Understanding that the information presented may include uncertainties or unpleasant truths.
- Not passing on the responsibility for making decisions about your own care to family members, friends, doctors, nurses or others if you are competent to make those decisions yourself.
- Not demanding services that violate the bounds of acceptable practice or draw upon a limited resource for which you have no claim.
- Not demanding that any health professional violate his or her moral beliefs, by asking that professional, for example, to help you commit suicide.

phisticated treatment and constant monitoring from the ICU's specially trained staff.

Following intervention at either the ambulatory care or hospital care level, the patient faces one of three possible outcomes: a return to health, death or the need for rehabilitative or long-term care.

Thus, for many people, interaction with the health-care system doesn't end with their discharge from the hospital. They may require skilled nursing or custodial care in an institutional setting (nursing-home care), home nursing or perhaps physical, occupational or speech therapy on an outpatient basis.

Many people believe that as they move along the continuum to higher levels of intervention, they must play an increasingly passive role. This mistaken belief causes patients and their families to let health professionals take over too much of the responsibility for making decisions. By doing so, patients may jeopardize the quality of their care.

When you, the patient, interact with health professionals, keep in mind the concept of *informed consent*—you have the right to accept or reject treatment on the basis of your beliefs and in furtherance of your goals; also, you have both the right and the responsibility to be fully informed about your condition (see box).

As treatment becomes more intensive, it is even more important for patients to participate in planning and decision-making, to ask questions, and to investigate treatment options and their benefits, risks and costs. In theory, the continuum of care is the appropriate model for the management of a patient's health complaints. In reality, however, the continuum is less an integrated model than a loosely linked array of health services not necessarily managed as a system.

Find Yourself on the Continuum

As you can see, whether experiencing optimum health or illness, every person is actually operating at some point along the health care continuum. Thus, everyone needs the skills to be an effective medical consumer.

The average person can expect to experience some medical problem on one out of every three days. These problems include such common complaints as headaches, sore throats and rashes, as well as more serious symptoms. In each instance, a decision must be made to either seek professional advice or do without it.

Most people are called upon to make other treatment decisions as well. For example, they may need to respond to an emergency, or manage a chronic condition—either their own or that of a family member. And unfortunately, they don't always make those decisions knowledgeably.

The lack of needed decision-making skills within

the general population is evidenced by the fact that, on average, people see a physician five times a year—yet 40 percent to 70 percent of those visits have been deemed unnecessary.

Unnecessary doctor visits do more than waste time and money. They subject people to unneeded tests and procedures and all of the accompanying risks, which include possible false test results, misdiagnosis, infection and exposure to X-ray radiation.

However, lay people can learn how to make good decisions about seeking care, and when appropriate, they can learn to apply home treatments.

Donald M. Vickery, M.D., has pioneered the development of educational materials that lead people through the medical decision-making process. In addition to *Taking Part: The Consumer's Guide to the Hospital*, his books *Take Care of Yourself* (co-authored with James F. Fries, M.D.) and *Taking Care of Your Child* (co-authored with Fries and Robert H. Pantell, M.D.) contain guidelines and algorithms (problem-solving charts) for treating common medical problems and making decisions about hospitalization and surgery. These books should be required reading for every medical consumer. (See box.)

Example of a clinical algorithm for diagnosing common medical complaints.

Colds and Flu

Any of the following in a child? (a) Rapid or difficult breathing (b) Wheezing (c) Marked irritability or lethargy	YES ▶	SEE PHYSICIAN NOW

NO ▼

Is ear discomfort more than mild?	YES ▶	SEE PHYSICIAN NOW

NO ▼

Has the cough produced thick, foul-smelling, rusty, or greenish sputum?	YES ▶	CALL PHYSICIAN TODAY

NO ▼

Is the throat more than mildly sore?	YES ▶	See **Sore Throat** (Problem 19)

NO ▼

APPLY HOME TREATMENT

Vickery D. and Fries J. *Take Care of Yourself.*
Copyright 1986. Addison-Wesley Publishing Co., Inc.
Reprinted with permission.

Controlled studies using Vickery's materials have resulted in a 17 percent decrease in doctor visits for all reasons and a 35 percent reduction in visits for minor illnesses, such as colds and the flu. What's more, a recent study described in the professional journal *Medical Care* showed a 15 percent decrease in doctor visits by Medicare recipients when self-care materials were used. These results are indicative of patients having confidence in their ability to take responsibility for their health.

Writing in the *American Journal of Health Promotion*, Vickery states, "It has been conclusively demonstrated that both training and communications interventions can [have a] beneficial impact on self-care behaviors. The potential for improving health and reducing the cost of traditional medical care is enormous."

Making good decisions about seeking treatment is just one of the skills you will need to be a prosumer now and in the future, when you may have to proceed along the health care continuum.

The Right Doctor for You

Most people enter the formal health care system by contacting a physician. Because your choice of a physician can greatly affect the quality of your care, it is important to choose carefully.

If you are a healthy adult under age 40 you may not need a personal physician. Any screening tests that you require can be performed by other health professionals, perhaps in a clinic or health-fair setting. But you should know how to find an appropriate doctor when you need one.

Of course, the kind of physician you select depends on your need. But in most instances, the patient first sees a primary care physician, one who is a specialist in family practice, internal medicine, pediatrics, or obstetrics and gynecology. If the patient is older, it might be wise to seek a physician who treats many older patients.

The primary care physician can provide routine screenings, treatment for minor illnesses and injuries, information on lifestyle management and preventive care and referrals to other medical specialists for more serious problems.

The physicians commonly labeled "specialists" are internists and surgeons who have limited their practices to particular areas of expertise. There are many specialties in medicine; some that might sound familiar are ophthalmology (diseases of the eye), plastic surgery, cardiology (the heart), dermatology (the skin) and psychiatry. Sometimes the patient makes contact initially with the specialist. In other instances, he or she is referred to the specialist by a primary care physician.

The Consumer's Hospitalization Checklist

In his book *Taking Part: The Consumer's Guide to the Hospital*, Donald M. Vickery, M.D., provides a list of questions that can help you make wise decisions about hospitalization or surgery.

• Are the tests, procedures or therapy necessary?
• Can they be performed outside the hospital?
• Have the benefits, costs and risks of hospitalization been explained?
• Do you understand your right to accept or reject health care on the basis of your own personal values and in furtherance of your own personal goals (informed consent)?
• Is testing recommended simply because it is routine? This is not an acceptable indication for testing.
• Are drugs used only when needed?
• Is an outside medical consultation needed?
• Have the benefits, costs and risks of surgery been explained?
• Can the surgery be done on an outpatient basis?
• Are you seeking to use the hospital for an inappropriate reason, as for a rest?

But whether for primary care or a specialized need, be sure that your physician is well qualified and someone with whom you feel comfortable. Vickery offers these suggestions for choosing a doctor:

• Ask your friends who their doctors are, and what they like or dislike about the care they receive.
• Ask physicians, nurses and other health professionals which doctors they use. If you need to see a surgeon or other specialist, ask your primary care physician to recommend someone.
• Call a teaching hospital in your area, and ask the chief resident in a particular specialty for a recommendation.
• Look for membership in a professional organization of physicians in that specialty, and affiliation with the hospital of your preference.
• If transportation is a problem, choose a doctor whose office is not far away.

Think about the style of practice that you like best, too. Do you prefer the team approach of a group practice, or the opportunity to get to know one physician well that a solo practice offers?

Economics also play a role. The type of health insurance plan that you elect—or that your employer offers—may expand or limit your choice of medical services. Here are a few common plan arrangements:

• Under a traditional individual or **group indemnity plan**, people are free to choose any qualified practitioner. The patient is reimbursed for incurred medical costs according to a formula. The patient usually must pay a yearly deductible, as well as a percentage of medical costs once the deductible has been satisfied.
• In a **health maintenance organization** (HMO), the patient or employer pays a fixed (capitated) monthly fee for care instead of a separate charge for each visit or service. (Some HMOs charge a small per-visit co-payment). Care is provided by physicians who are employed by or affiliated with the HMO. In theory, the fixed fee serves as an incentive for physicians to discourage unnecessary tests and procedures, and to educate patients in preventive practices.

Two common HMO models are the **staff-model HMO** and the **independent practice association** (IPA). In a staff-model HMO, health professionals treat HMO members only. Often patients see their physicians at a centralized facility. The physicians who practice in an IPA see patients in their own offices. They may treat non-HMO patients as well.

• The **preferred provider organization** (PPO) is another approach. Here a network of health providers offers corporations discounted rates for their services. An employee who elects to use a physician or other medical services outside the PPO plan must pay a higher deductible and co-payment.

Your Side of the Story

Your active role as a medical consumer doesn't end once you have found a doctor and deposited yourself in his or her office. The physician cannot provide the best or most appropriate care without your help.

Your first job as a patient is to provide a clear, precise medical history. The doctor will want to know about the problem for which you are seeking help—your symptoms, when they began, and any other information that you think will aid in diagnosis.

If you are a new patient, the doctor will request a more lengthy history, one that includes past illnesses and injuries; any chronic conditions that you have, such as high blood pressure or diabetes; any medications that you are taking or those to which you are allergic; and serious illnesses that have occurred in your family.

The only way to have that information available and be sure that you don't forget something important is to keep careful records. See Appendix I for guidelines on preparing a personal or family health record. If it will help you to recall details, bring your health record along when you visit the doctor.

Remember, the physician needs information from you; but equally important, you need information from the physician. You need to know the diagnosis, treatment alternatives, benefits, risks and costs of each treatment option. Only then can you be an effective partner in planning your care.

Obtaining all of that information will require you to question your doctor carefully. Here are some examples of questions that you might want to ask:

- I didn't understand your explanation. Can you rephrase it in non-technical terms?
- Is that test or procedure necessary?
- Is there an alternative to hospitalization or surgery?
- When will I return to normal? Or, if there will be no "normal," then what can I expect?
- Should I be alert for any signs of trouble? What should I do if they occur?
- Would it be helpful to get a second consultation?

Some health professionals suggest writing down any questions that you have, and bringing your list to the doctor's office. Specifically, it has been found to be beneficial if a patient writes down three questions each time he or she goes to a physician.

Does Doctor Know Best?

Your doctor is a valuable resource for health information, whose responses to your questions can guide you in making most treatment decisions. But there are times when you will need more information. For example, suppose your physician recommends surgery, or suppose you are concerned that an older relative's doctor is not doing everything necessary to treat your loved one?

In instances such as these, it may be wise to solicit an opinion from another physician. By following this common practice, you are admitting neither disloyalty nor dissatisfaction with your doctor. Instead, you are exercising your right to make the best, most informed decision you can.

How do you find someone to provide the consultation (sometimes called a "second opinion")? One approach is to ask your primary care physician for a recommendation. However, keep in mind that the second doctor should be impartial—not a member of your doctor's group practice or part of the surgical team. Another approach is to follow the recommendations for choosing a physician listed on page 70.

But whatever your method, be frank with your doctor about your desire for another consultation. That way, he or she can make your records and test results available to the second physician.

Obtaining a consultation from another physician will result in added expense. However, in terms of peace of mind, it's money well spent. If the consultation confirms your doctor's opinion, you can be confident that you are making a good decision. If the second doctor recommends an alternate course of treatment, you might just save yourself from unnecessary hospitalization or surgery.

Wise Use of Medications

There is one more area in which skill is important—medication use. Whatever your level of interaction with the health care system, and whether the drugs you use were purchased over-the-counter or by prescription, your drug-taking habits can affect your health.

Drugs are potent chemicals that must be used carefully and stored cautiously. Even such common remedies as antihistamines can have side effects. What's more, aspirin and other drugs are a leading cause of accidental poisonings.

Follow these recommendations for safe medication use:

- Carefully dispose of any drugs that are outdated or no longer being used. Store all others in child-proof containers in a locked medicine cabinet.
- Make sure that your physician explains why each drug is prescribed, possible side effects and interactions, and how long you will be taking the drug.
- Be aware of the signs of a possible reaction to a drug. If you suspect a drug reaction, notify the physician.
- Take as few medications as possible. In some instances, lifestyle changes are a better option. For

example, a low-sodium diet might be tried to control blood pressure before a diuretic is prescribed.

- Standard adult dosages may be too high for someone who has grown smaller with age. And because aging alters the absorption, processing and excretion of drugs, medications can remain in the system longer.

- Overmedication, or taking too may drugs, is a particular hazard for people over age 65, who consume more drugs than other age groups. This unsafe practice can result in confusion, weakness and sensory decline—symptoms too often dismissed as part of "growing old."

  If you suspect overmedication, employ what William Ira Bennett, M.D., of Harvard Medical School calls the "paper-bag exercise": Place all of the medications being used in a paper bag, including over-the-counter items. Take them to the doctor's office, and tell the physician exactly how much of each has been used, how often, and the observed symptoms.

- Use generic drugs cautiously. These chemical "equivalents" of brand-name drugs are not necessarily less expensive, and their exact formulas may vary. Therefore, comply with your doctor's choice of drugs if he or she has a good reason for prescribing brand-name drugs.

- If you use prescription drugs regularly, perhaps as part of managing a chronic disease, look into mail-order suppliers, which can save you as much as 50 percent on medications. To find a reputable supplier operating in your state, contact your board of pharmacy. Choose a supplier with a staff pharmacist available to answer questions toll-free, and a computerized medication file for each customer.

Managing Your Health With Confidence

This chapter has outlined the basic skills needed to interact with the health care system knowledgeably and responsibly. With a good understanding of the fundamental aspects of medical consumerism, you'll be able to make wiser decisions about health care any time you face them.

Remember, wherever you find yourself on the health-care continuum, it is important to be an active, informed partner in your care.

Signs of a Possible Drug Reaction

- Rash
- Dizziness
- Confusion
- Upset stomach
- Headache
- Loss of appetite
- Dry mouth
- Lethargy
- Incontinence
- Shortness of breath
- Nausea
- Irritability
- Vomiting
- Unsteadiness
- Cramps
- Fluid retention
- Ringing in the ears
- Diarrhea
- Sore throat

CHAPTER SEVEN

LifeSkill Seven:
Use Health Screenings Only When Needed

Not long ago, the yearly checkup was part of routine medical advice and a ritual for many Americans. It made life simple: You saw the doctor once a year, submitted to a battery of tests and walked out with a clean bill of health.

Now physicians are recognizing that while the annual physical makes sense in theory, its value has not been demonstrated in practice. For one thing, it rarely happens that an apparently healthy adult will have a disease that can be detected and treated in its very early stages. Most diagnoses are made from the patient's medical history and physical examination, not test results.

Only 28 percent of physicians surveyed by the University of Maryland said that they thought having an annual physical was very important. Most physicians don't submit to checkups themselves, nor do they send their families.

As far as testing is concerned, decreases in many types of screening have been recommended by the National Academy of Sciences, a Canadian national task force, and the American Cancer Society.

Tests reassure patients, but they can be risky. For example:

- Risks from medical tests include exposure to radiation during X-rays and allergic reactions to contrast agents ("dyes" used to make structures visible on X-rays).
- An incorrect reading could result in your being subjected to unnecessary therapies or procedures, or denied appropriate treatment. The risk is highest when there is no real indication for the test.

Medical tests can be expensive, and many insurance plans do not cover the cost of tests performed as part of a routine physical. The average price of a chest X-ray in 1986 was $70; of an electrocardiogram (EKG), $40; of a bilateral mammogram, $90, according to Mark A. Moskowitz and Michael E. Osband, authors of *The Complete Book of Medical Tests.*

An important LifeSkill is the **appropriate** and **timely** use of medical tests that can help detect such specific risk factors as high blood pressure and the early onset of diseases like colon cancer. Within this chapter we'll discuss common medical screening procedures for health risks based upon age and sex.

When Should You Seek a Test?

A few disorders **can be** treated successfully if caught early. And if such conditions as high blood pressure, high blood cholesterol, tooth decay and gum disease are detected and treated early, the quality of life can be enhanced.

These are among the periodically necessary screening tests and examinations. It is important to keep such tests in mind; they can be performed independently of a comprehensive physical examination.

- **Blood Pressure Tests.** Hypertension, or high blood pressure, is a significant medical condition that gives little warning of its presence. If left untreated, it can result in a heart attack or stroke. The incidence of hypertension increases with age (see Section III, Chapter Nine), but anyone can have the condition. Everyone, regardless of age, is advised to have a blood pressure check once a year.

  Blood pressure can be tested easily by a nurse, physician's assistant or nurse's aide. If high blood pressure is found and a doctor confirms the diagnosis, the patient should attend carefully to the treatment regimen developed in cooperation with the physician. Those who have high blood pressure will need more frequent testing and may choose to monitor their own blood pressure at home (see page 74).

- **Blood Glucose Testing.** Non-insulin-dependent diabetes mellitus (NIDDM), or adult-onset diabetes, is linked to obesity, lack of exercise and family history, and shows up in later adult life. (See Section III, Chapter Six.) It's recommended that adults age 40 to 59 who are obese and/or have a family history of diabetes have blood glucose testing every five years, and every two years after age 60.

- **Pap Tests.** This simple, painless test detects cancer of the womb (cervix), which has a high cure rate if diagnosed and treated in its early stages.

  A scraping of the cervix and a sample of the vaginal secretions are obtained for study under a microscope. A *cytologist* (a trained technician) examines the specimens for the presence of tumor cells.

A Home Medical Test For High Blood Pressure

If you have hypertension, you should buy a blood pressure kit. The ability to do blood pressure readings as often as necessary is essential if you are to keep your blood pressure under control. People who do not have hypertension can obtain a reading once a year. Blood pressure screening programs are available through corporations, public health departments, fire departments and voluntary agencies.

How it works. A home blood pressure test kit measures the pressure on the walls of the arteries. The measurement consists of two numbers: the systolic pressure, when the heart is in contraction, and the diastolic pressure, when the heart is relaxed.

Most kits include a cuff, an aneroid manometer—a measuring device—and a stethoscope. The center of the cuff is placed directly on the pulse point of the artery in the upper arm. The cuff is wrapped around the arm just above the elbow and is inflated rapidly until it stops the blood flow.

With a stethoscope, the user listens for sounds in the artery to detect systolic and diastolic blood pressures and records the readings.

The American Heart Association and the American Red Cross recommend that aneroid manometers be recalibrated by the user once a year against a standard mercury sphygmomanometer in a physician's office.

Tips on use. Blood pressure is usually lower in the morning and increases from the afternoon on, so try to test at the same time each day. Always use the same arm for testing. Some people find their pulse is more easily felt on one wrist than the other. If this is true for you, test your blood pressure on that arm.

Inaccurate readings can be caused by extraneous noises affecting the listening device, anxiety, movement during measurement or an incorrectly placed or incorrectly deflated cuff. Eating, drinking, smoking or exercising before testing also can affect results. An average of three readings, five to 10 minutes apart, is more accurate than a single reading.

The standard size cuff fits arms up to 13 inches in diameter. People with larger arms should order a larger cuff.

Before beginning to monitor your own blood pressure, get instruction from your local chapter of the American Red Cross, a local high blood pressure control program or a health care professional. Written instructions should accompany all instruments.

There is some debate among medical professionals over how often Pap tests should be performed. A widely recommended regimen is for a woman to have her first Pap test at the age when sexual activity begins, or at least by age 21. After three consecutive yearly tests have been negative, tests every three years are sufficient.

- **Breast Examination.** Women over age 21 should examine their breasts every month, usually following the menstrual period, to detect any changes or lumps that might indicate cancer of the breast. Although most breast lumps are not cancer, women should report any suspicious changes to their physician.

  Here is the recommended procedure:

  1. Look at your breasts in a mirror, first with your arms at your sides, then with your arms over your head. Look for any changes in appearance, shape or size, or for dimpling of the skin. Sometimes a lump that is difficult to feel can be seen quite plainly.
  2. Next, lie flat on your back and examine the left breast, using the inner fingertips of your right hand. Press the breast tissue against the chest wall. Do not "pinch" the tissue: All breast tissue feels lumpy when you do this. Do not neglect the portion of the breast under the nipple or that which extends outward toward the underarm.

     Keep your left hand behind your head while you examine the inner half of the left breast and at your side when you examine the outer half. A small pillow placed under your left shoulder may help.
  3. Repeat this process to examine your right breast. Self-examination should be supplemented every five years by a manual examination by a physician until age 50. Because women with large breasts cannot practice self-examination as reliably as other women, they may want to discuss other screening procedures with their physician.

- **Mammography.** The benefit of routine mammography screening (X-ray examination of the breast) for most women under age 50 remains controversial. After age 50, mammography at least every five years and regular self-examination is recommended. Many authorities recommend screening every year after age 50 and every other year after age 40.

  Perhaps the best way to schedule mammography is according to risk as determined by the table at right. Women at high risk should have mammography screening annually. For women at moderate risk, once every three years is appropriate. Women with borderline risk should be evaluated once every five years. If there is no measurable risk, women have the option of testing every five years.

DESIGNATION OF BREAST CANCER RISK LEVEL

Risk group	Group criteria	Variable risk factors (VRF)
High risk	Previous breast cancer or maternal breast cancer or over age 50, plus any two variable risk factors (VRF)	(1) Previous other cancer (2) Other close relative with breast cancer (3) Onset of menstruation at age 10 or earlier
Moderate risk	Under age 50, plus any two VRF, or over 50 plus any one VRF	(4) No pregnancies (5) First live birth after age 30
Borderline risk	Under age 50 plus any one VRF	(6) Menopause after age 50 (7) Previous benign breast disease (other than in connection with lactation)
No measurable risk	No VRF	

Adapted from Carter et. al. *Preventive Medicine* 16, 19-34 (1987)

- **Rectal Examination for Prostate Cancer.** Digital examination to detect prostate enlargement should be conducted by a physician for men every three years from age 40 through 59. Thereafter, every two years is appropriate.

- **Self-Test for Testicular Cancer.** Testicular cancer accounts for only 1 percent of all cancers in males, but it is the most common form in men between the ages of 29 and 35.

  Because testicular cancer can be treated effectively if detected early, men should examine themselves regularly for lumps, nodules, swelling or a change in the consistency of the testes.

  The best time to perform the exam is after bathing, when the scrotal skin is relaxed. Roll each testicle gently between the thumbs and fingers of both hands, and be sure to examine the entire surface of each testicle. Ask your physician to demonstrate the correct technique if you are uncertain. Anything unusual should be reported.

- **Occult Blood.** A test for occult, or hidden, blood within the stool is used to detect possible cancer of the colon. However, a positive result does not necessarily point to cancer. Blood may appear in the stools from such causes as bleeding gums, hemorrhoids, ulcers, diverticulitis, colitis or polyps. *False-positive* results may be caused by several factors, including dietary iron supplements and certain foods and medications. *False-negative* results can be caused by a high intake of vitamin C or laxatives containing mineral oil.

  Occult blood tests are recommended every other year after age 50.

- **Sigmoidoscopy.** Regular *sigmoidoscopy* (examination of the colon) has proven to be an effective method for detecting and treating colorectal cancer. In this procedure, the physician inserts an instrument into the sigmoid colon to view the interior surface.

  Colon cancer is almost as common as lung cancer in the United States; it occurs primarily in men and women over age 50. Therefore, people in this age group should have a baseline examination. If the test is negative, testing every three years is optional.

- **Blood Cholesterol Tests.** Elevated blood cholesterol is a controllable risk factor for coronary heart disease. A simple blood test can tell you whether your blood cholesterol level is cause for concern.

  Scientific studies have shown that people with high blood cholesterol levels have a greater chance of developing coronary heart disease than do people with lower blood levels of cholesterol. The chances of developing heart disease increase in proportion to the amount that the cholesterol is elevated. For example, someone with a blood cholesterol level of 265 milligrams per deciliter of blood (mg/dl) has four times the risk of developing heart disease as those with a level of 209 mg/dl or lower. The average blood cholesterol level for middle-aged adults in the United States is 215 mg/dl, but this is regarded as too high—a result, in part, of the high-fat American diet. Ideally your blood cholesterol should be below 200 mg/dl.

  To measure your blood cholesterol, a small blood sample is taken, and the amount of cholesterol it contains is determined in a laboratory or by a portable blood analyzing unit.

  The frequency with which the test should be performed varies. The National Heart, Lung, and Blood Institute recommends that all adults have an initial cholesterol check. If the result falls between 200 mg/dl and 239 mg/dl, you should go on a low-fat diet and exercise. The test should be repeated every three years. If the test is 240 mg/dl or higher, despite

Advice From The Dentist

Many people are uncertain about the correct way to brush and floss their teeth. Here are the methods recommended by the American Dental Association:

• **Brushing.** Gently "scrub" your teeth with a short back-and-forth motion, holding the toothbrush at a 45 degree angle against the gum line. Brush the outside, inside and chewing surfaces of each tooth. When brushing the inside surface of your front teeth, hold the brush vertically and tilted, and make several up-and-down strokes on the tooth surface with the tip of the brush. Don't brush too hard. Finally, brush your tongue to remove bacteria and freshen your breath.

• **Flossing.** Flossing removes food particles and plaque from between the teeth and under the gum line, areas the toothbrush can't reach. Use a long piece of dental floss (about 18 inches) and hold it tightly between your thumbs and forefingers. Using a gentle sawing motion, slide the floss between your teeth. At the gum line, guide the floss along the "C" curve at the top of each tooth, sliding it in gently until you feel resistance. Floss the sides of all your teeth, including those in the very back of your mouth.

A Few Words About Dentures

People who lose permanent teeth will require replacements, to make eating easier, to protect the integrity of the remaining teeth and jaw and to improve their appearance. Partial or full dentures are removable replacements that require minimal care.

Dentures take some getting used to. New wearers will have to learn how to eat and speak with them, and perhaps begin wearing them according to a predetermined schedule.

Dentures should be cleaned daily and soaked while you are sleeping, in water or a special cleaning solution. Wearers will need to see the dentist if they experience problems with comfort or fit. Otherwise, the dentist will want to check the fit every few years.

good diet and exercise habits, your physician will need to monitor your cholesterol level more regularly and will probably recommend cholesterol-controlling medications.

• **Vision Tests.** People who experience vision problems (corrected or uncorrected) should discuss an examination schedule with an *optometrist* (a licensed, trained primary eye-care practitioner) or an *ophthalmologist* (a physician who specializes in diseases of the eye) to detect or modify vision problems that can often develop gradually, thus escaping notice.

Presbyopia is the name given to the natural loss of sharp, clear vision that occurs with age. Without proper prescription lenses to compensate for its effects, presbyopia can contribute to headaches, extreme fatigue at the end of a work day, poor performance in tasks requiring near vision and difficulty in such social situations as eating in restaurants and shopping.

Glaucoma is a disease that can cause blindness. Most physicians believe that early treatment can prevent further damage to the eye. In glaucoma, the normal drainage of the fluid circulating in the front chamber of the eye is obstructed. The build-up of fluid creates pressure that damages such delicate structures as the optic nerve. Screening by ophthalmoscopy (performed by an ophthalmologist) is recommended yearly beginning at age 40 for those with a family history of glaucoma and every three years beginning at age 44 for those without such a history.

A comprehensive eye examination includes the following:
— A complete health history.
— Discussion of any current vision problems.
— Tests of ability to see clearly at all distances.
— Checks of eye coordination, muscle control and focusing ability.
— A test for glaucoma as indicated by age and family history.

• **Hearing Tests.** By the time you're 50, you can expect to experience some hearing loss, probably in your ability to detect high-pitched sounds. Hearing impairment is a common problem among older people and not only affects their quality of life, but can be misconstrued as a sign of being cantankerous, or even "senile." People who experience a hearing problem that affects their everyday activities should have a hearing test. This test can be performed by an *audiologist* (a trained hearing expert) or an *otologist* (a physician who specializes in the ear).

• **Dental Examinations.** People who want healthy teeth should visit their dentist every six months to have calcium deposits and *plaque* (bacterial film) cleaned from their teeth and for the dentist to perform a visual examination of the mouth.

Dental X-rays, like all X-rays, pose a risk from radiation. They should not be a part of every checkup. The optimal length of time between dental X-rays has not been determined, but it is probably between one and five years, and more likely closer to five years.

Immunizations for Adults

For most adults a tetanus booster every 10 years is sufficient to protect against the likelihood of contracting tetanus (lockjaw). However, a new booster is recommended if a cut or wound is particularly dirty and you haven't received a tetanus shot within the past five years.

Diphtheria boosters are not needed for most adults (assuming childhood vaccination) unless they run a high risk of exposure; for example, if they work in a hospital. In this case, a booster shot every 10 years is recommended.

Finally, the national Centers for Disease Control recommend that adults age 65 and older have an annual influenza (flu) shot. However, this may be unneccesary for apparently healthy older adults, unless they suffer chronic illnesses related to the respiratory and cardiovascular systems.

Summary of Recommended Screening Tests

The following table can help you determine which screening tests to have, and when. Be sure to refer to it periodically.

Know Which Screening Tests to Have

Knowing which screening tests to have is an important self-care skill. The following schedules are recommended for adults:

Test	Age 18 to 24	25 to 29	30 to 34	35 to 39	40 to 44	45 to 49	50 to 59	60+
Blood Pressure	YEARLY (Those who have high blood pressure will need more frequent testing.)							
Pap Smear (test for cancer of the cervix)	If sexually active, three consecutive yearly tests. Otherwise, three consecutive yearly tests after age 21. Thereafter, every three to five years if previous tests have been negative.							
Testicular self-exam	MONTHLY							
Breast self-exam		MONTHLY						
Manual exam of the breast by a physician	Every five years until mammography begins, then in conjunction with mammogram.							
Mammogram (X-ray of the breast)					Every one to three years for those in high-risk groups.		Every five years for low-risk groups.	
Glaucoma					Annually from age 40 with family history. Every three years, from age 44 with no family history.			
Dental check-ups	Teeth cleaned and examined every six months							
Sigmoidoscopy							Every three years.	
Digital exam (detect prostate enlargement)					Every three years.		Every two years.	
Blood Glucose					Every five years for those who are obese and/or have a family history of diabetes. Every two years > age 60.			
Occult Blood							Every two years	
Cholesterol	Initial baseline test. If 200 mg/dl to 239 mg/dl—every three years. Test of 240 mg/dl or higher—physician-recommended schedule.							
Vision	People who experience vision problems (corrected or uncorrected) should have an eye examination.							
Hearing	People who experience a hearing problem that affects their everyday activities should have a hearing test.							
Immunizations	Tetanus booster every 10 years; Diphtheria (childhood), 10 years thereafter, for high-risk groups (i.e., hospital workers); Influenza—shot for 65+ if they suffer chronic illnesses related to respiratory and cardiovascular systems.							

CHAPTER EIGHT

LifeSkill Eight: Don't Smoke; If You Do, Quit

Smoking contributes to an estimated 350,000 excess deaths per year. Experts agree that the eradication of smoking would have a greater impact on our nation's health and longevity than any other health measure.

The following chart presents the percentages of deaths from various diseases that smoking cigarettes, cigars and pipes contributes to in the United States:

Lung cancer	75%-90%
Bronchitis and emphysema	85%
Mouth cancers	40%-75%
Pharynx cancer	40%-75%
Bladder cancer	30%-50%
Esophageal cancer	30%-75%
Pancreatic cancer	25%-40%
Larynx cancer	40%-75%
Heart disease	15%

(Cigars, pipes, chewing tobacco and snuff are also cancer-causing!)
Source: U.S. Department of Health and Human Services

Though you would think the numbers speak for themselves, 54 million Americans **choose** to smoke each day, with the likelihood of **losing** five to eight years of life due to their habit.

Significantly, experts, including the Surgeon General of the United States, now have determined that use of tobacco, because of its nicotine content, is a habit at least as addictive as the use of heroin, alcohol and cocaine—and perhaps even more so. The pain of withdrawal is a major factor in staying hooked. Moreover, as Tom Ferguson, M.D., points out in his book

The Smoker's Book of Health, nicotine is a powerful psychological tool that provides the smoker with many "desirable" effects, including the following:

- **Mood Thermostat.** Nicotine acts as a mediator for neurotransmitters, thus "tuning" a smoker's mood either up or down.
- **Improved Attention and Performance.** Nicotine influences adrenaline and dopamine, the principal transmitters responsible for attention in the limbic system of the brain. Thus, by regulating the dosage of nicotine, the smoker can control concentration.
- **Sustained Alertness for Boring Tasks.** Studies have shown that nicotine helps smokers concentrate better than non-smokers on boring, repetitive tasks.
- **Improved Long-Term Memory and Learning.** Nicotine enhances long-term memory by enabling the smoker to consolidate learned material, although "incidental" experience is remembered less well.
- **Help Controlling Anger and Anxiety.** Nicotine somehow, perhaps as a depressant to the limbic system, allows the smoker to deal more calmly with irritating conditions.
- **Help With Stress.** Though categorized as a stimulant, nicotine in some way helps an individual "relax" during stressful events.
- **Help Dealing With Pain.** Nicotine numbs the person's awareness of pain and can thus serve as an analgesic.
- **A Sense of Control.** Smokers feel they have a significant degree of control over their moods and arousal through the proper dosage of nicotine. The average smoker takes between 200 and 300 nicotine "hits" per day, thereby controlling mood, attention, stress, pain, etc.

Smoking cessation techniques must address what Ferguson calls the "smoker's dilemma"—"trading off short-term psychological benefits for long-term physical hazards."

Walking Away Forever From Cigarettes

Since 1964, when the first Surgeon General's report was published linking tobacco with cancer, more than 35 million individuals have quit. Ninety-five percent have done it on their own, without formal cessation classes, acupuncture, aversive therapy or hypnosis. Most have done it cold turkey. But unless a smoker can find ways to replace nicotine's mental and physical benefits, relapse is likely.

Getting Started

Gandhi once said, "Don't give up anything until you don't need it anymore." What this means to the smoker is finding other LifeSkills that provide the same psychological benefits as nicotine, but are less harmful. The following smoking-cessation program includes proven techniques for success. The program is divided into five sections: **Pre-Conditioning, Setting a Quit Date, Preparing to Quit, On the Day You Quit**, and **After You've Stopped**. You don't have to use all of the techniques given here, but be wary of selecting only the easiest. You may be choosing failure!

Step One: "Pre-Conditioning": Are You in Reasonable Shape Before You Quit?

Many smoking-cessation programs view exercise, eating right and learning to relax almost as afterthoughts to the quitting process. These core LifeSkills, however, can provide benefits similar to those identified with nicotine use. For example:

- Regular exercise is an effective modifier of stress and tension.
- Relaxation exercises can help control moods, concentration and attention.
- Also, proper diet and exercise can help avoid extra weight gain, a common obstacle to quitting for good.
- Practice of these three core LifeSkills demonstrates a tremendous degree of self-management, a prerequisite for remaining smoke-free.

Even before you establish your quitting date, becoming a non-smoker begins with "getting in shape": incorporating into your lifestyle regular physical activity (*formal* aerobic exercise) a minimum of three days a week; analyzing your eating habits and making the necessary nutritional adjustments; and learning to relax at will through appropriate self-control exercises. Refer to Chapters One through Three of this section for specific recommendations. **Begin your pre-conditioning program 30 to 45 days prior to your quit date.**

(Warning: If you have been physically inactive or have other health problems, read Chapter One on the need for medical advice prior to starting an exercise program.)

Step Two: Setting a Quit Date

Trying to ease out of the habit by smoking less and less over months may not work well. It may just prolong withdrawal symptoms. Switching to brands low in tar and nicotine may not help either, because many people compensate by smoking more cigarettes, inhaling more deeply, and smoking the cigarette down farther toward the butt.

A modified cold turkey approach seems best: Cut down for a few weeks and then stop. Set a date for stopping completely—about 30 to 45 days off—and don't let anything change it! To motivate yourself, list all the reasons you want to quit.

Examples:

- A two-pack-a-day habit can cost more than $1,000 a year—enough for a week at a resort, new suits, a video cassette recorder or other luxuries. List what pleasures you will buy—for real—with your savings.
- People who smoke may develop facial wrinkles sooner than non-smokers.
- Smokers pay more for life insurance.
- Smoking affects your ability to taste and smell.
- Smokers use more sick days than non-smokers.
- The health costs of smokers are significantly greater than those of non-smokers.
- Smoking causes cancer, emphysema and heart disease.

Step Three: Preparing to Quit

First, use the "Pack Wrap" below or a smoking diary to monitor your smoking behavior.

The Pack Wrap Record is designed to give you a

- -

YOUR PACK WRAP RECORD
(Photocopy this form)

	Morning	Afternoon	Evening	Total
S				
M				
T				
W				
T				
F				
S				

- -

simple measure of how much you're smoking. Wrap it around each cigarette pack. Every day, keep a tally of the number of cigarettes you smoke in the morning, afternoon and evening, as well as the daily total. As you gradually cut down, you'll have a record of your progress.

Another technique is to keep a diary of every cigarette you smoke, and why you smoke it. On a sheet of lined paper, draw five columns: **Time**, **Need**, **Place** or **Activity**, **With Whom**, **Mood** or **Reasons**. Then, every time you smoke, record the factors that made you light up. In the column marked **Need**, use numbers to rate the cigarettes you feel you had to have (5), those you could easily have done without (1), and all those in between (2-4).

At the end of the day, review the diary for any patterns. Perhaps you smoke only with certain people, after meals, at parties or when you're anxious.

Try these tips to cut down:

- Postpone lighting your first cigarette by 15 minutes the first day and 15 minutes more each day thereafter.
- Assess your stress style (see Chapter Three); make appropriate adjustments to negative responses.
- Don't light up as soon as you crave a cigarette. Try distractions. Start a conversation; find something else to do; drink a glass of water.
- When you get the urge to smoke, breathe deeply, close your eyes and imagine yourself in your favorite spot.
- Set aside "non-smoking hours" and then extend those hours gradually.
- After a meal, quickly leave the table and take a walk or brush your teeth.
- When you have a strong urge to smoke, exercise. Exercise will help you relax and distract you until the urge to smoke disappears. (Refer to Chapter One.)
- Practice a self-control relaxation exercise daily.
- Switch to a brand you hate.
- Try not to smoke two packs of the same brand in a row.
- Buy cigarettes only by the pack. Finish one before buying another.
- Make it harder to get at your cigarettes. Wrap them in paper, lock them in a drawer . . . or roll them yourself.
- Try smoking with the hand you don't normally use.
- Smoke only half of each cigarette.
- Stop carrying matches or lighters.
- Chart your progress. Seeing is believing. Your daily records will encourage you as you count down toward cold-turkey day.
- Start sitting in non-smoking areas in restaurants, airplanes and other places when you have a choice.
- View smoking cessation as a positive move rather than a sacrifice. Tell yourself that you are becoming a non-smoker.
- Tell others you're quitting. They'll support you and encourage you to succeed.
- Make a bet with someone that you will stop smoking on your target date.
- Form a "Quit Team."
- Ask your spouse, a friend or co-worker to quit with you.
- Don't empty ashtrays. Stale cigarettes are a turnoff to smoking. At the end of each day, for about a week, save your butts in a glass jar.
- Drink more fluids than usual and get plenty of rest.
- Think of not smoking for one hour at a time.
- Avoid parties with people who smoke.

Step Four: On the Day You Quit

The trick is to focus on what you are doing rather than on what you are not and to build pleasures into the day.

- Reward yourself for stopping. Buy something you've had your eye on or do something special to celebrate. Keep rewarding yourself with little things—a paperback, or a movie.
- Continue to practice the "Big Three": regular exercise, proper nutrition and relaxation.
- Make sure all your cigarettes are gone. Hiding them is cheating.
- Keep busy. Go to the movies, exercise, take long walks or go biking.
- Spend as much free time as possible in NO SMOKING areas.
- As much as you can, avoid stressful situations if you can't apply appropriate stress-management techniques.
- Have your dentist clean your teeth.

Step Five: After You've Stopped

You may not need all of the following helpful suggestions, but being unprepared when the urge strikes can lead to "panic smoking," when you have to smoke because you don't know what else to do.

- Take it one day at a time.
- Practice "The Big Three": regular exercise, proper nutrition and daily relaxation exercises.
- If you link certain foods or drinks with smoking (see your diary) try to avoid them, at least for now. After you've quit for a while, you will be able to ease back to them.
- Avoid situations in which people are sure to smoke. Try to be with non-smokers.
- If you feel your will weakening, take a few deep breaths, light a match and then slowly blow it out. Crush it in an ashtray as you would a cigarette.

- If you have trouble keeping your hands busy, fiddle with a paper clip, worry beads, a pencil, etc. Keep busy with things you love to do—except smoking cigarettes.
- When the desire to smoke is strong, wash your hands or take a shower.
- If you miss having something in your mouth, buy a fake cigarette or keep toothpicks handy.
- Keep sugarless gum, mints, apples, celery or carrots handy.
- Drink lots of water and juice. Some ex-smokers swear by orange or tomato juice.
- Make a calendar for the first 90 clean days. Cross off each day and record the money saved by not smoking.
- Beware of the notion that just one cigarette won't hurt. That's the way most people start smoking again. But don't make this a self-fulfilling prophecy. If you yield to temptation and have one, don't view yourself as a failure or a permanent smoker. **Stop again immediately**. **You will succeed.**
- Most important, keep rewarding yourself for succeeding. Each day of not smoking takes effort, and you deserve a pat on the back.

If you are tempted to resume smoking because you start to pick up a few pounds, you should know that there is some evidence that the drugs in cigarette smoke increase metabolism and burn more calories. When you stop smoking, there may be a tendency toward weight gain because you are no longer using these drugs. The use of cigarettes to stay slim is simply the use of drugs to create disease that may cause loss of weight.

If weight gain occurs, the most successful solution is regular exercise and a change in your eating habits.

It Don't Come Easy, But You Can Do It: 35 Million Others Have

As the Ringo Starr song goes, ''You know it don't come easy,'' but with proper planning, incorporating support skills that help you deal with the problems of withdrawal, and finding new ways to satisfy your mental and physical needs, you can take the most positive step in prolonging your life. Go for it!

CHAPTER NINE

LifeSkill Nine: Drink Alcohol in Moderation or Not at All

For centuries, alcohol has been the most widely used and abused psychoactive drug in the world. Products of fermentation, beers and wines, with alcohol contents averaging 5 percent and 12 percent respectively, were the primary alcoholic drinks for thousands of years. Alcohol not only was used as a social lubricant, but for religious ceremonies and medicinal purposes.

With improved distillation techniques in the 17th century, the percentages of alcohol could be as high as 40 percent and 50 percent, creating a much more potent drug and increasing the opportunity for abuse.

The average American now consumes about 2.6 gallons of pure alcohol per year. It is estimated that more than 20 million Americans have serious drinking problems, with up to 10 percent of all workers in that group. Because of alcohol's serious health and social ramifications, the prudent use of this substance is a LifeSkill that cannot be ignored. This chapter will discuss the consequences of alcohol abuse and present recommendations for addressing this problem.

Factors Related to Blood Alcohol Concentration

A depressant, alcohol rapidly enters the bloodstream and directly affects the brain, lungs and kidneys. Metabolized in the liver, it is broken down at the rate of one drink per hour into acetaldehyde, then into acetate, and finally into carbon dioxide and water. Blood alcohol concentration is dependent upon a number of factors:

- **Dosage.** The stronger the drink, the faster the blood alcohol level will increase.
- **Rate of drinking.** Rapid drinking compresses the rate of intoxication, because the liver does not have

adequate time to metabolize the alcohol in the blood.
- **Food in the stomach.** Food slows alcohol absorption, whereas an empty stomach results in rapid absorption.
- **Tolerance level.** Levels of tolerance for alcohol vary from person to person. Regular drinkers and alcoholics metabolize alcohol faster than non-drinkers. Therefore, it takes higher quantities to affect them.

The Behavior of Alcoholics Endangers Themselves

The consequences of alcohol abuse are many. Alcoholics and problem drinkers are prone to early deaths, accidents, suicide and disease. Their life expectancies are estimated to be 10 to 12 years shorter than those of non-alcoholics. Their mortality rate is at least two and one-half times greater, and they suffer a disproportionate number of violent deaths. Alcoholics are 10 times more likely to die from fires, and between five and 13 times more likely to die from falls than non-alcoholics. More than half of all motor vehicle accidents are alcohol-related. Pedestrians with 0.10 blood alcohol levels—who would be considered legally intoxicated if driving in most states—are twice as likely to be hit by moving vehicles.

Alcoholics commit suicide between six and 15 times more frequently than non-alcoholics.

Alcoholics are also at increased risk for serious diseases, including cancer of the throat, mouth, breast, stomach, pancreas and liver. They are more likely to be malnourished and to have profound mental disturbances. Cirrhosis of the liver, one of several diseases common to alcoholics, causes nearly 30,000 deaths each year.

The Behavior of Alcoholics Endangers Their Families, Friends and Co-Workers

It is estimated that every alcoholic has a direct effect on another four people—primarily family members, friends and co-workers.

Excessive use of alcohol is a factor in about 50 percent of all divorces. Drinking is involved in 45 percent to 68 percent of spouse-abuse cases and up to 38 percent of child-abuse cases.

The negative consequences of alcohol abuse span the generations. Children of alcoholics develop alcoholism more frequently than children of non-alcoholics. Studies of juvenile delinquents have found that at least half of them come from homes where there are drinking problems. Finally, studies show that fetuses can be damaged by their mothers' habitual drinking. Fetal alcohol syndrome (FAS) is now considered one of the three leading causes of prenatal mental retardation in the United States. It is conservatively estimated that 1,800 to 2,400 infants are born with FAS every year.

A drinking problem is, in many ways, both a behavioral and social problem. Someone with a drinking problem seldom changes this habit alone; outside assistance and support are usually needed.

It's important first to be able to observe your drinking behavior and how it affects your relationships and well-being.

There are several methods you can use to decide if you or someone you care for has a drinking problem and how serious it is. One of these is the CAGE questionnaire. The acronym CAGE stands for **C**utting down, **A**nnoyance by criticism, **G**uilty feelings, and **E**ye-openers, the four key criteria being measured.

First, ask yourself the following questions about the behavior of the one you care for:

1. **C—Cutting down.** Has this person ever mentioned a need to cut down on drinking?
2. **A—Annoyance by criticism.** Have you ever felt moved to criticize your friend's drinking? Was he or she annoyed by it?
3. **G—Guilty feelings.** Has the person ever mentioned guilt feelings about drinking?
4. **E—Eye opener.** Have you ever noticed the person taking an "eye opener" in the morning?

NOW—go back and ask the same questions about **yourself!**

Studies suggest that if the answer to even one question is "yes," the individual may have a drinking problem. If the answer is "yes" to two questions, the studies show a possibility of alcoholism. The possibility gets still higher with three or four "yes" answers.

Here is another way to judge drinking behavior. Which of the following drinking categories do you or the party in question identify with?

A normal (social) drinker:

• Drinks slowly—no fast gulping.
• Knows when to stop drinking; doesn't get drunk.
• Eats before or while drinking.
• Never drives after drinking.
• Respects non-drinkers.
• Knows and obeys laws related to drinking.
• Drinks for reasons that don't lead to excessive use.

A problem drinker:

• Drinks to get drunk.
• Tries to solve problems by drinking.
• Becomes loud, angry or violent.
• Drinks when he or she shouldn't—before driving or going to work.
• Causes other problems—harms himself or herself, family, friends and strangers.

An alcoholic:

• Spends a lot of time thinking about drinking and planning where and when to get the next drink.
• Keeps bottles hidden for quick pick-me-ups.
• Starts drinking without consciously planning to and loses awareness of the amount of alcohol consumed.
• Denies drinking.
• Drinks alone.
• Needs to drink to face a stressful situation.
• May have "blackouts"—cannot remember what occurred while drinking although he or she may have appeared normal to other people at that time.
• Suffers from malnutrition and neglect.
• Goes from having hangovers to more dangerous withdrawal symptoms, leading to delirium tremens ("DTs"), which can be fatal.

Getting Help

The most important step in addressing a drinking problem is for you or the party in question to admit that a problem exists and that outside assistance is needed. It is common, unfortunately, for the alcoholic to deny his or her dependence to the bitter end.

Therefore, it is usually someone close to the person—a spouse, child, friend or co-worker—who is able to break through the facade of control and steer the victim to seek help. Rarely does the abuser seek help without confrontation or crisis, such as losing a job or facing a marital break-up.

If you or someone you care about has a drinking problem, it is important to seek help now. This is one LifeSkill that affects all of us.

The most successful resource for assisting an alcoholic to recovery is Alcoholics Anonymous (AA). Community-based, AA uses a self-help group format in helping the recovering alcoholic come to grips with the reality and consequences of alcoholism. Al-Anon and Alateen are also available in communities to teach and support family members in dealing with the alcoholic while protecting themselves.

Other resources to explore include public health departments, alcohol treatment programs, family physicians, clergy, mental health agencies and, if available, your company's employee assistance program.

Alcohol and Health

Clearly, alcohol abuse and its effects on the individual, family, co-workers, friends and society are serious and far-reaching. However, some studies have suggested that alcohol has positive effects on heart disease and longevity. A few studies have shown that moderate alcohol consumption, defined as no more than two drinks per day, increases high density lipoprotein cholesterol (HDL), the so-called good cholesterol. It has also been found that moderate drinkers live not only longer than heavy drinkers, but also longer even than teetotalers.

Although the data on the relationship between alcohol and health are inconclusive, it does seem safe to infer that moderate alcohol consumption—no more than two beers or glasses of wine, or one mixed drink per day—does not seem to have any long-term detrimental health effects.

The key here is moderation, with the drinker not allowed to save tickets for the weekend or a night on the town! Binge drinking itself is a sign of a problem drinker and should be addressed.

However, be careful! Even moderate drinking can impair the average person's judgment and coordination when driving a vehicle. Two drinks within an hour for a 150-pound male would raise his blood alcohol level above .05, which legally would make him guilty of driving "under the influence" in most states.

CHAPTER TEN

LifeSkill Ten: Stay Substance-Free

The use of illicit substances, such as cocaine, heroin and marijuana, in America has reached epidemic proportions. The National Institute of Drug Abuse has estimated that in 1986, 15 percent of the national population had experimented with cocaine, with nearly 40 percent of those aged 25 to 30 having done so. With the deaths of such celebrities as basketball star Len Bias, Americans, especially younger adults, have been given grim reminders of the consequence of drug use. Substance abuse not only abuses life, it takes it away.

This chapter focuses on the use of illicit drugs and prescriptive medications that are associated with abuse.

What Is Substance Problem?

A person has a substance problem when one or more of life's primary functional areas, be it the personal, family, work or community area, is repeatedly impaired by the use of a psychoactive substance—any agent that can act as a stimulant, depressant or hallucinogen.

Stimulants are substances that activate the nervous system, increasing one's energy and alertness. Caffeine in coffee, tea or cola drinks, and nicotine in tobacco are examples of widely used stimulants. Although there are health concerns about too much caffeine consumption as well as the recognized health risks from tobacco smoking, more concern generally has been focused on the use and abuse of such other stimulants as cocaine, amphetamines and antidepressants.

Depressive substances, in contrast, decrease central nervous system activity, narrow the field of perception and thus act as sedatives and pain-killers. Alcohol, narcotics, barbiturates, tranquilizers and volatile inhalants (solvents, aerosols or nitrous oxide) are powerful depressants and quite addictive.

Substances such as marijuana, LSD, PCP and psilocybin (magic mushroom) produce mild to strong hallucinations and sensory distortions, which can vary from euphoria (marijuana) to violent behavior (PCP). (See symptoms and signs of drug abuse, page 87.)

Substance Dependence

All psychoactive substances have a potential for dependence (described in the previous discussions of alcohol and nicotine), even if it is just development of a strong habit. Such drugs affect receptor sites in the central nervous system, which become accustomed to their presence. In time, greater amounts of the substance are required to register the desired effect. As in smoking and alcohol abuse, a tolerance is developed. In the absence of the substance, the central nervous system may react in such a way that the person experiences mental and/or physical discomfort—withdrawal symptoms.

Depressive substances, such as narcotics and tranquilizers, have a great potential for abuse. They are physically addicting, creating severe mental torment and physical discomfort when use is discontinued. There is mounting evidence that use of cocaine, a stimulant, can not only create a psychological dependence but also cause irreversible damage to the central nervous system.

Dependence on the Substance Experience

People can become dependent upon the process of using a substance just as much as they become dependent upon the substance itself. This is referred to as *dependence upon the substance experience*. Someone can not only become "hooked" on the drug but also on the lifestyle associated with it. A cocaine abuser, for instance, can get pleasure from and develop a dependence on the status of being a user, the risks involved in securing the drug, and the "party" atmosphere associated with it. As Richard Miller, Ed.D., of the University of Rochester, explains, "Getting hooked on the cocaine effect is quite possible, but it's the substance experience that intensifies that possibility."

How Does a Substance Abuse Problem Develop?

A substance abuse problem develops when a person has difficulty telling the difference between a personal experience and a substance experience. Some studies suggest that certain people have predisposed sensitivities to such things as the intoxication from alcohol or the "high" from marijuana. This predisposition, along with a substance-oriented lifestyle, increases the risk of developing a drug-abuse problem. According to another school of thought, dependency is entirely a matter of lifestyle and a negative response to a stressful world. Both groups of experts agree, however, that a learning process takes place, in which the person tries to eliminate or lessen pain (physical and/or emotional) through the substance experience. Eventually, however, drug use creates a vicious cycle, causing more pain than that which the person was trying to avoid.

Do You Have a Substance Abuse Problem?

How substance-free is your lifestyle? The following checklist is designed to identify the psychoactive substances you are currently using and how you perceive their effect on your moods or behaviors. Be honest with yourself.

Which of these psychoactive substances do you currently use?

Stimulants	Depressants	Hallucinogens
caffeine	alcohol	marijuana
nicotine	narcotics	LSD
amphetamines	barbiturates	PCP
antidepressants	tranquilizers	psilocybin
cocaine	inhalants	and others

Does your substance use:

	Yes	No
Make you forget your problems?	___	___
Usually occur when you feel troubled?	___	___
Make you feel good about yourself and life?	___	___
Prevent you from fulfilling responsibilities?	___	___
Discourage you from trying new things?	___	___
Prevent you from interacting with non-users?	___	___
Have to be done on a regular basis?	___	___
Make you uncomfortable when you stop using?	___	___
Make you intolerant of schedule changes that affect your use?	___	___
Make you ignore many changes and events in your life?	___	___
Lessen in effect or experience with time?	___	___
Make you feel bothered about the thought of stopping?	___	___

The more you answer "yes" to the questions on this page, the more likely it is that you have a substance-abuse problem. The wise decision is to find out for sure by seeking professional help. Talk to a community, employee assistance or religious counselor. The following section will help you get started.

Seeking Help: The First Step to Recovery

There is no cure for substance dependence; the **urge** can persist for much of your life. However, it can be controlled. Successful rehabilitation or recovery can be expected for 50 percent to 70 percent of all substance abusers. Treatment for substance dependence entails therapeutic counseling, group support and withdrawal from the substance. During treatment, efforts are made to restore healthy eating habits, increase physical activity, and learn to cope effectively with stress.

After treatment, you are expected to maintain a lifelong plan of recovery. This requires you to move from a therapist-supervised support group to a self-help group, such as Narcotics Anonymous.

Self-help groups can be located easily by referring to your Yellow Pages (look under alcohol or drugs), or by contacting your physician, community alcohol/drug abuse services, your employee assistance program or a pastoral counselor.

Symptoms and Signs of Drug Abuse

Hallucinogens

(LSD, psilocybin, mescaline, PCP, STP, MDMA, Bromo-DMA)

Signs of Severe Intoxication	Symptoms of Withdrawal
Pupils dilated	None
Rapid pulse	
Elevated blood pressure	
Face flushed	
Visual hallucinations	
Distorted vision and sense of time	
Slurred speech	
Increased heart rate	

With PCP:

Extreme hyperactivity
Drooling
Impulsive, often violent behavior

Central Nervous System Stimulants

(Amphetamines, cocaine, methylphenidate, phenmetrazine, phenylpropanolamine, most anti-obesity drugs)

Signs of Severe Intoxication	Symptoms of Withdrawal
Pupils dilated	Muscle aches
Rapid pulse	Abdominal pain
Shallow breathing	Chills and tremors
Hyperactive, easily excitable behavior	Intense hunger
Rapid speech	Extreme depression
Dry mouth	Anxiety
Sweating	Increased sleep
Impulsive behavior	Suicidal behavior

Cannabis Substances

(Marijuana, hashish, THC, hash oil)

Signs of Severe Intoxication	Symptoms of Withdrawal
Bloodshot eyes	Irritability
Increased appetite	Anxiety
Euphoria or anxiety	Nausea
Dreamy, fantasy state	Inability to sleep
Time-space distortions	Restlessness
Increased heart rate	

Opioids-Narcotics

(Heroin, morphine, codeine, meperidine, methadone, hydromorphone, opium, pentazocine, propoxyphene)

Signs of Severe Intoxication	Symptoms of Withdrawal
Pupils constricted	Abdominal cramps
Reduced breathing rate	Muscle jerks
Decreased body temperature	Flu symptoms
Reflexes diminished or absent	Vomiting
Decreased blood pressure	Diarrhea
	Trembling
	Anxiety
	In overdoses:
	Stupor or coma
	Convulsions

Central Nervous System Sedatives

(Barbiturates, chlordiazepoxide, diazepam, flurazepam, glutethimide, meprobamate, methaqualone)

Signs of Severe Intoxication	Symptoms of Withdrawal
Decreased blood pressure	Trembling
Reduced breathing rate	Sweating
Slow motor reflexes	Collapse of cardiovascular system
Drowsiness or coma	Delirium
Loss of muscular coordination	Hallucinations
Slurred Speech	Disorientation
Delirium	Inability to sleep

Anticholinergics

(Atropine, belladonna, henbane, scopolamine, trihexyphenidyl, benztropine mesylate, procyclidine, propantheline bromide)

Signs of Severe Intoxication	Symptoms of Withdrawal
Pupils dilated and fixed	Gastrointestinal disorders
Increased heart rate	Musculoskeletal disorders
Temperature elevated	
Flushed, dry skin and mucous membranes	
Confusion	
Visual hallucinations	

Source: *The Medical Letter on Drugs and Therapeutics*, Vol. 27, September 1985. Published by the Medical Letter, Inc., New Rochelle, New York.

CHAPTER ELEVEN

LifeSkill Eleven:
Keep Personal Safety in Mind

Personal safety, the prevention of accidents and the protection of life and property, is a LifeSkill, too—one often neglected or ignored until an accident or loss occurs.

Accidents are the leading cause of death for people one to 44 years of age, and a major cause of injuries in all age groups.

Personal injuries can usually be prevented through careful planning and simple maintenance schedules. Preventing burglary and personal assault is often a matter of home security. In this chapter, we will present general guidelines to help you and your family be more safety conscious.

Vehicular Safety

Close to 50,000 people die each year in motor vehicle accidents. This is the equivalent of a 727 passenger jet crashing every day. Drunk drivers are responsible for half of these deaths and for another 500,000 injuries. To reduce the risk of accident and injury, practice the following:

1. Drive within the designated speed limit, and slower when weather conditions require it. The National Research Council in Washington, DC, estimates that more than 4,000 lives per year have been saved since the 55 mph speed limit was demanded by federal legislation. (Recently, the 55 mph limit was increased to 65 mph on "low density" interstate highways.)
2. Wear seat belts and require all passengers to do so whenever a vehicle is in motion. Seat belts reduce the risk of injury by an estimated 66 percent.
3. Consider purchasing an air bag with your new car.

4. Don't drive after drinking or using drugs, illegal or prescriptive, which can make you drowsy or alter your sensory and motor skills.
5. Make sure your vehicle is in good mechanical order. Periodically check tire wear, brakes and headlights.
6. Obey all regulations when operating other vehicles, such as motorboats, motorbikes or bicycles. Wear an approved safety helmet when riding a motorbike or bicycle and a flotation vest when on the water.

Being Safe at Home

Accidents in the home contribute to more than 20,000 deaths and more than 3 million disabling injuries every year.

To avoid home accidents and subsequent injury, take precautions, act with foresight and expect the unexpected. Don't put off making your home a safer place. The following strategies will help you eliminate the most common hazards from your home.

Preventing Falls

In any given year, more than one million people are injured by falling. Half of the annual home-accident deaths result from falls. Those who fall are frequently over age 65 or under age five. To reduce the risk of falls:

- Don't store objects on stairs.
- Don't hang pictures on walls next to stairs.
- Cover stairs with rubber treads, abrasive strips or skid-resistant paint.
- Install skid-resistant shower or bathtub mats.
- Place lights at the top and bottom of stairways.
- Maintain a clear field of vision when carrying things up and down stairs.
- See that handrails and stairs end at the same point.
- Clear ice and snow from outdoor steps.

Watch Where You Walk!

You can avoid slipping, tripping and stumbling by being on the lookout for unexpected lubricants, such as:

- Water or another liquid that has spilled. If you see it, wipe it up immediately.
- Oil, grease or mud on garage floors. Absorbent chemicals available in hardware stores can take care of oily spills.
- Floor wax that has not dried.
- Icy patches on streets and sidewalks.

Injuries are compounded if the individual falls against, and breaks, a glass door or window. Therefore, make certain that sliding glass doors, glass entrance doors, large windows, and shower and bath enclosures are made of safety glazing materials.

Also, place a small decal at eye level to make the glass more visible.

Ladder Safety

Ladders come in handy, but mishaps with ladders account for 60,000 fall-related injuries a year. Therefore, if you need to use a ladder, learn to do so properly before taking your feet off the ground.

When you buy a ladder, check its maximum load rating (usually between 200 and 250 pounds), which includes the total weight of you and your materials. Choose a wooden or fiberglass ladder if you work near power lines or with electrical tools.

Make sure your ladder is long enough and that an extension ladder is placed one-fourth the usable length from the wall. This means understanding the difference between total and usable length. The top three rungs of a straight or extension ladder, or the top step and top platform of a stepladder, should not be used to support your weight.

Fires: Prevention and Preparation

Nearly 3 million fires occur in the United States each year, resulting in more than 7,600 deaths and 200,000 burns and other injuries. The following are among the most common causes.

Smoking: The Number-One Killer

Quitting smoking is the best way to eliminate this danger. But in the meantime, smokers can use these tips to make their homes safer:

• Have plenty of large, steady ashtrays with center grooves for holding cigarettes, and use them. Do not rest a cigarette on a countertop, sink edge, or any other place from which it may roll.
• Check chair and sofa cushions for smoldering cigarettes before going to bed.
• Wait until the next day to empty ashtrays. Never dump ashes that could still be hot into plastic waste baskets or paper bags, or on top of other trash.
• Never smoke in bed.
• Keep matches, lighters and other smoking supplies out of children's reach.

Caution in the Kitchen

Stove tops, ovens and broilers can take the heat, but you won't be able to if you treat them carelessly. Observe these safety rules:

• Keep curtains, wall hangings and paper towels away from the stove at all times, even if its burners are turned off.
• Never wear loose-fitting or flowing garments while preparing food.

• Turn pot handles inward so children can't reach for them and adults can't knock them over.
• Keep the burners and oven clean and grease-free.
• Treat toasters, toaster ovens and counter-top broilers with the same care as regular ovens and stoves.

How should you extinguish a fire on the stove? The National Safety Council (NSC) recommends turning off the burners and covering the flames with a pot or pan lid. NSC advises having the correct size lids handy while cooking.

Baking soda also can put out a fire, but you might not have enough on hand to do the job. Never douse flames with flour or other flammable substances.

Electrical Fires

• Do not overload electrical outlets, which can cause wires to overheat, damaging their insulation and igniting fires.
• Watch for blown fuses and circuit breakers; they indicate circuit overloads and possible overheating.
• Replace frayed cords.
• Never run cords alongside door jambs or across high-traffic areas.
• Inspect electrical cords and outlets periodically.
• Check the area around your television set; heat from the back of a TV can ignite accumulated dust or papers stored nearby.

Fireplaces and Wood Stoves

• A fireplace or wood stove should be installed by a professional. A wood stove should always sit on a fireproof base, away from combustible materials.
• Watch out for loose bricks and creosote buildup. All fireplaces, chimneys and stoves should be cleaned and checked yearly by a reputable servicing company.
• Make sure the metal fire screen is closed to stop sparks or, better yet, install a glass door.
• Never stack newspapers or magazines near the fireplace or stove.

Space Heaters

Portable electric or kerosene heaters are used by many people, especially older men and women, to save on heating bills. But they can be dangerous!

• Children's hands can fit between the protective bars of some portable electric heaters, letting little fingers touch red-hot coils. Protective covers help, but they don't eliminate the danger. Those coils can reach 500° F, so watch children carefully.
• Don't let your heater come in contact with such combustibles as papers, curtains and upholstered furniture.

For a kerosene heater:

- Make sure the heater's design prevents it from tipping over easily or leaking fuel. Does it have an automatic flame cutoff if the heater is bumped or knocked over?
- Do not put the heater in high-traffic areas.
- Know how to refuel the heater correctly. Let it cool first. Remember that kerosene **expands** with heat— if you add too much, some will overflow.
- Use only high-quality kerosene. Never use gasoline.
- Keep children and all combustibles at least three feet away from the heater.
- Open a nearby window one inch or more to permit air to circulate.

Plan Your Escape

Even if you take every possible precaution, a fire may still break out. It is important to know in advance what to do in an emergency.

The National Fire Protection Association recommends these steps:

- Plan an emergency escape route.
  - Make sure there are two escape routes from as many rooms as possible in your house.
  - Place a portable escape ladder in each upstairs bedroom, loft or den.
  - Have announced and unannounced fire drills. Schedule some drills between 11 p.m. and 6 a.m., hours when fires frequently occur.
- Plan an alarm system for your family to use in case of fire. For instance, you could use a special whistle or bell.
- When escaping a fire, stay low—on your hands and knees—to avoid breathing smoke or heated air.
- If a smoke detector awakens you, don't stand up. You could expose yourself to smoke and fumes, which rise. Instead, roll out of bed and crawl to safety.
- Feel the temperature of doors before you open them. If a door's hot, leave it closed. If it's cool, open it slowly, but be prepared to shut it again quickly at the first sign of smoke or heat.
- If smoke comes in around a closed door, block its entry with clothing or blankets.
- Agree now on a post-escape meeting place. That way, you'll know who's accounted for.
- Do not re-enter a burning building for valued possessions or even pets.
- Call the fire department from a neighbor's house.
- When you stay in a hotel, note the locations of exits and stairways. Always count the number of doors between your room and an exit so that you can find your way out even if smoke obstructs your vision.

Smoke Detectors Save Lives

According to U.S. Fire Administration statistics, smoke plays a role in three-fourths of all fire deaths. Smoke and poisonous gases can quickly render victims unconscious. They then suffocate or burn to death as the fire spreads.

The National Bureau of Standards' Center for Fire Research estimates that smoke detectors could prevent 55 percent of fire deaths by alerting residents early, before escape becomes impossible.

Smoke detectors are inexpensive, easy to install and battery operated. At least one detector for each level of the house is recommended. In most major metropolitan areas, the law requires the landlord to maintain working smoke detectors in all rented dwellings.

In your home or apartment, place each smoke detector on the ceiling or on a side wall, 12 inches below the ceiling. Never place a smoke detector in a corner where walls and ceiling come together—air doesn't circulate there. Similarly, be sure that smoke detectors are at least three feet from heat registers and air vents.

Finally, make sure to test your own and your parents' smoke detectors to make sure they're in working order.

Home Fire Extinguishers

In all but very small fires, a fire extinguisher's purpose is not to put out the fire. Rather, it is to slow the spread of flames, giving you more time to escape.

Experts recommend a dry chemical extinguisher for home use. It should be "triple rated," for use on class A, class B and class C fires. This means it will be effective on burning wood, textiles or paper (class A); flammable liquids (class B); and electrical equipment (class C). The Underwriters' Laboratories (UL) or Factory Mutual (FM) seal of approval ensures that a fire extinguisher meets rigid standards of construction and performance.

But even the best fire extinguisher won't help if you can't use it. Remember, you won't have time to read the instructions on your extinguisher when faced with a fire, so read them carefully now, and see that you understand them.

And to be sure you can count on your extinguisher when you need it, check it every few months.

Power Tools and Appliances

Each year, chain-saw and power-saw accidents cause 100,000 injuries. Slips with other home-workshop tools cause an added 25,000. Improper use of power mowers and hedge trimmers leads to another 42,000.

For safe use of any electrical power tool, follow these steps:

- Read the owner's manual before using the tool.

- Make sure the tool's safety guards are in place.
- Check the tool for faulty insulation or wiring.
- Wear approved safety goggles.
- See that your work area is dry.
- Be sure the tool has a three-pronged, grounded plug. Insert it into a three-pronged socket.
- Another caution—the noise of power tools can be hazardous to your hearing. Consider wearing earplugs.

Chain Saws

Two kinds of chain-saw injuries commonly occur: contact with sharp, fast-moving chains causes serious cuts and even amputations; and wood fragments that fly toward the user can cut or bruise skin, or injure unprotected eyes.

To prevent a chain-saw accident, heed these suggestions from the U.S. Consumer Product Safety Commission:

- Buy a saw that you can control easily. If possible, choose one with a low kickback chain or plastic cover on the guide bar.
- Test the saw to see that the chain stops as soon as the trigger is released.
- Wear sturdy shoes, heavy pants and safety glasses.
- Place logs to be cut firmly on the ground. Hold the saw parallel to the ground.
- Turn off the motor before walking with the saw or leaving it unattended.
- Keep children away from your work area.
- Use a lightweight hand saw, not a chain saw, for trimming branches.

Portable Power Saws and Table Saws

Most injuries that involve portable power saws and table saws result from contact with a blade. Injury is especially likely if the blade guard has been removed from a portable saw, or if a table saw is operated without a push block (a piece of wood used to push the item being cut). Here are some safety guidelines for working with these tools:

- Always keep blade guards and other devices in place.
- Use a push block when making straight cuts with a stationary saw.
- Allow the saw to operate at its own speed—don't try to force it forward.
- Unplug any saw before cleaning or repairing it.

Lawn Mowers and Hedge Trimmers

Sixty-eight percent of the injuries that involve power mowers result from hand or foot contact with whirling blades. Twenty percent are caused by rocks, twigs and other objects thrown by the blades. These are often eye injuries. Almost all hedge-trimmer accidents involve contact with moving blades. These accidents frequently occur when the gardener tries to change hand positions while the tool is turned on.

It's important to purchase a power mower that has the appropriate safety features. Learn to use it properly and wear protective goggles.

Care With Kitchen Appliances

Thousands of people are injured every year while operating blenders, garbage disposals, food processors and other kitchen appliances. The major cause? Contact with rapidly moving blades.

Take these precautions:

- Make sure all parts are properly connected before you turn on the appliance.
- Do not insert utensils into the blades of mixers, blenders or food processors, or adjust parts while the machines are turned on or plugged in.
- Keep your hands away from moving blades.
- Avoid operating portable appliances near sinks or wet areas. Unplug machines for cleaning, and never immerse them in water.

Poison Patrol

Each year, 4,000 Americans die from accidental poisonings, but 1 million are involved in non-fatal poisonings. Usually toxins are swallowed, but they can be inhaled or absorbed through the skin. Most poisonings occur in the home, and most victims are children under age five. Therefore, the best way to prevent a poisoning is to child-proof your home—even if you don't have young children. You never know when youngsters may visit.

If a Poisoning Emergency Occurs

A poisoning requires fast action. The longer poison remains in the body, the more damage it does. If you suspect a poisoning has taken place, even if you're not sure, seek medical attention promptly. Call the nearest poison control center, and follow their instructions. Keep the number posted near your phone with other emergency response numbers.

Depending on what was swallowed, the poison control center may ask you to administer an emetic, a substance to induce vomiting, such as syrup of ipecac, which is available without prescription. Keep this substance in your home pharmacy.

Inhaled Poisons

Toxins that enter the body through the respiratory system account for about 1,800 deaths per year. Most of these deaths are caused by carbon monoxide, a colorless, odorless gas found in motor-vehicle exhaust and fumes from faulty heating systems and burning charcoal.

You probably cannot rid your home of carbon monoxide, but you can keep it from reaching dangerous levels. Here's how:

- Open the garage door before warming up or tuning up your car engine. If the motor is on and the garage door is closed, you're asking for trouble.
- Have your heating and ventilation systems checked yearly by a certified heating and cooling specialist.
- Never burn charcoal in a garage or other closed area.

Emergency care for those who have inhaled poison is simple and standard: Get the individual out of the hazardous environment and into fresh air. But take care not to be overcome yourself—if you don't think you can rescue someone safely, call for trained personnel.

Finally, remember that even if they appear to recover quickly, victims should seek medical attention to prevent complications.

Contact Poisoning

The toxins most likely to enter the system through the skin are insecticides, rat poisons and corrosives, such as oven cleaner, gasoline and other petroleum products.

Signs and symptoms of contact poisoning include nausea and vomiting, burned skin, and difficulty breathing.

Prevent contact poisoning by adopting these two rules:

- Wear a mask, gloves and long sleeves when working with toxic substances.
- Don't let children play in recently sprayed areas.

If contact poisoning does occur, call a poison control center immediately.

Preventing Burglary

A major step in preventing burglary and possible assault is making it difficult for a crime to happen. An unlocked window or door is an open invitation to a crime. The National Sheriffs Association recommends using the following checklist to ensure your residential security. Use it to go through your home and that of your older relatives to see that no one is inviting a burglary.

Doors:

- Can all of your doors, including basement, porch, French and balcony doors, be securely locked?
- Do your basement doors have locks that allow you to isolate that part of your house?
- Are your locks in good repair?
- Do you know everyone who has a key to your

house, or are some keys still in the hands of previous owners or tenants?
- Are window locks properly and securely mounted?
- Do you keep windows locked when they are shut?
- In high-hazard locations, do you use bars or ornamental grills?
- Are you as careful with basement and second-floor windows as you are with those on the first floor?

Garage:

- Do you lock your garage door at night and when you are away from home?
- Do you have good, secure locks on garage doors and windows?
- Do you lock your car and take the keys out even when it is parked in your garage?

When You Go on a Trip:

- Do you stop all deliveries or arrange for neighbors to pick up papers, mail or packages?
- Do you leave some shades up, so that the house doesn't look deserted?
- Do you arrange to keep the lawn and garden in shape?

Safe Practices:

- Do you plan so that you don't need to "hide" a key under a doormat?
- Do you have a list of the serial numbers of watches, cameras, typewriters and similar items?
- Do you have a description of other valuable property that does not have a serial number?
- Have you recorded credit card numbers as well as the numbers to call if they are lost or stolen?
- Have you told your family to leave the house undisturbed and call the police if they discover a burglary has been committed?

Safety Concerns for Older People

According to the National Safety Council, 23,000 persons over age 65 die every year from accidental injuries. Another 750,000 are disabled. Older people are disproportionately represented when it comes to falls. Although they account for 12 percent of the population, they are involved in 21 percent of all falls. And the fire-death rate for this age group is about five times higher than that of the general population.

Impaired vision, slower reaction times and poor balance can make older people more accident prone than other age groups. Moreover, a mishap that might merely inconvenience a young person can put an older one out of commission for a long time.

Therefore, safety concerns should not only include guidelines outlined earlier, but also the additional ones that follow:

- **Lighting.** For those with reduced vision, adequate lighting is particularly important. The American Optometric Association recommends that everyone maintain soft overall lighting indoors, and use auxiliary lamps for tasks requiring more light—reading, sewing, cooking or taking medications. People over age 60 are advised to increase overall room lighting. Also, incandescent lights may be more comfortable than fluorescent.
  — Place night-lights in bedrooms and bathrooms, to safeguard against falls.
  — The head and foot of stairways should be well lit.
  — Make lights convenient to use: Switches should be located at room entrances. Fixtures should be easy to clean, with bulbs easy to change. Do not block electrical outlets with furniture.
- **Furniture.** Furniture can be hazardous. Remove pieces that are rickety, have outlived their usefulness or pose a potential threat.
  — Furniture should be easy to move for cleaning.
  — Furniture with rounded edges will prevent bruising.
  — Chairs should support the lower back and neck for long periods.
  — Furniture should be arranged for ease of maneuverability between rooms and for quick exit in an emergency.
  — Place a table at the bedside for a lamp, a telephone and water.
- **The Bathroom.** The combination of wet, slippery surfaces, hard floors and fixtures, and glass enclosures makes the bathroom one of the most hazardous sites in the home.
  — Place rough-surfaced adhesive strips in the bathtub to provide needed traction.
  — See that non-skid mats cover the floor.
  — Install grab bars over the tub or in the shower if needed.
  — To prevent scalding, install hot and cold mixing controls in the shower.
  — See that tub or shower enclosures are made from a safety glazing material.
- **Steps and Stairways.** Stairs can be hazardous, particularly for those with impaired vision or balance problems.
  — Use those stair coverings that provide the highest level of slip resistance and the most uniform traction: rubber treads, abrasive strips or skid-resistant paint. Steer clear of slippery waxes, and remember that even carpeting can be hazardous.
  — Install handrails on both sides of the stairway.
  — Avoid hanging pictures or other eye-catchers along stairway walls. While they may look pretty, they can distract and disorient stair climbers.
  — Don't use stairways for storage.

  — Keep a supply of rock salt handy for clearing icy steps, or arrange for someone to remove ice and snow.
- **Floors.** To further reduce the likelihood of falls in the home, eliminate treacherous floor surfaces.
  — Carpets, rugs and linoleum should lie flat and be smooth at the edges.
  — Eliminate sills or thresholds between rooms, to prevent tripping, if possible.
  — Choose carpeting with a low, tight pile. People are less likely to catch a heel in this type than in the deep-pile variety.
  — Place non-skid mats in spots that are frequently wet, such as entrance ways and the kitchen-sink area.
  — Replace any scatter rugs that do not have skid-resistant backings or pads.

  These precautions are particularly important for those who use walkers or wheelchairs.
- **The Kitchen.** Because of possible vision problems and slower reaction times, older people must take extra care in the kitchen. Here are some ways to alleviate kitchen hazards:
  — Keep all combustible items away from the stove.
  — Don't place or store potholders, dish towels or plastic utensils on or near the range. Be sure no curtains brush against heat sources.
  — The stove top and burners should be clean and free of grease.
  — Don't wear long, loose sleeves while cooking. They can catch fire or hook on pot handles.
  — Don't use any overhead cabinets that are more than 12 inches deep or 72 inches from the floor, and don't store items on shelves over the stove or refrigerator. These precautions will eliminate the need to use a stepstool and risk falling.
  — All pots, pans and bowls should be lightweight.
  — Mark burner controls with bright colors to indicate the "on" and "off" positions. This is helpful for those with poor vision.
  — Periodically check the contents of the refrigerator. This is especially important for someone with impaired senses of sight and taste.

Moving Around Safely

Automobiles represent a vital link with the outside world, but are a leading cause of accidental deaths among older people.

The American Association of Retired Persons and the National Retired Teachers Association recommend that older drivers be aware of changes in reaction time and vision.

Most older people can continue to drive safely by

making allowances for these physiological changes. Follow these guidelines:

- Have yearly eye examinations. Ask whether the optometrist or ophthalmologist detects any vision changes that could affect driving.
- Allow time to become accustomed to new lenses before driving.
- Wear good-quality sunglasses during daytime hours to reduce glare.
- Restrict your driving to daylight hours if you have difficulty seeing at night.
- Keep a window open slightly to hear sirens, horns or other warnings. Don't let the radio drown outside noises.
- Take frequent breaks to rest your eyes, stretch your muscles and renew your energy on long trips.
- Be sure that any medications you are taking will not impair your driving ability.
- Older drivers should consider taking a safe driver training course. Many states, as well as the American Automobile Association, offer them. Frequently, the completion of such a course entitles people to savings on insurance.
- Wear your safety belt all the time, whether driver or passenger.
- Don't drink and drive.

Those who use buses for transportation should:

- Hold onto seat backs and vertical supports in the center aisle.
- Limit the number of packages carried so that one hand is always free and vision is not obstructed.
- Stay seated until ready to exit.
- Check the street surface for irregularities before stepping down from the bus.

Reduce the likelihood of being struck by a vehicle while crossing the street. Here are some recommendations from safety experts:

- Stand on the sidewalk while waiting to cross, not in the street.
- Look to the right and left before entering an intersection.
- Wear light-colored or reflective garments when walking at night.

Avoid being victimized by crime by taking care not to walk in unfamiliar or unlit areas. Watch purses and wallets, and do not carry large sums of money. Never risk physical assault to safeguard cash: Don't struggle with the thief.

Take time to educate yourself about common safety hazards. Go through the house and look for ways to make it safer.

CHAPTER TWELVE

LifeSkill Twelve: Practice Safe Sex When in Doubt

Before the age of AIDS, sexually transmitted diseases, such as syphilis, gonorrhea, herpes and chlamydia, were the risks one took if one wanted to join the sexual revolution. Today, the game has changed. In some metropolitan areas, such as Manhattan and San Francisco, AIDS has become the leading cause of premature death for males 30 to 39 years of age. AIDS (acquired immunodeficiency syndrome), is a world-wide health concern that has fatal consequences and no cure. Since the disease was discovered in 1978, AIDS cases have risen to more than 70,000 (1988) with more than 40,000 deaths. Another 200,000-plus people are sick from AIDS-related complex (ARC), a collection of symptoms that do not meet the appropriate diagnostic category for AIDS.

AIDS is caused by the human immunodeficiency virus (HIV), which suppresses the immune system, leaving the body susceptible to normally rare disorders, including Pneumocystis pneumonia and Kaposi's sarcoma (a form of skin cancer), and other *opportunistic* diseases (diseases that take advantage of the body's defenselessness).

The symptoms of AIDS include persistent fatigue, unexplained fever, drenching night sweats, unexplained weight loss, swollen glands, persistent diarrhea and dry cough. However, it can take years before any of these symptoms appear.

Modes of Transmission

The AIDS virus is transmitted primarily through sexual intercourse—oral, vaginal or anal—when semen or vaginal fluids are exchanged and the virus finds an entry into the blood stream, usually through a tear in the mucous membrane.

A second mode of transmission is through the sharing of needles or syringes with an infected person.

The AIDS virus has not been shown to be spread from saliva, sweat, tears, urine or feces. You will not get AIDS from such casual contact as working with someone with AIDS. A kiss, a telephone, a toilet seat or a swimming pool will not spread AIDS. However, babies of infected women may be infected themselves during pregnancy or through breast feeding.

Some hemophiliacs and others have become infected because of transfusions of contaminated blood. However, with the development of HIV screening techniques, the probability of receiving infected blood is small and there is absolutely no risk in donating blood.

Who's at Risk?

As of mid-1988, the majority of AIDS cases were concentrated among male homosexuals, bisexuals and intravenous drug users. Approximately 4 percent of cases have been attributed to heterosexual contact.

At this writing, it is not clear whether AIDS is spreading within the heterosexual community. However, among intravenous-drug users there is an alarming increase, and experts believe that this may be the main means of transmission within the heterosexual population in the future. It is important to stress that though AIDS has been predominant in certain groups (i.e., gay men and intravenous drug users), it's not who you are, it's what you do, that increases your risk of infection. Therefore, reducing risky behavior is the first step to preventing and controlling the spread of AIDS.

Risky behaviors are the following:

- Sharing drug needles and syringes.
- Anal sex with or without a condom.
- Vaginal or oral sex with someone who shoots drugs or engages in anal sex.
- Sex with a stranger (pick-up or prostitute) or with someone who is known to have multiple sex partners.
- Unprotected sex without a condom.

Preventing AIDS

Currently, a number of researchers are testing AIDS vaccines. However, a vaccine for mass inoculation is not on the immediate horizon. Some experts believe that it may be extremely difficult to provide an effective vaccine, because HIV is a retro-virus. This means that it periodically changes its genetic code, thus requiring a different vaccine for each new strain.

Therefore, the primary means of prevention are:

- Celibacy.
- Maintaining a monogamous relationship with an uninfected person.

- Practicing safe sex in relationships where risk of infection is questioned.
- Not sharing needles and/or syringes or, even better, not shooting drugs.

Safe sex involves the use of a latex condom before, during and after oral, anal and vaginal intercourse. Condom use is found to be safe with a water-based lubricant. Do not use petroleum jelly, cold cream or baby oil as a lubricant. These products weaken the latex and can cause it to break. A recent study has shown that the use of a spermicide containing nonoxynol-9 in conjunction with a condom may provide further protection from HIV infection if the condom breaks.

Treatment

There are more than 70 drugs currently being tested that are designed to slow or stop the AIDs virus or help bolster the body's immune response. To date, zidovudine (formerly AZT) is the most promising drug and has shown positive results in extending the longevity of AIDS victims. However, it is not a cure.

For the foreseeable future, the best way to prevent AIDS is to avoid risky behavior and practice safe sex when in doubt of your partner's status. Individuals who engage in risky behavior should consider having a blood test to detect the presence of HIV antibodies. Confidential HIV testing is offered through county health departments, hospitals, blood banks, sexually transmitted disease clinics and your personal physician.

Sexually Transmitted Diseases
Be Safe—Be Smart

AIDS is in the media spotlight these days, but there are a number of other sexually transmitted diseases (STDs) that can have serious consequences.

All of these conditions are passed along through intimate sexual contact. They are among the most frequently occurring infectious diseases in the United States today. If you are sexually active, you need the facts about STDs.

Disease	Type of Infection	Symptoms	Diagnosis	Treatment	Special Concerns
Gonorrhea	Bacterial	Males—discharge from penis, burning on urination. Females—usually none. There may be vaginal discharge and abdominal discomfort.	Microscopic examination of vaginal discharge or culture from a suspected infection.	Can be cured with antibiotics.	If left untreated, gonorrhea can develop into pelvic inflammatory disease, a serious condition in women, or cause infertility, arthritis or other problems.
Syphilis	Bacterial	Initially a sore called a *chancre*, usually located in the genital or anal area, or mouth. Later symptoms include a rash, slight fever and swollen joints.	Examination of fluid from a chancre; blood test.	Penicillin or other antibiotics.	If syphilis is not treated, it can cause severe problems many years later, including blindness, brain damage and heart disease.
Genital Herpes	Virus	Painful sores, or blisters, in the genital area; possibly fever, enlarged lymph glands and flu-like illness. The sores heal, but tend to recur.	Physical examination; Pap smear; laboratory tests.	Medications can ease symptoms, but there is no cure.	Genital herpes is most contagious during an outbreak. Avoid sexual contact at these times. Genital herpes can cause complications during pregnancy and may be passed on to an infant during vaginal birth. For this reason, a Cesarean section may be advised.

Disease	Type of Infection	Symptoms	Diagnosis	Treatment	Special Concerns
Chlamydia	Bacterial	When present, symptoms are similar to those of gonorrhea.	Microscopic examination of vaginal discharge; culture.	Can be cured with antibiotics.	Chlamydia that is not cured can lead to pelvic inflammatory disease, infertility in women and complications in pregnancy.
Genital Warts	Virus	Small, fleshy growths (called *condylomas*) in the genital or anal area. Internal growths are soft and reddish. External growths are firmer and darker.	Physical examination.	Large condylomas may be removed surgically. A caustic preparation may be applied to burn off condylomas.	Genital warts can recur following treatment.
Pubic Lice	Parasite	Itching that is worse at night; lice visible in pubic hair; eggs, called "nits" attached to pubic hair.	Physical examination.	Medication to kill lice.	None
Acquired Immuno-deficiency Syndrome (AIDS)	Virus	Unusual susceptibility to illness; development of rare, "opportunistic" diseases; persistent fatigue; fever; night sweats; unexplained weight loss; swollen glands; persistent diarrhea; dry cough.	Blood test to check for antibodies to the AIDS virus; medical history.	No effective treatment. The experimental drug **zidovudine** shows promise in prolonging longevity, but it is not a cure.	AIDS is a fatal illness. Experts now think that AIDS-related complex, a less serious set of symptoms, will develop into AIDS.

CHAPTER THIRTEEN

LifeSkill Thirteen: Get Enough Sleep

The American Medical Association estimates that up to 20 percent of adults experience chronic sleeplessness, with twice as many women suffering insomnia and as many as one-third of adults over age 60 complaining of sleep problems. Some data suggest that the quality and quantity of sleep is related to longevity and to the immune system's ability to fight illness.

As individuals age, their sleep requirements usually decrease, with the seven to nine hours of shut-eye required by the 35-year-old decreasing to five to seven hours by age 65. However, individuals' sleep requirements vary, with genetics believed to play a role.

Sleep can be broken down into two major stages that alternate throughout the night. Non-rapid eye movement sleep (NREM) is characterized by the absence of eye movement, a moderate reduction in muscle tension and an association with sleep that is "deep and dreamless." NREM usually lasts for an hour and then "shifts" to rapid eye movement sleep (REM), which is characterized by 20 to 30 minutes of deep muscle relaxation and vivid dreaming. An individual will usually alternate between NREM and REM two to three times a night.

How to Sleep Better

It's common to experience occasional nights of sleeplessness. When insomnia becomes chronic, however, it's best to try the following sleep-inducing techniques:

- Associate your bed only with sleeping. Avoid using your bed for lounging, watching TV or reading.
- Avoid the consumption of alcohol and caffeine-containing drinks, such as coffee, tea and cola, after 6 p.m. or 7 p.m.

- Control your sleep environment. Adjust room temperature, humidity and noise level. Be sure tight bed linens do not restrict your movement. Check the firmness of the mattress.
- Go to bed only when you're tired.
- Don't toss and turn. Get up and read a good book in an armchair or listen to soothing music.
- Fix a light snack, such as warm milk and a piece of toast with jam.
- Avoid heavy exercise in the late evening (after 9 p.m.); move your exercise to the middle of the day or early evening.
- Practice a deep muscle relaxation exercise. Visualize a beautiful scene.
- To avoid oversleeping and ease "clock eye" (repeatedly waking to check the clock), use an alarm clock to awaken you at a predetermined time.

A Word on Medications

Every year an estimated 6 million to 9 million adults use medications to help counteract insomnia. However, sedative use is not recommended in treating chronic insomnia, because a tolerance to the medication develops, eventually leaving it ineffective while creating a dependency on its use.

Nevertheless, sedatives such as valium are used as a temporary treatment for those who are experiencing extreme stress during such periods as bereavement or hospitalization. Sedatives have also been effective in helping people adjust to jet lag or swing shifts.

Most over-the-counter (OTC) sleep aids are antihistamines, which, when used in moderation, can assist the individual in becoming drowsy. As with prescription sedatives, however, the body can build up a tolerance to OTC sleep aids within a matter of days, thereby hindering their effectiveness. Caution should also be exercised in the use of OTCs by older men and women, who tend to be more sensitive to drugs and thus more subject to undesirable side effects, such as dizziness and confusion, which can be misinterpreted as other problems.

CHAPTER FOURTEEN

LifeSkill Fourteen: Avoid the Sun

Though the "tan look" is associated with health and fitness, prolonged exposure to the sun or artificial tanning devices increase one's risk of skin cancer, wrinkling and pigment changes. As these facts gain currency, the cosmetic appeal of a year-round tan may give way to concern over excessive wrinkling, freckling and, most importantly, cancer risk.

Basal cell and squamous cell carcinoma are the most common forms of skin cancer and are usually treated quite easily if detected early. (Melanoma, in contrast, is the deadliest form of skin cancer and is not necessarily associated with sun exposure). Skin cancer can develop even where the sun doesn't shine, but caution should still be exercised regarding sun exposure.

Consult a dermatologist if any moles or blotches become irregular in shape, change their texture and/or change to a mixture of colors.

Use Appropriate Sunscreens

Sunscreens are designed to absorb ultraviolet light, which comes in two wave lengths: UVB (short wave) and UVA (long wave). UVB radiation causes most sunburns and is usually concentrated between l0 a.m. and 2 p.m. in summer, and 11 a.m. and 3 p.m. in temperate climates. UVA radiation is common throughout the day and is the major cause of skin damage and premature wrinkling, as well as skin cancer. A study published in the *Archives of Dermatology* estimates that the use of an appropriate sunscreen (SPF I5) during the first 18 years of life would decrease the lifetime incidence of basal and squamous cell carcinomas significantly.

Sunscreen preparations that contain either benzophenones or anthranilates protect the skin from both UVA and UVB radiation.

Most commercial sunscreens are rated by their "sun protecting factor" (SPF value), which signifies the mean ratio of time required to produce minimal skin burn with a sunscreen to the time required to produce the same degree of burn without sunscreen. SPF values can range from 2 (minimal protection) to as high as 50. However, SPF 15 is usually the highest value needed.

Considerations for use are the following:

- The fairer the skin, the higher the SPF value. However, most experts believe that SPF 15 should be the value of choice.
- Sunscreen should be applied 30 minutes to one hour prior to sun exposure.
- Sunscreen should be reapplied after swimming, toweling off or sweating. Be forewarned that reapplication does **not** lengthen your protection period.
- The higher the altitude, the greater the ultraviolet radiation. Always use a higher SPF value or a sunblock, such as zinc oxide, at high elevations.
- Regular use of sunscreens, especially by older people, blocks the production of vitamin D. This can lead to vitamin D deficiency.
- Whenever possible, wear dry, light-colored clothing when exposed to the sun for extended periods. Wear a hat that shades the neck and appropriate sun shades. (See Section III, Chapter Three.)

CHAPTER FIFTEEN

LifeSkill Fifteen: Use a Self-Management Plan

To this point, we've talked about specific LifeSkills that enhance health and longevity. We hope some of this information caught your attention and made you think, "I should be taking better care of myself," or, "I wish that could be me." This chapter will help you decide which LifeSkills you want to improve and show you how to achieve your goals through a personalized action plan.

Principles of Self-Management

Knowledge is everything. Teach people what they need to know and they will behave accordingly.

Well, not exactly. Don't we wish changing behavior was that easy! Unfortunately, it isn't. Knowledge is important in making decisions, and to a great extent our behavior is linked to what we know. For example, we don't deliberately eat contaminated food, because we know the consequence would be illness. But behavior, especially health behavior, is not always simple to change, because the consequences of our actions, such as smoking, may take years to come to light. In turn, many behaviors that have a negative impact on our health (including alcohol abuse, smoking and overeating) may serve as primary methods of coping with stress, or may provide temporary gratification. Because of perceived benefits, it's sometimes hard to convince oneself, let alone someone else, that other choices exist that can provide the same perceived benefits.

Health behavior is affected by our feelings, values and attitudes, the opinions of other people, and how achievable we perceive a healthy behavior to be. The facts we know are only part of the equation. The other part involves converting this knowledge into usable skills that change desired behavior.

One proven technique that can help you adopt new health behaviors is the development of a *self-management plan* (SMP), a "road map" that clearly defines where you want to go and how you intend to get there. Though not a guarantee for success, a formal planning process increases your chances. It challenges you to commit on paper (and to an outside observer) goals and a strategy for achieving success.

The following self-management planning sequence is designed to help you clarify your goals while developing an action plan that takes advantage of your positive behaviors and minimizes or eliminates factors that slow your progress. It incorporates an element of play by using appropriate rewards and penalties and the power of your imagination.

How to Develop Your Self-Management Plan

Step 1. To begin, identify the LifeSkills you feel good about. Focus on what you are satisfied with in your lifestyle; then recognize how these attributes can best be used to propel and reinforce your changes in less satisfying areas.

List two behaviors that you're satisfied with for each LifeSkill area:

Physical Activity _____

_____

_____

_____

Nutrition/Weight Control _____

_____

_____

_____

Stress Management _____

_____

_____

_____

Social/Mental Health _____

_____

_____

_____

Financial Health _____

_____

_____

_____

Other _____

_____

_____

_____

Step 2. Next, identify two behaviors in each Life-Skill area that you feel need improvement.

Physical Activity _____

_____

_____

_____

Nutrition/Weight Control _____

_____

_____

_____

Stress Management _____

_____

_____

_____

Social/Mental Health _____

_____

_____

_____

Financial Health _____

_____

_____

_____

Other _____

_____

_____

_____

Step 3. Once you have identified your "needs improvement" areas, it's necessary to narrow your choices further. Which three LifeSkills from Step 2 do you feel need the greatest improvement at this stage of your life?

List them in order of importance.

1st Priority _____

_____

_____

_____

2nd Priority _____

_____

_____

_____

3rd Priority _____

_____

_____

_____

Step 4. Goal Clarification. Now that you have targeted the LifeSkills you want to improve over the next six months, it's important to establish definable goals. **This means being able to narrow each goal to measurable objectives within a realistic timetable.**

For example, "getting in shape" is a broad-based goal. But, it doesn't define how you will "get there," or how long you plan to take.

A clearer goal would be: "I intend to get in shape over the next 12 weeks by accomplishing the following objectives:

1. Being able eventually to jog five days a week for 30 minutes per session.
2. Increasing my upper body strength until I can bench press my body weight.
3. Losing 15 pounds."

In this example, "getting in shape" has been broken down into three measurable objectives to be met within a 12-week period. These three sub-goals can be further clarified if they are broken down into intermediate goals. The reason? While keeping sight of your long-term goal of getting in shape is important, it's necessary to experience and celebrate "mini-victories." These behavioral milestones encourage you, reinforce you and direct your future efforts.

For example, one appropriate intermediate goal for someone wanting to jog continuously for 30 minutes would be: "To jog for two 10-minute periods with a three-minute walk in between. By week nine, I will jog for three 10-minute periods, with a one-minute walk in between."

In the spaces provided, clarify each of your goals, with an affirmative sentence that contains measurable objectives and a set time frame. Finally, break down each objective into intermediate goals. If you need help establishing measurable goals, refer to specific LifeSkills chapters for more information.

Goal One: _____

_____

_____

What are your intermediate goals?

Time Frame	Goal
_____	_____
_____	_____
_____	_____

Goal Two: _____

_____

_____

What are your intermediate goals?

Time Frame	Goal
_____	_____
_____	_____
_____	_____

Goal Three: _____

_____

_____

What are your intermediate goals?

Time Frame	Goal
_____	_____
_____	_____
_____	_____

Step 5. May The Force Be With You: Eliminating Obstacles to Your Goal. The best made plans or inten-

tions almost always go awry. We're creatures of habit, after all. It's not easy to break old habits or adopt new ones, and we tend to stumble upon real or imagined obstacles. These obstacles can be unrealistic goals, negative "self-talk" or a reluctance to ask for help.

Moreover, in developing your overall SMP, it's important to be able to identify those forces that can help you achieve a specific goal and those that hinder your progress. Here's a popular problem-solving technique used by managers, called "Force-Field Analysis." It enables you to identify your helping and hindering forces.

In a nutshell, you have a better chance of succeeding if you start from a position of strength—maximizing your helping forces—than from weakness—being blocked by your hindering forces. Often we fail to recognize our helping forces and think we face insurmountable obstacles. We may feel that our goals are out of reach. Listen to the self-talk that ensues: "I know I can't do this," or, "Look at all the road blocks!" All we see are the negatives, and we fail to acknowledge our strengths.

Here is an example of a force-field analysis for getting in shape:

Helping Forces	Hindering Forces
1. Established measurable objectives and time frame.	1. I'm too busy.
2. Created intermediate goals.	2. Too many last minute projects.
3. I've enjoyed jogging in the past.	3. I pulled a muscle in my leg the last time I jumped into an exercise program.
4. There's a health club close to the office.	4. It's been two years since I really worked out.
5. My spouse is supportive.	5. I'm self-conscious about the roll around my waist.
6. I feel much more productive when I'm fit.	6. I just want to relax on weekends.
7. My clothes fit much better when I'm fit.	
8. I feel more confident.	

Which hindering forces from the above list can be modified or eliminated? For example, time constraints seem to be important obstacles to starting an exercise program. How can effective time-management principles help this person exercise on a regular basis? He or she is also self-conscious about exercising in front of other people at the health club. Perhaps wearing a baggy sweatshirt would hide the "spare tire" and ease the self-consciousness.

Once your hindering forces have been addressed, think about additions that can be made to your helping strategies. Can each helping force be strengthened? What would you need to do?

Finally, appoint a "referee." Peer support can be a powerful motivator. Moreover, a friend can be a staunch ally. By sharing your SMP with someone else, you're putting your commitment on the line. Ask a friend to be your referee, to track your progress, encourage you and mete out your rewards and penalties. Once your plan is in writing, ask your referee to sign it and keep a copy. This contract formalizes your personal commitment.

Force-Field Analysis

For each goal, list the helping and hindering forces that influence your desired outcome.

Goal One: _____

_____

Helping Forces

_____

_____

_____

_____

Hindering Forces

_____

_____

_____

_____

_____

Goal Two: _____

_____

Helping Forces

_____

_____

_____

_____

Hindering Forces

_____

_____

_____

_____

_____

Goal Three: _____

_____

Helping Forces

_____

_____

_____

_____

_____

Hindering Forces

_____

_____

_____

_____

_____

Step 6. Every Good Person Deserves Favor: The Power of Reinforcement. Behavior is largely dependent upon rewards and punishment. Behavior modification theory indicates that if a behavior is rewarded, it will be repeated; if it is ignored or punished, it will decrease. Planning rewards and/or penalties is, therefore, an important motivator in shaping and achieving success.

Rewards are preferred by behaviorists, but self-contracted punishment or penalties can be effective deterrents to undesired behavior. An effective penalty must be the right thing meted out in the right amount, and at the right time. For example, a $5 donation to charity for each week that a pre-determined goal is not met might be an effective motivator. For someone else, a reward of $5 might be a better incentive.

In establishing your reward system, consider these questions:

- What internal satisfaction (reward) would be derived from achieving your goal? Imagine how you would **feel** once you achieved it. What would you be able to do then that you cannot do now?
- What external rewards (materialistic incentives, such as money or a new outfit) would help you succeed?
- What would be a good way to penalize yourself that would discourage behaviors that keep you from your goal?

Here is an example of a reward system for our "getting in shape" scenario:

1. **My Internal Satisfactions (Rewards) Are:**
   - Greater self-control and discipline.
   - Knowing that I'm taking care of myself.
   - Feeling better about myself.
   - Being more productive.
   - Looking more attractive.
2. **Grand Prize**
   If I achieve my goal and get in shape, I will reward myself with a new sport jacket.
3. **Intermediate Rewards**
   For every 10 exercise sessions I make, I will reward myself with a new compact disc.
   For every two pounds I lose, I'll put $10 into my "sport-coat fund."
   For every 10 pounds of weight I am able to increase in my bench press, I will contribute $5 to a theater-ticket fund for my spouse and me.
4. **I Will Penalize Myself By:**
   For every milestone that I miss, I will contribute $10 to an organization that I don't necessarily believe in. If I miss my goal altogether, I will donate an extra $25.

(Keep in mind that your reinforcement plan should emphasize enjoyment and satisfaction. Use your imagination and creativity to make your rewards and punishments match your needs and personality.)

Establishing Your Reward System

Now that your preliminaries are complete, create a reinforcement plan for each goal.

Goal One:
1. My Internal Rewards Are:

_____

_____

_____

2. My Grand Reward Will Be:

_____

_____

_____

_____

3. My Intermediate Rewards Will Be:

_____

_____

_____

_____

4. I Will Penalize Myself By:

_____

_____

_____

_____

Goal Two:
1. My Internal Rewards Are:

_____

_____

_____

2. My Grand Reward Will Be:

_____

_____

_____

_____

3. My Intermediate Rewards Will Be:

_____

_____

_____

_____

4. I Will Penalize Myself By:

_____

_____

_____

_____

Goal Three:

1. My Internal Rewards Are:

_____

_____

_____

_____

2. My Grand Reward Will Be:

_____

_____

_____

_____

3. My Intermediate Rewards Will Be:

_____

_____

_____

_____

4. I Will Penalize Myself By:

_____

_____

_____

_____

My Referee Is:

_____

_____

Step 7. Stay Focused on Your Goals. A philosopher once said, "When it comes a choice between will power and imagination, imagination always wins." In other words, the power of your mind in directing action is very strong. As your Force-Field Analysis illustrated, many forces that hinder you are products of your imagination—irrational thoughts and observations that can create negative self-talk and, therefore, negative action.

Imagination is a powerful tool, one that can be used to direct a positive outcome. High-jumper John Thomas, a former world record holder, was a strong advocate of mental rehearsal. It's said that he drew a line seven feet high on his bedroom wall. Then he mentally practiced making that jump hundreds of times as he lay in bed at night.

You can use the same approach to remain focused on your goal. Here is an example of a mental-rehearsal sequence. It's best to do your visualization when you have some quiet time, perhaps before going to sleep.

• First, relax by breathing slowly and rhythmically; relax your muscles, starting with your toes and moving to your legs, hips, chest, arms, shoulders, neck and head.
• Beginning with each intermediate step, visualize yourself gradually achieving each goal. Picture yourself 20 pounds lighter, being smoke-free or running your first 10-kilometer race.
• Imagine the benefits of your new behavior.
• Imagine yourself sharing and enjoying your goal with friends.
• Tell yourself that you are getting closer to your goal every day.

Step 8. Sticking to It. It's human nature to backslide into old, familiar behaviors. Don't consider this failure. When you begin to feel yourself slipping into old habits, go back to this self-management exercise and review each step. Re-evaluate and clarify your values and goals. Re-assess your helping and hindering forces, and your reward system. Increase the use of visual imagery in affirming your will to succeed. Finally, don't avoid seeking support and help. Good luck!

Section III

Common Chronic Ailments

of Older People

INTRODUCTION

Common Chronic Ailments of Older People

The stooped posture of osteoporosis, the cane or walker of the stroke victim and the persistent cough of obstructive lung disease rob some older men and women of quality of life and contribute to the negative image of aging.

You may confront chronic disease in a parent, spouse or other loved one. If so, you will need to know enough about the condition to help that person get suitable medical attention, to administer daily treatment, and to monitor signs and symptoms.

It's also possible that you have a chronic disease yourself. In fact, the early signs of such conditions as high blood pressure and hardening of the arteries may be detected as early as the 20s, when steps can be taken to reverse or minimize their effects.

Section III contains chapters on 14 common chronic conditions of older life: Alzheimer's disease, arthritis, cancer, cataracts, depression, diabetes, hearing loss, heart disease, high blood pressure, kidney disease, obstructive lung disease, osteoporosis, periodontal disease and stroke. Each chapter lists risk factors, preventive measures, symptoms, diagnostic tests, treatments, and outlooks. Self-care guidelines for the prevention or management of each condition when applicable (see box), are emphasized. The key to managing a chronic condition is to minimize its impact, in order to live as normally as possible. These guidelines will help you.

Look through these chapters now, to become familiar with the information they contain and the tips for prevention. Refer to them again in the future, should questions or problems come up.

LifeSkills that Contribute to the Prevention or Management of Chronic Ailments

	Alzheimer's Disease	Arthritis	Cancer	Cataracts	Depression	Diabetes	Hearing Loss	Heart Disease	High Blood Pressure	Kidney Disease	Obstructive Lung Disease	Osteoporosis	Periodontal Disease	Stroke
Staying Active	●	●	●		●	●		♥	●	●	●			●
Proper Nutrition /Weight	●	●	●		●	●		♥	●			●	●	●
Stress Management	●	●	●		●			♥	●					●
Social/Mental Activity	●	●	●		●			♥	●					●
Financial Planning	●	●	●	●	●	●	●	♥	●	●	●	●	●	●
Medical Consumerism	●	●	●	●	●	●	●	♥	●	●	●	●	●	●
Periodic Medical Screening			●		●	●		♥	●				●	●
Not Smoking			●					♥	●		●	●	●	●
Moderate Alcohol Intake			●		●			♥	●			●		●
Avoiding Drugs			●		●			♥	●	●	●			●
Personal Safety	●	●										●		
Safe Sex			●		●									
Adequate Sleep			●		●			♥	●					●
Avoiding the Sun			●	●										

CHAPTER ONE

Alzheimer's Disease

Alzheimer's disease is a progressive and irreversible deterioration of mental abilities caused by a loss of brain cells and characterized by *amyloid plaques*—waxy formations in the victim's brain. Although it begins gradually, Alzheimer's disease leads inexorably to complete disorientation and memory loss, and ends, perhaps 10 years later, in death. The process is a devastating one not only for the person, but for his or her family.

Alzheimer's disease afflicts about 2.5 million Americans. More than 100,000 die of it each year, making it the fourth leading cause of death in older adults. Most of its victims are over 65 years of age, although it can affect persons as young as 40. In the over-80 population, approximately 20 percent suffer from Alzheimer's. It strikes without regard to race or class, but it affects more women than men—primarily because women outlive men. The cause of Alzheimer's disease is not known, but scientists think that genetic factors, immunologic changes, unusual virus-like agents and environmental factors may all play a role. Evidence is growing that Alzheimer's can run in families. While someone in the general population over 65 has a 2 percent to 3 percent chance of developing Alzheimer's disease, the likelihood increases to about 7 percent or 8 percent if a parent or sibling is already afflicted. Clearly, more than genetics is at play in most cases, because one identical twin is no more likely to develop Alzheimer's disease if the other is afflicted than is a fraternal twin. Many scientists suspect that several genes may be involved, and that a person may inherit a predisposition to the disease that can be triggered by environmental factors such as viruses and toxins.

The discovery of excessive levels of aluminum in the brain cells of Alzheimer's patients fueled speculation that the disease could be caused by ingesting aluminum or using aluminum household products. However, epidemiologic studies have ruled out such a simplistic explanation and aluminum's role remains a mystery.

The earliest sign of Alzheimer's disease is forgetfulness. At first it may be scarcely noticeable, with the family compensating for small lapses or dismissing them as amusing eccentricities. Over a period of months and years, however, memory lapses begin to interfere with work and household tasks.

In addition, the victim may become confused, irritable and agitated, given to cursing or tantrums. Figures and words become hard to read; familiar terrain becomes terrifyingly alien; time unravels; judgment and concentration ebb; the ability to participate in routine activities slips away. Eventually memory loss becomes so profound that the victim cannot remember the previous sentence in a conversation. Ultimately, the victim recognizes no one, not even himself or herself.

Although the pattern of mental deterioration differs for each patient—one person may still be able to play the piano, or another to cook, despite profound memory loss—those in the final stages of Alzheimer's disease are typically apathetic and disoriented. Some take to wandering off. Occasionally, though not always, they become incontinent in the final months of life. (See "Understanding Incontinence.")

Most people occasionally experience forgetfulness, and many healthy individuals develop minor memory difficulties as they age. Such lapses are apt to flare up when the individual is under pressure; they may be triggered by fatigue, grief, stress or illness; and they may be minimized by reminders, lists and other memory aids. Recent research indicates that mental decline is least likely—disease apart—in older people who have maintained lively intellectual interests. Moreover, training programs that stimulate mental skills actually have reversed intellectual losses.

Unlike such minor but "normal" memory impairments, the memory loss of Alzheimer's dementia rapidly gets worse. When signs of forgetfulness, confusion and disorientation appear, it is important to seek a diagnosis—not so much to confirm Alzheimer's disease, which cannot be cured, as to search for another source of the symptoms, which may be treatable.

Alzheimer's Disease

Risk Factors

- Age
- Family history

Preventive Measures

- None known

Symptoms

- Progressive memory loss
- Confusion and disorientation
- Personality changes

Diagnosis

- Medical history
- Physical examination
- Tests of memory and reasoning
- Neuropsychological evaluation
- Laboratory tests to rule out other diseases

Treatment

- A supportive and orderly environment
- Mental, physical and social stimulation
- Drugs to alleviate agitation or depression

Outlook

- Gradual loss of mental abilities
- Eventual loss of some motor ability
- Life expectancy, typically, of 10 years

Understanding Incontinence

One of the main reasons for institutionalizing persons with Alzheimer's disease is loss of bladder control. However, incontinence affects many older people—perhaps one in 10. Nonetheless, having "accidents" is not a normal part of aging, and about 70 percent of cases of incontinence can be treated or controlled.

Incontinence can have many causes. It can be the first sign of a urinary-tract infection, which will clear up with treatment. Stress incontinence, the leakage of urine during coughing, laughing or other body movements that put pressure on the bladder, is more common in women. Overflow incontinence describes the dribbling of urine from a constantly filled bladder; it may occur in older men who have an enlarged prostate gland or in persons who have lost normal bladder contraction due to diabetes. The type most often associated with dementia, the inability to hold urine long enough to reach a toilet, is called urge incontinence.

The first step in treating incontinence is a medical examination to determine the cause. The possible treatments include medications, biofeedback training, exercises to strengthen pelvic muscles, surgery to correct an abnormally positioned bladder or an enlarged prostate, implantable prosthetic devices that control urine flow, indwelling catheters and external drainage bags. Failing all else, absorbent undergarments only slightly more bulky than normal underwear can prevent the embarrassment and inconvenience of incontinence, and allow the victim to carry on a normal social life.

For More Information

The Simon Foundation provides information on incontinence, including a quarterly newsletter. Their number is 800/23-SIMON.

There are 100 reversible conditions that mimic the symptoms of Alzheimer's disease. Among them are other brain diseases, including tumors; anemia; vitamin deficiencies; thyroid problems; some infections; and some blood clots. Two major sources of dementia-like symptoms in older people are side effects from drugs—many older people take multiple medications for chronic conditions—and depression. Even a minor head injury or a high fever can temporarily upset the normal activity of sensitive brain cells.

It is also important to distinguish Alzheimer's disease from the second-greatest cause of mental impairment in old age, multi-infarct dementia. Multi-infarct dementia occurs when small arteries in the brain become clogged, blocking blood flow and causing brain cells to die, creating an area of infarct (dead or dying tissue). Although damage due to an infarct cannot be reversed, the progress of multi-infarct dementia (which often occurs in stages, in contrast to the steady decline in Alzheimer's) can sometimes be slowed or halted by therapy directed at the underlying causes, such as high blood pressure or vascular disease.

The only way to make a definite diagnosis of Alzheimer's disease is by examining brain tissue at autopsy. A brain biopsy can provide tissue samples, but this is seldom done because of risk to the patient. However, a probable diagnosis can be deduced through a meticulous physical and mental evaluation. In addition to a list of past illnesses and the family medical history, the doctor will want the family to describe the person's symptoms and their progression, as well as how well the patient copes in day-to-day activities. The doctor can also use several simple sets of questions to assess the patient's mental functioning. Depending on the results of the history and physical examination, supplemental blood tests, urinalysis and X-rays may be performed. Together, these investigations will reveal most reversible conditions.

Depending on the circumstances, the diagnosis can be further narrowed with a variety of supplementary tests. These include a brain scan with computerized axial tomography (CAT) or magnetic resonance imaging; an electroencephalogram; neuropsychological evaluation of sensory and motor abilities, as well as of verbal, reasoning and other mental functions; speech and language analysis; and, if depression is suspected, a formal psychiatric assessment.

A diagnosis of Alzheimer's disease becomes more certain when mental changes worsen between one examination and the next.

Living with Alzheimer's

Although Alzheimer's disease is said to halve a person's remaining life expectancy, many victims are otherwise fairly healthy and may live for many years.

When death comes, it is likely to be from a disorder that complicates the profound brain disorder, such as pneumonia or pulmonary embolism.

At least in the earlier stages of the disease, most people are cared for at home, usually by a spouse or adult child. The caregiver's goal is to provide a safe and familiar environment that is stimulating but not overwhelming. The patient should be encouraged to perform to his or her fullest potential, to maintain a full daily routine, and to keep up social contacts. Memory aids for use in day-to-day living—a prominently placed calendar, lists of daily tasks, written reminders about routine safety measures, and directions to and labeling of frequently used items—may be employed.

The atmosphere should be one that helps the Alzheimer's victim maintain his or her dignity. The caregiver must not assume that because an individual cannot express thoughts properly, he or she cannot think or feel. And the caregiver must learn not to take expressions of anger or displeasure personally.

While there is no treatment for the underlying brain-cell loss of Alzheimer's, the judicious use of certain drugs may alleviate some symptoms. For instance, tranquilizers may lessen agitation, anxiety and unpredictable behavior; antidepressants may improve sleeping patterns or lighten the depression that often accompanies Alzheimer's. However, as mentioned on page 72, overmedication can produce undesirable side effects that can further impair a person's mental skills. Therefore, care is advised.

During the past decade, several experimental drugs have been tried in Alzheimer's. Lecithin, for example, has been used in an attempt to increase levels of acetylcholine, a brain chemical important to memory that is deficient in Alzheimer's patients. Most such drugs show little if any benefit, although research continues.

Help for the Caregiver

The demands on the family of the Alzheimer's patient—and on the professional caregiver, too—are immense. Caring for the patient can be physically exhausting and emotionally trying, as well as financially disastrous. Often the family will find it necessary to make major adjustments in its entire way of life. And family members are often beset by feelings of grief, anger and self-pity as they watch a loved one turn into a stranger before their very eyes.

No one should attempt to shoulder these burdens alone. The principal caregiver should arrange for respite care, enlisting the help of other family members and friends on a regular basis. Professionally provided respite care may be available in your community. Additionally, the recently passed catastrophic health care bill makes provisions for some respite services.

Legal and Financial Considerations

A diagnosis of Alzheimer's disease generates numerous legal and financial repercussions. Although it may be emotionally difficult, the patient and his or her family need to discuss what arrangements are to be made for the patient's life and assets in the future. This should be done as soon as the diagnosis is made, while the patient is still able to participate in decisions and remember where important documents and objects are located. Making plans together not only assures family members that they will be acting with regard for the patient's wishes, it also eases the patient's worry about what lies ahead.

It is usually wise to seek professional advice. The patient will need to designate someone to assume legal responsibilities—although it should be understood by all that the patient is giving up only those responsibilities that he or she can no longer manage. A power of attorney allows the designated "attorney in fact" to do almost anything on behalf of the victim, but is valid only so long as the one granting it remains mentally competent. A *durable* power of attorney remains in effect even after the person is considered no longer competent, but it must be arranged while the patient is still of sound mind. (See pages 220 and 221.)

Other points to discuss with a professional include establishing a living trust, which manages someone's assets during his or her lifetime; writing a will, which determines how assets will be distributed at death, and a living will, which stipulates an individual's wishes with regard to life-prolonging medical procedures.

If the patient is employed and covered by medical insurance at the time that symptoms appear, it is important to obtain an extension of such coverage to take care of any other illnesses or injuries that may occur. Insurance will likely cover diagnostic work-ups for Alzheimer's disease. However, most insurance programs, including Medicare, reimburse only for acute conditions; since dementia is a chronic disorder, most services—including nursing-home care—generally are not covered. (Refer to Section IV for further discussion of long-term care planning.)

Caregivers should also draw on the resources of local support groups. As the disease progresses, it may be helpful to employ aides with nursing or homemaking skills. Eventually the victim may need constant supervision and medical care; if a nursing home is necessary, and financially possible, the caregiver should be able to make the decision to institutionalize the patient without becoming paralyzed by guilt. (See discussion of nursing homes in Section IV.)

For More Information

Alzheimer's patients and their families can obtain excellent information, guidance and support from the Alzheimer's Disease and Related Disorders Association, Inc. (ADRDA), which has more than 1,000 family support groups in cities across the country. It publishes a newsletter and brochures on various aspects of Alzheimer's disease, supports research and lobbies for improved legislation. Its toll-free number is 800/621-0379 (in Illinois 800/572-6037); the address is 70 East Lake Street, Chicago, IL 60601.

Another important source of information and help is the National Institute on Aging (NIA). NIA publications include *Q & A: Alzheimer's Disease, Senility: Myth*

or Madness and *Progress Report on Alzheimer's Disease: Volume III*. In addition, NIA supports Alzheimer's Disease Research Centers at 10 medical centers around the country. For more information, write to the NIA Office of Public Information, Bethesda, MD 20892.

Understanding Alzheimer's Disease, Miriam K. Aronson, ed. (New York: Scribners, 1987), is available through ADRDA.

The Loss of Self: A Family Resource for the Care of Alzheimer's Disease and Related Disorders, by Donna Cohen and Carl Eisdorfer (New York: W. W. Norton & Co., 1986), is available at libraries and bookstores.

Losing a Million Minds, a 1987 report prepared by the Congressional Office of Technology Assessment, can be obtained from the Superintendent of Documents, Government Printing Office, Washington, DC 20402.

The Myth of Senility, by Robin Marantz Henig, can be ordered from American Association of Retired Persons Books, Scott Foresman and Company, 1965 Miner Street, Des Plaines, IL 60016.

The 36 Hour Day, by Nancy Mace and Peter Rabins (Baltimore: John Hopkins University Press, 1982), is available at libraries and bookstores.

CHAPTER TWO

Arthritis

Arthritis, strictly speaking, is an inflammation of the joints. More commonly, the term arthritis refers to a large group of rheumatic diseases—disorders not only of the joints but also of the connective tissues around the joints, which include muscles, tendons and ligaments. Most are chronic diseases that can be controlled but not cured. Three of the most prevalent types are osteoarthritis, rheumatoid arthritis and gout.

The most common form of arthritis, *osteoarthritis*, is caused by degeneration of the cartilage that cushions bones where they move against one another in joints. It is characterized by pain and stiffness, typically in the large weight-bearing joints—knees, hips and spine—and in the joints of the fingers.

Osteoarthritis is not usually very serious. It typically develops in older people and occurs twice as often in women as in men. It may occur at an earlier age in athletes who have injured joints during sports activities, and it seems to be aggravated—in the knee, especially—by obesity. The affected joints tend to hurt most after they have been overused, or after long periods of remaining still.

Osteoarthritic finger joints are more common in women, especially in those whose mothers had the condition. The joint becomes reddened, swollen and tender. After several months the pain goes away, but lumps, called nodes, remain. The process usually occurs first in one finger, then the others. When these lumps affect the topmost finger joint, they are known as Heberden nodes; on the middle joints they are called Bouchard's nodes.

The diagnosis of osteoarthritis can often be based on a medical history and physical examination. If other types of arthritis need to be ruled out, the joint may be X-rayed or fluid may be drawn from the joint and examined.

Although osteoarthritis cannot be cured, the symptoms usually respond to anti-inflammatory drugs and exercises that help to preserve mobility. The traditional drug of choice is aspirin, which both relieves pain and reduces joint inflammation. So do such newer non-steroidal anti-inflammatory drugs (NSAIDs) as ibuprofen, naproxen and tolmetin, and such older NSAIDs as indomethacin. None of these drugs, however, is free of side effects, especially in the doses required to reduce inflammation, and therapy should be monitored by a physician. Heat (a hot shower, heat lamps, etc.) can help relax muscles and relieve soreness; cold compresses can help to numb painful joints.

Regular exercise is important for most people with osteoarthritis. While rest can ease inflammation, too much rest causes joints to stiffen. Walking and swimming are both good prescriptions for keeping joints flexible; recreational exercise programs specially designed for people with arthritis are available in some areas. However, exercise is not recommended when joints are constantly inflamed or exhibiting severe pain.

Canes, crutches or walkers can help take weight off damaged joints; so can losing excess weight.

Sometimes joint damage becomes so painful and disabling that the best remedy is surgery. Damaged tissue can be removed through a small incision with the aid of an arthroscope. More extensive surgery is used to correct bone deformities or to realign bones. Or, in an increasingly common procedure, the damaged joint is replaced with an artificial one. Hips and knees are the joints most often replaced, but man-made parts are available for almost all major joints, including wrists, elbows, shoulders and fingers. Such surgery is not without its risks, including immediate infection, and its drawbacks, such as the possibility that the artificial joint may someday loosen. Still, several hundred thousand joint replacements are performed each year, usually bringing great relief to people who have been crippled by deformity and pain.

Rheumatoid arthritis, although less common than osteoarthritis, is more severe. Joints in the fingers, wrists, elbows, hips, knees or ankles—as many as 15 or 20 joints at a time—become painful, hot, red and swollen. (Usually joints on both sides of the body are affected symmetrically.) Rheumatoid arthritis can also affect other organs, including the lungs, spleen, skin and sometimes the heart.

Symptoms can include fatigue and weight loss. Bouts of inflammation alternate with symptom-free periods of remission, but about half of all people with the disease eventually develop joint deformities.

Rheumatoid arthritis often first appears between ages 30 and 40, and it affects three times as many women as men. Although its cause is not yet known, it is believed to result when an external factor, such as a virus, triggers an inherited susceptibility. It has been found that most people who develop the disease carry a genetically determined tissue marker, although not everyone with the marker develops the disease. The result is that the immune system responds inappropriately, turning its defenses on the body's own tissues. In this case, the main target is the *synovium*, the membrane that lines the joints. Normally smooth and velvety, the synovium becomes inflamed, rough, granular and swollen; cartilage and bone are destroyed.

A likely diagnosis of rheumatoid arthritis can be confirmed by blood tests. One such test shows the presence of abnormal antibodies known as rheumatoid factor found in about 80 percent of the cases, while another, the erythrocyte sedimentation rate, indicates chronic inflammation. Signs also can be detected in fluid drawn from an affected joint.

Like osteoarthritis, rheumatoid arthritis is treated with a combination of medication, rest, special diets, exercise, measures to protect the joints and, as a last resort, surgery. Because the symptoms of rheumatoid arthritis tend to be more severe, medications may need to be more potent. In addition to aspirin and NSAIDs, patients may be given oral corticosteroids, powerful hormone-like drugs that can cause numerous side effects, and corticosteroid injections, which are great for short-term relief but too dangerous to be repeated very often. Several types of agents begin to relieve symptoms only after they've been taken for at least one month and sometimes for six. These include gold injections or a gold compound taken orally, penicillamine, drugs used against malaria, drugs used to treat cancer.

As a chronic disease that can significantly alter the pattern of a person's life, rheumatoid arthritis can create psychological and emotional as well as physical needs. Most people with the disease benefit from talking openly about their concerns with their family and friends. Those who become depressed may find it helpful to work with a mental health professional. Support groups made up of arthritis patients can offer both practical advice and emotional solace.

Gout, or gouty arthritis, makes itself known with a sudden and excruciating pain, often in the big toe (or, less often, in joints of the finger, foot, ankle, elbow, wrist or knee). The inflamed joint is hot and swollen, the skin over it taut, shiny and purplish red.

The gout attack lasts no more than a few days, and a second may not occur for several years. If the condition isn't treated, attacks may come more often, last longer and involve more joints. Eventually joints suffer permanent damage, and so can the kidneys.

An attack of gout occurs when urate crystals—formed from an overabundance of uric acid in the body—settle in a joint, irritating the joint lining (the synovium) and causing inflammation. A slower build-up of urate crystals can produce lumps, called tophi, in bone, cartilage or even skin. Crystals also can accumulate in the kidneys, forming diffuse deposits or kidney stones. Uric acid precursors (e.g. purines) are present in many foods, but the high levels seen in gout have less to do with diet than with overproduction and faulty excretion of uric acid.

Gout runs in families and occurs almost exclusively in middle-aged men. An attack can be triggered by drinking alcohol, overeating, a crash diet, surgery or injury to a joint. The diagnosis can be confirmed by the demonstration of uric acid crystals in fluid drawn from the affected joint. Blood levels of uric acid, however, are not a reliable indicator.

During an acute attack, treatment is aimed at relieving the pain and inflammation. The classic gout treatment, colchicine, can be given intravenously or orally and usually brings quick relief; sometimes an NSAID such as indomethacin is used. Once the acute attack ends, the patient can take drugs that reduce uric acid levels, one type by blocking its manufacture, another by enhancing its excretion. These drugs also will gradually dissolve any tophi that may be present. By thus keeping the disease under control, it is possible to prevent any permanent damage.

Although it might seem logical to combat gout by limiting foods high in uric acid, restricting such foods (e.g., liver, mussels, sardines and beer) seems to offer little benefit. Rather, persons with gout do much better by losing excess weight and avoiding alcohol.

For More Information

The Arthritis Foundation is a national voluntary health agency whose local chapters throughout the country provide services and education for people with arthritis and their families. Some chapters offer exercises in swimming pools, easing movement and pain. Among the foundation's numerous publications are booklets on the various forms of arthritis, protecting joints, exercise, surgery, pain and stress. The national headquarters are at 1314 Spring Street, N.W., Atlanta, GA 30309.

Arthritis: A Comprehensive Guide, by James F. Fries, M.D., and its companion book, *The Arthritis Handbook*, by Kate Lorig, R.N., and James F. Fries, M.D., are available from Addison-Wesley, Reading, MA.

"How to Cope With Arthritis" is a booklet published by the National Institute of Arthritis and Musculoskeletal and Skin Diseases, Bethesda, MD.

The Independence Factory sells practical aids (such as zipper pulls, wide pencils and pens, and long-handled reaches) for those with hand and limb limitations. Their address is P.O. Box C, Middletown, OH 45042.

Arthritis

Risk Factors

- Family history (osteoarthritis, rheumatoid arthritis, gout)
- Age (osteoarthritis)
- Joint injuries (osteoarthritis, gout)
- Obesity (osteoarthritis, gout)

Preventive Measures

- Staying active (osteoarthritis)
- Staying trim

Symptoms

- Painful and stiff joints (osteoarthritis, rheumatoid arthritis)
- Knobby finger joints (osteoarthritis, rheumatoid arthritis)
- Multiple inflamed joints (rheumatoid arthritis)
- Sudden excruciating joint pain, often in big toe (gout)

Diagnosis

- Physical examination of joints
- History of symptoms
- X-rays
- Examination of joint fluids
- Blood tests (rheumatoid arthritis)

Treatment

- Drugs to reduce pain and inflammation
- Drugs to reduce uric acid levels (gout)
- Losing weight
- Rest to ease inflammation
- Exercises to keep joint flexible
- Measures to protect joint (canes, walkers, etc.)
- Joint surgery

Outlook

- Highly variable, from mild discomfort relieved by analgesics (more likely in osteoarthritis), to moderate deformity and severe disability (more likely in rheumatoid arthritis)
- In gout, treatment can prevent permanent damage

CHAPTER THREE

Cancer

Cancer comes in many shapes and forms. It can affect the blood or the bones, the lungs or the stomach or the skin—all of the body's organs and tissues are susceptible. Depending on the cancer's location and the type of cells involved, a person's symptoms—and the cancer's course—can vary enormously.

What all cancers have in common, however, is that each one is the result of cells growing out of control. The body's cells normally grow in an orderly fashion, reproducing themselves as needed. A cancer begins when the cells' growth instructions are disrupted. The cells multiply recklessly, eventually growing across boundaries that separate neighboring tissues and spreading through the bloodstream to set up colonies—metastases—at distant sites.

Not all abnormal growths are cancerous. In contrast to malignant, or cancerous, tumors, benign tumors neither invade adjacent tissues nor spread to distant sites. Nonetheless, some benign tumors can be dangerous; a benign brain tumor, for instance, may create damaging pressure within the rigid confines of the skull.

Cancer cuts a broad swath. The number of Americans developing cancer each year is approaching one million. Not only the absolute numbers but also the incidence rates continue to rise. Cancer is second only to heart disease as a cause of death; it claimed an estimated 476,700 lives in the United States in 1987. While it affects about equal numbers of men and women, for the most part it is a disease of middle and old age; three-fourths of all cases are diagnosed after age 55, and more than half after age 65.

The causes of cancer are many and complex. Substances interwoven in our lives—chemicals and tobacco smoke, sunlight and X-rays, viruses and hormones, foodstuffs and alcohol—can all, under certain circumstances, trigger changes in the genetic material of cells that disrupt their orderly growth.

Most cancers appear to result from interplay among environmental and hereditary factors. A few rare cancers involve a specific defective gene and are directly inherited. A tendency to develop some of the more common cancers—of the breast, colon and brain—also may run in families. More often, an individual probably inherits numerous genes that interact in shaping his or her response to specific stimuli in the environment.

The role of pollutants in the development of cancer is uncertain. A large number of pesticides, food additives and other chemicals have been shown to cause cancer in laboratory animals. In addition, a variety of chemicals—including arsenic, asbestos, benzene and vinyl chloride—are known to cause cancers in people exposed to high doses. However, it is difficult to trace the effects of erratic quantities of multiple potentially harmful substances on large populations—particularly when those effects may show up only years later.

Ironically, however, some of the most blameworthy carcinogens are avoidable. Smoking, for instance, is the single greatest cause of cancer death; it not only causes most lung cancers, it is also associated with cancers of the lip, mouth, larynx, esophagus and bladder. If smoking were eliminated, it would cut cancer incidence by a fourth.

Diets high in fat and/or low in fiber have been linked with cancers of the breast, uterus, prostate and colon; so has obesity. Alcohol abuse produces cancers of the liver and other organs. It has been estimated that simple dietary changes—keeping trim, eating a variety of foods low in fat and high in fiber, limiting alcohol consumption—could reduce cancer deaths by more than a third.

Most skin cancer is caused by excessive exposure to the sun. A straightforward solution is to wear protective clothing and use sunscreens.

The first signs of cancer are often subtle changes in the way a person feels or the way the body behaves. Such signs include changes in bowel habits, difficulty in swallowing, sores, a thickening or lump, an unusual discharge, and coughing or hoarseness.

Unfortunately, such symptoms are not very specific, and often occur only when the disease is fairly advanced. Several practices, however, can increase the likelihood of discovering a cancer while it is still in its early stages. These include, for women, a periodic Pap smear to check for cervical cancer as well as monthly breast self-examination and, for women at high risk of breast cancer, regular mammography; for men, rectal examination to look for changes in the

Cancer

Risk Factors

- Age
- Family history
- Use of tobacco
- High-fat, low-fiber diet
- Radiation exposure
- Environmental exposures
- Alcohol abuse

Preventive Measures

- Not smoking
- Low-fat, high-fiber diet
- Moderate alcohol use
- Staying trim
- Avoiding excess sunlight, unnecessary X-rays
- Self-examination of breasts, testes, skin
- Pap smear, sigmoidoscopy, tests for blood in the stool
- Surgical removal of precancerous lesions
- Protection against environmental exposures

Symptoms

- Can arise in any part of the body and vary widely, depending on the type of cancer
- Symptoms include:
  — Pain
  — Lumps
  — Sores
  — Bleeding
  — Coughing

Diagnosis

- Physical examination
- X-rays and scans
- Scoping procedures
- Tissue biopsy

Treatment

- Surgery
- Radiation
- Drug and hormone therapy
- Pain control

Outlook

- Depends on the type of cancer, the extent of spread at diagnosis, and the robustness of the individual
  — Full recovery
  — Months or years free of apparent disease
  — Death within weeks or months

prostate; and for both men and women, tests for blood in the stool after age 50, regular sigmoidoscopic examination of the rectum and lower colon after age 50, and regular self-examination of the skin.

When cancer is suspected, the doctor can use a variety of tests to narrow the diagnosis and/or determine how widely the cancer has spread. In addition to a thorough physical examination, these include laboratory tests, X-ray studies and other scanning procedures, such as computerized axial tomography and radioisotope scans.

Ultimately, a diagnosis of cancer requires a biopsy. Tissue is surgically removed (or cell-containing fluids are withdrawn through needles or tubes) and examined microscopically by a *pathologist*, a physician who specializes in the study of diseased tissues. Under the microscope, cells may appear normal, abnormal but not malignant, cancerous but confined to the area where they originated (cancer *in situ*), cancerous and growing into surrounding tissues, or cancerous and growing across tissue boundaries into nearby structures.

The first line of treatment for many types of cancer is surgery to remove the malignant growth. If the cancer has not spread (metastasized), surgery offers a good chance for a cure. Over recent years surgery has tended to become, to the extent possible, less extensive and less mutilating. With improvements in operating-room technology and postoperative nursing care, age itself is not usually a barrier to cancer surgery.

In some types of cancer—notably bodywide cancers of the blood and lymph systems—radiation and drugs constitute the first line of defense. High-energy radiation can be beamed at tissues from a machine such as a linear accelerator, or a radioactive material may be implanted for a few days in body tissues or cavities. Many anticancer drugs are toxic agents designed to kill rapidly growing cancer cells. Some are hormones; others are substances that stimulate the body's immune defenses.

In a few instances, radiation and drugs have proved successful as primary therapy. For example, three-fourths of the patients with the lymph-node cancer known as Hodgkin's disease can expect to be alive five years later without symptoms.

Radiation and anticancer drugs are also often proposed as an adjunct to surgery for patients whose cancer has already spread, or when cancer recurs following apparently successful surgery. Such treatment, which is usually coordinated by a cancer specialist (*oncologist*), may buy time for the patient by producing a remission. More often than not, however, the cancer eventually recurs. The question is, how soon?

Many anticancer therapies produce side effects that are dangerous—severe nausea, uncontrollable infections, bleeding, anemia—or, like complete hair loss, demoralizing. As a result, each patient will want to weigh the advantages and disadvantages of such therapy options.

A person's chances of recovering from cancer, or at least living for as long as 10 or 20 years after it is diagnosed, depend greatly on the nature of the specific cancer. Cancer of the lip is both slow growing and easy to notice; 95 percent of those with this cancer will be cured. Most women with breast cancer will survive more than five years, whereas most patients with lung cancer will be dead within six to 12 months of the tumor's discovery.

A person who has faced cancer—even one who appears to be cured—must contend with many emotional and physical strains. All surgery is painful and draining; cancer surgery also may have altered the patient's body and lifestyle very visibly, as is the case with a mastectomy or a colostomy. The individual lives with the possibility of recurrence, debilitation, pain and a life cut short. The cancer patient needs to be able to draw on the support of family and friends, as well as the counsel of the health care professionals who have participated in his or her care. Many cancer patients and their families also find it helpful to join mutual support groups.

For More Information

The National Cancer Institute's Cancer Information Service is an 18-hour-a-day telephone service that fields questions about all aspects of cancer and its treatment, as well as related subjects such as home health services and financial assistance.

The service will also send out free copies of more than 100 different NCI publications. The toll-free CIS number is 800/4-CANCER.

The American Cancer Society (ACS), a voluntary organization, offers a variety of patient services and sponsors several types of support groups. It is located at 261 Madison Avenue, New York, NY 10016 (212/599-3600). Local chapters are listed in the phone book.

Make Today Count, a self-help organization designed to provide emotional help to persons with incurable diseases and their families, has more than 200 chapters nationwide. The address is P.O. Box 222, Osage Beach, MO 65065 (314/348-1619).

Choices, by Marion Morra and Eve Potts (New York: Avon Books, 1987), written for cancer patients and their families, discusses, among other things, different kinds of cancer treatment, coping with pain and where to get help.

The American Cancer Society Cancer Book, Arthur I. Holleb, ed. (Garden City, NY: Doubleday & Co., 1986) is a comprehensive guide that covers prevention, detection, diagnosis, treatment and rehabilitation. It is distributed through local ACS chapters.

Lung Cancer

Cancer of the lung is a major cause of death in most Western countries. Most lung cancer is caused by smoking, and most is rapidly fatal. There were 150,000 new cases in the United States in 1987, and 136,000 deaths. The good news is that after years of rising steeply, the incidence of lung cancer in the United States has at last started to fall.

There are more than a dozen types of lung cancer, generally grouped as small cell lung cancers and non-small cell lung cancers. Small cell cancers, which make up about 25 percent of the total, have a tendency to spread so quickly that they have almost invariably metastasized by the time of diagnosis.

Risk Factors (proven)

- Smoking—risk increases with amount of smoking
- Exposures to asbestos, radon and other agents (risk many times higher in exposed individuals who also smoke)
- Secondhand tobacco smoke

Risk Factors (suspected)

- Air pollution
- Diet low in vitamin A (particularly for heavy smokers)

Outlook

- Generally bleak: Only 13 percent survive for 5 years; most patients die within the year
- For those patients with apparently localized non-small cell lung cancer (about 15 percent of all cases), the five-year survival rate is about 50 percent

Treatment

- For non-small cell lung cancers that are small and involve nothing more than local lymph nodes
  — Surgery to remove tumor (Surgery may remove a section of the lung, one lobe of the lung or an entire lung.)
  — Radiation to prevent possible brain metastases
- For non-small cell lung cancers that have spread into nearby tissues
  — Radiation to chest, usually combined with surgery
- For apparently limited small cell lung cancers
  — Combinations of anticancer drugs, with or without chest irradiation
- For cancers of either type that have metastasized
  — Treatment to shrink the tumor and relieve symptoms, usually radiation and sometimes chemotherapy

Preventive Measures

- Not smoking (Fifteen to 20 years after quitting, an ex-smoker's risk reverts to that of a non-smoker.)
- Avoiding air pollutants, including cigarette smoke and radon
- Diet high in fruits and vegetables, especially carrots and others that are yellow-orange in color

Symptoms

- From tumor in lungs and other chest structures
  — Chest pain
  — Cough
  — Shortness of breath
  — Pneumonia
  — Hoarseness
  — Difficulty in swallowing
  — Swelling of neck, face and upper extremities
- From metastases
  — Headache
  — Weakness
  — Bone fractures
  — Jaundice
- From hormones produced by lung cancer cells
  — Far ranging, from kidney damage to diabetes to neurologic abnormalities

Diagnosis

- Physical examination
- Chest X-rays
- Visual examination of airways through a bronchoscope
- Biopsy of tumor cells removed through bronchoscope, by needle aspiration or at surgery
- Biopsy of lymph nodes around breastbone
- Radioactive scans to detect metastases to brain, bone or liver
- Computerized axial tomography scans

For More Information

The National Cancer Institute's Cancer Information Service can provide publications on lung cancer, quitting smoking, and chemotherapy and radiation therapy. Call 800/4-CANCER.

Breast Cancer

Breast cancer usually develops in the tissues lining the breast's milk-producing ducts, or lobules, which are subjected to repeated pulses of hormones throughout a woman's reproductive life. It is the most common type of cancer (130,000 new cases annually) and the greatest cause of cancer death (41,000) in American women; one in 10 will develop it in her lifetime.

The most common sign of breast cancer is a lump, and most breast cancers are discovered by the woman herself. Most women have lumpy breasts, but most lumps are not cancerous; by practicing monthly breast self-examination, a woman can become familiar with the feel of her own breasts and thus be quick to discern unusual changes (see Section II, Chapter Seven). When the disease is localized at the time of diagnosis, five-year survival exceeds 90 percent.

Preventive Measures

- Low-fat diet
- Staying trim
- Early detection through regular breast self-examination
- Breast examination by a physician every five years up to age 50
- Mammography—reveals breast cancers that are too small to be felt, and that usually have not spread (Refer to Section II, Chapter Seven, for screening schedule.)

Risk Factors

- Female gender (Males get breast cancer, but rarely.)
- Age
- Family history (risk doubles when either a mother or sister has had breast cancer, and increases six-fold when they both have)
- Previous breast cancer or other cancers
- Hormonal factors:
  — Never pregnant, or first pregnancy after age 30
  — Early onset of menstruation
  — Late menopause
- High-fat diets
- Obesity

Symptoms

- Unusual lump—most often discovered by the woman herself either accidentally or during breast self-examination
- Discharge from the nipple
- Dimpling of the skin
- Retraction of the nipple

Diagnosis

- Breast palpation by health professional
- Mammography
- Biopsy of tumor and lymph nodes

Treatment

- Surgery
  — Modified radical mastectomy (removes the breast and some underarm lymph nodes but leaves chest muscles intact)
  — For small tumors, lumpectomy—takes only the tumor and a little surrounding tissue (Lumpectomy is typically supplemented by surgical removal or a sampling of underarm lymph nodes, and is often combined with radiation therapy.)
- Radiation to tumor area to prevent metastases
- Chemotherapy (for women whose lymph nodes are "positive"— they contain cancer cells, indicating likely bodywide spread)
- Hormonal therapy (for postmenopausal node-positive women whose tumor cells retain their sensitivity to female hormones)
- Surgery to reconstruct the breast's shape (an alternative to wearing an artificial breast form)

Outlook

- With early detection and treatment, five-year survival exceeds 90 percent
- Overall five-year survival is 74 percent

For More Information

A series of booklets discussing different aspects of breast cancer, from breast exams to living with advanced cancer, is available from the National Cancer Institute's Cancer Information Service, at 800/4-CANCER.

Reach to Recovery, a program of the American Can-

cer Society, uses volunteers who have had breast cancer to counsel women with newly diagnosed disease. They can be contacted through local ACS chapters.

Alternatives, by Rose Kushner (Kensington, MD: Kensington Press, 1984), provides a detailed discussion of biopsy and therapy options.

Prostate Cancer

Cancer of the prostate, the walnut-sized gland that produces much of the fluid in semen and surrounds the urethra in men, is the second most common cancer (after lung cancer) among American men, and is on the rise. Black men in the United States have the highest incidence in the world, but the fact that the high rate has developed only in recent decades suggests that it is due to changes in lifestyle rather than genetics.

Many older men have an enlarged prostate. Although this condition (benign prostatic hypertrophy) produces some of the same symptoms as prostatic cancer, it does not lead to cancer. If symptoms are severe, part or all of the prostate may be surgically removed.

Prostatic cancer often grows slowly, and signs of unsuspected prostate cancer are often found at autopsy. Very early cases may need no treatment other than regular follow-up. Surgery or radiotherapy can often cure limited disease.

Because traditional prostate cancer surgery nearly always causes impotence, sexually active men have often opted for radiotherapy, which usually does not impair potency. Now, a new surgical technique that preserves the nerves essential for erection is being adopted by many urologic surgeons.

Risk Factors

- Age—over age 50, and especially over 65
- High-fat diet
- Environmental exposure to carcinogens, including cadmium

Preventive Measures

- Low-fat diet
- Digital rectal exams every three years after age 40, and every two years after age 60

Outlook

- Excellent when disease is confined to the prostate: These men are just as likely to be alive 15 years later with no evidence of disease as men in the general population
- Fairly good if disease has not metastasized; overall five-year survival is 70 percent
- With metastatic disease, only 25 percent of the patients will still be alive in five years

Symptoms

- In early stages, often no symptoms
- Problems with urination
  - Weak or interrupted flow, frequent urination (especially at night), inability to urinate or difficulty in starting, painful or burning sensation
- Blood in the urine
- Persistent pain in back, hips and pelvis (from metastases)

Diagnosis

- Digital rectal exam
- X-rays, including intravenous pyelogram, which shows kidneys, ureters and bladder
- Urinalysis
- Biochemical tests (Blood levels of certain enzymes and other substances are often elevated in prostate cancer.)
- Biopsy of tissue removed by needle aspiration or surgery

Treatment

- When disease is limited to a few microscopic clusters of cancer cells discovered in tissue removed for benign hypertrophy
  - Follow-up examination every six months
- When cancer is confined to the prostate
  - Surgery (radical prostatectomy) to remove the entire prostate and seminal vesicles, or
  - Radiotherapy (usually high-energy external beams; sometimes implants of radioactive substances)
- When cancer metastases cause symptoms
  - Hormone therapy to relieve pain and shrink tumors (Options include surgical removal of testes or estrogen therapy.)

For More Information

The National Cancer Institute publishes brochures titled "What You Need to Know About Cancer of the Prostate and Other Male Genitourinary Organs" and "Research Report: Cancer of the Prostate." They can be obtained by calling the Cancer Information Service at 800/4-CANCER.

Colorectal Cancer

Cancer of the colon—the last five or six feet of the digestive tract—and the rectum—the last five or six inches of the colon—is common in the United States and other highly developed countries. Although the incidence continues to climb, death rates are decreasing; more than half the patients can expect to survive at least five years. And when the cancer is detected at an early, localized stage—as it was with President Reagan—long-term survival increases dramatically.

Risk Factors

- Age—risk increases at 40 years, and rises sharply after 50
- Intestinal polyps
- Family history, particularly of precancerous polyps (Almost 100 percent of these cases become cancer.)
- Chronic ulcerative colitis
- High-fat, low-fiber diet

Preventive Measures

- Diet low in fat and high in fiber
- Surgery to remove precancerous polyps
- Proctosigmoidoscopic examination of colon, every two years beginning at age 50
- Test for blood in stool, yearly after age 50

Symptoms

- Blood in the stool, either bright red or very dark
- Stools smaller in width than usual
- General abdominal discomfort
- Frequent gas pains
- A feeling that the bowel does not empty completely
- Unexplained weight loss
- Fatigue

Diagnosis

- Digital rectal exam
- Examination of stool for blood
- Visual examination of lower portion of colon with a proctosigmoidoscope
- Barium X-ray of large intestine (lower GI series)
- Visual examination of entire colon with flexible colonoscope
- Biopsy of tissue obtained through colonoscope, proctosigmoidoscope or at surgery

Treatment

- Surgery
  — Bowel resection to cut out diseased segment, plus surgical removal of area lymph nodes
  — Colostomy to remove lower portion of colon, including rectum, and create an opening (a stoma) through which wastes are routed out of the body

Outlook

- With early detection and treatment, the chance of long-term survival is very good
- Overall five-year survival exceeds 50 percent

For More Information

National Cancer Institute publications include "What You Need to Know About Cancers of the Colon and Rectum" and "Research Report: Cancer of the Colon and Rectum."

Persons who have had a colostomy can get information, advice and support from "ostomates" who make up the United Ostomy Association (36 Executive Park, Suite 120, Irvine, CA 92714, 714/660-8624). Local chapters are listed in the telephone book under "Ostomy."

Cancer of the Uterus

Cancer of the corpus, or body, of the uterus—the upper, broader part of the pear-shaped womb—usually arises in the inner lining, or endometrium, and so is known as endometrial cancer. Cancer also can develop in the lower, narrow end of the uterus, the cervix. Endometrial and cervical cancers differ in many respects.

Endometrial Cancer

Endometrial cancer is the fourth most common cancer in American women, although its incidence has been falling for decades. About 35,000 new cases are diagnosed each year; nearly 3,000 will die of it.

The incidence of endometrial cancer rose sharply in the 1970s. Once it was discovered that this increase was linked to the widespread use of estrogens prescribed to treat the symptoms of menopause, first estrogen usage and then the incidence of endometrial cancer decreased. The estrogen replacement therapy used today, in which much lower doses of estrogen are combined with progesterone, does not increase endometrial cancer risk. Women who have taken estrogen-progesterone oral contraceptives actually have a lowered risk of endometrial cancer.

Benign uterine tumors, called fibroids, often cause no symptoms and require no treatment.

Preventive Measures
- **Staying trim**
- **Low-fat diet**
- **Treatment of precancerous changes**

Risk Factors
- **Age—55 to 70**
- **Obesity—risk increases as weight goes up**
- **Diabetes and high blood pressure (Because both are also associated with obesity, it is not clear if they are separate risk factors.)**
- **Hormonal factors**
  - **Few or no children—more children mean less risk**
  - **Early onset of menstruation**
  - **Late menopause**
- **High-fat diet**

Symptoms
- **Abnormal vaginal bleeding, usually after menopause**

Diagnosis
- **Endometrial biopsy to obtain small tissue sample**
  or
- **Dilation and curettage (D&C) to obtain larger tissue sample**
- **Thorough pelvic exam, using endoscope and X-rays, to ascertain degree of spread (Distant metastases are rare.)**

Treatment
- **For mild endometrial hyperplasia (proliferation of endometrial tissue), a precancerous condition**
  - **In younger women, hormone therapy**
- **For severe hyperplasia, or mild hyperplasia in postmenopausal women**
  - **Surgical removal of the uterus (hysterectomy)**
- **For early-stage endometrial cancer**
  - **Surgical removal of uterus, usually along with the ovaries and fallopian tubes**
  - **Radiation therapy, either externally beamed or implanted within the uterus**
- **For cancer that has spread within but not beyond pelvic region**
  - **Radiation**
- **For more extensive or metastatic cancer**
  - **Progesterone (Approximately 30 percent to 40 percent of patients respond, and responses sometimes last for years.)**

Outlook
- **Good: Overall five-year survival tops 80 percent**

Cervical Cancer

The incidence of invasive cervical cancer and the number of deaths due to it have been declining steadily, thanks largely to the early detection of precancerous changes (dysplasia) and early, non-invasive cancer (carcinoma *in situ*) with Pap smears. (See page 73.)

Cervical cancer is more than twice as common in black and Hispanic women as it is in white women. It is more likely to have spread when discovered in older women.

Risk Factors

- Young at first intercourse
- Multiple sexual partners
- Mother who took DES during pregnancy

Preventive Measures

- Baseline Pap smear when sexually active or age 21; after three consecutive negative smears, every three to five years
- Minimizing number of sexual partners

Symptoms

- Irregular menstrual bleeding
- Bleeding after intercourse or pelvic exam

Diagnosis

- Pap smear
- Biopsy of areas that appear abnormal when stained or when examined through a colposcope
- D&C if larger biopsy sample is need
- Thorough pelvic examination
- Test for papilloma virus

Treatment

- For carcinoma in situ or very early stages of invasive cancer
  — Surgical removal, part of cervix
  — Surgical removal of uterus (hysterectomy)
- Radiation—usually a combination of external radiation and implants of radioactive materials
  — For early cancer in some older women
  — For cancer that has spread beyond the cervix
- Chemotherapy
  — For cancer that has spread extensively

Outlook

- For carcinoma in situ (45,000 cases a year), surgery is curative
- Two-thirds of the women with invasive cervical cancer (13,000 new cases each year) will be alive five years later

For More Information

"What You Need to Know About Cancer of the Uterus," "What You Need to Know About Dysplasia, Very Early Cancer, and Invasive Cancer of the Cervix," and "Research Report: Cancer of the Uterus" are available free of charge through the National Cancer Institute's Cancer Information Service, 800/4-CANCER.

Skin Cancer

Skin cancers fall into two broad classes. Melanomas are fairly rare but potentially deadly cancers that often begin in a mole. Non-melanoma skin cancers—chiefly basal cell and squamous cell cancers—are much more common and more curable.

Most skin cancers are caused by the sun's ultraviolet rays. They are especially common in people who spend lots of time outdoors, and they become more common with age. The most susceptible persons have fair skin that burns easily.

Melanoma

Melanoma is a cancer of *melanocytes*, skin cells that produce the dark pigment melanin. Some melanomas develop from moles (a true mole, or nevis, is a cluster of melanocytes); others arise spontaneously. They can

Preventive Measures

- Limiting exposure to sunlight (especially between the hours of 10 a.m. and 2 p.m. (standard time, roughly an hour later for daylight saving time), when the sun's rays pass through less ozone (the protective atmospheric layer)
- Using a sunscreen
- Wearing protective clothing
- Avoiding tanning salons and sunlamps, which emit the same types of ultraviolet rays as the sun
- Avoiding unnecessary X-rays
- Self-examination of skin
- Treatment of actinic keratosis (It can be cleared up by applying an anticancer agent directly to the skin.)

Risk Factors

- Extensive exposure to sunlight's ultraviolet radiation
- Fair skin/freckling
- Tendency to burn/inability to tan
- Living closer to the Equator, where ultraviolet radiation is more intense
- For melanoma
  — Atypical moles known as dysplastic nevi
  — Large brown moles at birth
  — Family history (In certain melanoma-prone families, persons with dysplastic nevi are virtually assured of developing melanoma.)
- For basal and/or squamous cell cancers
  — X-ray treatments for skin conditions such as acne
  — Environmental exposure to ionizing radiation or certain chemicals
  — Burn scars
  — Certain genetic diseases, including albinism
  — A precancerous change known as actinic keratosis (red, rough patches on sun-exposed areas of skin)
  — Previous skin cancer (One patient in four will develop repeat cancer every two years.)

Symptoms

- A mole, birthmark or beauty mark that
  — Changes color
  — Increases in size or thickness
  — Changes in texture
  — Is irregular in outline
- A spot or growth that continues to itch, hurt, crust, scab, erode or bleed
- A skin growth that increases in size and appears pearly, translucent, tan, brown, black or multicolored
- An open sore or wound on the skin that does not heal, or heals and reopens

Diagnosis

- Thorough examination of the skin
- Biopsy to determine if cells are cancerous (In melanoma, the biopsy also shows how thick the growth is; thin lesions seldom metastasize and so need less extensive treatment.)

Treatment

- Surgery—removing growth and small border of normal skin (Depending on how extensive the surgery is, or where the cancer is located—on the face, for instance—the patient may require skin grafting or other plastic surgery.)
- Electrosurgery (destroying the cancer with high-frequency current applied through a needle electrode)
- Cryosurgery (destroying tissue with intensely cold liquid nitrogen)
- Radiation therapy
- For metastatic disease
  — Chemotherapy or radiotherapy

Outlook

- For melanoma
  — Five-year survival is 80 percent and better than 90 percent in Australia, where incidence and awareness are both very high
- For non-melanoma skin cancers
  — The prognosis is excellent; the death rate is less than 1 percent

appear anywhere on the body, but most show up in areas exposed to the sun.

Worldwide, the incidence of melanoma has been doubling every decade; in the United States it now strikes about 26,000 people a year. Fortunately, greater awareness and earlier detection have kept mortality rates from skyrocketing; still, the annual death toll approaches 6,000.

Non-Melanoma Skin Cancers

Non-melanoma skin cancer represents the most common type of cancer in the United States, with more than 400,000 new cases each year. However, it is so readily cured it is frequently not counted in cancer statistics. Nonetheless, this cancer is not always discovered before it spreads; each year it claims about 2,000 lives.

Squamous cells make up most of the skin's surface. Basal cells, which are fewer in number, are located in the lowest part of the skin's outer layer, or epidermis. Basal cell cancer is 10 times more common, but squamous cell cancer is much more likely to metastasize, and metastasize sooner, within a matter of months. Both occur frequently on the face, head and neck.

For More Information

The Skin Cancer Foundation publishes a variety of brochures, as well as a quarterly newsletter called *Sun and Skin News*. The Foundation's address is 245 Fifth Avenue, Suite 2402, New York, NY 10016.

A brochure titled "Melanoma/Skin Cancer" is available from the American Academy of Dermatology, P.O. Box 3116, Evanston, IL 60204; a stamped, self-addressed envelope should be enclosed.

"What You Need to Know About Melanoma" and "What You Need to Know About Cancer of the Skin" are National Cancer Institute brochures that can be obtained by calling 800/4-CANCER.

CHAPTER FOUR

Cataracts

A cataract is a cloudy or opaque area in the lens of the eye, which, if it becomes large or dense enough, interferes with vision. The normal lens, located just behind the pupil and iris, is transparent.

Cataract means "waterfall," and it is an apt name, because seeing through a cataract can be like trying to look through a waterfall. Cataracts result from a change in the chemical composition of the lens. However, the exact cause of this change is still not known.

A recent study has linked prolonged sun exposure to an increased probability of cataracts in later life. The study also showed that a brimmed hat and sunglasses reduced ultraviolet light significantly.

There are several types of cataracts, including congenital cataracts and those caused by certain drugs (chiefly cortisone), trauma and radiation. Cataracts can also develop as complications of certain eye disorders or illnesses, including diabetes.

Only 5 percent of people between the ages of 52 and 62 show some signs of cataract; in persons 75 years of age or older the number rises to around 46 percent. A tendency to develop cataracts at a relatively early age appears to run in some families.

Cataracts may affect one eye or both, and they often progress at a different rate in each eye. They develop gradually, without pain, redness or tearing. The chief sign is hazy, fuzzy or blurred vision. Sometimes double vision occurs, but this usually goes away as the cataract worsens. Some people actually experience a temporary improvement in reading vision—"second sight"—but this, too, disappears as the cataract progresses. Very often cataracts cause problems with light and glare; night driving may become problematic, or it may be difficult to find the right amount of light for reading or close work.

Although some cataracts remain small and do not seriously affect vision, most steadily progress. Untreated, they can cause serious impairment; cataracts are the third leading cause of legal blindness in the United States.

Cataracts can be diagnosed by an ophthalmologist, a medical doctor who specializes in diagnosing and treating eye disorders.

The only effective treatment for cataracts is surgery. Cataract surgery—in which the clouded lens is removed—is a relatively routine operation that succeeds in restoring near-normal vision in more than 90 percent of the cases. Indeed, most people are enthusiastic about the results. Cataract surgery should be performed by an ophthalmologist with experience performing such surgery day in and day out.

The procedure takes only an hour or so, and is usually performed under local anesthesia. Of more than one million cataract extractions performed each year in the United States, most are done on an outpatient basis; recovery and adjustment take six to eight weeks. When both eyes are affected, they usually are treated in two separate procedures, with time between to allow the first to heal.

The lens removed at surgery must be compensated for with a replacement lens. This may be achieved with glasses, with contact lenses or—as is more and more often the case—with a lens implanted in the eye at the time of surgery. These *intraocular* lenses, made of clear plastic, cannot be felt by the wearer and need not be removed or changed. Contact lenses may be appropriate for some younger cataract patients, because the implanted lens has not been in use long enough for its very long-term effects to be known; older patients, in contrast, may find contacts difficult to handle. Thick-lensed cataract glasses, for many years the only option for cataract-surgery patients, still are used in some cases, but they can cause visual distortion and a loss of peripheral vision. It is important for the cataract patient to discuss alternatives with the eye surgeon and arrive at a decision prior to surgery.

Individuals who needed corrective eyeglasses before the cataract developed will need them afterwards as well. And, of course, cataract surgery may not bring much benefit to a person whose eyesight is seriously impaired by another eye disease.

Surgery, however, is never completely without risks. Thus, cataract surgery usually is postponed until the cloudiness in the lens progresses to the point where it interferes significantly with the person's daily activities—when, for instance, reading or watching television becomes difficult, or vision is reduced in bright sunlight or darkness, or there is a significant loss of depth perception. Watchful waiting neither reduces the potential improvement in vision nor damages the eye. If the cataract is a slow-growing one, however, surgery may be put off 10 or even 20 years.

Each patient should decide with the help of his or her doctor at what point the benefits of cataract surgery outweigh the risks. Patients may want to get a second consultation about the advisability of surgery and perhaps also about the most appropriate substi-tute lens to use after surgery. And, although Medicare may pay for most of the operation's costs, the patient should establish what those costs will be—for diagnostic tests, for the surgeon, for the hospital or outpatient facility, for the anesthesiologist, for laboratory work and for follow-up care—and how much of the charges will be billed to the patient.

Cataracts

Risk Factors
- Age
- Family history
- Diabetes
- Excessive sun exposure

Preventive Measures
- Sunglasses and brimmed hat
- Avoidance of sun

▼

Symptoms
- Hazy, fuzzy or blurred vision, developing gradually and painlessly in one or both eyes

▼

Diagnosis
- Eye examination

▼

Treatment
- Monitoring the cataract's development
- Surgery to remove the clouded lens
- Replacement lens—either glasses, contacts or surgically implanted lens

▼

Outlook
- With surgery, restored vision
- Without surgery, possible blindness

For More Information

"Cataracts" is a brochure prepared by the National Eye Institute, Building 31, Room 6A32, Bethesda, MD 20892. The NEI, part of the National Institutes of Health, conducts research into the causes, treatment and prevention of cataracts and other eye diseases.

"The Aging Eye: Facts on Eye Care for Older Persons" is a publication of the National Society to Prevent Blindness, 500 E. Remington Road, Schaumberg, IL 60173 (312/843-2020). Some of the Society's local chapters sponsor Cataract Clubs, which put persons facing cataract surgery into contact with individuals who have completed it.

Cataracts: A Consumer's Guide to Choosing the Best Treatment is a large-print book available from the Public Citizen's Health Research Group, 2000 P Street N.W., Suite 708, Washington, DC 20036.

CHAPTER FIVE

Depression

Depression can be defined as a loss of pleasure in life. The depressed person becomes incapable of enjoying anything, loses interest in his or her surroundings, and lacks energy and drive.

Although anyone can feel "depressed" on occasion, depression is considered an illness when the symptoms are intense enough to interfere with ordinary daily activities and last at least two weeks. Bereavement, however, is an exception. When a loved one dies, it is not unusual for feelings of depression to last for several months. Depression is considered a major disorder when less severe or intermittent symptoms persist for two years or more.

Between 4 percent and 10 percent of the American public suffers from a clear-cut depressive disorder. Many more have "depressive symptoms." Over the course of a lifetime, perhaps a quarter of the population will suffer a major depressive episode.

In general, depression is twice as common in women as in men. In women, it peaks between the ages of 45 and 55; in men, it increases with advancing age. And aging men are increasingly likely to commit suicide; the rate is more than twice as high among men who are over 85 than among those who are between 35 and 44.

About half of the people who experience serious depression have a single major episode. For the rest, depression recurs at varying intervals. Sometimes the episodes grow more frequent with advancing age. Usually, even serious episodes of depression are self-limiting. Without treatment, they may last a year or more; with treatment, they may clear up in about a month.

Mental health professionals distinguish between unipolar disorder, in which the person experiences depression only, and bipolar disorder, also known as manic depression, in which episodes of depression alternate with episodes of mania (a mood of exaggerated euphoria, a "high," often accompanied by hyperactivity). Bipolar disease usually makes its first appearance when persons are in their 20s and 30s.

Unipolar depression is further categorized as endogenous or non-endogenous. Endogenous depression is suspected to have a more direct relationship to biological factors, though it can be triggered by a painful event. Today the term describes a particular set of symptoms that are likely to respond favorably to drug therapy.

The risk of depression is higher not only in women, but also in lower socioeconomic classes, the unmarried and unattached, and those who have recently experienced a personal loss. Heredity, too, can play a role; bipolar depression in particular has been shown to have a genetic component.

Research has uncovered several biological components of depression. In the brain of a depressed person, several of the chemical messengers known as neurotransmitters are present in abnormal quantities; so are various enzymes that break down such neurotransmitters, and certain hormones. Depression can also alter brain-wave patterns during sleep and may disrupt biological rhythms.

A number of illnesses, including Parkinson's disease, thyroid disorders, pernicious anemia, uremia and even influenza can trigger depression. In some illnesses, notably cancer of the pancreas and certain brain tumors, depression can even be the first symptom. Nearly half of the people who suffer strokes develop depression within the year.

Depression can also occur as a reaction to a variety of other conditions. Cardiovascular disease regularly produces severe depression, as does a diagnosis of cancer. The loss of function and independence that accompanies many chronic diseases, such as arthritis, diabetes and glaucoma, may also plunge someone into severe depression.

Serious depression can also be caused by medication, including the drugs used to treat high blood pressure, Parkinson's disease, arthritis and cancer.

Disruptive changes in one's social circumstances—so-called life events—are yet another source of depression. (See Section II, Chapter Three.) The most common is the death of a loved one, particularly a spouse. Divorcing, moving, losing a job or retiring can also precipitate a bout of depression.

Depression can occur at any age. Remarkably, considering the litany of losses that can accompany advancing age (loss of vigor, health, mental powers, employment and financial security, friends and relatives), the incidence of depression in older people is not very different from that in other age groups. Overall depression has been estimated to affect between 10 percent and 15 percent of the over-65 population, with rates higher among those with physical illnesses. Recent epidemiologic surveys of community-based populations suggest that severe depression is even less common in older people than in younger groups. However, fairly large numbers of older persons—a fourth to a half—complain of some depressive symptoms.

Biological changes may also contribute to depression in the older population. Several researchers have shown that levels of certain important chemical messengers, or neurotransmitters, decrease in the aging brain, while the level of an enzyme that degrades such neurotransmitters increases.

A diagnosis of clinical depression usually rests on the presence of at least four of eight main symptoms—loss of appetite, weight and sleep disturbances, hyperactivity or lethargy, anxiety, crying, slowed thinking, thoughts of death or suicide, and feelings of worthlessness, hopelessness and guilt. In older people, clinical depression is especially likely to be associated with signs of agitation, physical complaints, hypochondria, delusions of persecution and poverty, thoughts of dying and suicide, and confusion.

Detecting depression in the aging is complicated by a number of factors. Many older people, as well as members of their families, accept depressive symptoms as a part of aging or illness. Other older people do not believe that it is appropriate to discuss their feelings with their doctor, or do not realize that their symptoms can be treated.

Depression in older people is, in fact, often caused by a physical disorder or medications. At the same time, the symptoms of a serious illness can mask even a severe depression. In some older people, depression appears in the guise of minor complaints about bowel functions, urinary frequency, dizziness, or various aches and pains that have no apparent physical basis. Insomnia, common in the elderly, is also a sign of depression.

The first step in diagnosing depression is to uncover any possible physical causes, through study of the patient's medical history and appropriate diagnostic tests. A careful drug history is also essential.

In older men and women, depression must always be distinguished from dementia. The term "pseudo-dementia" describes a true depressive condition in which the thinking process is so muddled that the patient appears demented. This condition will usually have been preceded by symptoms such as irritability, worry and discouragement, whereas a true dementia,

such as Alzheimer's disease, tends to have a more insidious onset. A family history of either depression or dementia, as well as the patient's own medical experience (a history of small strokes, for instance), may suggest treating the patient for depression; a person is twice as likely to be depressed as demented. If the trial fails, little has been lost.

Treatments for depression fall into two broad categories—physical and psychosocial. Often several approaches are combined.

Many depressed people respond favorably, some even dramatically, to antidepressant drugs. These include a group of drugs known as tricyclic antidepressants, others called monoamine oxidase inhibitors (MAOIs) and several types of a new generation of antidepressant drugs. Lithium is a drug that is effective in bipolar depression.

The usual practice is to try an antidepressant drug for four or five weeks. If the first drug proves ineffective, a second drug can then be tried.

However, antidepressant medications must be used with caution, because different drugs produce a wide range of side effects. Some create a sense of dizziness or faintness when one moves to sit up or to stand up. Known as postural hypotension, this condition can lead to falls and broken bones—a particular danger for older people—as well as heart attacks and strokes. Antidepressant drugs can also trigger a toxic reaction that increases restlessness and decreases mental acuity; if the reaction proceeds, the person can develop hallucinations and even seizures. Yet another adverse effect of significance for older people is constipation.

An innovative approach to therapy is sleep deprivation. This technique consists of keeping the depressed person awake for 36 consecutive hours, once or twice a week, up to eight times. It works by altering the patient's biological day-night rhythm, which apparently affects the production of specific hormones.

Several types of psychotherapy, often combined with antidepressive medication, can also be helpful in treating depression. Behavior therapies, which attempt to identify troublesome practices and then train the person to develop new habits, are particularly appropriate in depressions that are linked to severe anxiety. Cognitive therapy is aimed at changing excessively negative feelings and self-talk about the world, helping him or her to overcome apathy by becoming more active and learning how to minimize unpleasant situations. Probing, insight-seeking psychotherapy, however, is not generally recommended for depression; particularly in older people, this approach can shatter coping mechanisms that may help to shield the individual from a harsh reality.

Finally, regular physical activity has been associated with decreased levels of mild to moderate depression in particular individuals. However, physical activity should be viewed as an adjunct to professional treatment when severe depression is diagnosed.

Family members or the family physician can be of help by providing a sympathetic ear along with reassurance that the feelings of depression are very likely to disappear with time, and express confidence in the person's capabilities. Because depression is so often rooted in a sense of helplessness and worthlessness, the depressed person should be encouraged and helped to exert as much control over his or her life as possible. Family members should assist an ailing person in making the best use of whatever physical capabilities remain and encourage his or her participation in physical activity programs, which, by improving physical endurance, lead to greater independence. Finally, they can bolster the person's sense of self-worth by treating him or her with respect and dignity.

For More Information

"Helpful Facts About Depressive Disorders" and related pamphlets can be obtained from the National Institute of Mental Health, 5600 Fishers Lane, Rockville, MD 20857.

Depression

Risk Factors
- Physical illness
- Medications
- Psychosocial stresses
- Family history (bipolar depression)

Preventive Measures
- Physical activity
- Cultivating a positive point of view
- Maintaining social contacts

Symptoms
- Loss of appetite
- Sleep disturbances
- Hyperactivity or lethargy
- Anxiety
- Crying
- Slowed thinking
- Thoughts of death or suicide
- Feelings of worthlessness, hopelessness and guilt

Diagnosis
- Medical and family history
- Tests for physical illness
- Drug history
- Confirmation that several symptoms are persisting

Treatment
- Drugs
- Sleep deprivation
- Psychotherapy
- Physical activity

Outlook
- In three-fourths of the cases, symptoms will go away in a month with treatment, or in about a year without treatment.
- In half of the cases, symptoms will eventually recur.

CHAPTER SIX

Diabetes

Diabetes (diabetes mellitus, or "sugar diabetes") is a complex disorder of body chemistry. Normally the body converts dietary sugars and starches (carbohydrates) into a form of sugar called glucose, which it can burn for heat and energy. In diabetes, the storage and use of glucose is significantly impaired.

The trouble lies with insulin, the pancreatic hormone that controls the conversion of blood glucose into energy. In some cases the pancreas doesn't produce enough of the hormone; in others, the available insulin is somehow prevented from working properly, a condition known as insulin resistance. Either way, the result is high levels of glucose in the blood, which can severely damage many organs, including the heart, blood vessels, eyes, kidneys and nerves.

These two situations—lack of insulin or ineffectual insulin—account for the two major types of diabetes, insulin-dependent diabetes mellitus (IDDM), or juvenile diabetes, and non-insulin-dependent diabetes mellitus (NIDDM), or adult-onset diabetes. IDDM, which typically develops during childhood or young adulthood, is the more severe of the two, but it is much less common, accounting for less than 20 percent of all cases. Treatment requires daily injections of insulin, as well as a controlled diet, exercise, and careful monitoring of glucose levels in the urine or blood. NIDDM usually occurs after age 40, and usually can be controlled with diet and exercise. Both types, however, can cause the same long-term health problems.

Approximately 10 million Americans have diabetes; the typical diabetic is middle-aged and overweight. Diabetes occurs more often in blacks and Hispanics than in whites and becomes more common with age. Estimated to be the nation's seventh leading cause of death, diabetes doubles the risk of heart disease and stroke, accounts for one-quarter of all new cases of kidney failure, and is the leading cause of blindness in middle-aged Americans. Diabetic nerve disease causes leg and foot ulcers that may require amputation.

The cause of diabetes is unknown. IDDM is suspected of being an autoimmune disease, one in which the immune system mistakenly attacks body tissues—in this case, the insulin-producing beta cells of the pancreas. Experimental work also suggests that a virus may play a role in the development of at least some cases of juvenile diabetes.

NIDDM has a strong genetic component. A person's risk of developing diabetes is 14 percent if one grandparent had it, 22 percent if one parent had it, and 60 percent if both a parent and grandparent (or aunt or uncle) had it.

NIDDM, moreover, is closely linked with obesity. Approximately 80 percent of those who develop diabetes are overweight; being 20 percent to 30 percent overweight clearly increases one's risk. The risk continues to increase with the severity and duration of obesity. Furthermore, the chances of developing diabetes appear to be higher if the excess fat is carried in the central body—the waist and belly—than in the extremities—the buttocks, thighs and arms. Obesity itself, it is now known, can cause insulin resistance even in people who are not diabetic, but they compensate by making more insulin. When they lose weight the situation reverts to normal. Persons who are obese, or who have a family history of diabetes, should have their blood glucose tested every five years if they are between the ages of 40 and 59, and every two years if they are 60 years or older.

Typically, the first signs of diabetes are frequent urination, excessive thirst and weight loss, as the body tries to flush excess glucose out of the system. Other symptoms may include blurred vision, weakness, lack of ability to concentrate and loss of coordination. Sometimes the disease develops so gradually that the first hint may be a problem related to the complications of diabetes—numbness in the feet and legs, or infections that are slow to heal.

If symptoms are ignored and blood sugar levels are not controlled, IDDM may turn into a life-threatening emergency. Very high levels of blood sugar can cause a diabetic to go into a coma (also called diabetic ketoacidosis). Before insulin became available, ketoacidosis was a frequent cause of death in juvenile diabetics. Today, diabetic coma is treated with intravenous fluids and large doses of quick-acting insulin, and death is rare.

Alternatively, very low levels of blood sugar (hypoglycemia) can make a diabetic lose consciousness,

Diabetes

Risk Factors

- Obesity
- Age—40 and over
- Family history (NIDDM)

▶

Preventive Measures

- Staying trim
- Physical activity

▼

Symptoms

- Frequent urination
- Excessive thirst
- Weight loss

▼

Secondary Symptoms

- Numbness or sores in legs and feet
- Blurred vision

▼

Diagnosis

- History of symptoms
- Family history
- Elevated blood-sugar levels
- Test for glycohemoglobin

▼

Treatment

- Insulin injections (IDDM and NIDDM)
- Both non-insulin-dependent and insulin-dependent diabetes
  - Weight loss
  - Controlled diet/spaced meals
  - Physical activity
  - Monitoring of blood-sugar level
- Oral hypoglycemic drugs (NIDDM only)

▼

Outlook

- In non-insulin-dependent diabetes mellitus, a lifelong diet and exercise program usually controls symptoms; if controlled, there is only a small chance of developing serious complications
- In insulin-dependent diabetes mellitus, a large percentage will develop serious complications; many of these will die prematurely of heart disease; others will require kidney dialysis; and still others will undergo amputations

convulse and even die. Hypoglycemia may be brought on in people taking insulin or oral diabetes drugs by not eating enough food to balance the effects of the insulin or drugs, or exercising too strenuously. The symptoms, which include heavy sweating, hunger and headache, call for a quick snack or a drink containing sugar. A person who is unconscious needs an injection of glucose or a substance called glucagon. (An identification bracelet explaining that the wearer has diabetes is a wise precaution for persons who depend on insulin or drugs.)

A diagnosis of diabetes is based on elevated blood-sugar levels as well as the presence of symptoms such as thirst and frequent urination, risk factors such as obesity and a family history of the disease, or signs of complications such as heart disease.

Several different tests can be used to measure levels of sugar in the blood and urine. To minimize the effects of what and when a person has eaten, blood tests are usually done in the morning (a fasting blood sugar test), or two hours after a meal (a postprandial test). More reproducible results can be obtained with a glucose tolerance test, which measures blood glucose before and after a person ingests a liquid containing a measured amount of glucose and sometimes other sugars.

However, blood glucose levels not only fluctuate throughout the day, they also tend to increase, quite normally, with age. Because the standards for glucose tolerance tests were originally developed using college students, for a while many older people were erroneously diagnosed as "diabetic." Standards now in use usually take age into account.

The goal of treatment is to control glucose levels so as to prevent symptoms. For the juvenile diabetic this means a daily routine of insulin injections, a controlled diet, exercise and regular testing for glucose in the blood or urine—perhaps several times a day. (A number of kits on the market make testing easy; paper strips or tablets change color when exposed to urine or to a drop of blood.)

For adult diabetics the mainstays of treatment are exercise and diet. Both help to control weight and to normalize blood-sugar levels. As weight drops, blood glucose levels usually show a remarkable tendency to move toward normal.

Exercise, in addition to burning off calories and curbing the appetite, helps the body to combat insulin resistance. It also reduces the diabetic's high risk of coronary heart disease. However, any exercise program must take into account an individual's possible physical frailties. Besides being overweight and out of shape, a diabetic may be a candidate for heart attack, a detached retina or foot damage. The important thing is to select a form of exercise that, in addition to being safe, is sufficiently enjoyable to do frequently, and to

continue to do for life.

A vital component of any weight-loss program is a nutritionally balanced diet limited in calories—usually some 500 to 1,000 calories below daily requirements. Diabetics can test blood or urine to follow their progress in controlling blood sugar, but until they achieve normal levels, they should plan to see their doctor often. Once weight and blood sugar are acceptably low, a diabetic can further reduce the risk of heart disease by limiting total fat intake to less than 30 percent of calories, and saturated fat to less than 10 percent of total calories—but the first and overriding goal is to shed pounds.

In addition to losing weight, some people will have to pay special attention to their eating patterns—avoiding too many carbohydrates (sugars and starches) at one time, and spreading calories throughout the day by eating several small meals rather than a single big one. Sugar, however, is no longer a forbidden food.

Because losing weight is never easy, many people find it helpful to participate in programs that offer behavior therapy, group support and nutritional counseling. Structured exercise programs may help, too. Diabetics also may want to consult with a nutritionist or dietitian; names can be obtained from local chapters of the American Diabetes Association, the American Heart Association or the American Dietetic Association, or from a local hospital or medical school.

In the rare cases in which weight control alone fails to bring blood glucose levels under control, it may be necessary to take insulin injections or drugs, known as oral hypoglycemics, that lower blood sugar. The latter are no panacea, however. They can make nerve damage worse and may increase the risk of a heart attack. As a result, many physicians prefer to use insulin injections. Blood glucose levels can sometimes be upset by stresses, either physical—such as illness or surgery—or emotional.

It is believed—but not yet certain—that controlling blood-sugar levels will reduce the risk of damage to body organs. An extensive study now in progress is evaluating the possibility of slowly preventing or reversing blood-vessel damage in juvenile diabetics by very careful control of blood sugar, insulin given by injection three or four times a day or continuously with an insulin pump, frequent self-monitoring of blood glucose, and an initial hospital stay followed by clinic visits once a month (rather than the standard every three months). Unfortunately, previous attempts to control blood sugar closely either failed or produced too many problems with low blood sugar.

No one knows which diabetics will go on to develop serious complications, although these are more likely to occur in people who have IDDM and those who have had the disease for many years. Such complications as heart disease, stroke and kidney failure are often linked with other distinct risk factors, including obesity, high blood pressure and smoking. The earliest diabetic changes are believed to be abnormalities in small blood vessels and nerves.

Changes in blood vessels that supply the retina, the light-sensing tissue at the back of the eye, cause diabetic retinopathy. An early sign is blurred vision. Because the changes can be arrested with laser treatment, they now proceed to severe visual loss in only a very small percentage of all diabetics.

Changes in vessels and nerves (diabetic neuropathy) in the legs reduce blood supply to the legs and feet, setting the stage for sores and ulcers that become infected and are slow to heal. Alternatively, diabetic neuropathy can cause intense pain. The peripheral vascular complications of diabetes account for more than 40 percent of all non-traumatic amputations.

Diabetic nerve damage can also affect digestion and blood pressure, and it can cause impotence. Diabetics are also more susceptible to infections and periodontal disease.

For More Information

The American Diabetes Association is a voluntary organization that provides printed materials on many aspects of diabetes and information on support groups, and publishes a newsletter. Its National Service Center is located at 1660 Duke Street, P.O. Box 25757, Alexandria, VA 22313 (703/549-1500).

"Noninsulin-Dependent Diabetes" is one of several publications available through the National Diabetes Information Clearinghouse, a program of the National Institute of Diabetes and Digestive and Kidney Diseases. The address of the Clearinghouse is Box NDIC, Bethesda, MD 20892.

The American Dietetic Association is a good source of referrals for help in developing a weight-loss program. It is located at 430 North Michigan Avenue, Chicago, IL 60611 (312/822-0330).

CHAPTER SEVEN

Hearing Loss

The job of the ear is to convert the mechanical energy of sound waves into electrical impulses comprehensible by the brain. When the ear is working properly, sound waves strike the delicate eardrum, are amplified as they traverse three tiny bones that make up the middle ear, and enter the snail-shaped cochlea. Within this fluid-filled canal, hairlike sensor cells transform the incoming vibrations into electrical impulses. The electrical impulses excite nearby wave cells, which relay the signals along the auditory nerve to hearing centers in the brain.

Hearing losses fall into three major categories:

- **Conduction loss** occurs when sound waves are blocked by obstructions—such as earwax—or infections in the outer or middle ear. Voices and other sounds are muffled or faint.

- **Sensorineural hearing loss,** or nerve deafness, results from damage—or wear and tear—to the delicate workings of the inner ear. Sensorineural deafness makes it difficult to understand what is being said; it may also create an intolerance for loud sounds.

- **Central deafness** reflects damage to the auditory nerve or to the hearing centers in the brain, perhaps the result of trauma, stroke or lengthy illness with a high fever. Although sound levels are not affected, understanding of language is.

It is estimated that more than 20 million Americans have some degree of hearing impairment. Almost 2 million, including 200,000 newborns and young infants, are profoundly deaf. More often, hearing loss is partial and develops gradually. It frequently has a hereditary component.

Presbycusis is the name for hearing loss associated with aging. Thirty percent of persons 65 through 74, and 50 percent of those 75 and older are noticeably hearing-impaired.

However, hearing loss is not an inevitable consequence of growing old. In some remote and very quiet cultures, both men and women retain excellent hearing in old age. These people differ in many ways from their American counterparts—they have less stress, different diets, lower blood pressure. One of the principal differences is their quiet environment.

Often the first sign of presbycusis is an impression that people are mumbling. High tones are usually the first to go, and high-pitched sounds are crucial for understanding speech; some of the highest sounds in English are the widely used consonants t, p, k and s, which do not employ voice. As one loses the ability to distinguish between small differences in pitch, especially at high frequencies, it becomes harder and harder to tell what is being said, even when volume is adequate.

It seems clear that lifelong exposure to noise can contribute to presbycusis. Even a brief burst of very loud sound, such as from gunfire, can produce a temporary loss of hearing. Continued exposure to loud noise erodes the hair cells and damages hearing permanently.

People of all ages should avoid loud and prolonged noise. Ear protectors or ear plugs can be a good defense not only against environmental din, but also in shielding the ears against loud household noises such as vacuum cleaners, lawn mowers and chain saws. Another source of danger is a cordless phone that, after being answered, continues to ring shrilly into the ear until a switch is flipped.

In addition to noise, many factors can lead to hearing loss. At the top of the list are disorders affecting the circulation and, thus, the blood supply to the ear. These include diabetes, cardiovascular disease, emphysema and certain kinds of kidney disease. Tumors that affect the auditory nerve—so-called acoustic neuromas—can produce hearing loss or ringing in the ears, as well as dizziness and facial numbness. Aspirin in the large doses used to treat arthritis, antibiotics such as streptomycin, and certain diuretics can damage hair cells or other vital parts of the inner ear, as can anticancer drugs. Alone among these, aspirin-induced damage can often be reversed if it is detected early enough and dosage is reduced.

Hearing Loss

Risk Factors
- Noise
- Age
- Family history
- Circulatory disorders
- Tumors
- Medications
- Ear wax
- Trauma

Preventive Measures
- Avoiding noisy environments
- Wearing ear protectors or ear plugs

▼

Symptoms
- Sounds are muffled or faint
- Difficulty in understanding speech
- Inability to hear certain sounds—violin notes, bird songs
- Continuous hissing or ringing sounds

▼

Diagnosis
- Physical examination, including ears
- Ear examination by otologist
- Hearing test by audiologist

▼

Treatment
- Irrigation (ear wax)
- Surgery (perforated eardrum, otosclerosis, tumor)
- Hearing aid
- Assistive hearing devices

▼

Outlook
- When hearing loss affects the part of the ear that conducts sound, treatment can usually restore hearing
- When it affects structures that interpret sound, the loss is usually irreversible

Although presbycusis is usually associated with change in the inner ear or brain, it can also be the result of conduction defects. Sometimes sound is blocked by a buildup of ear wax. In some persons the eardrum grows thicker and less flexible; in others, it is perforated by injury, sudden pressure change or infection. Middle ear disease—otitis media—can affect adults as well as children and be triggered by allergy as well as respiratory infections. In a hereditary condition known as otosclerosis, sound waves are impeded when the small bones of the middle ear become fixed by an overgrowth of spongy bone.

Some people, most of them middle aged or older, develop a constant ringing or buzzing in the ears or inside the head. Known as tinnitus, this condition can range from annoying to totally disruptive. Temporary episodes of tinnitus can be triggered by excessive amounts of aspirin or related drugs; cautious use is advised.

The ramifications of hearing loss can be enormous. The impaired person guesses at what is being said, feels embarrassed if the guess is wrong, balks at having to ask someone to repeat, resents missing the punchline, grows suspicious of people who don't speak up. He or she may not be able to hear the high-pitched voices of grandchildren, to follow conversations in group settings, to speak on the telephone, or to enjoy television shows. He or she may be unable to hear the phone or the doorbell, musical notes or bird songs. In the face of such frustrations, some people retreat from the social scene. Mislabeled as confused or uncooperative, they may grow depressed. It is not known how many hard-of-hearing people are mistakenly diagnosed as "senile."

The first step toward diagnosis of hearing impairment is a visit to the family physician. In addition to looking for ear wax, the doctor can rule out such possible problems as drug reactions, infections or other diseases.

More complicated cases call for the expertise of a specialist, either an otologist or an otolaryngologist. In addition to obtaining a family history and a medical history, the specialist will conduct a thorough ear examination, perhaps supplemented by laboratory tests or X-rays of the head.

Hearing tests are usually conducted by audiologists, professionals educated in the science of hearing. Using specialized equipment in a soundproof room, the audiologist conducts a battery of tests designed to evaluate both what one can hear and how well one understands what is being said.

Hearing loss due to conduction defects can often be reversed. Treatment can be as simple as irrigation to remove impacted ear wax, or as sophisticated as microsurgery to reconstruct a perforated eardrum. Otosclerosis can often be remedied by surgery that removes the excess bone and replaces all or part of one of the small middle ear bones with an artificial substitute.

When an acoustic neuroma is detected early, surgery to remove the tumor can often reverse the hearing loss; diagnosed at a later stage, such tumors may be inoperable, or surgery itself may impair hearing. For the most part, however, nerve deafness is permanent and irreversible.

Hearing aids, which work by amplifying sound, help some but not all people who are hard of hearing. When volume is a problem, as it is with conductive hearing loss, amplification is more likely to be of benefit. Hearing aids can help some people with nerve deafness by emphasizing a particular range of sounds, such as high frequencies, and filtering out sounds in other ranges.

To the disappointment of many who get them, hearing aids do not restore natural hearing. Because many hearing aids amplify sounds in a limited range of frequencies, they can sound mechanical rather than natural. They can distort sounds, and they amplify distracting background noise as well as speech. Nonetheless, even an imperfect hearing aid can be an invaluable ally in preserving links to one's social environment.

A small number of people who are profoundly deaf have received a so-called cochlear implant. This is a surgically implanted device that transmits electrical impulses directly to the acoustic nerve, bypassing the damaged hair cells of the inner ear. The sound it creates is distorted, and the wearer must learn to interpret it. As technology improves, however, the cochlear implant may eventually become an important treatment option for the hearing impaired.

In addition to hearing aids, people who are hard of hearing may benefit from a variety of "assistive listening devices." Some provide a direct link to tape players and television sets; others amplify sound in large meeting rooms and other public settings, such as churches and theaters, and can relay them to people wearing hearing aids or carrying receivers. Telecaptioning adapters, attached to a television set, generate written dialogue on the screen. Some devices use radio waves or infrared waves to transmit sound between speaker and listener. Various types of equipment make it easier for hearing-impaired people to use the telephone. Others convert sound—such as a doorbell or the ring of a telephone or an alarm clock—to visual or tactile signals, helping to ensure the individual's safety and independence.

Many hard-of-hearing people can also benefit from speechreading. Speechreading training develops skills in picking up visual clues from lip movements as well as facial expressions, body posture and gestures.

Family and friends can help a hearing-impaired person by speaking slightly louder than normal, slowly and clearly. Overarticulating, however, distorts sounds and masks visual clues. The speaker should try to stand or sit three to six feet in front of the person, in a good light that makes it easy to see lip movements, facial expressions and gestures. It's also a good idea to keep sentences short and simple.

For More Information

Self Help for Hard of Hearing People (SHHH) is a volunteer organization that promotes educational and lobbying efforts and conducts local and national meetings. In addition to a bimonthly journal, SHHH publishes articles and books. SHHH is located at 7800 Wisconsin Avenue, Bethesda, MD 20814 (301/657-2248).

The American Speech-Language-Hearing Association, a professional and scientific group, and its consumer affiliate, the National Association for Hearing and Speech Action, respond to queries on hearing loss and hearing aids—and provide local listings of certified audiologists—both by mail and through their toll-free number, 800/638-8255. The address is 10801 Rockville Pike, Rockville, MD 20852.

"Hearing Loss: Hope Through Research" is available from the Office of Scientific and Health Reports, National Institute of Neurological and Communicative Disorders and Stroke, Bethesda, MD 20892.

The National Institute on Aging's Information Office has prepared an information sheet, "Hearing and the Elderly." NIA, Bethesda, MD 20892.

Hearing Aids

Hearing aids—all of which come with a microphone, amplifier, receiver and earmold—come in a bewildering variety of styles. The largest and most powerful type, the body aid, encases the microphone and amplifier in a flat box worn on the chest and is linked to the ear via a wire that runs up the side of the neck. Other aids are worn behind the ear; some are built into eyeglasses; some fit snugly into the ear canal. Generally the smaller aids are less powerful.

Hearing aids are not custom made (although the earmold can be custom fitted). Rather, the dealer attempts to meet the individual's needs by combining and adjusting available components. The advice of an audiologist can be very helpful, too, but the ultimate choice should suit the individual's needs in terms of comfort, convenience and quality of sound.

Because hearing aids require adjustments, maintenance and repairs—and learning to use one requires instruction and counseling—the quality of dealer service is an important consideration. Many dealers offer a free trial period of up to 30 days.

New types of hearing aids promise to overcome some of the drawbacks of older models. For example, the "say-it-again" aid, like the black box in airplane cockpits, records everything that is said and will play back the most recent. "Directional" hearing aids contain a tiny high-fidelity microphone that makes it easier to focus on desired sounds and screen out background noise. And in a few years digital technology may make prescription hearing aids—containing a microprocessor that adjust sounds to the wearer's needs—a reality.

CHAPTER EIGHT

Heart Disease

Coronary heart disease occurs when the blood vessels that supply the heart muscle become blocked, cutting off supplies of oxygen and nutrients. The coronary arteries encircle the heart like a corona, or crown. When an artery is partially blocked, blood flow is diminished, creating a condition known as ischemia and producing chest pain known as angina pectoris, or simply angina. When an artery is completely blocked, heart muscle downstream from the blockage dies. This is a myocardial infarction, or a heart attack.

The condition underlying coronary heart disease is atherosclerosis. In a process that begins early in life but rarely produces symptoms until middle age, fatty deposits accumulate in the walls of the coronary arteries, and scar tissue and debris build up to create lesions called plaques. The inner walls of the arteries, normally smooth, grow thickened and irregular, and the artery channels narrow. Most heart attacks occur when a blood clot, or thrombus, builds up on a rough or fissured plaque and shuts down the already narrowed blood vessel.

More than 5 million Americans have significant coronary heart disease, and 1.5 million will have a heart attack in a given year. More than one-third of these heart attacks will be fatal, making coronary heart disease the nation's leading cause of death. But thanks to preventive efforts and better therapy, mortality rates have been declining steadily for the past two decades.

Heart disease is more than twice as common in men as in young and middle-aged women. However, the incidence in women rises after menopause, and by age 65 a woman is as likely as a man to have a heart attack. Overall, risk increases with age; heart disease is two times more likely in persons over age 65 than in those between ages 45 and 65. The risk of heart disease is also higher for a person with a family history of heart disease. Blacks, disproportionately afflicted with hypertension, are also at higher risk.

In addition to gender, age and family history, a number of other factors strongly influence the development of heart disease. The three major controllable risk factors are cigarette smoking, high blood pressure and high blood cholesterol. Each one can raise a person's risk independently, and when more than one are present they multiply each other's effects. A person with all three has a risk eight times that of a person with none.

Cigarette smoking nearly doubles the risk of coronary heart disease. The more one smokes, the higher the risk. Smoking is particularly dangerous, in terms of heart disease, for women who use oral contraceptives.

The risk for heart disease increases as a person's blood pressure reading rises above the normal level of 120/80. At 150/95, the risk doubles.

Cholesterol, a waxy substance essential to cell structure and function, is both manufactured by body cells and derived from foods, primarily saturated fats. It is carried in the bloodstream in transport packages known as lipoproteins, primarily by low-density lipoproteins (LDLs). When LDL particles are present in excess, they are deposited in tissues and form a major part of atherosclerotic plaques. Plaque formation is inhibited, however, by high-density lipoproteins (HDLs), which transport fat to the liver to be broken down.

Higher cholesterol levels mean higher risk. Total cholesterol levels between 200 and 239 milligrams per deciliter of blood (mg/dl) are considered borderline, those above 240, high risk. The ideal level at which heart disease is unlikely is below 150 mg/dl. Someone with a level of 265 mg/dl has four times the risk of developing heart disease as someone whose total cholesterol is 190 mg/dl or lower.

Total cholesterol is not the whole story, however. The proportion of HDL, the "good cholesterol," is also important. HDL levels above 75 mg/dl are considered protective, while HDL levels below 35 mg/dl are a danger signal—as are LDL levels over 160 mg/dl.

Other factors that raise the chances of developing heart disease include obesity, diabetes mellitus, family history, physical inactivity and perhaps behavior pattern (the impatient and angry "Type A"). Clearly, several risk factors—inactivity, high cholesterol, obesity, high blood pressure, diabetes—may coexist.

Atherosclerosis develops silently, seldom producing symptoms until an artery is at least two-thirds

Coronary Heart Disease

Risk Factors

- Gender—males are more susceptible
- Age
- Family history
- Smoking
- High blood pressure
- High blood cholesterol levels
- Diabetes
- Obesity
- Sedentary lifestyle
- Type A behavior

Preventive Measures

- Not smoking
- Diet low in saturated fats and cholesterol
- Staying slim
- Regular physical activity
- Control of diabetes and high blood pressure
- Stress management

Symptoms

- Chest pain, sometimes radiating to jaw and arms, or back pain
- Loss of consciousness

Diagnosis

- Electrocardiogram at rest and during exercise
- X-rays, ultrasound
- Radioisotope scans
- Cardiac catheterization

Treatment

- For angina: vasodilators, calcium channel blockers and beta blockers
- For heart attack: oxygen; defibrillators; drugs to dissolve clots, to reduce workload of heart, to prevent pain and irregular heart rhythms
- For atherosclerosis: diet, drugs and exercise to reduce cholesterol in the blood and plaques in the arteries, or surgery to open or bypass clogged vessels

Outlook

- Unpredictable. One-third of all heart attacks are fatal; the majority develop without warning obstructed. Angina—typically a dull, sometimes crushing pain beneath the breastbone—often develops following exercise, which increases the heart's demand for oxygen. It lasts from a minute or two to perhaps 20 minutes, and it is nearly always relieved by rest and/or tablets of nitroglycerin, a drug that relaxes the coronary blood vessels and reduces overall oxygen demand.

The pain of a heart attack is characteristically more severe and more persistent than angina, and it is not relieved by nitroglycerin or rest. Most heart-attack victims feel pain in the chest, but it differs from one person to another. Sometimes the pain spreads to the neck, jaw, shoulder or back, or down the arm. Many victims experience weakness, shortness of breath, nausea and sweating.

The extent of damage from a heart attack depends on which vessel is blocked, how large the vessel is, and whether the heart muscle in that area can be supplied by other branches of the coronary arteries. Once a section of muscle has died, it can no longer contract and expand, so the heart loses some of its effectiveness as a pump. Moreover, if the damage extends to an area housing the heart's electrical pacing system, heart rhythms can be dangerously disrupted.

Doctors have at their disposal a wide array of methods for diagnosing heart disease and evaluating its extent. At the simpler end, these include listening to heart and lung sounds with a stethoscope, taking a pulse and measuring blood pressure. A chest X-ray can show heart enlargement. An electrocardiogram (ECG), which measures the electrical activity of the heart, can reveal irregular heart rhythms, called arrhythmias, and provide information on the kind, extent and location of injury produced by a heart attack. An exercise electrocardiogram, graded exercise test (GXT), or stress test, measures the heart during activity (typically walking or jogging on an uphill treadmill); it can show problems that occur only when the heart is experiencing physical stress—but it must be done under carefully controlled conditions, lest it trigger a heart attack. A portable ECG called a Holter monitor makes it possible to monitor heart activity as someone goes about his or her daily activities.

An echocardiogram uses ultrasound to depict the heart's structure and motion. Radioisotopic scans, which detect radioactivity emitted by substances that have been injected into the bloodstream as they travel through the heart, can help to evaluate blood supply, heart size, blood volume and muscle damage. A blood test can reveal an enzyme released by heart muscle that has suffered permanent damage; high levels of this enzyme can distinguish a true heart attack from severe angina.

The most complete view of the coronary arteries can be obtained by cardiac catheterization and angiography. A flexible, hollow catheter is inserted into a blood vessel in the leg or arm and threaded up into the heart; its progress is monitored on X-ray and documented on film. When dye is injected, it can be seen flowing through the chambers of the heart and the coronary arteries, disclosing areas of narrowing or blockage.

It is possible to have a heart attack with no symptoms at all; the damage will be diagnosed only later on the basis of electrocardiographic abnormalities. At the other extreme, about one-fourth of all heart attacks give no warning, but cause sudden death.

A heart attack is a medical emergency, yet many people tend to deny the possibility of anything as serious as a heart attack. The average heart-attack victim waits three hours before seeking help; but if symptoms persist more than a few minutes the emergency rescue service should be called. When heartbeat and breathing have stopped, cardiopulmonary resuscitation (CPR)—using mouth-to-mouth resuscitation to supply oxygen and chest compression to maintain circulation—should be performed until an ambulance arrives. Ambulances carry defibrillators, devices that can shock a stopped heart into beating or turn chaotic heartbeats into smooth rhythms. They also can provide oxygen, ECG monitoring and medication to relieve pain and relax the patient.

The newest emergency tools are drugs that dissolve blood clots. Injected while the attack is in progress, they can dissolve any thrombus that is causing blockage, in hopes of preventing irreversible damage to the heart muscle.

In the hospital, a person who has experienced a heart attack has his or her vital signs—blood pressure, heart rate, temperature, respiration—intensely monitored. Treatment may include drugs to relieve pain, control blood pressure and help the heart to beat regularly. Other drugs can lessen demand upon the weakened heart by blocking cardiac stimulation during periods of stress and exercise. If all goes well, after a day or so in coronary care the patient graduates to a location that provides monitoring, but at a less intensive level.

Exercise is an important part of recuperation. Patients begin arm and leg exercises while still in the coronary care unit, and are up and walking about in a few days. Once home, they resume normal activities at a pace that does not tire them. In the weeks following the attack, most people have a stress test to evaluate their heart's capabilities. Many gain their strength and improve their cardiovascular fitness by participating in medically supervised cardiac rehabilitation exercise programs several times a week.

Many people who have had a heart attack continue to experience bouts of angina. A variety of drugs can be used to control chest pain, lessen the demands placed upon the heart muscle and decrease the likelihood of another heart attack. In addition to nitroglycerin, these include various long-acting nitrate preparations, some in the form of skin patches. Beta blockers, such as propranolol, reduce oxygen consumption by blocking cardiac stimulation during periods of stress and exercise. Calcium channel blockers, such as verapamil and nifedipine, relieve symptoms of angina by relaxing coronary artery spasm and reducing cardiac oxygen consumption. Other drugs that thin the blood or reduce the stickiness of blood platelets, including heparin and aspirin, are given to discourage the formation of clots.

When angina cannot be controlled satisfactorily with medication, surgery may help. A technique known as percutaneous transluminal coronary angioplasty, or balloon angioplasty, involves inserting a catheter—the same way it is done for coronary angiography—into the coronary arteries. When the catheter reaches an area of blockage, a small balloon within the catheter is inflated, crushing back the obstruction.

A more dramatic but increasingly commonplace solution is coronary artery bypass surgery. This involves grafting a section of a blood vessel so that it connects to the coronary artery above and below the point of blockage, rerouting blood flow around the occlusion. However, bypass surgery is not without risks; the mortality rate from the surgery itself averages between 1 percent and 3 percent. It is of greatest benefit to those who have blockages in two or three of the coronary arteries and severe angina; persons with less severe symptoms are usually just as well served with medical and lifestyle interventions.

Heart transplants represent a last resort for people with severely diseased hearts. Like other transplants, they require the use of potent drugs to minimize the chance that the heart will be rejected. These drugs can make the individual susceptible to life-threatening infections. Approximately 1,500 heart transplants were performed in 1987; about three-fourths of the recipients could be expected to be alive two years later.

A more prosaic but also more effective way to treat heart disease is to attack atherosclerosis through exercise, diet and drugs. Lowering blood cholesterol reduces the risk of coronary heart disease; every 1 percent reduction in cholesterol level brings a 2 percent reduction in high risk individuals. Indeed, lowering cholesterol can slow or even reverse the progression of atherosclerotic plaques.

The cornerstones of a cholesterol-lowering plan are exercise and diet. Exercise contributes to cardiovascular fitness in several ways. In addition to improving the efficiency of the heart and lungs, it combats heart disease by raising the HDL level and lowering the level of LDL. Exercise lowers blood pressure, diminishes the risk of diabetes, helps one cope with stress and makes it statistically more likely that a person will cut down or stop smoking. By curbing the appetite as well as burning up calories, regular exercise helps control weight. Physically active people are not only less likely to suffer a heart attack, they are more likely to survive one when they do. (See Section II, Chapter One, "Stay Active.")

A healthy-heart diet is low in cholesterol and saturated fats (which the body converts to cholesterol). In fact, in terms of coronary risk, the saturated fat in foods seems more important than dietary cholesterol. Losing weight also reduces cholesterol levels. (See Section II, Chapter Two, "Eat Healthy.")

For persons whose cholesterol levels remain elevated after six months of following a diet low in cholesterol and saturated fats, increasing fiber intake and staying physically active, cholesterol-lowering drugs may be an option. Some have been shown to lower heart attack rates; the effects of others on heart disease are still under study. All of them, however, appear to work much better when they are combined with a low-fat diet.

For a man or woman with heart disease, therapy centers around a healthy lifestyle—a low-fat diet, regular physical activity, weight loss and not smoking.

For More Information

The American Heart Association publishes dozens of booklets and fact sheets on heart disease, smoking, diet, exercise and high blood pressure. Its 1,500 local chapters conduct educational programs and provide information about community resources. The national center is located at 7320 Greenville Avenue, Dallas, TX 75231.

A variety of informative brochures is available from the National Heart, Lung, and Blood Institute, Bethesda, MD 20892.

CHAPTER NINE

High Blood Pressure

Blood pressure is the amount of force the blood exerts against the walls of the arteries as it flows through them. It is measured when the heart beats—the systolic pressure—and when the heart rests between beats—the diastolic pressure.

A so-called normal blood pressure reading is a systolic reading of 120 and a diastolic reading of 80, but generally the lower the pressure, the better. High blood pressure, or hypertension, is defined as levels above 140/90. In older people, just the systolic reading may be high, the result of increasing vessel rigidity with age.

Pressures normally fluctuate during the course of a day, dropping with sleep, rising with activity and soaring with stress. Hypertension is not, however, a disease of people who are tense; it is a sustained rise in blood pressure, and it can easily occur in calm, relaxed individuals.

High blood pressure develops when the small arteries that regulate blood pressure contract, forcing the heart to pump harder. In a few cases, hypertension can be traced to tumors or diseases, usually kidney problems, that cause the body to produce substances that make the blood vessels constrict or increase the volume of blood in circulation. In the vast majority of cases, however, the source of high blood pressure remains a mystery. This is known as "essential" or "primary" hypertension.

High blood pressure is both commonplace and dangerous. It is estimated that 58 million Americans—one in every four—has blood pressure high enough to need some form of treatment or monitoring. High blood pressure appears to run in families, and is more frequent—and more severe—among blacks. For women, the incidence increases after menopause. It is more likely to affect a person who is overweight, uses a lot of salt and/or drinks a lot of alcohol.

Although high blood pressure develops without any overt symptoms, it ravages the body. Forced to overwork, the heart can enlarge, weaken and fail. The stressed blood vessels lose elasticity and become scarred and narrowed, setting the stage for heart attacks and strokes. Diseased blood vessels in the kidneys lead to death of kidney cells and ultimately to kidney failure. Severe and longstanding hypertension can cause hemorrhage in the eyes, resulting in loss of vision. And the rare condition known as acute, or malignant, hypertension can itself create a life-threatening emergency.

The diagnosis of hypertension is straightforward. Blood pressure is measured with a sphygmomanometer, an instrument that consists of a cuff with a gauge attached. The cuff is wrapped around the arm and inflated until the pressure in the cuff exceeds the pressure in a large artery in the arm, cutting off its blood flow. As the cuff is slowly relaxed, a small amount of blood squirts through the artery; the artery snaps open and closed, making a sound that can be heard with a stethoscope. The first point on the gauge at which the sound can be heard represents the systolic pressure. The sound continues until the artery is fully open; the point at which the sound disappears is the diastolic pressure.

Even though measuring blood pressure is eminently simple, many people have high blood pressure without knowing it. Because hypertension can be treated effectively, and the treatment of even mild disease is beneficial, this is one situation where early detection—screening—makes sense. Everyone should have his or her blood pressure checked once a year. The doctor's office is not the only, nor even the best, place to do it, since the stress of visiting the doctor can itself raise blood pressure. Blood pressure checks are available without charge through public health departments, voluntary health agencies and corporations.

A single high reading is not synonymous with hypertension—at least one-third of those whose first reading is high will subsequently be normal—but it is reason to measure the blood pressure several more times. Someone diagnosed as having hypertension should have a complete examination to rule out the possibility of any underlying conditions, and to check other factors, such as blood sugar, blood cholesterol and kidney function, that contribute to heart disease, kidney disease, diabetes and stroke.

Although it is possible for a person who is trim and athletic to develop high blood pressure, lots of people

High Blood Pressure

Risk Factors

- Age
- Gender—males more than females
- Race—blacks more than non-blacks
- Family history
- Obesity
- Sensitivity to sodium
- High alcohol intake
- Sedentary lifestyle
- Stress

▶

Preventive Measures

- Blood pressure screening (yearly)
- Staying trim
- Exercise
- Limiting sodium and alcohol intake
- Stress management

▼

Symptoms

- Usually none

▼

Diagnosis

- Blood pressure measurement

▼

Treatment

- Diet to control weight, curb sodium and alcohol
- Exercise
- Drugs
- Stress management

▼

Outlook

- If controlled, prognosis is good
- If uncontrolled, increased likelihood of heart attack, stroke, congestive heart disease or kidney failure

with high blood pressure are overweight and sedentary. Many of them could lower their blood pressure by losing weight and exercising regularly; both exercise and weight loss work independently to reduce hypertension. Stress management techniques have also been found to be effective.

For some people, no other treatment will be necessary. For others medication will be needed.

The recent discovery that some anti-hypertensive drugs can produce a number of side effects that boost the risk of heart disease, including increases in blood cholesterol and blood sugar, has renewed interest in controlling high blood pressure with physical activity and diet alone. Studies of people taking drugs for less severe hypertension have shown that about two-fifths of them can discontinue drug therapy and keep their blood pressure controlled by following a diet that limits weight as well as sodium and alcohol intake. Many, but not all, people are sodium sensitive. Dietary sodium increases their blood pressure, while restricting sodium intake can help lower their blood pressure. Numerous studies have shown that heavy drinking—consuming more than four ounces of alcohol a day—also raises blood pressure significantly.

Numerous types of blood pressure medications are available, and many patients take more than one type. Some are diuretics that help rid the body of excess fluid and sodium; these are usually the first drugs to be tried. Others, known as vasodilators, help expand the blood vessels, while yet others prevent blood vessels from constricting. Often different drugs need to be tried to find those that work best. Sometimes one drug may be fine for a few years but may then need to be changed.

Some studies have indicated that calcium supplements may help to lower blood pressure, but the data are not all in. Biofeedback and relaxation techniques have been shown to be beneficial.

One of the biggest problems with treating high blood pressure is convincing the person who has it to take the condition seriously. Although it can readily be controlled with exercise and diet and/or medications, many people abandon therapy because they can detect no symptoms or wrongly presume it has been "cured." High blood pressure is never cured; controlling it is a lifelong proposition. It is, therefore, essential to work out a regimen that is compatible with one's daily routine, home life and work schedule.

The core of any program should be diet, exercise and stress management. If medications are necessary, they should be taken faithfully. The person taking them should be alert to any possible side effects. It is a good idea to have a home blood pressure kit, and make frequent checks on one's progress (see Section II, Chapter Seven). It also helps to enlist the support of a close friend or relative—preferably someone in the same household—to provide reminders and encouragement.

For More Information

Among the several publications on high blood pressure available from the American Heart Association are "About High Blood Pressure," "An Older Person's Guide to Cardiovascular Health," and "Buying and Caring for Home Blood Pressure Equipment." Local chapters of the American Heart Association are listed in the phone book.

The National Heart, Lung, and Blood Institute (Bethesda, MD 20892) publishes brochures on "High Blood Pressure" and "Questions About Weight, Salt, and High Blood Pressure."

CHAPTER TEN

Kidney Disease

The kidneys, a pair of bean-shaped, fist-sized organs located behind the abdominal cavity, are responsible for keeping the body's chemistry in balance. They do this by filtering waste products out of the blood and returning substances the body needs back into the bloodstream. They also secrete hormones that help to control blood pressure and produce red blood cells as well as vitamins.

Each normal kidney contains about one million functioning units called *nephrons*. Each nephron consists of a tuft of tiny blood vessels called the *glomerulus*, plus a looping tubule. The glomerulus filters fluid out of the blood flowing through it into the tubule, where chemicals and water are added or removed, according to the body's needs. Every 24 hours the kidneys filter about 200 quarts of fluid; about two quarts are excreted as urine, while the rest are recycled.

When the kidneys are damaged by disease, the body's delicate chemical balance is jeopardized. Waste products from the breakdown of protein fluids, such as urea and creatinine, and the fluids themselves accumulate, causing a variety of symptoms, including swelling, or edema. In advanced or end-stage kidney (or renal) disease, kidney shut-down causes a potentially deadly buildup of toxins known as *uremia*, or uremic poisoning. In order to survive, a person must either rely on kidney dialysis to cleanse the blood artificially or have a kidney transplant.

There are many types of kidney disease—congenital, hereditary, acquired, acute and chronic. Kidney disorders range from infections to kidney stones to progressive kidney failure; all told, they affect 13 million Americans and cause 80,000 deaths a year. Approximately 90,000 persons with end-stage renal disease are on dialysis; 9,000 or more each year receive kidney transplants.

The most common types of kidney disease involve an inflammation of the glomerulus, or glomerulonephritis. Acute glomerulonephritis usually follows an injury or a bacterial infection. Such infections often affect children, and can clear up spontaneously. Chronic glomerulonephritis, in contrast, causes progressive damage and is the most important cause of kidney failure.

Sometimes chronic glomerulonephritis is preceded by a condition known as the nephrotic syndrome, in which the quantity of protein in the blood decreases sharply. The upshot is severe fluid retention, resulting in swollen legs and increased urination at night. As kidney function declines, the affected person can experience any of a wide range of non-specific symptoms, including nausea and vomiting, loss of appetite, weakness, easy fatigue, itching, muscle and leg cramps, and anemia.

Chronic glomerulonephritis, with its silent and gradual scarring of the kidney, can have many causes. In some cases it is a primary disorder of the kidney, while in others it is secondary to another illness. High blood pressure can bring on kidney disease, making the vessels of the kidney thick and rigid and burdening the heart, so that blood supplies to the kidney diminish, just as the kidney disease itself can induce high blood pressure.

Often the nephrotic syndrome and the subsequent damage of chronic glomerulonephritis are associated with diabetes. In fact, diabetes now ranks as the single greatest cause of kidney failure. Diabetes not only damages the blood vessels of the kidneys, it increases the likelihood of high blood pressure. Moreover, people with diabetes are particularly susceptible to kidney damage from medications containing ibuprofen.

After 15 years of disease, about one-third of those with insulin-dependent diabetes and one-fifth of those with non-insulin-dependent diabetes will show signs of kidney disease; after an average of five to seven years of kidney disease, approximately 50 percent of the former and 10 percent of the latter will develop end-stage renal disease.

When blood and urine tests reveal decreased kidney function, for example, by detecting changes in blood albumin, blood urea nitrogen (BUN) or creatinine, the first step is to look for underlying conditions. In addition to diabetes and high blood pressure, these may include urinary-tract infections or abnormal bladder function. Certain drugs, including heavy doses of pain killers for many years, can also damage the kidneys.

When no underlying cause is found, treatment focuses on slowing the progress of kidney damage. Some cases of the nephrotic syndrome respond to corticosteroids, others to diuretics that reduce swelling and blood pressure. Keeping blood pressure in the normal range is very important in slowing the loss of kidney function. Current research is assessing claims that a diet low in protein and phosphate may be beneficial.

Once the kidneys have failed, three types of treatment are possible: hemodialysis, peritoneal dialysis or kidney transplantation. The choice of treatment depends on many factors, and many patients receive each of the three at various times. Dialysis is performed in the hospital, in special dialysis facilities or—after a person has received training—at home.

Hemodialysis, the most common form of treatment for end-stage renal disease, uses an artificial kidney machine to remove waste products from the blood and restore the body's chemical balance. First an artery, usually on the arm or the leg, is surgically connected beneath the skin to a vein, to create a large arterialized vein, or fistula. Needles inserted into the fistula carry blood through plastic tubing to and from the machine, where wastes and excess water are washed away and substances such as calcium or sugar can be picked up. The length of a dialysis session varies for each patient; the average treatment lasts three to four hours, and must be repeated three times a week.

In peritoneal dialysis, a special solution is introduced into the abdominal cavity through a surgically implanted soft plastic tube. The fluid is allowed to remain in the cavity for a few hours, so that waste products can seep into it from the surrounding blood vessels. Then it is drained and discarded, and replaced with fresh solution.

One form of peritoneal dialysis, continuous ambulatory peritoneal dialysis, uses gravity rather than a machine to draw the fluid in and out. A bag containing the solution is suspended at shoulder level to let the fluid flow in, or placed on a low surface to allow it to drain out. This procedure, which takes about 45 minutes, is repeated four times every day. While the fluid is in the abdomen, the individual is free to go about everyday activities. Another form of peritoneal dialysis uses a machine to deliver and drain the fluid, but this process, too, can be carried out at home—usually overnight.

Dialysis is a life saver but no panacea. It relieves many but not all of the symptoms of kidney failure, and some people benefit more than others. Problems—in addition to those of discomfort, inconvenience and loss of time—abound. Hemodialysis patients in particular must be attentive to diet, carefully

balancing types of protein and other nutrients. Persons undergoing dialysis face bone disease, disorders of nerve function, anemia, high blood pressure, acceleration of arteriosclerosis and disturbances of sexual function. Artificial kidney machines can cause problems with blood clotting and infection. The average mortality rate for persons on dialysis is 10 percent per year.

About one-third of the people on dialysis are considered to be healthy enough to make good candidates for kidney transplantation. In the past 25 years, this procedure has become increasingly widespread and, with the development of new drugs to lessen the chances that a transplant will be rejected by the body's immune system, increasingly successful. However, the supply of donor organs is never adequate to meet needs; at any given moment, about 10,000 persons are on waiting lists for donor kidneys.

In a three-hour operation, a new kidney—either from a relative or from the body of a person who has just died—is placed in the lower part of the abdomen and attached to the recipient's blood vessels and bladder. It goes to work almost immediately, filtering blood and putting out urine, but the recipient spends the next few weeks in the hospital, being closely watched for signs of infection or rejection.

Transplants succeed—as measured by their continued ability to function two years later—in 60 percent to 90 percent of the cases. Kidneys from living relatives are the most successful. However, transplant recipients need to take potent and costly immunosuppressive drugs for the rest of their lives and report for regular checkups. Should the kidney fail, the person returns to dialysis; some will have a second transplant.

The success of these various treatments, and the quality of life they ensure, vary widely. Most transplant patients feel well, are able to return to work, can travel and participate in sports. Many dialysis patients also feel well and resume working, but others experience complications. Counseling helps many patients and their families to handle the emotional ups and downs that come with the dependency of dialysis. Patients on continuous ambulatory peritoneal dialysis have the advantage in arranging work and travel schedules; those who rely on mechanical dialysis also can travel by making advance arrangements at dialysis centers in the cities or countries they visit.

All of these remedies are expensive. The expense of dialysis averages $25,000 or more a year. Transplant surgery involves a one-time cost of about $25,000 plus immunosuppressive drugs at several hundred dollars a month. The government pays 80 percent of the charges for dialysis and transplant surgery; much of the remainder is covered by private insurance or state assistance programs. The cost of immunosuppressive

Kidney Disease

Risk Factors

- For chronic kidney disease
  — Diabetes
  — High blood pressure
  — Certain kidney-damaging medications
- For acute glomerulonephritis
  — Infections
  — Injury

Preventive Measures

- Control of diabetes
- Control of high blood pressure
- Judicious use of pain killers

Symptoms

- Burning or difficult urination
- Frequent urination, particularly at night
- Bloody urine
- Puffiness around eyes, swelling of hands and feet
- Pain in small of back
- High blood pressure

Diagnosis

- History of symptoms
- Blood and urine tests for protein and protein breakdown products
- Tests of blood sugar
- Blood pressure measurement

Treatment

- Treatment of underlying disorders
- Diuretics to reduce swelling
- Drugs to lower blood pressure
- Diet low in protein and phosphate (under study)
- Regular physical activity
- For end-stage renal disease
  — Hemodialysis
  — Peritoneal dialysis
  — Kidney transplantation

Outlook

- Gradual progression of disease
- With end-stage renal disease, life will be severely disrupted for some, near normal for others
- Life expectancy approaches normal for many patients; however, about one-tenth of those on dialysis die each year
- Under the best circumstances, the one-year survival for transplant patients is about 90 percent

drugs, however, must be borne by the individual.

Regular exercise has been shown to provide special benefits for persons being treated for kidney failure. Specifically, it improves strength, stamina and energy by increasing the proportion of red blood cells. This helps to counteract the anemia that leaves many people with kidney failure feeling tired and weak. Of course, exercise can also help control hypertension, blood lipids, blood sugar and weight—and thus diabetes and heart disease. (At the same time, the possibility of complicating conditions makes it essential to use prudence and consult one's doctor in designing an exercise program.)

For More Information

The National Kidney Foundation provides information on kidney disease, dialysis, transplantation, nutrition and rehabilitation. Through its affiliates around the country, the Foundation sponsors information and referral programs for patients and their families, drug banks, support groups, transportation services and counseling, as well as direct financial assistance to needy patients. The Foundations's address is 2 Park Avenue, New York, NY 10016 (800/622-9010).

Information about research into kidney diseases is available from the National Institute of Diabetes, Digestive and Kidney Diseases, Bethesda, MD 20892. The Institute has established six centers that specialize in research into kidney and urinary diseases.

CHAPTER ELEVEN

Obstructive Lung Disease

Chronic obstructive lung disease (COLD) comprises two separate but closely related and usually coexisting conditions, emphysema and chronic bronchitis. Together, by damaging delicate lung structures, they prevent the lungs from performing their main job, which is to bring in oxygen and expel carbon dioxide.

The exchange of gases between the lungs and the bloodstream takes place across the extremely thin walls of millions of tiny air sacs called alveoli. In emphysema, the walls separating the alveoli break down, permanently transforming them into larger spaces where fresh air cannot readily reach the circulating blood.

Chronic bronchitis, for its part, inflames, scars and clogs the airways. The walls of the larger air passages, the bronchi, thicken, and excessive amounts of mucus are secreted. The hallmark is a persistent, sputum-producing cough.

In chronic obstructive lung disease, stale air gets trapped in the alveoli and gas exchange becomes less efficient. At the same time, the job of pushing air out through the obstructed airways becomes more and more difficult. The person feels, at first, short of breath, and later, starved for air.

More than 10 million Americans have COLD, most of them former or current smokers. The more one smokes, the greater the chances of developing the disease. COLD is the fastest-rising major cause of death in the United States, and the greatest brake on normal daily activity; many COLD victims are so seriously handicapped they are no longer able to work or maintain a household. COLD is much more common in men than in women, but women, who are smoking more, are catching up. The tendency to develop COLD also runs in families.

The condition develops slowly; it may take 20 years or more for full-blown disease to appear. It then continues to grow worse. Consequently, most serious disabilities and deaths occur among persons over age 65.

Long before serious symptoms appear, however (actually within a month of beginning to smoke), inflammatory changes begin to develop in the small airways, the bronchioles. If a smoker quits after a short time, before lung changes become extensive, these tissue changes revert to normal. Smoking also greatly accelerates the small, normal decline in lung function that occurs with age. Quitting can prevent further rapid decline of lung function, but it won't restore function that has been lost. Yet, ex-smokers have lower death rates from COLD than people who continue to smoke.

Air pollution contributes to emphysema by aggravating the lung damage produced by smoking. Respiratory infections, which are common in people with emphysema, may add to the problem, because secretions released by microbes or by body cells fighting the infection may also injure lung tissues. A particularly severe form of emphysema occurs in people with an inherited deficiency of an enzyme that protects the lungs from destructive chemicals.

Early symptoms of COLD include mild shortness of breath and a slight morning cough; the symptoms get noticeably worse during infections such as colds. Sputum may turn yellowish green, and episodes of wheezing may develop.

Gradually, shortness of breath becomes more marked; a slight exertion can trigger severe breathlessness. Minor respiratory infections become a major problem. In order to breathe, many people sleep half sitting up, and often wake to cough and clear their lungs.

As the disease progresses, its effects spread. The heart, working hard to pump blood into the lungs, can become enlarged; this condition, known as cor pulmonale, leads to fatigue, chest pains, and, when the heart is especially stressed, swollen legs and ankles.

The body, trying to compensate for too little oxygen, boosts its supplies of oxygen-carrying red blood cells, but the excess of cells thickens the blood, creating new problems, including cyanosis, a bluish tinge to the skin and lips. When the nervous system, including the brain, is beset by the combination of too little oxygen and too much carbon dioxide in the blood, the results are headaches, insomnia, impaired mental acuity and irritability. Breathing becomes increasingly labored.

A variety of measures of lung function can be used in diagnosing COLD: the volume of air expelled into a machine called a spirometer in a single breath, the force with which it is expelled, the amount of air forcibly expelled in one second (FEV/1), and the quantity of air that remains after exhaling. Another indication of COLD comes from blood levels of oxygen and carbon dioxide—the former falling, the latter rising as the disease progresses. Since no single measure tells the whole story, several tests are usually used in concert.

The first line of defense against COLD is to quit smoking. Although lung tissue destroyed is gone forever, quitting prevents further rapid deterioration and markedly decreases the inflammation of chronic bronchitis. The damaged lungs should be protected in other ways, too—by avoiding exposure to dust and fumes, avoiding air pollution (lying low during air-pollution alerts), protecting oneself against respiratory infections (staying clear of people who have colds or flu, and perhaps getting vaccinated against flu and pneumonia), and avoiding extremes of temperature or very high altitudes (air that is too hot, too cold or too thin).

Medications called corticosteroids can improve airflow, while antibiotics can cut short respiratory infections. Many over-the-counter drugs combine an assortment of ingredients, including expectorants and sedatives as well as bronchodilators. These mixtures may help, but may create side effects.

A variety of techniques has been devised to keep air passages clear. Secretions can be thinned by inhaling bland aerosols (often made from solutions of salt or bicarbonate of soda) for 10 to 15 minutes three or four times a day. Drinking lots of water also helps to keep secretions liquid. Clapping the chest and back helps dislodge secretions, lying in certain positions enlists the help of gravity to drain them, and controlled coughing techniques can be learned to help bring them up.

Physical training also can benefit a person with COLD. In addition to general exercises to improve overall physical fitness and tone respiratory muscles, breathing exercises can help to slow the respiratory rate, coordinate the breathing effort and decrease the work of breathing. Learning to use the diaphragm and abdominal muscles instead of the chest muscles al-lows the person to make the best use of a limited breathing capacity.

Many people with advanced disease need supplementary supplies of oxygen from tanks of compressed gaseous oxygen, containers of liquid oxygen or devices that concentrate oxygen from room air. Small units with shoulder straps can be carried about outside. Although the person is tethered to the equipment and the treatment is costly, home oxygen therapy can provide many benefits. It not only improves a person's physical and mental abilities and reduces symptoms such as sleeplessness, irritability and headaches, it also curbs the overproduction of red blood cells. Intermittent oxygen therapy may suit someone whose oxygen needs increase only during sleep or exercise.

Survival is closely tied to how severe the impairment is and how rapidly function continues to deteriorate. The FEV/1 is a fairly good predictor of disability and early death. Among persons under age 65 whose FEV/1 has diminished to approximately one-third of normal, two out of three will probably be alive five years later. About half of those can be expected to survive an additional five years.

For More Information

The American Lung Association disseminates information on lung-related diseases, including flyers instructing the COLD patient on physical therapy, breathing training, exercising and home respiratory equipment. It is also the source of ''Help Yourself to Better Breathing,'' a 24-page manual for COLD patients. The Association is headquartered at 1740 Broadway, New York, NY 10019 (212/315-8700); local chapters are listed in the phone book.

The National Jewish Center for Immunology and Respiratory Medicine provides publications and information on chronic respiratory diseases through its LUNG-LINE, 800/222-LUNG. It is located at 1400 Jackson Street, Denver, CO 80206.

''Chronic Obstructive Pulmonary Disease'' is a moderately technical discussion of COLD prepared by the National Heart, Lung, and Blood Institute, Bethesda, MD 20892.

Information on help in quitting smoking is available from the Office on Smoking and Health, Public Inquiries, Park Building, Room 1-58, 5600 Fishers Lane, Rockville, MD 20857 (301/443-1575).

Obstructive Lung Disease

Risk Factors
- Smoking
- Gender—males are more susceptible
- Family history
- A rare genetic defect
- Age

Preventive Measure
- Not smoking
- Staying active

Symptoms (early)
- Mild shortness of breath
- Slight morning cough
- During colds, greenish sputum, wheezing

Symptoms (late)
- Severe breathlessness, aggravated by exertion and infections
- Chest pain, palpitations, fatigue
- Bluish skin and lips
- Headache, insomnia, impaired thinking, irritability

Diagnosis
- History of symptoms
- Smoking history
- Lung function tests
- Blood levels of oxygen and carbon dioxide

Treatment (to slow advance of disease)
- Not smoking
- Avoiding air that is polluted, too hot, too cold or too thin
- Taking precautions against respiratory infections, including vaccines against flu and pneumonia

Treatment (to relieve symptoms)
- Antibiotics
- Inhaled aerosols, high liquid intake to keep secretions thin
- Physical maneuvers to clear lungs
- Breathing exercises
- Fitness training
- Home oxygen therapy

Outlook
- Initial improvement in lung function with treatment
- Gradual worsening of symptoms
- Length of survival closely tied to initial level of impairment

CHAPTER TWELVE

Osteoporosis

Osteoporosis is a thinning of the bones with age that causes bones to break easily. For many older persons, particularly older women, osteoporosis can transform an everyday gesture or action into the cause of a crippling and even life-threatening fracture. And when weakened vertebrae splinter, they produce not only back pain but also a shrunken and stooped appearance.

Living bone constantly renews itself, with new bone being formed and old bone being reabsorbed. In children and young people bones grow stronger, with more calcium, which makes bones hard, being added than removed. Bones attain peak bone mass—their maximum density and strength—around the age of 35; thereafter that bone mass begins to diminish. The exaggerated bone loss of osteoporosis is the work of many complex factors, including heredity, numerous hormones, nutrition and inactivity.

Osteoporosis is a common condition, affecting one in four women over the age of 60. It develops in men, too, but much less frequently. In part this is because men have heavier bones to begin with. In addition, bone loss in women accelerates sharply during the eight to 10 years following menopause, when the ovaries curtail the output of estrogen, the female hormone secreted during childbearing years that helps to ensure a strong skeleton and a ready reserve of calcium for breast milk.

Women most prone to osteoporosis are apt to be those who start out with a low peak bone mass. Statis-tically, osteoporosis is most likely to strike postmenopausal white or oriental women who are thin and have small frames. The danger of osteoporosis is especially marked for women who experience early menopause (before the age of 45), either naturally or through surgical removal of the ovaries.

The development of osteoporosis also can be influenced by several dietary components. Chief among these is calcium. When someone takes in too little calcium, the body draws what it needs for many vital functions, including muscle contraction and the beating of the heart, from the bones. Surveys indicate that older people typically do not consume enough calcium to meet minimum daily requirements. The problem is compounded by the fact that, starting at about age 40, the body becomes less efficient at absorbing calcium from food.

In order to absorb calcium properly, the body requires vitamin D. Most people get enough from their diet and from normal outdoor activities. The body manufactures vitamin D in response to sunlight. However, people who are confined to a nursing home, for instance, may suffer from a vitamin D deficiency.

Bone density also is influenced by physical forces, such as body weight and the action of muscles working against gravity. It is known that inactivity leads to bone loss; prolonged bed rest produces rapid bone loss, even in the young. Osteoporosis may prove a special problem for persons whose mobility is limited by a condition such as arthritis, or who are bedridden. Weight bearing exercise, however, strengthens bone in the young and, thus, although it has not been proven, seems a likely way to diminish bone loss later in life.

A number of other factors may influence someone's risk of developing osteoporosis. These include a family history of the disease; heavy cigarette smoking, which reduces estrogen production; excessive alcohol intake; high caffeine intake; and a diet that is almost exclusively protein. Bone loss also can be the byproduct of certain drugs and diseases—the anticoagulant heparin, cortisone, thyroid conditions, diabetes, kidney disease, certain cancers and imbalances in calcium metabolism.

Osteoporosis often gives no warning until a bone breaks—often with little cause. There are no laboratory tests that pick up the disease in its early stages, although some tests can help to rule out other diseases that might be contributing to bone loss. By the time skeletal changes can be seen on an X-ray, about one-quarter of the bone mass is already lost.

Several new techniques to measure bone density are being explored; these include an adaptation of computerized axial tomography (CAT) scanning to assess bone mineral content in the spine, and a proce-

Osteoporosis

Risk Factors

- Early menopause, particularly after surgery
- Race—whites more susceptible
- Gender—females more susceptible
- Slight build, fair skin and fair hair
- Low calcium intake
- Inactive or sedentary lifestyle
- Family history
- Smoking
- Excessive alcohol use

Preventive Measures

- Estrogen replacement therapy
- Diet high in calcium and adequate in vitamin D
- Weight-bearing exercise
- Not smoking
- Moderate alcohol use

Symptoms

- Sudden back pain
- Loss of height
- Humped back
- Sudden bone fracture

Diagnosis

- Otherwise unexplained bone fractures
- Decreased bone density on X-rays (advanced disease)
- Decreased bone density on computerized axial tomography or photon absorptiometry

Treatment

- Estrogen replacement therapy
- Ample intake of dietary calcium
- Calcium supplements
- Weight-bearing exercise
- Safety precautions

Outlook

- Continuing threat of unexpected fractures
- With hip fracture, curtailed mobility
- Depending on time between start of treatment and onset of menopause, possibility of rebuilding bone mass or preventing further bone loss

dure called photon densitometry (or photon absorptiometry) in which the amount of radiation absorbed by bone serves as a measure of the bone's chemical composition. Such tests, which are available only at certain medical centers and tend to be very expensive, can be helpful in assessing high-risk patients or monitoring therapy. However, there is no evidence that using them to screen premenopausal women will identify those who will eventually develop fractures.

Sometimes the first indication of osteoporosis is a loss of height or the beginnings of a humped back produced by the collapse of weakened vertebrae. Such crush fractures, as they are called, occur most often in women between the ages of 55 and 75. They can be caused by something no more strenuous than bending over to make a bed, lifting a bag of groceries from the trunk of a car or even getting up out of a deep chair. Sometimes crush fractures cause a sudden, sharp back pain, but even when they are not immediately painful they can trigger painful spasms in back muscles trying to compensate for a partially collapsed spine.

In contrast to spinal fractures, fractures of other parts of the skeleton, which consist mostly of a different type of bone, tend to occur in men and women who are about 10 years older than the women who get crush fractures. Broken wrists are common. So are hip fractures, which can be disastrous in older people. Many older individuals never fully recover their mobility after a hip fracture, and nearly one-fifth will not survive a year. The outlook should improve, though, as better surgical and rehabilitation techniques increase the likelihood that a hip fracture will be repaired promptly, enabling the patient to be up and moving about in a matter of days.

Treating osteoporosis is basically a matter of preventing bone loss. Young women can try to give themselves a head start by boosting their peak bone mass with high levels of calcium and regular exercise; for middle-aged and older women and men, the goal is to minimize bone decline.

The mainstays of therapy are hormones, nutrition and exercise. Oral estrogen, taken in the years following menopause, slows or halts bone loss throughout the body, and women who take estrogens have fewer fractures than women who do not. However, estrogen replacement therapy has its own drawbacks. Given alone, estrogen can increase the risk of endometrial cancer, although combining estrogen with another female hormone, progestin, eliminates this risk. Generally estrogen replacement therapy is recommended only for women who are at moderate to high risk of osteoporosis and who are free of such conditions as endometrial or breast cancer, stroke or unexplained vaginal bleeding.

Calcitonin, a thyroid hormone that inhibits bone breakdown, has been officially approved for the treatment of severe osteoporosis. It is administered in daily injections, along with calcium and vitamin D. Unfortunately, it is very costly.

Ample calcium intake appears to be yet another important way to protect against osteoporosis, although the results of research studies are not all in agreement. Experts believe that most adults need about 1,000 milligrams of calcium a day: postmenopausal women not taking estrogens need 1,500 milligrams a day.

The best source of calcium is dairy products, where its bioavailability—the amount absorbed and used by the body—is certain. One cup of milk contains about 300 milligrams. So do 1.5 ounces of cheddar cheese, 2 cups of cottage cheese and 1 cup of yogurt. Choosing dairy products such as skim milk and low-fat yogurt helps keep dietary fat within bounds. Other foods rich in calcium include fish, shellfish and dark green vegetables such as kale and broccoli.

People who find it difficult to get enough calcium from their diet may want to consider a calcium supplement. There are dozens on the market, but it is important to read the product label, because different formulations contain different amounts of elemental calcium. Calcium carbonate, for instance, is only 40 percent calcium (so a 100-milligram tablet contains only 40 milligrams of calcium). Calcium lactate is 13 percent calcium; calcium gluconate is 9 percent. Calcium supplements are not recommended for persons who have kidney stones.

Weight-bearing exercises, which include running, walking, aerobics and tennis, appear to be another way to slow bone thinning. Anyone starting an exercise program needs to use common sense, beginning slowly and building up gradually. Persons who have heart or joint problems would be wise to check out their exercise plans with their doctor. Even when more rigorous exercise is out of the question, walking can be extremely beneficial.

Persons who have osteoporosis need to minimize the threat of fractures. They should accident-proof their homes by eliminating slippery floors or rugs that are easy to trip over, increasing the brightness of lighting, adding handles to bathtubs and railings on stairways. And they have to learn to move with deliberation—no lurching, wrenching or lifting while stretching. Still, they cannot let fears of falling keep them house or chairbound. For both physical and mental well-being, the most important rule is to remain as active as possible.

For More Information

A detailed booklet, ''Osteoporosis: Cause, Treatment, Prevention,'' is available from the National Institute of Arthritis, Musculoskeletal and Skin Diseases, Bethesda, MD 20892.

The National Osteoporosis Foundation is a non-profit voluntary health organization that supports public and professional education programs. It is headquartered at 1625 I Street N.W., Suite 1011, Washington, DC 20006.

Fitness for Life, written by Theodore Berland and published by the American Association of Retired Persons, presents an exercise program for people over 50. AARP can be contacted at 1909 K Street N.W., Washington, DC 20049.

CHAPTER THIRTEEN

Periodontal Disease

Periodontal, or gum, disease affects the structures that support the teeth. First the gums become inflamed, then the underlying bone—to which the teeth are attached—degenerates. Teeth grow loose and eventually fall out.

Most of the 23 million Americans who have lost all of their teeth are the victims of periodontal disease. So, to a lesser degree, are an estimated 94 million others. Although toothlessness has grown less common in recent years, particularly in middle-aged persons, more than 40 percent of those over 65 are missing all of their teeth, while only 2 percent of older people still own all 28 of their permanent teeth. Nearly half of all older people, and more than 40 percent of adults in the work force, show signs of gum disease.

Periodontal disease develops when masses of sticky bacteria—known as dental plaque—are allowed to accumulate on the teeth. If the bacteria are not removed by regular brushing and flossing, first the bacteria themselves and then the body's antibacterial immune defenses begin to erode the gums and, eventually, the jawbones.

Although most periodontal disease gets its start with poor oral hygiene, the risk of periodontal disease is increased by certain conditions in which body metabolism is altered. These include pregnancy and diabetes. The course of the disease is erratic, plateauing and flaring up. It does not even affect all parts of the mouth equally.

In the earliest stage of periodontal disease, known as gingivitis, plaque grows along the teeth and edges beneath the gums. The bacteria irritate the gums, causing redness and swelling. Gradually the redness and swelling become more obvious, and the gums bleed easily—often during toothbrushing.

If the inflammation is not controlled, the disease progresses to the next stage, periodontitis. Bacterial plaque hardens into calculus and extends to the tooth root. The gums gradually become detached from the teeth, creating spaces, or pockets. Such pockets, which often occur between adjacent teeth where a toothbrush cannot reach, become infected and fill with pus. Infected pockets often cause bad breath.

As the gums recede, connective-tissue fibers that fasten the teeth to the jawbone are destroyed. The bone itself disintegrates, and the tooth is lost.

For the most part, periodontal disease develops painlessly. The swollen and bleeding gums that signal the condition may be noticed by the individual, or they may be detected during a dental checkup. Diseased gums typically bleed when probed gently with a dental instrument. Probing also can reveal the presence of pockets, and measure their depth. Bone destruction will show up on dental X-rays.

The cornerstone of both prevention and treatment is to keep the teeth free of plaque through good dental hygiene—fastidious brushing, flossing and sometimes irrigation. (Plaque can be "disclosed" with mouth rinses containing vegetable dyes.) Teeth should be brushed and flossed after every meal, if possible, but at least once a day. In a healthy person, good self-care will maintain healthy gums.

Home care needs to be combined with dental visits—semi-annually for persons who do not have gum disease, more often for those who do. The dentist or periodontist (a dentist who specializes in gum disorders) can remove plaque from otherwise inaccessible areas, scrape away calculus, remove dead tissue and clean out pockets.

In advanced disease, after regular flossing has failed to improve the condition, various surgical procedures may be used in an effort to prevent tooth loss. Diseased gum tissue can be excised, while tissue from another area of the mouth can be grafted onto an uncovered tooth surface. Sometimes a short course of antibiotics is helpful in quieting the destructive bacteria.

Alternatively, some dentists recommend massaging the gums with an antibacterial paste made by mixing baking soda and hydrogen peroxide, applying fluoride toothpaste or a fluoride gel, or irrigating under the margins of gums with an antibacterial solution, such as saturated salt water. Whatever the treatment, though, its ultimate success depends on frequent and meticulous self-care.

People who have already lost some or all of their teeth also need to practice good oral hygiene. Dentures, either partial or full, need to be kept clean and free from deposits that cause stains, bad breath and gum irritation. The dentures should be brushed with a denture-care product once a day, and removed from the mouth and placed in water for at least six or eight hours each day. It's also a good idea to rinse the mouth with a warm salt water solution in the morning, after meals and at bedtime.

For More Information

Information about periodontal disease and peri- odontal research is available from the National Institute for Dental Research, Bethesda, MD 20892.

Information on general dental care can be obtained from the American Dental Association, 211 E. Chicago Avenue, Chicago, IL 60611. Names of dentists who specialize in the care of older persons can be obtained from the American Society for Geriatric Dentistry at 1121 W. Michigan Street, Indianapolis, IN 46202.

Periodontal Disease

Risk Factors
- Poor oral hygiene
- Diabetes

Preventive Measures
- Regular and meticulous brushing and flossing
- Regular professional dental cleaning

Symptoms
- Reddened, swollen gums
- Bleeding with toothbrushing

Diagnosis
- Visual inspection
- Gentle probing to detect bleeding or pockets
- X-rays to detect bone loss

Treatment
- Professional dental cleaning to remove plaque and calculus
- Fastidious oral hygiene
- In advanced cases, surgery to prevent tooth loss

Outlook
- Good oral hygiene can arrest disease in early stages
- In later stages, good care can delay disease progression; slipshod care will result in tooth loss

CHAPTER FOURTEEN

Stroke

Stroke is a sudden interruption in blood flow to part of the brain. Deprived of oxygen and nutrients, brain cells wither and die. The effect depends on the area of brain injury as well as its extent. Strokes can impair memory and thinking, speech and comprehension, the senses and behavior. Most strokes diminish control of the body's muscles, creating weakness (paresis) or paralysis, typically on just one side of the body.

Some stroke victims suffer no more than a mild slurring of speech, while others become crippled and yet others are almost totally incapacitated. Stroke is responsible for a large number of admissions to nursing homes. Many victims—nearly one-third—die from the initial stroke.

Although the number of deaths due to stroke has been nearly halved over the past two decades (the fruit of more healthful living patterns), stroke remains the country's third leading cause of death. About 400,000 Americans have a stroke each year, and the number of stroke victims still living approaches two million.

Strokes mainly affect older people. One younger group at increased risk consists of women who both take oral contraceptives and smoke. Strokes are more common in men than in women, and much more common in blacks than in whites—to some extent perhaps because more blacks have high blood pressure.

Strokes are brought on when an artery in the brain or neck becomes obstructed, or when a blood vessel in the brain ruptures. Most strokes are a byproduct of atherosclerosis, the narrowing of arteries by fatty plaques and the formation of clots. (See Chapter Eight, "Heart Disease.") One of the most common forms of stroke, cerebral thrombosis, occurs when an artery—typically narrowed by atherosclerosis—is blocked by a clot, or thrombus, in much the same way that a thrombus in a coronary artery can cause a heart attack. Cerebral embolism results when a piece of a clot from another part of the body, usually the heart or the arteries of the neck, breaks away and is carried by the blood until it wedges in and blocks a smaller artery in the brain. (Embolus means "plug.") Other strokes are attributed to stenosis—severe narrowing of the artery.

Hemorrhagic strokes occur when a defective artery in the brain bursts, flooding surrounding tissues with blood; not only is the brain's supply of blood interrupted, the spilled blood floods and flattens nearby tissues. Some hemorrhages are created by the bursting of an aneurysm, a weakened area of the artery wall that balloons out into a little pouch. (Aneurysms, which are present from birth, occur in about 10 percent of the population, but the vast majority never rupture.) Most cerebral hemorrhages are associated with high blood pressure (see Chapter Nine, "High Blood Pressure"), but some are related to head injury.

High blood pressure is the single greatest risk factor for strokes caused by clots, emboli and hemorrhage. Having either diabetes or a high red blood cell count also increases a person's chances of having a stroke. So does a diseased heart, which, besides pumping inefficiently, becomes a source of emboli. Alcohol, even in moderate amounts, increases the risk of hemorrhagic stroke, independent of its relationship to blood pressure. And a person who has already had one stroke is at increased risk for having another.

Some strokes take the victim completely by surprise. Others are preceded by little strokes, or transient ischemic attacks (TIAs). Caused by a brief interruption of blood flow to the brain, TIAs produce sudden temporary weakness or numbness on one side of the body, temporary trouble speaking or understanding speech, or temporary loss of vision. In older people, dizziness can sometimes signal a TIA.

Some studies have suggested that drugs that interfere with blood clotting, including heparin and aspirin, may help to reduce the risk of stroke in someone experiencing TIAs, or who has already had a mild stroke. Surgery, too, has been tried. Endarterectomy, for example, is a procedure to remove clots from arteries in the neck. However, surgery can reach only a small percentage of the clots that threaten stroke, and the surgery itself sometimes dislodges emboli that set off strokes.

The symptoms of stroke are similar to those of a TIA—one-sided weakness, loss of speech, dimmed

Stroke

Risk Factors

- High blood pressure
- Heart disease
- Age
- Gender—males are more susceptible
- Family history
- Race—blacks are more susceptible
- Diabetes
- Prior stroke
- Transient ischemic attacks
- High level of red blood cells
- Sickle cell disease
- Smoking
- Stress
- Overweight
- Oral contraceptives with smoking

Preventive Measures

- Control of high blood pressure
- Promoting cardiovascular fitness through a diet low in saturated fats and cholesterol, weight loss, exercise and not smoking
- Control of diabetes

Diagnosis

- Physical examination
- Medical history
- Electroencephalogram (EEG)
- Computerized axial tomography (CAT)

Symptoms

- Loss of muscle control on one side of the body
- Loss of ability to speak or understand speech
- Diminution of vision

Treatment

- Drugs to minimize a stroke in progress
- Physical, occupational and speech therapy
- Aspirin or (rarely) surgery to diminish the risk of future strokes

Outlook

- Nearly one-third of stroke survivors resume their pre-stroke level of activity
- More than one-half manage to carry on activities of daily living, though they may need assistance
- About 15 percent require constant care
- Approximately one-fourth will have another stroke

vision—but rather than disappearing, they persist or worsen. Diagnosis is based on recognition of the evolving symptoms. In addition to a physical examination and a medical history, tests may include an electroencephalogram (EEG), which measures nerve-cell activity in the brain, and a computerized axial tomography (CAT) scan, which can reveal the extent of stroke damage.

While a stroke is in progress, the patient may be given drugs—anticoagulants for a thrombotic stroke, drugs to lower blood pressure or encourage clotting for a hemorrhagic stroke—in an attempt to prevent continuing damage to brain cells. Usually, though, a stroke runs its course undaunted. The acute phase can last from minutes to hours or, rarely, days.

In the two or three days following a severe stroke, brain tissue starts to swell, threatening further damage. Speech and paralysis may improve and then worsen. Some patients rally and improve; others grow worse, or slip into a coma. It is a period of anxious watching and waiting for the family. Doctors will make frequent checks on the patient's reflexes, mobility and feeling, but only time can tell how extensive the damage will be.

When stroke has injured the left side of the brain, paralysis occurs on the right side of the body. In addition, the person will often have difficulties with speech and language, and he or she is apt to be cautious, anxious and disorganized. A person with right-brain damage and left-sided paralysis, in contrast, often experiences difficulty with spatial perceptions, and may behave impulsively and overconfidently. A stroke so massive as to affect the entire body is usually fatal.

Many stroke victims experience a condition known as hemispheric neglect. Damage to one half, or hemisphere, of the brain cuts off input from half of the body. They may be unable to see things in the left (or right) field of vision and neglect objects on that side. Sometimes they fail to use or even acknowledge the limbs on that side of the body.

Many stroke patients lose some control over their emotions, crying or laughing inappropriately, moaning, or lashing out in anger. In addition, some months after a stroke, a person may develop post-stroke depression. This often severe reaction, characterized by anxiety, sleep disturbances, and loss of energy, weight and appetite, appears to be at least as much a part of the brain's response to stroke injury as it is a psychological phenomenon.

A common complication of stroke is aphasia, the inability to use or to make sense of spoken and written language. Aphasia does not, however, affect intelligence; the individual can remain mentally alert even if his or her speech is jumbled or incoherent. Some people know what they want to say but cannot find the words. Others may speak fluently but make little sense. In milder cases, the person may just be unable to come up with the correct names for persons, places or things.

Fortunately, stroke symptoms tend to improve with time. To maximize recovery and to prevent the muscle deterioration that sets in with immobility, rehabilitation and physical therapy should begin as soon as the patient is out of danger. Physical and occupational therapists, social workers, speech and language specialists, and other experts can be called on to help the patient relearn how to walk or sit, improve balance and/or speak clearly.

Many patients recover quickly, reaching their full potential within weeks. For others, recovery is a long, drawn-out process, and some never fully regain their former abilities. However, it is possible for even seriously paralyzed stroke patients to make remarkable progress, and the goal of rehabilitation is to allow each person to lead as independent and productive a life as possible. Stroke victims usually continue rehabilitation therapy after they leave the hospital; some enroll in programs at rehabilitation institutes.

Families, too, can benefit from consulting with trained counselors. Family support and encouragement are essential to the patient's recovery, but family members need to understand what the patient is experiencing. They need to learn how to tap into community resources. And they have to help the patient work out measures to compensate for impairments, obtaining self-help devices and making adjustments around the house. Stroke Clubs, sponsored by area hospitals and/or local chapters of national health organizations, are a good source of information, encouragement and enjoyment for both patients and their families.

For More Information

American Heart Association publications, available from local chapters, include "Recovering from a Stroke," "Strokes: A Guide for the Family," "Up and Around: A Booklet to Aid the Stroke Patient in Activities of Daily Living," and an excellent discussion of physical and behavioral changes written by Roy S. Fowler, Jr. and W. E. Fordyce, "Stroke: Why Do They Behave That Way?" Four times a year AHA publishes "Gaining Ground," a newsletter for stroke patients and their families. Chapters compile information about local sources of stroke treatment and rehabilitation, financial assistance and equipment. They also sponsor Stroke Clubs.

"Stroke: Hope Through Research" and "Aphasia: Hope Through Research" are available from the National Institute of Neurological and Communicative Disorders and Stroke, Bethesda, MD 20892.

The National Easter Seal Society is concerned with treatment and rehabilitation for persons with physical disabilities and speech and language problems. It also sponsors Stroke Clubs. The address is 2023 West Ogden Avenue, Chicago, IL (312/243-8400).

Information concerning federal benefits and services for rehabilitation can be obtained from the Clearinghouse on the Handicapped, Switzer Building, Room 3132, 330 C Street S.W., Washington, DC 20202.

Section IV

Preparing for Long-Term Care

INTRODUCTION

Preparing for Long-Term Care

Perhaps you have been involved in the care of an older relative, directly or indirectly, at some time in your life. You may be responsible for someone's care at this moment: a parent, an in-law, a spouse. Your "care" may involve taking Aunt Mary grocery shopping once a week, or it may mean participating in the family decision to admit Dad to a nursing home, because his Alzheimer's disease is too much for Mother.

As life expectancy has risen, the 65-and-older group has become the fastest-growing segment of our nation's population, and has already outstripped teenagers in number. Increased longevity, however, brings new diseases—illnesses we rarely heard about 30 years ago. Such degenerative diseases as Alzheimer's and osteoporosis have become household words—and worries.

At the same time, increased life expectancy is associated with good health practices. And while advances in medical services help us better manage such chronic ailments as arthritis, diabetes and hypertension, older people remain dependent on formal and informal care systems that provide a range of services from household chores to skilled nursing facilities.

As more people join the ranks of the 65-and-older group, the formal and informal care systems will be stretched to provide appropriate, high-quality care.

Aging, however, has many dimensions in addition to caregiving. For example, corporate America is studying the repercussions of an aging work force on such issues as health care, pensions, productivity and a dwindling young work force.

The Travelers Companies are acknowledged leaders of this corporate thrust. 1979 marked the founding of the Travelers' Older Americans Program, a multi-faceted approach to a changing population. Among its projects are:

- A Meals-on-Wheels program operated out of The Travelers' corporate kitchen.
- A Retirees Job Bank, which enables The Travelers' retirees to work as much as 40 hours a month without pension penalties.
- Sponsorship of seminars and symposia on such issues as older workers and productivity, employment, health and retirement.
- A retiree exercise program that meets twice a week in Hartford, CT.
- Retirement-planning programs for employees and their spouses.
- Financial support and stewardship of research in health care, "wellness," and caregiving.
- Geriatric fellowships that encourage physicians to enter the field and stimulate medical research.

The corporation has also established The Travelers Center for Geriatrics and Gerontology at the University of Connecticut Health Center, and has supported such aging-related research as the 1984 *Study of Older Women: The Economics of Aging*.

Aging is inescapable, and long-term care needs to be examined outside the area of retirement planning. Planning for long-term care must be viewed as a survival skill. Here is why:

- A majority of Americans believe that Medicare pays for custodial nursing home care, when, in fact, it only pays for limited skilled nursing. The average single adult who enters a nursing home is impoverished within 13 weeks.
- The average annual nursing home bill in 1988 was $24,000.
- Eighty percent of caregiving is provided by a family member, usually a wife or daughter.

The burden of caring for an older relative is compounded by the fact that the caregiver is usually "sandwiched" between the needs of an elderly relative and the demands of raising his or her children.

A pioneer study by The Travelers Companies of a 20 percent sample of 7,060 employees over 30 years of age found that 52 percent of their caregivers were in the 41-to-55 age group. Caregiving was defined by The Travelers as caring for a relative or friend age 55 or older "in need of the employee's time or help," and involved a wide range of activities, from telephone calls and visits to choosing a nursing home. Forty-four percent of the care recipients still lived in their own houses or apartments, although 20 percent lived with

the caregiver and 15 percent in a nursing home.
Some other findings were:

- Forty-six percent of those cared for were mothers of the caregiver.
- Overall, 69 percent of those receiving care were female.
- Sixty-three percent of the caregivers were themselves female. Moreover, 18 percent of the male care providers relied on their wives to do most of the work.
- The average age of those receiving help was 77.2 years.
- Thirty-one percent of the caregivers were between the ages of 30 and 40; 72 percent of them had children under 19 living at home.
- Of the 52 percent of the caregivers who were between 41 and 55 years old, 41 percent still had children under 19 at home.
- The average number of hours spent by the employee in caregiving per week was 10.2, with female employees averaging 16.1 hours. Other relatives in or outside the household spent 17.6 hours, and the time of paid help was an average 30.3 hours.
- Twenty percent of the caregivers felt that caregiving interfered with "social and emotional needs and family responsibilities . . . frequently or most of the time"; 60 percent felt that caregiving interfered most of the time.
- Eighty percent of those surveyed by The Travelers felt they did not know enough about available community resources.

In fact, in a study funded by the National Institute of Aging, researchers from Boston University found, through interviews with 635 people requiring care and 429 of their caregivers, that in 27 percent of the cases, available formal care services were not being used. The study concluded that family caregivers needed to know more about such services and to make greater use of them.

These studies not only emphasize the fact that family caregiving is a growing concern, but with the added demand envisioned in the near future, building awareness of resources and delivering services to the caregiver will be major challenges.

This section is written to help you, as a caregiver, address some basic questions involving long-term care. These questions include:

- What are the options, besides a nursing home, for taking care of an older relative?
- What resources are available to me, as the caregiver, and to the care recipient?
- What are the financial ramifications of a specific care option? Who pays?
- What happens if my relative is incapable of making decisions on his or her own? What are an older person's legal options?
- What assistance and support are available to help me, the caregiver, cope with the problems and issues that exist?

This section is not intended, nor should it be perceived, as an exhaustive reference on long-term care issues. Rather, it should be viewed as a primer, an introduction to six CareSkill areas: 1) understanding long-term care, 2) long-term care planning, 3) long-term care resources and support services, 4) financing long-term care, 5) legal concerns and 6) help for family caregivers.

By familiarizing yourself with these basic areas, you will be better able to understand the complex issues of long-term care planning, so that you can make informed decisions for yourself and your loved ones.

CHAPTER ONE

CareSkill One:
Facing Up to a
Predictable Life Event

"Bill and I had planned that when our youngest graduated from college, we would put the house on the market, buy a condo closer to the city, and start doing more of the things we like to do together.

"But then Mother became ill, and our plans were forgotten. I couldn't move farther away from her. Tending to her needs takes up so much time that Bill and I have less freedom now than when the children were little.

"I shouldn't complain. After all, she took care of me when I was growing up. But it's hard to adjust when your life is disrupted. I get so tired and depressed!"

Unfortunately, when planning for the future, many people close their eyes to a significant fact of life: One day they may be faced with the responsibility of caring for a loved one.

Thanks to medical advances, people are living longer than in years past. However, research indicates that these added years are not necessarily healthy ones. For example, in a survey conducted by the national Center for Health Statistics, nearly half of those age 65 and older reported having arthritis. High blood pressure was reported almost as often. Moreover, because this survey did not include hospital or nursing-home patients, the actual incidence of chronic ailments within this age group is likely to be significantly higher. A chronic condition may not necessarily restrict activities, but often the interaction of several conditions will make daily chores difficult or impossible.

Writing in the *Statistical Bulletin* (April-June 1988), James B. Weil states, "It is known that Americans are living longer, but are the added years of life years of vigor and independence or years of frailty and [excessive] dependence? Unfortunately, trend data do not show dramatic gains in the health status of the aged. Instead, it appears that while life expectancy slowly moves up, Americans are rapidly increasing the number of years that they live with significant disabilities. . . . Long-term care is becoming a predictable life event for an increasingly large part of the population."

The reality of disability in a parent, spouse or other loved one is always a terrible blow. Caring for that loved one often requires an enormous commitment of time. It can cause stress, isolation and depression; and it can deplete financial resources.

Family caregivers are often ill-prepared to deal with day-to-day caregiving responsibilities. Our culture offers very few educational or life experiences to teach people how to care for a disabled or frail older person. These skills are developed through trial and error.

Moreover, caregiving can continue for years without any predictable end. The true costs of caregiving are hidden, and cannot be measured in dollars and cents. Though it is not generally acknowledged, the financial costs of home-based care can equal or **surpass** those of nursing-home care!

Does the magnitude of caregiving's impact surprise you? If so, perhaps you have accepted some common misconceptions about who is caring, and not caring, for America's older people.

Myth vs. Reality

When asked to picture an older person requiring care, many people conjure up images of a frail, confused man or woman spending months or years in a nursing home, receiving few, if any, visitors. Somehow this stereotype has become imbedded in our collective consciousness and has given rise to the myth that America has abandoned its older people.

Yet contrary to this widely held belief, 80 percent of those who can no longer remain independent are cared for by family members, most often their spouse or an adult child. The level of care provided varies according to need, from such simple assistance as transportation to shopping areas and appointments to help with complex medical treatments, eating and bathing. The fact is, only 5 percent of the aged are in nursing homes, and most of these people are age 85 or older.

Nevertheless, an estimated 2.3 million people did spend time in nursing homes in 1988, and this number is expected to **triple** by 2018. As the proportion of the population over age 85 increases, nursing homes may not be able to meet the added demand. As a result, some of the "old-old" will have limited care options.

Technology may also play a role in keeping some members of this age group out of nursing homes. The need to reduce the cost of health care, coupled with the escalating older population, has provided an incentive for medical-equipment companies to modify hospital devices for home use. Already, technological advances are enabling many people to obtain sophisticated therapies and treatments outside of an institutional setting. For example:

- Kidney dialysis machines, which once filled an entire room, now can sit on a bedside table, thanks to the development of microprocessors.
- Cardiopulmonary monitors can alert care providers in the home to abnormalities in a patient's breathing or heart rate.
- Computerized pumps can control the drip rate of intravenous (IV) medications and detect problems within the IV line.
- Devices called *oxygen concentrators* can filter oxygen from room air and deliver it directly, through tubes, into the patient's nose and mouth.

These advances are not intended to cure, but to allow sufferers from chronic conditions to remain in a familiar setting. People receiving such sophisticated treatments will still have to depend on a caregiver, usually a family member.

In addition to these complex, sophisticated technological devices, there are simpler technical aids that facilitate day-to-day tasks. They may help the person with low vision or hearing loss or any other of the deficits that often come with age.

As such innovations proliferate, families will come to rely on the support of skilled home-care professionals and the spectrum of long-term care services aimed at promoting independence and optimal functioning.

A Network of Alternatives

Just as it is a myth that most older people are cared for in nursing homes, it is also not true that families have only one alternative to nursing-home care—to take in an aging relative and provide all of the care themselves.

There is a loosely linked array of services to meet the needs of older people with significant health problems or loss of physical, psychological or social functions. These range from services in the home and community-based programs to institutional care. They can be as simple as friendly visiting and congregate-meal programs, or as complex as round-the-clock medical care in a skilled nursing facility.

Experts call this range of services the *spectrum of care*. (See box.) This general phrase offers a good way of thinking about long-term care options—as if, like a spectrum of colors, long-term care services could be lined up

The Spectrum of Care

Think of the spectrum of care as a variety of living arrangements, with supportive services offered in the home, in the community or in an institutional setting. Some services do not fit neatly into one category. For example, in congregate housing arrangements ("retirement homes") the individual maintains private living quarters but receives services in a centralized location. Refer to Chapter Three for descriptions of these services.

Services Provided in the Home

- Emergency response systems
- Telephone reassurance
- Friendly visiting
- Chore services
- Home-delivered meals
- Companion services
- Homemaker-home health aides
- Skilled home care
- Respite services
- Hospice care

Community-Based Services

- Congregate meals
- Senior centers
- Adult day care
- Board and care homes
- Congregate housing
- Group homes
- Shared living

Institutional Care

- Nursing homes:
  — Custodial care
  — Intermediate care
  — Skilled nursing

in order, from least invasive or restrictive to most intensive. All of the services along the spectrum share two goals: improving the quality of life and keeping older or disabled people as independent as possible.

Many older people take care of themselves as well as they ever did and require little, if any, outside aid. Some benefit from minimal assistance—a friendly telephone call, a ride to the supermarket, someone to wash the windows. Others need help preparing meals, caring for their homes and maintaining social contacts. Some may benefit from the protective and therapeutic environment of an adult day care center. Still others may require regular assistance in complying with prescribed medical treatments and therapies, or with such daily functions as dressing, bathing, toileting and eating.

At every stage of life, feelings of personal control— being able to live independently and make one's own decisions—contribute to fulfillment and well-being. Inability to control events is highly stressful and can lead to both physical and emotional illness. Time does not alter our need for control. In fact, as we age, maintaining independence becomes even more important in preserving self-worth. We often try to ensure that we do not compound losses—some physical or mental limitation does not mean that a person loses the ability to make decisions.

The spectrum of care can be thought of as a system of living arrangements, in which caregiving services complement the individual's own capabilities and the assistance of family members on an ongoing basis, to provide the highest degree of independence possible. While they do not make caregiving a simple task, long-term care services can ease the burden and normalize life **as much as possible** for caregivers and care recipients alike.

The U.S. Health Services Administration sums up the long-term care network as a system consisting of "those services designed to provide diagnostic, preventive, therapeutic, rehabilitative, supportive and maintenance services for individuals . . . who have chronic mental and/or physical impairments in a variety of institutional and non-institutional health-care settings, including the home, with the goal of promoting the optimum level of physical, social and psychological functions."

Barriers to Long-Term Care

Ideally, each person would receive the most appropriate long-term care services as needed throughout the later years. Yet at present several obstacles stand in the way of this objective:

- **Ignorance of available services.** Before you can take hold of a helping hand, you have to know that it is outstretched and waiting. Regrettably, a large number of older people and their families are not aware of available services that could provide an alternative to institutional care.

The same research that measured the extent of caregiving in our society also demonstrated a need for more knowledge about available services. For example, in The Travelers' survey, four out of five caregivers expressed a need for more information about community resources, insurance coverage and related issues.

Lacking such information, family members often shoulder a heavy load until the burden becomes unmanageable, when they reluctantly decide to place their loved one in a nursing home. When nursing-home admission is appropriate, an older person's health and quality of life can actually improve, and the family can gain a release from the stress and guilt of not being able to care properly for the older person. But viewing the nursing home as the **only** alternative to family-provided care benefits neither caregiver nor care recipient. In this situation, family members become exhausted and guilt-ridden, believing they have let down their aging relative. In turn, the older person is denied the opportunity to live as normal a life as possible. It is important for all caregivers to know that most communities have senior information and referral services. The number should be listed in the phone book.

- **Rejection of services**. Sometimes older people refuse to accept care and thus build their own barrier against independence. They may see their refusal as proof that they can function unassisted and view care services as the route to dependence rather than self-direction.

When these people do ask for assistance, it is frequently too late. Their insistence on doing without needed services has resulted in malnutrition, a broken bone suffered in a fall, or some other impediment to independent functioning. These individuals could benefit from the thoughtful attention and intervention of a social worker.

- **Gaps in the spectrum of care.** The spectrum of care exists more in theory than in practice. The size of a community may limit the number and variety of services available. Home health and chore services are common gaps in many communities. Some services might already be filled to capacity. Nursing homes may have long waiting lists or may not be close to the family.

- **Financial realities that create gaps, too.** Long-term care can be expensive. Currently, the average cost of nursing-home care is $24,000 per year. Skilled home care costs range from $15 to $35 per hour. Under some conditions, health insurance,

Medicare and Medicaid will help pay for these services—but often not as much as people think. And there are no guarantees that care will be provided: Some nursing homes are unwilling to care for patients who have become eligible for Medicaid, for example.

According to a House Select Committee on Aging staff analysis, more than 200 million Americans are underinsured for long-term care, often because they are not aware of Medicare's exclusions. Remember, Medicare is designed to cover acute, not chronic, care. Medicaid does cover long-term care, but only if your income is **very** low. Unfortunately, many people "spend down" most of their income and assets to become Medicaid-eligible.

So bear in mind that the spectrum is not always complete. It may very well contain significant gaps. It's important to pay attention to new legislative efforts to ensure a basic floor of protection for all Americans and, if you have the resources, check around for one of the new private long-term care policies.

A Topic Too Often Ignored

There is an additional barrier: Reluctance to face up to harsh realities. No one likes to think that he or she will one day require such assistance or become a "burden" to family members. No one likes to think loved ones are going to change. Hence, the eventuality of long-term care is a neglected issue in many families.

Even those willing to face these possibilities hesitate to bring up the subject for fear that they will be misunderstood. "We don't want Dad to think we are prying into his financial affairs"; "We don't want Aunt Mary to think we are eager for an inheritance"; "We don't want Mom to see our concern as an attempt to take away her independence."

It's much easier to ignore the topic and hope that everyone will remain well or assume that you will work things out when the time comes. Such tactics are unrealistic and can lead to heartbreak. Long-term care possibilities need to be talked about frankly, even with parents who have always enjoyed optimal health.

As Barbara Silverstone and Helen Kandel Hyman, authors of *You and Your Aging Parents*, point out, "It's wonderful to be able to say, as some fifty-year-old sons and daughters can, 'Mother's eighty but she looks sixty-five and does everything for herself. Last year she traveled to Europe alone.' " Yet, the authors warn, "The strong possibility is that this eighty-year-old will run into difficulty before she's finished unless a massive stroke, a fatal heart attack, or a plane crash makes it possible for her to die with her boots on."

In other words, for an older person to die swiftly and without warning is the exception rather than the rule. Eventually, just about everyone who lives long enough can expect to lose some ability to function that could create a need for assistance from others. It may simply be a decline in vision or hearing, or the onset of a chronic disease, such as diabetes, hypertension or arthritis.

Chapter Two, "Planning for Long-Term Care," outlines the planning process, which can help you minimize the stress and financial impact of caregiving and point the way to maximizing independence and quality of life for all family members.

CHAPTER TWO

CareSkill Two:
Planning for Long-Term Care

Your widowed mother has just had hip surgery and is ready to come home. What are you going to do?

Often people don't even begin to plan for long-term care until such an emergency strikes. It sometimes takes a crisis to uncover the need for such arrangements, but by then families are anxious and overwhelmed, and find it difficult to make decisions.

This situation can be avoided if people start thinking early about long-term care options. In other words, even if there's no need now, it's wise to begin laying the groundwork. Talk with your mother or other older relative; listen to his or her ideas and preferences; evaluate the probable nature of future needs and determine whether financial resources are available. A clear knowledge of your relative's values—before the need arises—will help you enormously when you have to make decisions later.

Discussing such sensitive issues isn't easy, but it may not be as difficult as you think, particularly if you approach it thoughtfully. Show your concern and love. Start with a question: "Mom, I worry sometimes. Suppose you get to the point that you can't manage alone, what do you plan to do? Is there some way that I can help you?" You might be surprised to find that your mother or other loved one has given the matter great thought and already has plans.

Even so, it's wise for you to know what those plans are and whether they will be adequate to meet future needs. Look at the available options and consider all aspects of the older person's life. The following considerations will help you cover all of the bases.

- **Preferred lifestyle.** Would the older person be willing to move to be closer to the family? Would he or she **prefer** to remain in the same home or to investigate alternative living arrangements? Does he or she want to pursue special activities or hobbies?

- **Financial considerations.** What are the older person's resources? Should a nursing home be needed, will there be funds to supplement Medicare? Does your loved one want to look into long-term care insurance to protect his or her assets should institutional care be required?

- **Legal considerations.** Does your relative have an up-to-date will? What will happen if he or she becomes mentally incapacitated? Should the need arise, here are some things to consider: A *power of attorney* gives a designated individual limited authority to handle financial matters for another, so long as the person is able to enter into any contracts made on his or her behalf. Should your mother or another older person become mentally incapacitated, that power of attorney is automatically terminated. A *durable power of attorney*, however, remains valid even in the event of incapacity. In many states a *durable power of attorney for health care* will allow a designated person to make treatment decisions. A *living will*, legal in most states, specifies whether heroic measures are to be used to keep that person alive. (See Chapter Five for more information on the legal aspects of long-term care.)

  Discussions of this nature should include a clarification of values. It's important to understand and respect the older person's views.

- **Available services.** Make sure your relative is aware of the various services that are available within the home, in the community and in an institutional setting to meet specific needs. If you, yourself, are not sure of what's available, check it out. Talk to someone at a senior center, your local information and referral service, or your Area Agency on Aging. (Refer to Chapter Three.)

  Tell your loved one about the services that will help him or her maintain the greatest degree of independence.

- **The informal care network.** Often this—a cadre of family members, friends and neighbors—is the best solution, if these people can pitch in and help with such needs as transportation, housekeeping and, most of all, companionship. These "networks" can be extended to include the members of social, recreational and religious groups or clubs.

- **Maintaining health—and independence.** Encourage the older person to practice appropriate Life-Skills, such as not smoking, remaining physically active, eating well, maintaining social contacts and having periodic medical screening tests. Stress that these will help maintain vigor and independence and guard against a premature need for long-term care.

- **Safety.** Older people are more likely than others to suffer serious injuries from falls and other accidents. Be sure your relative's home is safe. (See Section II, Chapter Eleven, for details on personal safety.)

- **Preparing for an emergency.** Ask your loved one to furnish you with the names and telephone numbers of his or her primary care physician, any specialists who may also be providing care, and his or her attorney; the names and dosages of all medications being taken (prescription and non-prescription); his or her hospital of preference; and the location of insurance policies, financial records, a will and any other legal papers.

- **What is to happen in the event of death?** Because they are in the later years of life, many older people have thought about their funerals. Your relative may have definite wishes about such issues as the kind of religious service to be held, how much the funeral should cost, and decisions on interment. Also, he or she may prefer cremation to burial, or wish to make an anatomical gift.

Though these topics may be difficult to discuss, addressing them now can help ensure that your loved one's wishes are understood and that they will be honored. In addition, it can spare family members the stress and burden of making funeral arrangements in the midst of mourning.

If the older person is unfamiliar with funeral costs and practices, suggest that he or she do some comparison shopping. Funeral directors are required by law to quote prices over the telephone, and to provide an itemized list of their charges on request.

If the older person wishes to leave funeral instructions in writing, a "letter of last request" can be prepared. One copy can be retained by family members and a second held for safe keeping by a member of the clergy, attorney or other trusted individual. Funeral arrangements should not be outlined in a will, because wills often are not read until after the deceased has been laid to rest.

Your loved one can also arrange to leave his or her body to a medical school or to donate the corneas, kidneys or other organs for transplant or research. Anyone wishing to bequeath a body can receive information on the procedure to follow by calling a local memorial society. To obtain a Uniform Donor Card, which is to be signed and carried by someone planning to make an anatomical gift, contact the Living Bank, P.O. Box 6725, Houston, TX 77005.

What Are Your Needs? How Much Will You Be Able to Handle?

The older person's needs will be paramount in an emergency, but you should be realistic in deciding how much help you can give by weighing the needs of your **own** family and your personal priorities. Here are some questions to help you weigh the effect caregiving may have on you.

- Will it prove too much for you? Are you already under a great deal of stress at home or at work? Do you have the physical and emotional energy for caregiving?
- How much time can you spare?
- What will the financial impact be? Would you be required to reduce your work hours, or take a leave of absence?
- How might caregiving affect your marriage or other important relationships?
- If you have children, do they need a lot of supervision? Could your family handle your divided attention? Would they resent your absence? Would you be unhappy over the loss of some family time?
- Do you have a good relationship with the older person? Could it stand the added tensions that would arise?
- Do you have good friends in whom you can confide? Are you able to talk out your feelings?

Should the Older Person Come Into Your Home?

This is not a question to be taken lightly or answered quickly. Try to imagine what the impact would be on your family—your spouse, your children and yourself. Discuss these issues with family members.

While multi-generational living can make for happy families, sharing one roof can also create friction. If you should move your loved one into your home and it doesn't work out, what then? Hurt, guilt and stress would surely arise. An older person who then had to move out—to a retirement or nursing home—would face yet another adjustment. Such changes tax everyone's emotional stamina.

So, be careful. Don't make hasty or ill-considered decisions, and above all, don't make promises you can't keep. If your relative wants to move in and you don't think it will work, say honestly, but not harshly, that it would not be a good idea for anyone concerned, that such an arrangement could jeopardize relationships too precious to damage.

Discussing such issues requires delicacy and a sensitivity to the desires of your loved one. Remember, it's not your life; therefore, what the older person does—unless he or she is mentally incapacitated— must be his or her choice. Your role is to make sure that the older person has all of the necessary information to make an informed decision.

Sometimes, it is better for one adult child to talk to an aging parent; in other instances, a family conference is more effective. Follow the family style and do what seems most comfortable for all concerned. No matter what, be sure your loved one knows the concern is shared by everyone. And remember, building strong lines of communication now will help in care planning later. Most importantly, respect your aging relative as you would want to be respected yourself.

When the Crisis Comes—What Now?

Whether the disability is sudden and major, or gradual, it's heartbreaking to realize that this loved one may never be the same; it is distressing to know that he or she can no longer remain independent, as before. You may feel like an emotional shipwreck, but if you have done your preplanning, you won't feel completely lost at sea. Your accumulated knowledge, understanding and support can act as your "navigational charts" in providing for your loved one's care.

Once the disability has been recognized and the immediate crisis has passed, the family will need to institute an action plan that will help the older family member live as independently and comfortably as possible within the limitations of his or her condition.

The following six-step problem-solving technique, adapted from Xerox Corporation's employee involvement program, is an effective way to establish a viable care plan:

1. Identify the problem.
2. Analyze the problem.
3. Generate potential solutions.
4. Choose the best solution.
5. Implement the solution.
6. Evaluate the solution.

Let's look at each of the steps in detail and see how they apply to long-term care issues.

Step One: Identify the problem. A problem cannot be solved until it has been clearly defined. You must progress from realizing that, generally, "Something is wrong," to understanding specifically what that "something" is.

The goal of Step One is to state the problem briefly, in a single sentence, as objectively as possible. This is not the time to list any reasons for the problem or possible solutions to it, but to look at the problem itself. (Refer to the "Care Management Planning Guide" at the end of this chapter to review some common caregiving problems.)

Sometimes there is more than one problem. If you state the problem as accurately as possible and your sentence still seems too general, try breaking the problem down.

Your stated problem might be similar to one of the following:

1. "Mr. McCarthy has suffered a significant loss of mobility. He is unable to speak, and his memory may be impaired."

2. "Aunt Rose's clothes are not clean. Her refrigerator contains many old or outdated food items, and her sheets have not been changed in some time."

Once you have defined the problem, compose a second statement, one that expresses the "desired state"—the goal that you expect to achieve by solving the problem.

Here are some examples of how people identifying the need for long-term care might state their goals:

1. "Mr. McCarthy regains as much of his lost ability as possible."

2. "Aunt Rose continues to live in her apartment, which is kept clean and safe."

Step Two: Analyze the problem. This is the stage at which you investigate the cause or causes of the problem. To begin, you might ask yourself, "What's keeping us from reaching the desired state?" This will point you in the right direction as you look for more information.

When gathering your data, strive for objectivity. Stick to the facts and try to separate opinions based on emotion from objective observations. People's **opinions**, while well intended, may be clouded by personal involvement and may not reflect what's best for their loved one.

In cases where the loss of functioning is severe, a formal assessment should be done in conjunction with a physician, nurse, social worker, geriatric case manager, hospital discharge planner or your Area Agency on Aging (AAA).

This assessment will evaluate the individual's ability to complete several *activities of daily living* (ADL), common functions that are necessary for self-care and independent living. At the most basic level, the activities assessed are eating, being able to move in or out of a chair or bed, dressing, bathing, and attending to oneself at the toilet. The health professional performing the assessment will determine whether the patient can perform each activity unaided, with assistance or not at all.

A more advanced scale would assess such activities as handling personal finances, preparing meals, shopping, traveling and doing housework.

The results of this assessment will aid in determining the most suitable long-term care services, the level of skill required, the need for environmental support and whether a change in housing is warranted. They may also provide justification for Medicare reimbursement.

When the changes you observe in an older person

do not appear to be major, you can perform your own informal assessment.

Begin the assessment by asking several general questions:

- Can the person carry out chores alone, or is help needed?
- Are chores harder to perform today than they were six months ago?
- Does the individual fail to perform chores or other activities more often than he or she did six months ago?
- Does the older adult feel safe at home and in the community?

Next, zero in on specific tasks. Observe how well your relative performs these activities:

- Bathing, dressing and grooming.
- Preparing meals and performing housekeeping chores.
- Completing minor household repairs.
- Getting around the house.
- Shopping and running errands.
- Driving a car or using public transportation.
- Walking and climbing stairs.
- Taking medications.
- Paying bills and handling other financial matters.
- Doing outdoor yard work.

Questions to ask the older person's spouse, relatives and friends include indicators of emotional well-being. Ask if the older person:

- Has trouble getting out of bed in the morning.
- Feels overwhelmed by problems.
- Has withdrawn from social activities.
- Experiences more interpersonal conflicts.

Your assessment will give you a clearer idea of the problem. In some circumstances, your informal assessment may help you to realize that a professional assessment is needed.

Once you have analyzed the situation, return to your original statement describing the problem. Very likely it will need to be revised.

Here's how our earlier statements might be revised after the assessments are carried out:

1. "Mr. McCarthy's stroke has caused paralysis on his right side, has left him unable to speak intelligibly and has affected his short-term memory. He will require assistance with many activities of daily living as well as physical and speech therapy" (following a formal assessment).

2. "Because of her declining vision, Aunt Rose doesn't notice items that are soiled or unsafe. She lacks the strength to perform certain chores, such as lifting a mattress to change a fitted sheet" (following an informal assessment).

Step Three: Generate potential solutions. This is the "brainstorming" stage, when you investigate every possible way to meet the older person's care needs.

Your original investigation of formal and informal resources, conducted during the preplanning stage, can serve as your starting point. You can begin by contacting the agencies and individuals you identified at that time, to determine what services they might provide and, if applicable, the costs of those services and whether there is a waiting period. (Refer to the "Care Management Planning Guide" at the end of this chapter to help you identify possible resources for addressing specific problems.)

Quality is also very important. Check out credentials, get references for facilities such as nursing homes and make on-site inspections.

You should never feel that the job of investigating potential sources of help is one that you must undertake alone. It's much wiser to take advantage of the ideas and expertise of others—family members and friends as well as caregiving professionals.

- First and foremost, the older person should be involved in the planning process to the extent that he or she is able, to express preferences, share ideas and fully understand the available options.
- Relatives and friends can sometimes offer creative suggestions or tell you about ways other families have met similar care needs. Some may even volunteer to perform needed tasks.
- If your older relative is being discharged from a hospital or another care facility, solicit suggestions from the physician, hospital discharge planner or social worker. This person may have helped assess your loved one's ability to function, and thus may be especially sensitive to his or her needs.
- Your Area Agency on Aging (AAA) is a source of much information (see box). Established by Congress in 1973 under an amendment to the Older Americans Act, AAAs maintain a complete listing of available services, both government-sponsored and private. AAA staff can assess the older person's functioning and recommend the most appropriate resources to meet his or her needs.
- The geriatric case manager is a new kind of professional, specially trained in services for the aging. The geriatric case manager can be particularly helpful when there are multiple needs (see page 185). He or she can coordinate social services for the patient, keep the family informed, make daily or weekly visits, check on personal needs, help fill out Medicare forms and perform other needed services. Not surprisingly, however, such services have a price. The cost of an initial consultation may range from $40 to $100, although local mental health agencies

Your Area Agency on Aging: What It Can Do for You

The approximately 650 Area Agencies on Aging (AAAs) in the United States were created as a result of amendments to the 1965 Older Americans Act. Your AAA is the local extension of a network that includes the Administration on Aging at the federal level as well as your state unit on aging.

AAA plans, develops and coordinates services to meet the short-term and long-term needs of older people living in your region. Sometimes AAA provides those services directly, but often it monitors and funds local service providers.

AAA helps all people age 60 and older obtain needed services, but preference is given to those with the greatest economic or social need. Contributions are welcome, but no one is denied AAA's assistance because of inability to pay.

Although services vary in different communities, your AAA can generally help you locate the following:

- Adult day care
- Assistance with shopping
- Employment opportunities
- Escort services
- Friendly visiting
- Home-health aides
- Homemakers and chore services
- Housing services
- Information and referral services
- Legal assistance
- Mental health services
- Nursing home/adult home placement
- Nutrition programs
- Ombudsman services
- Respite care
- Retirement planning
- Senior centers
- Telephone reassurance
- Transportation
- Visiting nurses

and Area Agencies on Aging may have less expensive case-management resources.

You can locate a geriatric case manager by looking in the Yellow Pages under Aging Services, Social Services or Social Workers. Also, an information and referral service, senior center, Area Agency on Aging office, visiting nurse agency or hospital discharge planner may be able to recommend someone.

But be careful: This is a new field, and its practitioners are not regulated or licensed. Check out the practitioner's credentials, experience and knowledge of community resources. Get personal and business references. Be certain you understand the fee structure, what the charges cover, and who is responsible for your loved one's case.

Also, don't turn over all responsibility to the case manager. Whenever possible, your older relative should be an active partner in his or her care plan, with you providing support.

If the older person is unable to make decisions regarding care, one person should be designated to represent his or her interests in discussions with the case manager, physician and any other health professionals. Family members who take on this responsibility sometimes hesitate to make any decisions for fear of making the wrong one. Caregiving professionals often counsel that it is better not to view health care decisions in terms of "right" or "wrong," but to make the best decision you can given the facts as they are known.

Returning to the problem-solving process, let's look at the potential solutions that were generated for Mr. McCarthy and Aunt Rose.

- For Mr. McCarthy, it was determined that there were two nursing-home options that offered the custodial care he needed. Windhaven, just 20 miles from his son's home, had a four-to-six-month waiting list. Hillside Manor, 100 miles away, could accommodate him immediately.

  Another, less expensive, option was home care. A home-health aide could help with such tasks as bathing, dressing and shaving, and a physical therapist and speech-language pathologist could visit the home periodically.

  The family could also provide some custodial care, and as Mr. McCarthy improved, he could spend some time in an adult day care center.

- The first step for Aunt Rose was an eye exam, to see if new glasses would aid her vision. Her care options included a housekeeper once a week to do general cleaning and laundry, and, on occasion, a chore service to take care of heavier tasks.

  A niece and a nephew could have performed these tasks themselves, but they lived 90 minutes away and both worked full time. They could not visit every week.

A neighbor was willing to visit every few days to keep an eye on Aunt Rose's functioning and ask about her needs. The neighbor also volunteered to take Aunt Rose shopping and invite her for dinner occasionally.

Step Four. Choose the best solution. Your search will probably turn up more than one way to meet your relative's needs. The patient and all involved family members must weigh the advantages, disadvantages and costs of each alternative and see how each measures up against several criteria:

- **The older person's needs and preferences.** When there is more than one way to meet a particular need, look at the added benefits of each service. For example, an older person who is not getting adequate nutrition might benefit from home-delivered meals or from congregate meals served at a senior center or other centralized location. If the adult is able to get out of the house without difficulty and longs for social contact as well, the congregate meal program is the better choice. However, a homebound individual would require the delivery service. Always try to find out what his or her priorities and preferences are.

- **Available financial resources.** Most often, this is the deciding factor. For those receiving Social Security and a fixed pension who do not have long-term care insurance, the $24,000 or more per year that a nursing home would cost makes it truly a last resort. Home care in some cases is less expensive, but it, too, is costly when the individual needs a great deal of supervision. Family members must sometimes decide whether they can contribute some of the costs, or whether they must perform some custodial services themselves, perhaps feeding, dressing and bathing the individual. Either way, the direct and indirect costs of family caregiving can limit care options quickly. For many families, the only option becomes that of "spending down," mentioned earlier. Although it allows the older person to qualify for Medicaid, it is often psychologically painful. In some states, the threshold for Medicaid eligibility is so low that it is very difficult to qualify.

- **What family members are willing and able to commit in the way of time, money and direct assistance.** Many families must make difficult decisions regarding the impact of caregiving on their present way of life and their plans for the future. Also, some may be willing to help, but live too far away to provide needed assistance themselves.

The severity of the older person's disability will affect the selection process, too. In the case of Aunt Rose, for example, the decision-making was easy. The homemaker and chore services were not too expensive, and they could satisfy Aunt Rose's needs better than her niece and nephew could; but her younger relatives were still able to visit once a month. The neighbor's kind offer of companionship was gratefully accepted.

Things weren't so simple for Mr. McCarthy's family, though. They had to decide between the demands of caring for a severely disabled person at home, which, even with outside help, would be taxing, and the expense and emotional turmoil of placing someone they cared about in a custodial-care facility.

When deciding is difficult, Barbara Silverstone and Helen Kandel Hyman, authors of *You and Your Aging Parent*, recommend calling a family conference, primarily to avoid some of the too-frequent unhappy outcomes of long-term care decision-making: one family member taking matters into his or her own hands, relatives blaming one another for the process's outcome, and the older person making a poor adjustment to an institution he or she may feel forced to enter.

It's important to emphasize that the family conference should be directed at helping the older relative to reach a solution about care unless he or she is incapacitated, in which case a coordinator and spokesperson should be appointed. This is especially important when dealing with medical issues, because information flowing from the physician, nurse, therapists and other members of the medical team should be directed toward one family member.

A family conference "provides the forum for open communication between all members, including the older person himself," say Silverstone and Hyman. "Here is the opportunity to air all objections, discuss all disagreements, and consider all preferences."

A special effort should be made to include family members who live far away. Even though they say, "Do what you think best," they are just as likely as anyone else to have preferences and suggestions, and to resent being left out.

Step Five. Implement the solution. Once you have evaluated all of the options and selected the solution, or care plan, that seems most appropriate, you are ready to put your plan into practice.

It is crucial to remember that you can't be sure the plan will work until you try it. So avoid being too optimistic, but take some initial steps to help ensure success; and be prepared, so that if your plan doesn't work out as expected, you won't be back at square one.

Make sure that everyone understands the plan. Just because you have explained the care plan to other family members, don't assume they understand it. It may help to follow some advice from experts in inter-

Caring From Afar

When infirmity or illness strikes an older person, family caregivers who live far away face a special set of problems. Often, they cannot afford to commute between their home and that of their loved one to provide needed care. Their attempts to pull together resources from far afield are frustrating. They often feel guilty about not doing enough.

Long-distance caregiving is a manageable task, but it is one that requires your best organizational skills.

Caregiving professionals offer these suggestions:

- Talk with your older relative, and work together to assess needs, solve problems and develop a care plan.

- Observe your loved one during visits. Pay attention to his or her diet, interaction with others, mobility and handling of financial matters.

- Explore the informal care network that may already exist. Friends, neighbors, and members of social and religious groups may be willing to help or may already be assisting your relative in some ways. Perhaps these individuals can do more. For example, a neighbor who occasionally brings groceries may be able to stop by more frequently.

    Write down each person's name, address and telephone number before you head home, and be sure each one knows how to contact you.

- If you are unfamiliar with available services in the area, speak with someone at a local senior center, information and referral service, or Area Agency on Aging, or enlist the help of a geriatric case manager or social worker. In large cities, there are reputable social workers who can supervise care.

    When you contact service agencies, explain the older person's needs as specifically as possible. Be sure that you and the group communicate when needed. Call in periodically to show your appreciation and get an update on your relative's situation.

- Continued checks through thank-you notes and calls let caregivers know that although you live far away, you are still deeply involved in your loved one's care.

personal communication, and ask the others to restate the plan to you, using their own words. That way, any misconceptions should become evident.

Another idea is to get the plan down on paper. Ask the other family members to read it over, and solicit their questions and comments.

Get clear commitments from others. Ask the other family members to specify the roles they will play in carrying out the plan. For example, if someone volunteers to take your older relative shopping, find out how often, and when. If another agrees to provide telephone reassurance, try to work out a schedule. To avoid future misunderstandings, write down each person's commitment alongside the care plan.

Throughout the implementation process, follow up on whether each person is fulfilling his or her commitment.

Have a contingency plan. If one way of meeting the older person's needs doesn't work out, have a second plan ready to implement, if possible.

For example, Mr. McCarthy's family chose not to place him in a nursing home right away, but to try caring for him at home, with outside help. However, they put his name on the waiting list at the nursing home in case things did **not** work out.

Step Six. Evaluate the solution. Your task in Step Six is to determine whether the long-term care plan you have selected and implemented is meeting the older person's needs.

One way to do this is to return to your description of the desired state, composed in Step One: How much improvement has Mr. McCarthy made? Does the assistance Aunt Rose is receiving enable her to live independently in a clean, safe environment? If the older person seems no closer to the desired state than before the plan was implemented, can you determine why?

There are some other questions to ask when evaluating your care plan:

- Is the older person happy with the arrangements that have been made? If not, can you identify the factors that are causing the unhappiness?
- How about the other family members—are they comfortable with their roles in providing care?
- Have the older person's needs changed since the care plan was implemented? For instance, it may be time to consider hospice care for a terminally ill loved one, rather than to continue skilled nursing care. Or perhaps the older person's condition has improved, and he or she can begin spending some time in an adult day care center. Therefore, would it be helpful to obtain a new professional assessment at this time?

Planning Never Stops

As people change, needs change. This means that planning for care is an ongoing process. It's wise to evaluate your care plan periodically to see whether the older person's needs are still being met, or whether new needs have evolved.

If you determine that needs have changed, that is, if you perceive some decline or improvement in the older person's ability to function, it may help to return to Step One of the problem-solving process, and begin again to identify your problem.

As a process, long-term care planning can be cyclical, in that the final step, evaluating your plan, can lead you back to Step One. Knowing how to plan for long-term care will enable you to make effective decisions, whether you act independently or in partnership with health care professionals.

Long-Term Care Planning Checklist

You can't plan for something as complex as long-term care simply by checking off items on a list, but you can use the following checklist as a **guide**, to be sure that you cover the most important points.

Preplanning

These are the topics that need to be discussed:

* **Desired lifestyle**
  — Willingness to move
  — Favorite activities
  — Social/community network
* **Estate planning**
  — How assets should be used
  — Long-term care insurance
  — Up-to-date will
  — Funeral preparations
* **Legal issues**
  — Power of attorney, durable power of attorney or durable power of attorney for health care
  — Living will
  — Organ donations
* **Available long-term care services**
  — Home-based services
  — Services provided in the community
  — Institutional services—nursing homes and the like
* **Informal care network**
  — Family members who might be able to help
  — Friends and neighbors who could assist
  — Members of social and religious organizations
* **Healthy living**
  — Regular physical activity
  — Nutrition
  — Medical self-care
  — Not smoking
  — Being substance-free
  — Stress management
  — Financial planning
  — Personal safety

Geriatric Case Management

For frail and disabled older people requiring multiple long-term care services, geriatric case management can be a way to maintain the highest possible level of independence in the midst of what has been called "a fragmented, duplicative, and confusing non-system"!

If they are able and willing, clients can act as their own case managers, coordinating services themselves or in cooperation with a family member.

Another option is to enlist the services of a professional case manager, usually a nurse or social worker, who may be employed by a home-health care agency, hospital, nursing home or case-management organization, or who may be in private practice. Some insurance companies provide case-management services as well. Case managers are also called care managers.

1. **Assessing need.** The older person's health and ability to complete activities of daily living must be evaluated either informally or professionally, by a trained, multidisciplinary team.
2. **Planning care.** Available services must be identified, and a plan developed to address the older adult's needs.
3. **Implementing and coordinating program delivery.** Care can be provided either formally (e.g., homemaker services) or informally (e.g., a family member furnishing transportation). Respite services may be provided for the family caregiver.
4. **Follow-up.** The case manager monitors the quality and appropriateness of care, and how the patient is responding to that care.
5. **Reassessment.** The case manager remains alert to any change in the older person's status, and is prepared to implement or discontinue services as needed.

- **Emergency preparedness**
  — Names and telephone numbers of physicians (Refer to Appendix I, the Personal Health Record.)
  — Name and telephone number of attorney
  — Names and dosages of medications being taken
  — Hospital of preference
  — Location of legal and financial documents, the will and insurance policies

When Disability Occurs

Follow the six-step problem-solving process:

- **Identify the problem**
  — Define, or state, the problem
  — If necessary, break the problem down into smaller problems
  — Define the desired state

- **Analyze the problem**
  — Perform an informal assessment of your relative's abilities, if appropriate
  — Obtain a formal assessment of the your relative's abilities, if needed
  — Revise your definition of the problem

- **Generate potential solutions**
  — Contact agencies and individuals identified in the preplanning stage
  — Determine services provided, availability, costs and quality
  — Seek help finding other resources from your Area Agency on Aging, hospital discharge planner or social worker, information and referral service, physician, or geriatric case manager
  — Ask all involved family members, including the patient, for input

- **Choose the best solution**
  Match available services with:
  — The older person's needs and preferences
  — Available sources of funding
  — What family members are able to commit
  — Hold a family conference, if appropriate

- **Implement the solution**
  Make sure that:
  — Everyone understands the plan
  — Clear commitments have been obtained
  — There is a contingency plan

- **Evaluate the solution**
  — Is the older person living more independently and comfortably than before the plan was implemented?
  — Is he or she happy? If not, why not?
  — Are family members comfortable in their caregiving roles?
  — Have the older person's needs changed?
  — Is it time for a new assessment?

Information and Referral Services: An Important First Step

Information and referral services (I&Rs) provide exactly what their name implies: information on the types of assistance available in the community and referrals to specific agencies and organizations. For those who are unfamiliar with long-term care services, an I&R can serve as an important beginning resource.

You can find an I&R by looking in your telephone directory's "Guide to Human Services," or in the Yellow Pages under "Social Service Organizations." The United Way sponsors more than 400 I&Rs and, together with the Alliance of Information and Referral Services, has developed operating standards for these services. For more information, contact:

The United Way of America
National Agencies Division
801 N. Fairfax Street
Alexandria, VA 22314

If no I&R exists in your area, similar assistance can be obtained from your Area Agency on Aging or your State Unit on Aging, which may operate a toll-free information line.

Care Management Planning Guide*

   Identifying appropriate resources to meet a specific care need can be difficult. The following tables will help you identify common problems and specific resource options. Whenever possible we have cross-referenced each option to a particular service discussed at length in Chapter Three, "The Spectrum of Care," or to pages elsewhere in this text.

My Relative . . .	Services Needed	Options	Refer to Pages:
. . . needs to get out and do something.	Socialization/Volunteering—Programs designed to provide an opportunity to socialize with peers or to offer service without compensation	Nutrition sites Senior centers Adult day care Companion services YMCA/YWCA Recreation departments Retired Senior Volunteer Program AARP Talent Bank United Way	205 206 207 197 — — — 245 186
. . . can do light house-cleaning but needs assistance with heavy tasks.	Chore Services—Window washing, mowing lawn, roof repair, minor housing repair	Area Agency on Aging Churches or synagogues Fraternal organizations Youth groups Neighborhood clubs United Way	182 195 — — — 186
. . . has some legal matters that need attention.	Legal—Assistance with matters pertaining to law	Area Agency on Aging Legal Councils for the Elderly Legal Aid Banks Adult protective services	182 245 186 — —
. . . is grieving over the death of a loved one.	Bereavement Support—Dealing with the normal grieving process	American Association of Retired Persons National Association of Military Widows United Way Mental health association Home health agency or hospice	245 — 186 224-227 201
. . . cannot drive or use public transportation and taxicabs.	Transportation—Special transportation for older persons	Private transportation Handicapped transportation American Red Cross Local churches or synagogues Adult day care United Way	— — — 205 207 186
. . . is unable to remain in his/her present housing.	Housing—Special housing options are available to the elderly	Housing options Institutional settings United Way City or local government	202-203 212-215 186 —

(Care management is also called case management.)

*Adapted from *Care Management Guide, Caregivers in the Workplace*, American Association of Retired Persons, 1987.

Care Management Planning Guide* (continued)

My Relative . . .	Services Needed	Options	Refer to Pages:
. . . needs help with food preparation and/or house-keeping and/or laundry.	Homemaker Services—Non-medical service to help an older person remain in the home	Homemaker services United Way	198 186
. . . needs assistance with personal care (bathing, dressing, grooming, toileting).	Home, Health or Personal Care Aide—Personal and basic health care provided by a specialist	Homemaker-home health aide	198
. . . doesn't eat right.	Nutrition—Nutritious meals provided at home or in a group setting	Home-delivered meals Nutrition programs Senior centers United Way	196 205 206 186
. . . cannot be left alone during the day.	Friendly Visitors or Intermediate Care Facility—Volunteers who visit with the elderly or a facility that provides constant supervision	Adult day care Friendly visiting service Companion service United Way	207 194 197 186
. . . needs special services for physical limitation and impairments.	Handicapped Services	Disease-specific organization Local office for physical disabilities National not-for-profit health organizations United Way City or local government	243-244 — 240-242 186 —
. . . has health care costs that are unbelievable.	Health Care Cost Containment—Reducing cost of quality health care	Medicare-Social Security Office Medicaid department Private insurance carriers United Way	216-217, 241 217-218, 241 218-219, 241 186
. . . shows signs of depression, sadness, withdrawal.	Mental health—Evaluation of psychological and emotional health (also see Complete Geriatric Evaluation, below)	City/county mental health department Geriatric social workers Psychiatric hospitals Alzeheimer's Disease and Related Disorders Association Mental health association United Way	— 185 — 110-114 224-227 186
. . . has begun acting strangely and out of the ordinary.	Complete Geriatric Evaluation—Medical, psychological and social testing of older person	Have physician evaluate nutritional habits, health status and medications. Have mental health worker rule out depression. Have neurologist run diagnostic tests if above evaluations are negative.	180-181

Care Management Planning Guide* (continued)

My Relative . . .	Services Needed	Options	Refer to Pages:
. . . really needs 24-hour supervision even though he/she denies it.	Private Nurse or Nursing Home—Homes for the elderly offering 24-hour medical supervision	Private nursing organization Institutional homes United Way	199 213-215 186
. . . has a terminal illness and wants to return home instead of dying in the hospital.	Hospice—Medical and social services designed for terminally ill patients	Visiting Nurses Association American Cancer Society Hospice association Hospital social services Churches and synagogues United Way	199 — 210 — — 186
. . . needs my assistance but lives in another area.	Long Distance Care Management—Evaluation, coordination of services and monitoring of older persons living at a distance from caregiver	Local or state unit on aging Geriatric case manager	184-185 185

I Sometimes Feel . . .	Services Needed	Options	Refer to Pages:
. . . overwhelmed; I have so many unanswered questions about aging and services for the elderly.	Information and Referral—Method of providing knowledge of particular services and recommendations of places providing those services	Area Agency on Aging Case manager for the elderly City or local information and referral service American Association for Retired Persons United Way	182 185 186 245 186
. . . I need to share my feelings with someone who understands.	Counseling/Support—One-on-one consultation or meetings with other caregivers who share problems and coping skills	Support group for caregivers Churches or synagogues Family services Employee assistance program Mental health association United Way	243-244 — — — 224-227 186
. . . I need time for myself; caregiving is a 24-hour job.	Respite Care—Substitute caregiver in or out of home who allows the family time away from caregiving responsibilities	Area Agency on Aging Respite organizations Churches or synagogues Women's groups United Way Visiting Nurses Association	182 200 — 245 186 198-199
. . . other family members are not helping enough.	Family Meeting—Meeting of relatives to discuss responsibilities for elderly care	Family services agencies Private therapist Social workers Geriatric case manager Mental health association	243 — — 186 —
. . . my caregiving responsibilities are negatively affecting my work, personal life and health.	Physical Exam, Stress Management and Complete Medical Evaluation—Techniques designed to alleviate stress and/or increase coping skills	Company health promotion program Employee assistance program Private therapist Personal physician Mental health association	— — 137 — 224-227

CHAPTER THREE

CareSkill Three: Understanding the Spectrum of Care

This chapter describes 18 long-term care options, outlining the purpose of each, the services provided, funding sources and resources for further information.

Use these descriptions as part of long-term care planning, to become familiar with the kinds of services available in most communities. This knowledge should help you if you need to design a health-care plan or help an older relative match services to specific needs.

Services Provided in the Home

Home-based care can be simple or intensive, ranging from assistance with housekeeping to skilled nursing to hospice care for the terminally ill. Home-based services share a common goal—to enable older people to remain independent in a familiar, comfortable environment, preferably that of their own homes.

Who Can Benefit?

- Older people who live alone or spend long periods by themselves

▼

Purpose

- To link older people with emergency services in the event of an accident or medical problem

▼

Basic Services Provided

- A wireless control worn as a necklace or bracelet, which can send a signal to a hospital emergency room

▼

Costs

- $10 to $20 per month

▼

Resources

- Area Agency on Aging
- Lifeline Emergency Response Systems (800/451-0525)

Personal Emergency Response Systems

One afternoon, soon after Maxine began to take medication to control her high blood pressure, she became dizzy in her bathroom and fell. Fortunately, she wasn't hurt, and a change in her dosage corrected the dizziness. But the incident caused Maxine to worry: Suppose she had been hurt and unable to call for help? She began to think it might be dangerous to continue living alone.

Maxine learned about the emergency response system through a newsletter distributed by her community hospital and decided to sign up. Now she is linked to the hospital's emergency room by an unobtrusive signaling button worn as a piece of jewelry. Chances are, Maxine will never need to use the device, but knowing she can gives her peace of mind.

How It Works

Fear of being alone, having an accident or becoming ill threatens the independence of many older people, often causing them to give up their homes. Personal emergency response systems provide these people with a vital tie to the outside world.

A small, wireless device worn around the neck or wrist acts as an alarm system, which, when activated, causes the user's telephone to signal the emergency room of a nearby hospital. The emergency team will then attempt to call the person by telephone and/or notify a previously designated relative or neighbor to check immediately and advise the hospital if further assistance is needed.

What It Costs

In most areas, leasing emergency-response equipment from a local hospital costs between $10 and $20 a month. However, not all hospitals offer this service. You can check with your Area Agency on Aging, call various hospitals, or call Lifeline Emergency Response Systems at 800/451-0525.

Who Can Benefit?
- Older persons who live alone or spend long periods by themselves

▼

Purpose
- To provide regular telephone contact with older adults, to end social isolation or ascertain needs, health status and safety

▼

Basic Services Provided
- Daily, weekly or bi-weekly telephone calls, often at a regular time
- Confirmation of health and safety status
- Lifeline to emergency services
- Limited social contact

▼

Costs
- Usually free, although some for-profit organizations charge a fee

▼

Possible Funding Mechanisms
- Most often provided through voluntary agencies or organizations

▼

Resources
- Area Agency on Aging
- Church or synagogue
- Civic or social agencies
- Visiting nurse association
- Retired Senior Volunteer Program

Telephone Reassurance Programs

Dave Goldberg's job requires a lot of travel, and when he's on the road, he can't check on his aging mother as often as he would like. Both Dave and his mother appreciate the telephone reassurance program that their synagogue provides.

Every day at a scheduled time, a volunteer calls Mrs. Goldberg to chat briefly and to discuss any needs she might have. Now Dave's mother has an important link to the outside world, and Dave knows that if a call goes unanswered, the police and a trusted neighbor will be notified.

How It Works

Telephone reassurance programs provide a simple but important service. Through regularly scheduled telephone calls, a trained volunteer checks on an older person's health and other needs. This worthwhile program also provides valuable social contact for an isolated person.

What It Costs

Telephone reassurance programs often are free, provided through non-profit organizations and staffed by volunteers. Some are a service of for-profit companies, which charge a modest fee.

To locate a telephone reassurance program, contact your Area Agency on Aging, your church or synagogue, a civic or social agency, the Retired Senior Volunteer Program, or a visiting nurse association.

Who Can Benefit?

- Homebound older people who suffer from boredom, isolation and loneliness

▼

Purpose

- To provide homebound individuals with a regular visitor one or more times a week

▼

Basic Services Provided

- Regularly scheduled visits
- Conversation and company
- Help with writing letters, running errands and other light tasks

▼

Costs

- Usually free (if not, a nominal fee is charged)

▼

Resources

- Area Agency on Aging
- Community and religious organizations
- Universities
- Labor unions
- Retired Senior Volunteer Program

Friendly Visiting

Sometimes it seems to Frank that the hours from 7:30 a.m., when his daughter and son-in-law leave for work, until 6 p.m., when they return home, are a lifetime. His daughter always leaves a list of jobs for him to do—take meat from the freezer, dust the furniture, empty the dishwasher, etc.—but they occupy only a fraction of his time.

Frank calls his volunteer friendly visitor a "godsend." Two afternoons a week, she stops by to spend time with him. Sometimes they play cards or watch television together, but mostly they sit and talk. Frank looks forward to her visits; they brighten the loneliest part of his day.

How It Works

A volunteer visits the older person's home, according to a regular schedule. Conversation and companionship are the most valuable services offered, but the volunteer may also help out with shopping, errands, paper work and other light tasks.

What It Costs

Most friendly visiting programs are free, operated by community organizations, churches and synagogues, colleges and universities, and even labor unions. If a fee is charged, it is minimal.

Call your Area Agency on Aging to find out about visiting services near you.

Who Can Benefit?

- Otherwise-independent older adults who need help with minor household repairs and maintenance

▼

Purpose

- To provide home repair and maintenance assistance at a reduced cost to older adults who are incapacitated or have a low income

▼

Basic Services Provided

- Minor household repairs
- Yard work
- General maintenance

▼

Costs

- Costs vary from region to region, from minimum wage to $6 per hour or more

▼

Resources

- Area Agency on Aging
- The United Way of America
- The Yellow Pages
- Department of social services
- Chamber of commerce

Home-Based Chore Services

Christine hated to think of her Aunt Mildred giving up her comfortable house, but at age 81 and with severe arthritis, the older woman was unable to perform heavy household chores. Christine herself was 63 and had back problems, and so had to limit her own activities. There was no one to wash windows, hang screens or do yard work for her aunt until Christine found, through the local chamber of commerce, a bonded, reputable chore service to keep Aunt Mildred's home in good shape.

How It Works

Community-based chore services perform a variety of needed home-maintenance tasks for those unable to do the jobs themselves. The services provided include minor household repairs—fixing leaks, repairing steps and replacing broken windows; raking, mowing and other yard work; and general maintenance duties, including cleaning gutters, caulking windows and installing storm doors or screens.

What It Costs

In general, chore services cost about $5 per hour, plus materials, with labor performed by youth groups and/or retirees.

For information on available services contact your Area Agency on Aging or the United Way of America, or look in the Yellow Pages. For your own protection, **make sure** that any individual or agency you employ is **bonded** and a member of the Better Business Bureau or chamber of commerce.

Home-Delivered Meals ("Meals on Wheels")

Throughout their married life, James's wife did all the cooking. After she died, he began having his midday meal at a neighborhood coffee shop and snacking on a sandwich, or maybe a piece of pie, in the evenings. At age 73 and with poor eyesight, he wasn't about to start experimenting in the kitchen.

But one winter afternoon, James slipped on an icy sidewalk. He wasn't seriously hurt, but he was sore from the fall and reluctant to go out of the house. As a result, he often missed his hot lunch, and his food supply dwindled.

A concerned neighbor contacted the local senior center and helped James arrange for home-delivered meals. Now, every day from Monday through Friday, a friendly volunteer delivers a hot, nutritious lunch to James. She also brings a cold, light meal that he can keep in the refrigerator until evening.

James has recovered, but he continues to receive his "Meals on Wheels" because of its convenience and modest cost. He still eats out on weekends, but mostly for a change in routine.

How It Works

To someone with arthritis, impaired eyesight, or even poor balance, nutrition can be a serious problem. Preparing meals means carrying bulky bags of groceries, lifting heavy pots and pans, manipulating can openers and knives, and trying to read labels or the lettering on the stove.

Without assistance, the individual would be forced to sacrifice nutrition, health and, eventually, independence.

Five days a week, home-delivered meal services bring hot, nutritious meals to the older person's home, in most cases for midday consumption. A second, cold meal is often provided as well, usually a snack or light supper for the evening, and some programs provide boxed or frozen meals for weekend or emergency use.

What It Costs

The cost of home-delivered meals is modest and sometimes based on ability to pay. Some services charge between $2 and $4 per meal; others ask for voluntary contributions.

To learn more about home-delivered meal services in your area, contact your Area Agency on Aging; a local church, synagogue or community center; or the United Way. Commercial, for-profit meal services are listed in the Yellow Pages.

Who Can Benefit?

- Older adults who wish to remain in their own homes, but whose disability makes it difficult for them to buy groceries or cook

▼

Purpose

- To provide home-delivered meals to older individuals who are homebound and incapable of shopping or preparing meals

▼

Basic Services Provided

- Hot, nutritious meals delivered to the home once or twice a day, five days a week

▼

Costs

- $2 to $4 per meal, or a voluntary contribution, according to the individual's ability to pay

▼

Possible Funding Mechanisms

- The federal government
- The United Way of America
- Private donations/funds

▼

Resources

- Area Agency on Aging
- Local church or synagogue
- Neighborhood community center
- The United Way of America
- The Yellow Pages (for-profit, commercial services)

Who Can Benefit?

- Older persons who live alone or spend long periods by themselves

▼

Purpose

- To provide services that remove house-keeping and social-isolation barriers to independence

▼

Basic Services Provided

- Companionship
- Housekeeping
- Errands and essential shopping
- Meal preparation
- Respite care

▼

Services Not Provided

- Any services requiring medical supervision or assistance (e.g., administering medication)
- Personal care
- Heavy cleaning chores
- Transportation as a major and regular service

▼

Costs

- Hourly rates vary by geographic region, from minimum wage to $10
- Services may be free or based on ability to pay

▼

Possible Funding Mechanisms

- Community organizations
- Personal assets
- Local department of social services

▼

Resources

- Area Agency on Aging
- Department of social services
- Senior Companion Program under AC-TION
- State office on aging
- Visiting Nurse Association

Companion Service

Before her arthritis got so bad, Josephine didn't mind being alone while her daughter, Carol, went to work. But over time it became painful to use her hands, and she feared falling on the stairs or when she went out. Josephine was pleased, therefore, when Carol helped her find Gladys, her companion, who now comes in for three hours each weekday afternoon.

Gladys prepares Josephine's lunch, does some light housework, and chats with the older woman. She leaves when Josephine's granddaughter comes home from school. Occasionally, Gladys spends the evening with Josephine when Carol and her family have plans to go out.

Carol, too, is happy with the companion service. It provides respite and relieves her to know her mother is well taken care of.

How It Works

As its name implies, a companion service does just that—provides companionship to home-bound individuals who otherwise spend long periods alone. The companion may also prepare meals for the older person, assist with shopping and other errands, and perform limited household tasks. A companion is **not** trained to administer medical or personal care; nor does he or she do heavy house cleaning or provide regular transportation.

What It Costs

A companion charges an hourly rate, which can vary according to the region of the country and the level of care required. For specifics, contact your Area Agency on Aging or local department of social services.

Homemaker-Home Health Aide

Irv's emphysema had worsened until he could do little without getting winded. Such simple tasks as climbing stairs and bathing had become too much for him. His wife, Anne, did what she could, but Irv was a big man, and caring for him was difficult.

At the suggestion of their doctor, the couple hired a homemaker-home health aide, who comes to the house regularly to help Irv with his bath and oxygen therapy. She changes his bed linens, straightens his room and helps Anne with laundry and household chores.

While Irv's condition can never improve, the help he and Anne receive from the homemaker-home health aide enables him to remain at home and live as normal a life as possible.

How It Works

Those who are disabled by a chronic disease or recovering from illness or surgery are more comfortable and independent at home than in an institution. Homemaker-home health aides assist with light housework, laundry, shopping and meal preparation. They help the disabled person bathe and dress. While they cannot provide skilled nursing care, a growing number of homemaker-home health aides have received training in geriatric care and are certified to provide medical care at a basic level.

What It Costs

Most homemaker-home health aide services are covered by private health insurance, Medicare or Medicaid, but only under specific circumstances. The average costs range from $8 to $20 per hour. In some states, homemaker-home health aide services are funded through the Older Americans Act, and are available free or on a sliding scale to persons who qualify.

To be sure you receive competent, qualified, trustworthy care, investigate any home health agency that you are considering engaging: Make sure the agency is bonded and a member of either the Better Business Bureau or chamber of commerce. Be sure the aide has been trained to provide the care needed and is supervised by a health professional or social worker. Get and check references and make sure that you understand the charges you will incur.

Questions to Ask When Evaluating Homemaker-Home Health Aide Agencies

- Is the agency bonded, and is it a member of the chamber of commerce or Better Business Bureau?
- What are the costs and funding options?
- Does the aide have references that I can check?

Who Can Benefit?

- Disabled individuals or discharged hospital patients who require personal assistance and some health services within the home

▼

Purpose

- To provide personal care and some health services, such as the administration of oral medications in the home

▼

Basic Services Provided

- Light housework
- Laundry
- Shopping
- Meal preparation
- Help with dressing and bathing
- Oral medication compliance

▼

Costs

- An average of $8 to $20 per hour

▼

Possible Funding Mechanisms

- Medicare
- Medicaid
- Private funds
- Private health insurance
- Area Agency on Aging
- United Way

▼

Resources

- National Home Caring Council
- Social Security Administration
- Area Agency on Aging
- The Yellow Pages
- Hospital discharge planner
- Local department of social services
- Local health department
- Visiting Nurse Association
- Personal physician

- Is the aide trained to perform the services that I will need?
- Who supervises the aide? Will I have frequent contact with the aide's supervisor?
- What happens if I am not satisfied with the service?

Skilled Home Care

A few days after Bob Weber's stroke, when the extent of the damage had been determined, the doctor told his family that the care Bob needed—medication, physical and speech therapy—could be administered at home.

Bob's son, daughter-in-law and grandchildren were eager for him to return home and willing to care for him to the best of their abilities. But some of Bob's care needs could only be met by skilled health professionals. The hospital discharge planner therefore put the family in touch with a home-health agency.

Soon after Bob went home, an agency nurse came to assess his need and to see that his family understood the medication schedule prescribed by the doctor. Bob's home treatment included the services of a physical therapist to exercise his weakened limbs. A speech-language pathologist also came regularly to help him re-learn clear speech.

This skilled home care kept Bob out of a nursing home and he was able to regain much of his lost ability at home with his family.

How It Works

Too often, patients remain in the hospital or are admitted to a nursing home for care that could be administered at home. Skilled home care meets the needs of these people and, more importantly, encourages them to return to a higher level of functioning.

The registered nurses, physical and occupational therapists, speech-language pathologists, and other health professionals employed by home-care agencies provide a wide variety of services. They supervise the patient's medication, change dressings, catheterize the patient, give injections or monitor vital signs, such as blood pressure. Physical, occupational or speech therapists can come to the homes of those who need them.

Home-health professionals can also offer nutritional counseling for those on restricted diets, answer questions from the patient and family, and direct them to other health resources. A visiting nurse may also supervise the care provided by homemaker-home health aides.

What It Costs

Skilled care in the home costs, on average, $15 to $35 per hour. When the care has been ordered by a physician, the cost will be covered, at least in part, by private health insurance, Medicare or Medicaid.

Your personal physician, a hospital discharge planner, the Social Security Administration or a local social services agency can help you find a skilled home care agency.

Who Can Benefit?

- An older adult who is convalescing or suffering from a chronic illness

Purpose

- To provide skilled, supervised care, administered by a nurse, physical or occupational therapist, speech-language pathologist, or other health professional in the home

Basic Services Provided

- Administration of medication
- Specialized treatment procedures
- Nutritional counseling
- Health information and referrals
- Supervision of homemaker-home health aide

Costs

- Between $15 and $35 per hour (Hourly rates are based on the type of service provided and the level of care required.)

Possible Funding Mechanisms

- Medicaid
- Medicare
- Private health insurance
- Personal funds
- Private long-term care insurance

Resources

- Personal physician
- Social Security Administration
- Local department of social services
- Hospital discharge planner
- Visiting Nurse Association
- Private home-health care agencies

Respite Services

To Trudy, the most difficult part of caring for her aging mother was the isolation. As the older woman grew more frail and dependent, Trudy saw less and less of her friends. She rarely got out of the house. "This situation would cause anyone to get depressed," Trudy often told herself.

Although she had heard about the respite service sponsored by a community volunteer organization, she was reluctant to call for help. She didn't think her mother would welcome care from a stranger, nor did she think that someone else could do the job as well as she did.

But when a friend called and invited her to join a bridge club, Trudy relented. She hadn't played bridge in years and couldn't bear to turn down the invitation.

As it turned out, Trudy's mother was happy to see her go out and enjoy herself, and the respite service's trained volunteer provided care that met Trudy's high standards. More important, the evening out did wonders for Trudy's outlook and energy level. For a few hours, she was able to forget her responsibilities. She has decided to use the respite service regularly—for the sake of her social life and her peace of mind.

How It Works

This service is for caregivers! Respite services provide a "respite," or break, for family members who care for an older relative at home. A trained person can visit the home regularly for several hours each week, or for an occasional day or evening. Adult day care can also act as excellent respite option. Or, if a caregiver needs to be away for a few days, respite care may be available at a local nursing home or assisted living facility.

What It Costs

The cost of respite services is dependent upon the level of care required and can range from no charge for volunteer-provided services to $35 a day for adult day care or as much as $75 to $100 for an overnight stay in a nursing home or assisted living facility.

To learn more about respite services in your community, contact local churches and synagogues, volunteer organizations, civic or social agencies, or your Area Agency on Aging.

Who Can Benefit?
- People who carry a heavy, time-consuming caregiving load

Purpose
- To give family caregivers time off from their demanding responsibilities while ensuring that the older person is supervised and well cared for

Basic Services Provided
- In-home care for short periods
- Relief for family caregivers

Costs
- Costs vary depending upon level of care (The new catastrophic health care legislation will cover some respite services.)

Resources
- Area Agency on Aging
- Local church or synagogue
- Home health agency
- Civic or social agencies
- Volunteer organizations
- Nursing homes
- Adult day care

Who Can Benefit?

- Individuals who have been diagnosed as terminally ill, with less than six months to live

▼

Purpose

- To provide physical, psychological, social and spiritual care to the patient and his or her family. Hospice care aims to make the patient's final weeks as comfortable and as meaningful as possible. Hospice care can be administered in the home, in a hospital or nursing home, or in a free-standing facility.

▼

Basic Services Provided

- Medical care designed to reduce pain and suffering, rather than to prolong life through heroic measures
- A team of doctors, nurses, social workers, clergy and volunteers who provide medical, psychological, social and spiritual care and counseling
- Respite services

▼

Costs

- $50 per day in the home
- $200 per day in an institution

▼

Possible Funding Mechanisms

- Medicare—in a Medicare-approved facility. (The patient must choose hospice care instead of the traditional medical treatment for terminal illness covered by Medicare benefits.)
- Private health insurance
- Medicaid (in some states)

▼

Resources

- Your personal physician
- The Social Security Administration
- The National Hospice Organization
- Local church or synagogue
- Visiting Nurse Association

Hospice

Adeline had heard horror stories about people dying alone in hospital rooms, their bodies hooked up to tubes, wires and machinery. When she learned she had terminal cancer at age 66, she realized that she feared an undignified death more than death itself.

Adeline's physician referred her to a hospice program in a neighboring community. The hospice's nurses, counselors and volunteers helped Adeline and her husband, Al, enrich their final months together.

Al was taught to administer Adeline's pain medication on days when the nurse didn't visit. A volunteer, Mary, came regularly to talk with Adeline and help her bathe and put on makeup, which boosted her self-image. Mary's visits gave Al time to shop, run errands and keep the weekly bowling date that, for him, was an outlet for stress.

One day, Adeline told Mary that for years she had been saving family letters, dating from her parents' courtship. She had always meant to organize them, but never had the time. Now she didn't have the strength.

Mary found the box of letters in Adeline's basement. Each day, she read a few aloud to the dying woman and sorted them according to her instructions, sometimes with Al's help. It wasn't a big job, but it brought meaning to Adeline's final weeks and helped her reflect on her experiences and accomplishments.

How It Works

Hospices offer a special kind of care to dying people and their families. Some hospices are home based, while others are through in-patient facilities. Their goal is not to cure, but to improve the quality of life, relieving pain and incorporating the patient's wishes into the care plan.

The hospice team is diversified, including physicians, nurses, social workers, clergy and volunteers. Their goal is to meet the physical, psychological, social and spiritual needs of the dying person and his or her family.

If the patient wants to remain at home, the team will arrange for care to be administered in the home setting by nurses, aides and family members.

Home-health aides or volunteers assist with personal care needs, such as bathing and dressing, and help keep life meaningful by encouraging the patient to talk about the past, the present and death, and to keep in touch with the outside world, even if the person can do little more than enjoy the view from a familiar window or smell a bouquet of flowers.

The hospice team also provides respite service for family caregivers. Families are invited to join a support group, where they can talk with others in the same situation. When death comes, services don't stop. The hospice team stays in touch with the family and helps them work through the grieving process.

What It Costs

The costs of hospice care can vary from approximately $50 per day for care in the home to $200 per day or more for care in an institutional setting. Institutional care is likely to involve physicians to a greater degree than home hospice care does.

Medicare benefits will cover the cost of hospice care, if that care is provided by a Medicare-approved hospice-agency or facility. In such instances, the patient must elect hospice care instead of the standard hospital treatment for a terminal illness. Most private health insurance plans pay for hospice care and, in some states, so does Medicaid.

For a referral to hospice services in your area, contact your family physician, the Social Security Administration or the National Hospice Organization, a clearinghouse for hospice information.

Housing Options for Older People

A change in living quarters could improve the quality of life for an older person, freeing him or her from the responsibility and expense of home maintenance. The following are some housing options:

• **Condominiums.** A condominium, or condo, can be a unit in an apartment building or a townhouse. Living units are owned, up to and including the interior walls. Together the individual unit owners share ownership of the *common elements*—the grounds and any recreational facilities, such as a pool. Condo owners pay their mortgage and taxes as well as a monthly maintenance fee.

• **Cooperatives.** A cooperative, or co-op, is actually a non-profit organization that owns and manages a housing facility for the residents' benefit. Residents purchase not a single unit, but a share in the cooperative, which entitles them to live in a particular apartment. As in a condo, residents are permitted to vote on maintenance and other decisions affecting the facility.

• **Renting.** In exchange for a security deposit and monthly rent payments, the tenant is entitled to a place to live. The property owner, or landlord, is responsible for maintenance. The tenant must abide by the landlord's rules as set forth in the lease, which may forbid pets, limit visitors or require the tenant to obtain permission before making changes in the dwelling place.

• **Elder Cottage Housing Opportunity (ECHO Housing).** An ECHO unit or "Granny Flat" is a self-contained, temporary dwelling that can be situated on the land adjacent to a grown child's house. It is removed when it is no longer needed. ECHO units are inexpensive, but in many areas, zoning laws do not allow them. If you would like to install an ECHO unit, check local zoning regulations.

- **Retirement communities.** Specialized communities for older people can contain a mix of housing styles, recreational facilities, emergency response systems, adult day care, hospitals, shopping areas and places of worship; or they can consist of a single apartment building. The cost of living in a retirement community can vary greatly, depending on the community's location and the type of housing and services offered. Often, in addition to purchasing the living unit, the resident must pay a monthly maintenance charge and activity fee.

- **Continuing care retirement centers.** The continuing care retirement center (CCRC), or life care center, offers appropriate living conditions and care as residents needs change throughout their older years. Nursing-home care is available, and its cost is included in the hefty entrance fee (up to $100,000), with monthly fees of up to $1,200 common.

  Because a number of CCRCs have folded for financial reasons, those considering such an arrangement should investigate the company by calling the Better Business Bureau and the local consumer affairs office. The organization's financial records and the proposed agreement between the resident and the institution should be reviewed by an attorney before signing.

- **Federal housing programs.** In many locations, the federal government provides safe, adequate, affordable housing to people with limited incomes. Some federal housing is exclusively for people age 62 and older, although younger disabled people may be permitted to live there, too. Other units are for people with low to moderate incomes, regardless of their age.

  Some federal housing for seniors is designed for people who can live independently. In other places, residents receive assistance with transportation and housework, and perhaps dine communally.

  For more information on federal housing opportunities, contact the U.S. Department of Housing and Urban Development, the Farmers Home Administration (if you live in a rural area), or your local housing agency.

- **Group homes and shared housing.** Available in many communities, this system matches one older individual with another to share a large home. Or, an agency will maintain a special home for a group of older people. Your local AAA can tell you if there is such a program in your community.

- **LifeCare at home.** LifeCare at home (LCAH) is a new residential concept. In contrast to the CCRC resident, the LCAH enrollee remains in his or her own home. The LCAH resident pays a significantly lower one-time entry and monthly fee than the CCRC resident.

  Services such as medical care, nutrition programs and chore services are coordinated by care managers who develop specific care plans based on the enrollees' needs.

  The LCAH model is most attractive to middle- or higher-income people and can potentially serve up to 25 percent of the long-term care market.

  An LCAH can be sponsored by a single institution or be a co-venture involving local health providers, HMOs, hospitals or insurance carriers.

Services Provided in the Community

Community-based services form a vital link between the home and the outside world for many older people. Time spent in a senior center or adult day care center, for example, offers an opportunity to socialize and exercise mental and communication skills.

Community services aid family members, too, by providing respite and perhaps enabling the primary caregiver to work outside the home.

Nutrition Services—Congregate Meals

Bea and Carl liked living in the mobile home park close to their daughter, but leaving the city had required a big adjustment. They missed their friends and familiar neighborhood stores. In their late 70s and without a car, they depended on their daughter to take them shopping.

Then a new neighbor told Bea and Carl about the community senior center's nutrition program. They were delighted. Now, twice a week, for a modest cost, they enjoy a hot meal and the company of other people their age. The center's van picks them up and returns them home after each visit. They also use the center's van service to shop at a nearby supermarket.

The nutrition program provides a balanced meal and gives Bea a break from cooking. Twice a week Bea and Carl have a chance to make new friends—and they have become less dependent on their daughter.

How It Works

Several factors contribute to poor nutrition among older people, including health problems, gradual loss of taste and smell, difficulty shopping or preparing food, and loneliness—the company of other people is an important appetite stimulant.

Community-based nutrition or congregate meal services provide people age 60 and older with hot, nutritious meals in a group setting, as often as five times a week, usually at midday. Frequently, transportation is provided to and from the senior or community center, church or synagogue, school, or other facility where the meals are served.

Other services may be provided as well, including nutrition education, meal-planning tips and transportation to shopping areas.

What It Costs

Funded by government agencies and private donations, most nutrition services ask participants for a modest contribution, perhaps a dollar or more. However, anyone who cannot afford to make a donation will not be denied a meal.

To locate congregate meal services in your community, contact your Area Agency on Aging; a local church, synagogue, senior or community center; or the school district in which you live.

Who Can Benefit?
- Anyone age 60 or older who would like to enjoy hot meals in the company of others

Purpose
- To provide hot, nutritionally balanced meals in central locations

Basic Services Provided
- Hot meals, several times a week
- Transportation to and from the program site
- Nutrition education, meal planning and shopping expeditions (in some programs)

Costs
- A voluntary contribution of a little more than a dollar (No one is denied services if unable to pay.)

Possible Funding Mechanisms
- Federal and state agencies
- Private donations
- Personal funds

Resources
- Area Agency on Aging
- Local senior center
- Church or synagogue
- Community center
- School district

Who Can Benefit?
- Older individuals who are able to leave the home

▼

Purpose
- To provide opportunities for social interaction in a centralized location

▼

Basic Services Provided
- Planned social activities
- Health screening
- Educational programs
- Legal and financial counseling
- Congregate meals
- Transportation

▼

Costs
- Usually free (A small fee is charged for some services, but no one is denied participation based on inability to pay.)

▼

Resources
- Area Agency on Aging
- Social services agencies
- Civic organizations
- Churches or synagogues
- Mental health associations

Senior Centers

At one time, Everett, age 75, led an active social life. But after his wife died and friends left the area, he spent much of his time alone. He seemed to have lost interest in life and sat for many hours in front of the TV. His daughter worried about him.

At her insistence, Everett began spending one afternoon each week at a neighborhood senior center. The experience opened up his world again. He enjoyed talking with the men and women he met at the center. He even attended some of the center's planned parties and lectures. He signed up for a class in oil painting, something he'd always wanted to try. Best of all, it was good to have friends again.

How It Works

Senior centers offer older people a wide range of services and opportunities: a place to gather and spend time with others; parties and outings; health screenings, including tests of blood pressure and blood cholesterol; lectures and personal enrichment classes on a variety of topics; legal and financial counseling; congregate meals; and transportation to and from the center.

What It Costs

Most of the services provided by senior centers are available at no charge. For some, such as congregate meals, a minimal fee is charged. However, no one is denied services due to inability to pay.

To learn about senior centers in your community, contact your Area Agency on Aging or a local social services agency.

Adult Day Care Centers

Combining the demands of her job with caring for her aging mother-in-law became increasingly difficult for Martha Boone. The older woman became frailer every day. She needed help with her meals, with medications and even just getting around the house.

Martha considered quitting her job to stay home and care for Mrs. Boone, but to do so would create financial hardship for the family. Besides, she loved her job.

The employee assistance counselor at her office told her about adult day care centers, an alternative that had enabled other caregiving employees to continue working.

Now, Martha drops Mrs. Boone at the center on her way to work. Her husband, who gets home earlier, picks up his mother each afternoon. Mrs. Boone enjoys being with others. Because of the care she receives, she is happier and her family is able to live a more normal and satisfying life.

How It Works

There are many older people who are not homebound, but who require regular care. An adult day care center can benefit these individuals and their families as well: It permits the older person to get out of the house for part of the day and to interact with other people, yet still receive needed care. Family members get time away from caregiving duties, to take care of other responsibilities and possibly to work outside the home.

An adult day care center is not a "drop-in" service, but a structured program of care offered five days a week to the older people who are enrolled.

In addition to providing supervision, meals and custodial care, the center's staff organizes social activities, furnishes transportation and offers some rehabilitative assistance, so that the older person spends worthwhile time in their care.

Recently, intergenerational day care centers have begun to be offered within select communities. This concept combines child and adult day care within one facility and provides functional older adults the opportunity to interact with children.

What It Costs

The cost of adult day care can vary considerably. Those centers receiving federal assistance normally charge between $18 and $35 per day. Some charge fees based on ability to pay. However, privately owned facilities will charge more.

Medicare does not pay for the service, although in some states, **Medicaid** will pay the cost for those peo-

ple who qualify. However, most people pay for this service out of their own pockets.

To find out about adult day care services in your area, contact your Area Agency on Aging, county health department or an information and referral service.

Who Can Benefit?
- **Older adults who are able to leave the home setting but who require supervision as well as some care and assistance**

Purpose
- **To provide structured, daily, supervised care and social and rehabilitative services in a community setting**

Basic Services Provided
- **Supervision**
- **Meals and snacks**
- **Some custodial care**
- **Rehabilitation**
- **Social activities**
- **Assistance with medications**
- **Transportation**

Costs
- **$18 to $35 per day for centers receiving federal funding, higher fees in for-profit centers**
- **Some charge fees on a sliding scale**

Possible Funding Mechanisms
- **Medicaid**
- **Personal funds**
- **Private long-term care insurance**
- **Community or state programs**

Resources
- **Area Agency on Aging**
- **County health department**
- **Information and referral service**
- **National Institute of Adult Day Care, a division of the National Council on Aging**
- **Religious organizations**
- **Municipalities**
- **Hospitals, nursing homes**

Board and Care (Foster Care) Homes

At age 79, Leonardo was tired of living alone. Keeping up a three-bedroom house was expensive, and his arthritis caused him to dread home-maintenance chores. Besides, he often felt lonely in the evenings.

Leonardo's roots were important to him. He took comfort in the fact that he still belonged to the church in which he was married and where he and his family attended Mass together for so many years. Also, he enjoyed spending time with lifelong friends who lived nearby and who, like himself, were the children of Italian immigrants.

A counselor from his Area Agency on Aging helped Leonardo find a board and care home in his parish where he has his own room and a private bath, and where the staff takes care of his housekeeping and laundry needs. The other residents like to chat with him in the evenings, and he is able to maintain important ties to the community.

Leonardo and the counselor visited three board and care facilities before he chose his present home. In each, they carefully questioned the resident manager to learn the services provided and evaluate their quality.

How It Works

To some older people, a home or apartment symbolizes independence; to others, it is a burden. A board and care resident receives a room of his or her own with bathroom facilities, meals, laundry and housekeeping services. Transportation to shopping areas and other community services can also be provided. Daily contact with staff members and other residents helps ensure that social needs are met. Assistance with personal-care tasks, such as dressing and bathing, can be obtained if needed, at an additional fee.

Who Can Benefit?

- Older adults who require some assistance with daily functions and activities, but who are basically well and able to maintain some degree of independence

Purpose

- To provide residents with room and board as well as some assistance with activities of daily living

Basic Services Provided

- Room and board
- Housekeeping
- Laundry service
- Transportation
- Bathing and grooming (usually for an additional fee)

Sponsors

- Private operators
- The Veterans Administration

Costs

- Costs and quality vary widely, from $400 to $1,200 per month

Possible Funding Mechanisms

- Personal funds

Resources

- U.S. Department of Health and Human Services
- Area Agency on Aging
- Community consumer protection office
- State long-term care ombudsman
- The Veterans Administration

What It Costs

The cost of board and care homes varies widely depending on the degree of amenities offered and whether or not the home is state licensed. Homes that are either licensed or that offer extensive amenities, such as planned social activities or medication compliance, can cost as much as $1,200 per month. Unlicensed homes or those with fewer amenities range from $400 to $700 per month.

Exercise Caution

The quality of services provided by board and care homes can vary considerably. While some offer very good accommodations and care, others are substandard, don't comply with fire codes or are unsanitary. Licensing is not necessarily a guarantee of quality. In some states, licensing ensures close monitoring and on-site inspections of board and care facilities. In others, licensing is more a measure of size than quality: Homes with five or more residents, for example, may be required to be licensed.

Contact your Area Agency on Aging and your county office of adult protective services to determine whether complaints have been filed about any facilities you are considering.

Visit prospective board and care homes in person, preferably on a "drop-in" basis. Inspect the surroundings, meet the staff and residents, and question the staff thoroughly and carefully.

Questions to Ask When Evaluating Board and Care Homes

- Is the facility safe, clean and secure?
- Can a resident maintain existing social ties?
- Is the staff well trained and qualified?
- Do the staff members and residents seem pleasant and friendly?
- Do the rooms appear comfortable? Are the meals well cooked?
- What will happen if a resident needs help in an emergency?
- What services will the resident receive for the fee?

Congregate Housing— "Assisted Living Facilities"

Marie made excellent progress recovering from the stroke she suffered last year, but her left leg remained weak, and she walked with a cane. At age 76, Marie had always enjoyed independence and social activities, but it became difficult for her to shop and care for her house. Also, she couldn't get out often.

A retirement home—a congregate housing unit—was the answer for Marie and worth the several months spent on a waiting list. There, the staff helps with housekeeping, provides transportation to a nearby shopping mall, and prepares good meals. Marie has made friends among the other residents, yet she can spend time alone in her own apartment when she wants to, and prepare coffee and snacks in her kitchen.

How It Works

The residents of congregate housing facilities live in their own apartments—often with their own furniture—with a kitchen for preparing snacks and light meals. In addition, they have access to varied services within the facility, including meals served in a central dining room, transportation to and from shopping areas, and planned social functions. Some residents may receive additional help with housekeeping and aspects of personal care (bathing, dressing, etc.) as needed.

The facility is likely to employ a social worker or trained counselor, a registered dietitian, and an administrator to plan and oversee group activities.

What It Costs

The cost of congregate housing ranges from $500 to $1,000 or more a month and varies according to regional differences in the cost of living, the range of amenities offered, and the extent to which long-term care services are provided.

Questions to Ask When Evaluating Congregate Housing

- What are the fees?
- What services are available?
- Does the monthly fee cover these services?
- Can the kitchen accommodate special diets?
- Do the apartment units appear comfortable and in good condition?
- Is the atmosphere pleasant and friendly?
- Does the resident-to-be understand all of the terms of the lease before signing?

Who Can Benefit?

- Older people whose overall health is good, but who need assistance with meal preparation, transportation and other services to remain independent

▼

Purpose

- To provide supportive services for older adults in a communal setting without sacrificing personal privacy

▼

Basic Services Provided

- Separate apartment units with kitchens
- Central dining facilities for main meals
- Professional staff
- Transportation

▼

Sponsors

- Non-profit and for-profit organizations
- Government agencies

▼

Costs

- Costs vary widely and can range from $500 to $1,000 per month

▼

Possible Funding Mechanisms

- Personal funds
- Rent subsidy through local housing authority

▼

Resources

- Area Agency on Aging
- Local housing, welfare or religious organizations

Institutional Services

The major suppliers of institutional care for older adults are nursing homes. Most nursing-home residents are over age 85 and may require continuous health care for an extended period.

As in home and community care situations, the needs of nursing-home residents can vary considerably. Some require a supervised living environment and assistance with personal care. Others need an intermediate level of care: some medical assistance in addition to supervision and help with basic functions. A third group of nursing-home residents requires intensive medical care, 24 hours a day.

Custodial Care Facilities (Adult Homes)

Although she knew it would be difficult, Irene had decided several years ago to care for her husband, Harold, at home. But Harold had Alzheimer's disease, and had grown progressively worse. Irene could not continue to handle his care needs.

Harold no longer recognized members of the family. He had begun to wander through the house at night and neither Irene nor the home-health aide was able to watch him 24 hours a day.

Irene and her children reluctantly agreed that the time had come to place Harold in a custodial care facility. He did not require medical care, but he needed constant supervision.

Seeing Harold in the nursing home was not the devastating emotional experience that Irene thought it would be. Harold was well cared for and comfortable. She realized that the professional staff truly was better able to meet his needs than she. For Harold, the custodial care facility was the best long-term care option.

How It Works

Custodial care, or an adult home, limits its services to non-medical assistance for people who cannot perform fundamental activities of daily living—such functions as feeding, dressing, toileting and getting in and out of bed. The typical patient receiving custodial care might be in the advanced stages of Alzheimer's disease or have another organic brain disease requiring round-the-clock care.

What It Costs

Custodial care in a nursing home can be expected to cost between $37 and $55 per day. This kind of care is **not** covered by Medicare or most private health insurance policies. Medicaid will pay the tab for those who have exhausted their resources, but most custodial care is paid for out of personal assets, such as savings and Social Security benefits. Long-term care insurance is a new option that can help fund custodial care.

For specifics, contact your personal physician, the Social Security Administration, a financial counselor, a private insurance company, or the National Citizens' Coalition for Nursing Home Reform.

Because the quality of care provided in nursing homes can vary significantly, any facility under consideration should be visited, and its license, certification and general operations investigated. Use the checklist at the end of this section to help you evaluate nursing-home services.

Who Can Benefit?

- Individuals who require room and board and assistance with activities of daily living, but who don't require regular medical care

▼

Purpose

- To provide custodial care to individuals who need trained supervision and personal assistance, but who don't need medical care

▼

Basic Services Provided

- Room and board
- Social programming
- Assistance with activities of daily living

▼

Costs

- $37 to $55 per day

▼

Possible Funding Mechanisms

- Medicaid
- Personal funds
- Social Security benefits
- Private long-term care insurance

▼

Resources

- Personal physician
- Social Security Administration
- Financial counselor
- Private insurance carrier
- National Citizens' Coalition for Nursing Home Reform
- American Association of Homes for the Aging
- Veterans Administration

Intermediate Care Facilities

Abby, age 83, had recognized for some time that one day soon she would have to make other living arrangements. Caring for her apartment was becoming increasingly difficult, she suffered from frequent dizzy spells, and now that she no longer had friends nearby, she was lonely.

A social worker helped Abby make the decision to enter an intermediate care facility, where her meals would be prepared, her living quarters kept clean, and her nursing needs met. It was comforting to know that help was near, and she enjoyed interacting with the other residents.

How It Works

Intermediate care facilities serve people who are still fairly independent—who can get themselves up and dressed, and make their own way to the dining room—but who require some assistance, perhaps with taking medications or preparing meals. Residents can take part in planned social activities and outings.

A stay in an intermediate care facility can be short, as in the case of an older person whose family caregiver goes out of town, or long-term: for example, when an older person with no living relatives can no longer manage at home. In this instance, the nursing home becomes a residential setting, and the older person may even be permitted to bring favorite pieces of furniture.

It is important to investigate any intermediate care facility under consideration. (See the checklist at the end of this chapter.) The older person will be living in the facility for a definite or indefinite period, and will be dependent upon its staff for care. Therefore, the caregiver will want to be certain that the facility is well maintained, that the atmosphere is pleasant, and that the staff is friendly, attentive and capable of meeting the older person's needs. You may want to experiment with a "trial period" to see how the older person reacts to living in this setting.

What It Costs

Intermediate care facilities generally cost between $41 and $70 per day. The rate varies according to the region of the country and the type of care required. Currently, Medicare will not pay for this level of care. For those who qualify, Medicaid and Veterans benefits can offer assistance. Private long-term care insurance can cover some of the cost, but most intermediate care in nursing homes is paid for with personal assets.

To learn more about intermediate care facilities in your area, contact the older person's physician, your Area Agency on Aging, the National Coalition for Nursing Home Reform or the Veterans Administration.

Who Can Benefit?

- Individuals who are not able to live alone and who require some nursing assistance and minimal personal care

Purpose

- To provide non-intensive nursing and personal services within an institutional setting

Basic Services Provided

- Room and board
- Limited nursing care
- Social activities

Costs

- $41 to $70 per day

Possible Funding Mechanisms

- Medicaid
- Veterans benefits
- Private long-term care insurance
- Personal funds

Resources

- Personal physician
- Area Agency on Aging
- National Citizens Coalition for Nursing Home Reform
- Veterans Administration
- Private insurance carrier
- American Association of Homes for the Aging

Who Can Benefit?

- Individuals who require professional medical care, 24 hours a day

Purpose

- To provide round-the-clock medical care, often to patients who were recently discharged from the hospital

Basic Services Provided

- Room and board
- 24-hour nursing care supervised by a registered nurse, under the direction of a physician
- Medical director on call
- Pharmaceutical services
- Physical, occupational and speech therapy

Costs

- $65 to $140 per day

Possible Funding Mechanisms

- Medicare
- Medicaid
- Private long-term care insurance
- Veterans benefits

Resources

- Personal physician
- Social Security Administration
- Financial counselor
- Private insurance carrier
- National Citizens' Coalition for Nursing Home Reform
- American Association of Homes for the Aging
- Veterans Administration

Skilled Nursing Facilities

When Mike's Uncle Nathan was hospitalized at age 82 after breaking a hip, the physician told Mike that the older man's recovery would be slow. He recommended that Uncle Nathan be transferred from the hospital to a skilled nursing facility within the coming weeks for the appropriate level of medical and custodial care, as well as important social stimulation.

Mike and his wife, Sally, visited a number of nursing homes in their city to observe the quality of care, level of interaction between staff and residents, and general atmosphere. Of the two they liked best, one did not anticipate having space for Uncle Nathan within six weeks. Therefore, they were forced to choose the other facility.

Mike continued to visit his uncle regularly after he was moved to the nursing home. He and Sally were pleased to see that his care was good, he was always clean and alert, the staff members spoke pleasantly to him, and his meals were nutritious and well prepared.

In time, Uncle Nathan improved to the point that he was able to leave the nursing home and receive needed care in the home and community.

How It Works

Skilled nursing facilities treat people with complex nursing and rehabilitative needs—intravenous therapy, surgical dressing changes, oxygen therapy, and perhaps physical, occupational or speech therapy. Often these patients have had major surgery or have suffered a stroke. They require round-the-clock supervision and treatment, but they don't need the level of care that would be provided in a hospital.

Because the skilled nursing facility's goal is rehabilitation, stays are usually short. If a patient makes sufficient progress, he or she may return home. If not, a move may be warranted, to an intermediate or custodial-care unit, perhaps within the same facility. However, in many communities, a lack of alternatives can mean that a person starts in a skilled nursing facility when it's not necessary.

Besides receiving room, board and continuous supervision, the residents of a skilled nursing facility are under the constant care of health professionals who are supervised by a registered nurse. Should a medical emergency arise, a physician is on call. A skilled nursing facility's residents receive assistance from a varied health care team, which can include pharmacists, physical and occupational therapists, and speech-language pathologists.

What It Costs

The cost of care in a skilled nursing facility can range from $65 per day to $140 per day, depending on such factors as the region of the country and the type of care required.

Most of the cost of skilled nursing-home confinement is met by private funds: savings and other personal assets. Medicare pays a significant portion (see Chapter Four), and Medicaid and the Veterans Administration can help meet the expenses for those who qualify, once personal assets have been depleted. Currently, only a small percentage of the cost is met by private health insurance.

To learn about skilled nursing facilities in your region, contact your Area Agency on Aging, the Veterans Administration, the department of social services or a hospital discharge planner. Be sure to visit any facility under consideration and allow the older person to inspect it—or at least view its operations. This inspection is vitally important, because the commitment may be long-term.

Evaluating Nursing Homes

A nursing home will be "home" for your older relative—for a few months or, perhaps, for the rest of his or her life. Quality of care is crucial and can affect a person's general health, attitude and ability to function. Make personal visits to any custodial, intermediate or skilled nursing facility that you are considering.

The following checklist, based on guidelines from the American Association of Retired Persons, can help you select the most appropriate facility. Here is what you should look for:

- A state-licensed facility, with membership in either the American Health Care Association or the American Association of Homes for the Aging.
- Certification for Medicare or Medicaid reimbursement, as needed.
- A staff that includes an administrator, director of nursing, social worker and activities director.
- Nurse's aides who receive ongoing training.
- A facility and grounds that are clean, comfortable and well maintained.
- A clean, well equipped kitchen that can provide a varied or specialized diet.
- A pleasant atmosphere in the dining room, with assistance for residents who cannot feed themselves.
- A physician on call 24 hours a day and nurses on duty to carry out the doctor's instructions.
- The "Residents Bill of Rights" visibly displayed.
- An active committee or council representing the residents' interests.
- Cheerful, helpful and respectful interaction between staff members and residents.
- Residents appear clean, dressed, active and well cared for.
- Under the supervision of a social director, staff members and volunteers organize holiday celebrations, social activities and educational programs.
- Residents participate in religious services of their preference.
- Information on fees and a list of services provided.
- A contract that specifies which services are included in the basic fee and which cost extra, and what will happen if a resident depletes his or her resources and becomes eligible for Medicaid.
- A staff that helps residents apply for Medicaid.
- Residents are allowed to bring a few pieces of furniture from home. This encourages residents to have control over their environment.
- Many communities have undertaken independent evaluations of nursing homes. Ask your AAA. Additionally, there are nursing-home ombudsmen programs that can offer both insight and assistance.

CHAPTER FOUR

CareSkill Four: Understanding the Ins and Outs of Financing Long-Term Care

Gene and Clara Lawrence had looked forward to their retirement years. They never expected that Clara would have a stroke.

Upon her release from the hospital, Clara needed long-term custodial care— not skilled nursing care, but help with such basic functions as getting dressed, feeding herself and moving from a bed to a chair.

The Lawrences had always thought that Medicare, the Social Security system's health insurance plan, would pay for this kind of care. They were distressed to learn that they were wrong. They were forced to tap into their retirement savings and use a portion of their pension and Social Security checks.

Gene wanted the best possible care for his wife, but he worried that he wouldn't be able to afford it for very long.

As emphasized throughout this book, people are living longer than at any time in our history. It is that extended life span, together with harmful health habits, that gives prominence to such degenerative diseases as Alzheimer's and osteoporosis, and to chronic disorders like hypertension and arthritis.

Skyrocketing medical costs have put long-term care beyond the financial means of many families, creating catastrophic burdens. Medicare helps meet some of the bills, but is not, and was never intended to be, a primary funding source for long-term care.

The annual cost for nursing-home care usually sur-

passes a retired person's yearly income. A lifetime's savings can be wiped out in a matter of months, if not weeks. Recent studies have shown that half of couples over age 65 with one partner in a nursing home are impoverished within six months. Seventy percent of single patients reach the poverty level in as little as 13 weeks. This is called the "spending down" syndrome, and for those caught in it, the ordeal most often is devastating.

At present, there is no simple formula for avoiding such a disaster. Because legislators are uncertain how best to address the issue of health care financing, it is likely to be some time before any comprehensive federal funding is available. Private long-term care insurance, a new option to help ease the financial burden, is now available from large insurance companies.

It is important to understand that financial planning for retirement is not the same as planning to meet the costs of long-term care. Savings, a pension and Social Security are meant to finance day-to-day living (see Section II, Chapter Five). They are no match for the deluge of expenses that can accompany long-term care.

This chapter provides an overview of the major resources for care: Medicare, Medicaid, "medigap" insurance and long-term care insurance. You can learn more about Medicare and other forms of coverage by contacting the Social Security Administration or talking to a knowledgeable person in your company's employee benefits department, a qualified insurance agent or a representative of your state insurance department. Some companies are even looking into long-term care insurance as an employee health benefit, so ask about this, too.

The importance of financial preparedness cannot be overemphasized. Recently, a government task force on long-term care advised the U.S. Department of Health and Human Services **"to inform consumers that Medicare, medigap and acute health care insurance do not cover long-term care."** You cannot afford to be uninformed—or unprepared.

Understanding Medicare

Medicare is a health **insurance** plan, part of the nation's Social Security system. It serves those age 65 and older, along with some younger people who are disabled or suffering permanent kidney failure. The plan is financed by taxpayers, employers and the federal government.

People qualify for Medicare by turning 65, even if they continue working. People who apply for Social Security benefits are offered Medicare coverage at the age of 64 years and 9 months. Those who choose not to retire, and therefore not to begin receiving Social Security payments, must apply for their Medicare benefits about three months before their 65th birthday. Federal civilian employees must also file an application for benefits.

Medicare has two parts. Part A covers inpatient hospital care, as well as care in some skilled nursing facilities, home health care and hospice services. Part B, which is optional, covers such medical costs as physicians' fees, outpatient hospital care, medical supplies and some home health care.

Under Part A, Medicare's beneficiaries receive 100 percent coverage for 60 days of hospitalization after paying a yearly deductible of $590 (in 1990). The patient is required to pay co-insurance, or a portion of the cost, for the 61st through the 90th day of hospitalization. Medicare pays a portion of the cost for 100 days of skilled nursing or rehabilitation-facility services following at least three days of hospitalization. Medicare also pays for certain home health services, including part-time nursing care, physical therapy, the services of a medical social worker, intravenous drug therapy, and some medical supplies and rehabilitation equipment.

Medicare covers some hospice costs under certain conditions: A physician must certify that the illness is terminal; the patient must choose hospice rather than regular Medicare benefits; and services must be provided by a Medicare-certified hospice.

Part B, called "Supplemental Medical Insurance," is optional. However, anyone who chooses not to enroll must notify his or her Social Security office.

Among the services paid for under Part B are:

- Physicians' fees.
- Independent physical and occupational therapists.
- Supplies ordered by a physician.
- X-ray, laboratory and other diagnostic tests.
- X-ray, radium and radioactive isotope therapies.
- Surgical dressings, splints and casts.
- Ambulances.
- Rental or purchase of durable medical equipment.
- Artificial replacements for internal body parts (except dental items).
- Arm, leg, back and neck braces.
- Artificial legs, arms and eyes.

What does it all cost? Part A coverage is funded through contributions to the Social Security Trust Fund. Most people do not make monthly payments for Part A coverage. People who turn 65, but do not qualify for Social Security, must pay a monthly premium for Part A coverage. (See page 63 for an explanation of eligibility for Social Security.) For Part B, a monthly premium is always charged. That premium was $28.60 in 1990 for people whose coverage began at age 65. Part B's recipients must also pay a $75 deductible, while Medicare picks up 80 percent of the remaining tab. The other 20 percent is co-insurance and is the responsibility of the beneficiary.

The Short-Lived Catastrophic Care Act

In 1988, Congress passed legislation to make coverage for catastrophic care a provision of Medicare. The goal of the Catastrophic Care Act was to protect older Americans from the severe financial difficulties that can quickly follow a sudden, devastating illness. The new benefits also included limited protection against spousal impoverishment for nursing-home patients who became eligible for Medicaid, the health assistance plan financed jointly by the federal and state governments.

Almost immediately, the added coverage became controversial. Many older people said that its funding mechanism was unfair. All Medicare recipients were charged a monthly premium. Also, the two-fifths of eligible adults with the highest incomes were subject to a tax surcharge. Many people suggested that the cost be shared equally by all Americans, as it is for other social programs.

A second criticism concerned the coverage itself. It was argued that so-called catastrophic illnesses strike only a small number of people, while long-term, chronic conditions are a widespread problem and often just as costly. There was a growing consensus that the new coverage did not meet the needs of most older people.

In November 1989, Congress voted to repeal the new legislation, and Medicare returned, for the present, to its previous level of coverage, as described above. Two important provisions of the catastrophic-care legislation, which actually affect Medicaid and not Medicare, were retained. One is limited protection against spousal impoverishment. The other is a requirement that Medicaid pay Medicare deductibles and co-insurance for people who are below the poverty line but not poor enough to be eligible for full Medicaid coverage.

The federal government remains concerned about the high medical costs that many older people face. Legislators, organizations that represent older Americans, and the insurance industry are working to develop solutions that better meet people's needs. **Readers are advised to keep abreast of news reports regarding this important issue. Also, your regional Social Security office can answer your questions about current Medicare coverage.**

Medicaid's Helping Hand

In contrast to Medicare, Medicaid is a health **assistance** plan, financed jointly by the federal and state governments for those defined as medically indigent, a definition that differs from state to state. Medicaid helps the needy of any age, as well as the disabled.

This dual funding means that Medicaid programs differ from one state to another. The federal government demands only that each state adhere to certain baseline standards and services. For instance, each state must have a quality-control system to monitor its Medicaid program for fraud and waste. States must also offer physician, hospital and skilled nursing-home care; health screenings and follow-up for children; laboratory and X-ray services for those age 21 or older; nurse-midwife care; home health care; family planning services; and rural health clinics.

Other benefits are optional. These include dentistry, prescription drugs, eyeglasses, clinics, intermediate care facilities, and diagnostic, screening, preventive and rehabilitative services.

Those who qualify for both Medicare and Medicaid can merge the two services. There are several ways in which Medicaid can pay Medicare's leftover bills.

For those who qualify, Medicaid will pay:

- The $590 yearly deductible charged by Medicare for Part A coverage.
- The $75 yearly Part B deductible charged by Medicare.
- The 20 percent co-insurance not covered by Medicare.
- The monthly premium for Part B of Medicare (in most states).

To find out if you or a relative qualifies for Medicaid, contact your local or state department of social services. It is important to be aware, however, that many older people who face real financial hardship are not considered poor enough to qualify for Medicaid.

Filling the "Medigap"

To meet the costs that Medicare leaves uncovered, many older people have turned to supplemental, or "medigap," insurance policies, sold by private insurance companies. In fact, recent studies have revealed that 70 percent of older Americans own at least one medigap policy. The total yearly cost for these policies is more than $6 billion.

People often buy medigap policies because they fear that long-term hospitalization could wipe out their savings; yet the average hospital stay for Medicare recipients is seven days.

In actuality, medigap policies are most useful in filling other gaps: Medicare's deductibles; the cost of in-hospital, private-duty nursing; or the difference between a Medicare-approved charge and the actual fee for a doctor's services. Some medigap policies pay cash directly to beneficiaries; others make payments to the hospital or physician.

Medigap insurance can be a smart buy, but purchasing the right policy requires careful shopping. Always compare the benefits and costs of policies under consideration. Work with a trusted insurance agent who will be available to service the policy once it has been purchased. Some states also have health insurance counseling programs to provide objective information.

Consumers must be wary of fraudulent medigap policies. If you have any questions about a policy's legitimacy, contact your state or local consumer protection agency for information. Also, the United Seniors Health Cooperative, a non-profit consumer group located in Washington, DC, runs a computerized "Medigap Check-Up," which compares policies by cost and coverage. There is a small fee for the service.

Not everyone who turns 65 needs medigap insurance. An employer's insurance plan may offer excellent supplemental coverage for those entitled to it. Moreover, employers of 20 or more workers must offer the same health care benefits to their entire staff, regardless of anyone's age. Those who retire can choose to remain on their employer's group plan for up to three years, as can their spouses. Widows and divorced spouses are sometimes eligible, too, if they pay a premium.

Another group that may not need medigap insurance comprises those who are covered by Medicare but whose income is low. In the event of serious illness, they would very soon qualify for Medicaid.

Long-Term Care Insurance: The Wave of the Future?

Another option for more complete coverage is long-term care insurance. It can truly fill the gap, because it covers what Medicare and private health insurance do not: custodial (nursing home) services and home health care.

At present, long-term care insurance is the only form of coverage available to large numbers of people that is designed especially to help shield families and their assets against what has been labeled the "cruel" cost of long-term care. Experts have offered the following suggestions to help consumers obtain the most appropriate coverage:

- **Coverage for skilled, custodial and home care.** Most people seeking long-term care insurance want protection against the eventuality that they will one day require intensive, round-the-clock skilled care. But many people (stroke victims, for example) require long periods of custodial care -- help with basic functions of daily living. Insurance coverage that pays only for skilled care is of no benefit to them.

  Similarly, coverage for home care is important. But be sure that you don't have to spend time in a hospital or nursing home before you can receive home-care benefits. Not everyone receiving home care follows that route.

- **Adequate benefits.** Long-term care policies differ in the amount and duration of payments. In general, they pay from $50 to $150 per day for nursing-home care and approximately half that amount for care at home. To get a clearer idea of what an adequate payment would be, call several nursing homes and home health care agencies in your area and ask their rates.

The duration of benefits varies, too. Keep in mind that payment for three to four years of nursing-home care is adequate to cover most stays.

- **Guaranteed renewability.** Make sure that the insurance company is required to renew your policy as long as you pay your premium. "Conditional renewability" means that the insurer could cancel your policy if, for instance, it decided to cancel all similar policies in your state.
- **Protection against inflation.** What seems like enough coverage now may be woefully inadequate in five or 10 years. Look for policies that permit you to increase your coverage to keep up with inflation.
- **A policy with no prior hospitalization rule.** Avoid policies which specify that you must be hospitalized for a specific number of days before entering a nursing home to be eligible for benefits. A number of conditions, such as arthritis, do not warrant hospitalization but may lead to the need for care in a nursing home.

What's the Price Tag?

The cost of long-term care insurance varies according to age. Currently, those in their 50s will pay about $20 to $30 per month for a plan with a $50 daily nursing-home benefit, while those age 65 will pay $60 to $90 per month for the same coverage.

The advantage to buying young is that your premium will be lower and won't increase as you grow older unless it increases statewide. As a general rule, those approaching retirement should look into long-term care insurance. Individual policies are available through most insurance agents, and some employers now offer group plans. Those under age 50 should consider long-term care insurance as part of their overall financial plan. They might also want to consider long-term care insurance for an older relative.

Don't wait too long — if an illness or disability occurs before you purchase long-term care insurance, you may have difficulty getting coverage. Some companies will not pay benefits for care for pre-existing conditions, some set a lengthy waiting period before coverage for those conditions begins, and some simply will not insure you.

Most policies sold today cover the expenses incurred in caring for Alzheimer's disease, which may not be named specifically in the policy. If it is not, but there is a category called "mental and nervous disorders," ask if Alzheimer's disease is included in that category.

Don't buy any long-term care policy without reading it first. In a May 1988 evaluation of long-term care insurance, *Consumer Reports* found that insurance agents were sometimes unclear about what their policies covered. *Consumer Reports* advised, "If you get answers that are vague or contradict the sales literature, ask for a specimen policy. The policy will tell you what's covered and what's not, setting out all the limitations you need to know about." Also, "An agent may be reluctant to give you a specimen policy.... If that happens, write to the company. If a company doesn't give you what you need, go elsewhere."

One last word: As mentioned earlier, some employers now offer long-term care insurance through their benefit plans. A long-term care insurance option allows the employee to purchase coverage at a competitive price, and the premium can be deducted from his or her paycheck. Insurance usually can be purchased for the employee's spouse and parents as well. Consult your employee benefits department to learn if this coverage is offered or being considered.

A Special Kind of Planning

Many older people and their families recognize that they need help and protection from long-term care's monumental bills. But to rely on federally funded programs as they now exist is a dangerous mistake. Medicare was never intended to cover long-term, chronic care. It is an important and needed resource for paying medical bills, but depending on your needs, you might be wise to supplement it with medigap insurance (as long as it truly fills the gaps) and long-term care insurance. Finally, pay close attention to what candidates say about publicly funded long-term care benefits. This is an increasingly important aspect of the public debate about responsibility for health care.

CHAPTER FIVE

CareSkill Five: Understanding the Legal Aspects of Long-Term Care

Crucial to long-term care planning is the unpleasant prospect that you or a loved one may one day need help making decisions about money or medical treatment.

Discussing these issues in advance is essential. But talk isn't enough: Appropriate legal measures are needed to ensure that the wishes of the older person are carried out. Although an older adult may think that his or her intentions have been understood, relatives may still face confusion when the time comes to act in their loved one's behalf. In some circumstances, the law may prevent families from taking action without the necessary documents.

This chapter explains joint bank accounts, powers of attorney and conservatorships, arrangements that enable older people to have help managing their financial affairs; and living wills, which specify whether heroic measures are to be used to keep an individual alive. (A caution: State and territory laws may vary considerably and should be checked carefully.)

Wills are discussed in this chapter as well. While not directly related to long-term care, a valid will can ensure that an individual's assets are distributed as he or she would wish. In addition, the existence of a will, and what it specifies, can have an enormous effect on the quality of life for a surviving spouse, who may also one day require long-term care.

Managing the Money

A loss of mental ability is not a natural part of aging, but it can occur in such conditions as Alzheimer's disease or stroke, rendering the victim incapable of handling financial matters. Some disabilities—poor eyesight and arthritis, for example—can make paying bills and keeping records difficult.

There are several arrangements through which family members or others can help older people manage their money, and thus protect their assets, while maintaining a higher level of independence. Effective preplanning involves learning the advantages and disadvantages of each option and, if possible, making arrangements ahead of time, when consent can readily be given.

- **Joint bank accounts** allow another person to pay bills and withdraw funds for an incapacitated adult. This can prevent a shut-off of utilities, possible loss of property, disruption of health services and legal entanglements.

 Many joint accounts are held under *joint tenancy*. When one owner dies, the assets pass directly to the surviving owner. This arrangement can avoid probate, but if the account is large enough, estate taxes may be due. When the account's owners are *tenants in common*, however, each owns a specified percentage of the funds. The deceased owner's share is passed on to his or her heirs.

- **Power of attorney.** This legal arrangement enables someone else to act in a person's behalf. A power of attorney can be limited to paying bills or broadened to cover handling all finances, including investments.

 Regular powers of attorney become invalid if the person granting the right becomes incompetent. For this reason, a regular power of attorney is not the way for an older person to arrange for help with financial matters in the event of incapacity.

 To retain its validity in the event of incompetence, a power of attorney must be made *durable*; that is, it must contain a *durability clause*, stating that the power of attorney is to endure, even if the older person's ability to make decisions does not. A clause can also be written so that the power of attorney becomes active **only** in the event of incompetence.

 To be valid, a power of attorney must be witnessed and notarized as required by state law. Should you decide to revoke the power, you must file a formal, notarized document with the local recorder of deeds. Because the exercise of a power of attorney is not supervised, mismanagement of a life's savings can and does happen—more often as a result of ignorance than of maliciousness. So when choosing the best person to take on a power of attorney, an older adult must rely not on emotion, but on a careful assessment of the individual's experience and training.

- **Conservatorship.** The family of an older person who has become incapable of entering into a joint bank account or power of attorney agreement can still assist in the management of that person's affairs through a conservatorship, sometimes called a guardianship.

  In this arrangement, a family member or other caregiver petitions the court to appoint a *conservator* to manage the disabled person's finances and estate. The court may appoint a relative, close friend or attorney as conservator. If no one else is available, a *public guardian* may be appointed. The court will decide whether the older person still makes sound, informed financial decisions. The court does not assess overall competence.

  In this arrangement, a family member or other care acquires complete access to the disabled person's assets. The court requires the conservator to file a yearly report detailing every transaction made.

  Once a conservator has been appointed, the disabled person has no control over his or her financial affairs. Dealings are between the court and the conservator alone.

When Life Itself Hangs in the Balance

Medical science has altered simple notions of life and death. The ability to extend life for the terminally ill through technology has forced families to become philosophers.

The question of whether to prolong life through extraordinary or "heroic" measures is not a matter of "right" or "wrong." Deciding whether to continue such treatment reflects individual beliefs and preferences and the legal precedent in that state.

You and other family members may hold very different opinions about these issues, so it is important that they be discussed. However, your goal should not be to argue through to a common stance, but to know what each person wants done should tragedy strike him or her.

It is important, too, to reflect on your responses to others' wishes. If you and a loved one differed, whose desires would you honor? Could you feel comfortable acting upon a belief at odds with your own? Would you suffer guilt as a result?

A *living will* and a *durable power of attorney for health care* are two options for handling these crises.

- **Living wills.** These are legal documents that specify whether medical procedures aimed at delaying death should be used in the event that the patient is unable to make decisions about medical care. The living will can also specify whether surgery is to be attempted, whether pain medication is to be administered, and whether organs are to be donated.

  Living wills are legal in all states that have a Natural Death Act. Such a law allows a person to stipulate whether his or her life is to be prolonged artificially in the event of terminal illness. In most states where it is legal, a living will overrides the wishes of relatives and protects the attending physician against lawsuits.

  You do not need an attorney's help to draw up a living will. A sample living will form is contained in this book. (See Appendix VI.) One can also be obtained from your Area Agency on Aging. To be valid, a living will must be witnessed by two people who are neither relatives, heirs, nor the person's physician. Some states require that a living will be notarized; a few have additional stipulations.

  It is recommended that several copies of a living will be made. One should be kept by a close family member or friend, and others should be available to give to a hospital or physician as needed.

- **A durable power of attorney for health care.** This document goes beyond a living will to appoint an individual to make all health care decisions for a person who becomes incapacitated.

  It is possible to combine a durable power of attorney for health care with one for managing financial decisions, but this is advisable only if the person most qualified to make your personal health care decisions would be best at managing your financial interests as well.

  The concept of a durable power of attorney for health care grew out of a recommendation of the President's 1983 Commission for the Study of Ethical Problems in Medicine and Biomedical and Behavioral Research. Nearly all states have made such documents legal for individuals to create. Some states, however, require that a specific form be used. You may wish to discuss this with an attorney. (A sample durable power of attorney for health care form is included in Appendix VII.)

The Will—A Document No Adult Should Be Without

Currently, an estimated 50 percent of Americans die *intestate* (without a will). In these cases, the fate of the estate is determined in court, according to state laws.

When an individual dies intestate in most states, the surviving spouse receives one-third to one-half of the deceased's estate, with the balance going to the deceased's children. If the deceased has no children, portions could go to his or her parents, brothers or sisters.

The latter situation could result in financial hardship for the surviving spouse. And even if caring relations decided to return their portion of the estate, a stiff gift tax could be levied.

In a "community property" state—Arizona, California, Idaho, Louisiana, Nebraska, New Mexico, Texas or Washington—all assets acquired during the marriage are considered jointly owned. Therefore, the spouse would receive the bulk of the estate, but this could mean that surviving children might receive less than the deceased intended.

Without a will, an older person could not leave something to a special friend, a grandchild or even a favorite charity. His or her bank accounts and safety deposit box could be kept under lock and key for a year or more.

Writing a will correctly requires the services of an attorney—if possible, one who is experienced in estate planning. This can cost between $100 and $500, depending on the complexity of the estate, but the expense is offset by the knowledge that the will is not apt to contain a mistake that could cause it to be invalidated. Given the value of a home, pension and other assets, many in the middle class might now have an estate worth between $250,000 and $500,000. A few hundred dollars seems a small price to pay for protection and peace of mind.

The older person will need to appoint an *executor*—someone who has the legal obligation to see that the will's provisions are carried out. This is no small responsibility, so the matter should be discussed with the intended executor before the will is drawn. The executor often receives a fee from the estate, but is usually required to post a bond, which is an expense.

Some people think that a wife doesn't need a will, particularly if she never worked. However, a woman must always be protected. Were she to die shortly after her husband—before she'd had time to draft a will of her own—the fate of her estate would be decided in court, perhaps not according to her wishes. It's possible that a woman has jewelry and heirlooms that she would like to leave to a loved one. Wills cover such bequests.

A will is not something to be written and forgotten. It should be updated periodically to take into consideration changes in the estate or family circumstances, new state or federal tax-law provisions, the need for a new executor, or a move to a new state. Usually it isn't necessary to draft a completely new will; an amendment to an existing will, called a *codicil*, can be written.

Reviewing a will every three years is a wise practice. However, those whose wills were written before 1981 should make an extra effort to do so as soon as possible: The Economic Recovery Act of 1981 resulted in substantial changes in the laws regarding estate taxes. As a consequence, wills drafted before that year could be seriously outdated. Affected individuals should consult an attorney specializing in estate planning.

Is It Wise to Avoid Probate?

Financial planners disagree on this question. Some view *probate*, or the process by which a will is proven valid in court, as lengthy and expensive. It can take a year or more to complete, and lop off as much as 5 percent of the estate. Others see its value, stating that probate ensures the orderly passing of the estate to the heirs.

Even if someone does not need or desire to avoid probate completely, steps should be taken to minimize its impact on the estate, and to safeguard assets from heavy taxation. Joint ownership and trust funds—both living and testamentary—can help meet these needs.

- **Joint ownership.** Having the title to a major asset, such as a house or automobile, registered in joint ownership (between a husband and wife, for example) can ensure that complete ownership of an asset will pass automatically to the surviving owner in the event the other dies, thus bypassing probate.

  Joint ownership, however, does not negate the need for a will. Certain eventualities must be planned for. For example, there is always the possibility that co-owners could die simultaneously; if there were no mention of the jointly owned asset in a will, its fate would be decided by the court. Or if one owner died before the other, the asset would be inherited by the surviving owner's children and relatives upon his or her death—those of the owner who died first would be overlooked. Finally, thought must be given to whether either owner could manage the asset if left with the entire responsibility.

- **Trust funds.** A properly established trust fund could ensure that an asset is well-managed after the owner's death. Trusts can serve other purposes for your older relative, too. They can allow him or her to pass assets along to heirs while cutting taxes now and in the future, see that assets and inheritances are properly managed, simplify management of assets right now, and protect a life's savings in the event of catastrophic illness.

  What exactly is a trust fund? Basically, it's a legal arrangement whereby the ownership of money is transferred on behalf of a *beneficiary*, who could be one or more individuals, or a school or other institution. As *grantor*, the older person establishes the guidelines for management of the trust and distribution of the interest and principal. A *fiduciary agent*, or *trustee*, must also be assigned. This is the party, often a bank, with the legal responsibility for managing the trust's assets according to the grantor's specifications.

A *living trust* is one that can be set up now. It begins paying some interest to the beneficiary during the grantor's lifetime. After the grantor dies, the trust fund's principal can either pass automatically to the beneficiary or remain in the trust, whichever is specified. In either case, the trust escapes probate.

Living trusts can be *revocable* or *irrevocable*. A revocable living trust is one that the grantor has the power to dissolve; he or she must continue to pay taxes on the income it earns at his or her current tax rate. The funds in an irrevocable living trust cannot be taken back, but its income is taxed at the beneficiary's rate, which may be lower.

Some experts recommend establishing a revocable living trust initially. If the grantor is pleased with the way the bank or other trustee is managing the trust, it can be made irrevocable.

A *testamentary trust* is one established as a provision of a will. It doesn't start paying dividends until after the grantor dies. A testamentary trust doesn't avoid probate, but it assures the grantor that an inheritance will be managed according to his or her wishes.

At one time, the bulk of an estate was heavily taxed by the federal government. But the problem of federal taxes was significantly lessened by the Federal Tax Act of 1981, which specified that an individual could leave an estate to his or her spouse without it being federally taxed. As of 1987, the amount that could be left tax-free to others increased to $600,000. Therefore, most estates are not taxed.

But although a spouse can inherit tax-free, if his or her estate is worth more than $600,000, the survivors won't be so lucky. One way to avoid taxation in this situation is to place everything above $600,000 in a *bypass trust*. With this special arrangement, upon an individual's death, his or her spouse receives the income from the trust. When the spouse dies, the trust passes to the inheritors. They can also inherit the spouse's $600,000 estate.

A number of people plan to pass along assets to children as gifts. The Uniform Gifts to Minors Act permits an adult to give money or other assets to a child, yet remain the custodian until the child comes of age. This allows a family member to set aside funds for the child's education, for example, yet pay no taxes on them. While the child would be liable for any taxes, he or she would be taxed at a much lower rate or not at all.

A bank can help someone establish an account under the Uniform Gifts to Minors Act. Of course, the funds in this account are a gift and can't be taken back, but that also means they cannot be drained in the event that the giver experiences a catastrophic or long-term illness.

Monetary gifts are one way in which people requiring or anticipating long-term care have attempted to reduce their assets and thus qualify for Medicaid. While this may have worked well in the past, a number of states have tightened their regulations, requiring large gifts (normally $10,000 or more) to be made at least two years prior to Medicaid application. Therefore, an older person who wants to protect assets in this way should not wait until long-term care is imminent.

The Greatest Reward Is Peace of Mind

Facing up to the legal aspects of long-term care may be the most difficult part of preplanning, because it means acknowledging that life is finite and that one's ability to make decisions can diminish.

But someone who makes the necessary legal arrangements to cover decision-making in the event of incapacity, and who drafts a valid, up-to-date will gains assurance that his or her wishes will be respected when important decisions are made. Also, the loved ones are spared the guilt, anger and regrets that are so common when families must make these decisions unguided.

CHAPTER SIX

CareSkill Six:
Caring for the Caregiver

"By caring for Mother, I know I neglect my husband and kids. But what can I do? She can't manage without my help."

"I visit or call Dad every day, and do everything he asks of me. But I always worry that I'm not doing enough!"

"Most women in his generation didn't work. He can't understand that my family needs the money, or that my career is important to me."

"I wish I could get more help and understanding from the rest of the family. My brothers don't see any need to get involved."

"What about *my* needs?"

These are the frustrations commonly voiced by members of the "sandwich generation," those adults caught between the demands of their children, spouses and careers, and the needs of a chronically ill older relative.

Exhaustion, loneliness, depression, anger, stress, guilt, resentment, helplessness—many caregivers understand those emotional responses all too well. Thus, it's crucial that any care plan consider the caregiver. It must not just meet all of the older person's needs. It **must** also address the needs of the caregiver. But this can only happen if the caregiver is honest about his or her feelings and seeks necessary help from friends and family members (including the older person) and community organizations and services. Also, he or she must actively and assertively practice self-care and pursue outside interests.

The Ambivalent "Dutiful Daughter"

Those adults, and they are mostly women, who find themselves cast in the role of caregiver are subject to unrealistic or conflicting feelings.

Usually, they feel a responsibility to care for their older relative; often they want very much to help. But sometimes these feelings get out of hand, and the caregiver tries to live up to too high a standard—attempting to provide flawless care, be an ideal spouse and parent, hold down a job and keep a spotless home. Such high expectations can only lead to "burnout," guilt or anger that is either overt or repressed.

Occasionally, resentments harbored since childhood can cause adult children to approach caregiving with mixed emotions. As Barbara Silverstone and Helen Kandel Hyman, authors of *You and Your Aging Parent*, explain, "Childhood may seem an eternity away as people grow older and many memories are left behind, both pleasant and unpleasant. But the feelings developed in that early period are not so easily left behind. . . . Once a resentful child begins to live his own adult life, he may forget how angry he used to be with his parents. But just as the helplessness and disabilities of their old age can awaken feelings of tenderness and compassion untapped for years, their new dependency can rekindle old feelings of anger and resentment long thought to be dead and buried."

It is important for all caregivers to realize that negative feelings toward their responsibilities and even toward the older person they care for are normal. You can acknowledge these feelings without having to label yourself as selfish or uncaring. It may help to get them off your chest by talking with an understanding friend or relative.

But when negative emotions occur frequently, it is a sign that the caregiver needs help. The checklist at right can help caregivers assess their emotions.

Developing Your Own "Care Plan"

Completing the Caregiver's Emotional Checklist gave you an informal assessment of your needs. And just as the initial stages of long-term care problem solving included an assessment of the older person's requirements, taking an objective look at your own situation is the first step toward obtaining the appropriate support.

Analyze your responses to the questionnaire to learn what they tell you about yourself:

- Do you feel isolated, angry or depressed?
- Do you need someone to talk to?
- Would you benefit from occasional time off from caregiving?
- Are you carrying a heavy financial burden?
- Is caregiving affecting your health?

Caregiver's Emotional Checklist

	Often	Some-times	Not Very Often	Never
Indicate how often you feel this way:				
• Resentful of other family members who do not provide assistance.	☐	☐	☐	☐
• That the care recipient makes unreasonable, unnecessary demands.	☐	☐	☐	☐
• Stressed by conflicting responsibilities.	☐	☐	☐	☐
• Depressed about your caregiving situation.	☐	☐	☐	☐
• Worried about the care recipient's future needs.	☐	☐	☐	☐
• Strained relations with the care recipient.	☐	☐	☐	☐
• That caregiving has negatively affected your health.	☐	☐	☐	☐
• That caregiving doesn't allow you enough privacy.	☐	☐	☐	☐
• That caregiving limits your social life.	☐	☐	☐	☐
• Unappreciated by the care recipient.	☐	☐	☐	☐
• That the care recipient leans on you too much.	☐	☐	☐	☐
• That the care recipient is manipulative.	☐	☐	☐	☐
• That caregiving is causing you financial distress.	☐	☐	☐	☐
• The following emotions resulting from the relationship:				
— guilt.	☐	☐	☐	☐
— anger.	☐	☐	☐	☐
— resentment.	☐	☐	☐	☐

There is no "cut-and-dry" method for evaluating this checklist, but a majority of responses in the columns labeled "often" and "sometimes" is an indication that you should seek assistance.

Adapted from Zarit, S., *"The Burden Interview,"* 1985.

Once you have a clearer understanding of your problem, you can begin to investigate possible solutions. Assistance is available to caregivers either formally, through community organizations, or informally, from friends and relatives. Self-help is an important part of the picture, too.

Finding Someone to Listen

• **Support Groups**. It is a welcome relief to learn that other people are in the same situation. Membership in a support or self-help group can put you in touch with other caregivers, with whom you can share emotional support, understanding and suggestions for handling problems.

The group provides an atmosphere of acceptance, and it encourages members to express their feelings, communicate more effectively, view their situations objectively and find more appropriate coping strategies.

A typical support group is likely to meet regularly in a church hall or public building. Some meet in members' homes. And as employers are becoming more aware of caregiving's impact on their employee population, some support groups are being formed within the workplace.

Many groups employ a professional counselor to guide discussions and structure meetings. From time to time, experts in various aspects of caregiving might speak to the group.

You can find a support group in your area by contacting national or local clearinghouses or hotlines, your employee assistance program, or a church, synogogue, hospital or community organization. (Refer to Appendix III: Support Groups for You and Your Parents.)

- **Counseling.** Caregivers should not hesitate to obtain counseling if they feel a need for confidential, one-on-one assistance. Discussing problems with a clinical psychologist or social worker is nothing to be ashamed of or avoided.

To locate a licensed mental health professional, contact your county mental health agency, mental health association, a licensed mental health clinic or a clinical social workers' association. Many agencies charge fees on a sliding scale, based on ability to pay. Also, a workplace employee assistance program can help you determine whether you require professional help and provide referrals.

Respite Care: Some Well-Deserved Time Off

The demands of caring for an older relative leave caregivers with precious little time for themselves. In a recent study conducted by The Travelers Companies, 80 percent of caregivers responded that caring for an older adult had caused their social and emotional needs to go unmet. Thirty percent had not had time off from caregiving in more than a year.

To avoid the depression, fatigue and "burnout" that inevitably come from such stress, caregivers must acknowledge their own needs—particularly the need for a "break," or respite, from the responsibility.

Respite care can be provided by organizations in the community or informally, by relatives and friends. The kind of respite care that you choose will depend on the level of care that the older person requires and the services available in your community.

Respite services, often staffed by trained volunteers, are offered by churches or synagogues, nursing homes, home health agencies or volunteer organizations. A volunteer spends time with the older person in his or her home, so that the family caregiver can run errands, take part in social activities, or enjoy hobbies and other interests. Such a brief hiatus can make it far easier for the caregiver to sustain his or her role.

Other long-term care options can also provide short-term relief. For example, adult day care centers can take over for a caregiver who is employed. There are nursing homes and other residential facilities that will take care of people temporarily to give the caregiver a chance to get out of town for a business trip or vacation. These and other long-term care options are described in Chapter Three of this section.

Family members, friends and neighbors might be willing to provide respite care as well. Friends may offer to spend an occasional evening with the older person, while another family member can relieve the caregiver for a longer period, perhaps for a much-needed vacation.

Ease the Financial Burden

Unfortunately, there is no one resource or simple solution for family caregivers who are experiencing a heavy financial burden. But there are some self-help measures that are worth looking into:

- **Less expensive resources than those now being used.** It doesn't make financial sense to pay for an expensive private-duty nurse when a homemaker-home health aide can perform the needed caregiving duties. If you are unsure of the level of care required, a physician's office, social services agency or your Area Agency on Aging can arrange for a formal assessment of the situation.

- **Help from other family members.** Your brothers and sisters or other relatives may have no understanding of the costs of your loved one's care. You should not bear the total responsibility. Call a family meeting, at which you outline the financial situation and ask the others to chip in; or discuss other options, such as forgoing an inheritance or selling off property to meet the costs of care now.

- **Benefits for the older person.** It is no disgrace for your loved one to receive Medicaid or other forms of public assistance if he or she is entitled to these funds. Chapter Four, "Understanding the Ins and Outs of Financing Long-Term Care," discusses various sources of funding. Become familiar with these. Discuss your financial options with your local Social Security office, department of social services or Area Agency on Aging.

- **Resources for the employed caregiver.** Some caregivers leave their jobs or cut back on working hours to meet the demands of caregiving. This often results in financial hardship and almost always leads to anger and frustration. It not only robs the caregiver of money, but of the joy of the job and the social atmosphere of the workplace.

Quitting your job may simply compound an already stressful situation. Do not consider such a major step without checking into other options. Adult day care or companion services, for example, provide care that can enable you to stay on the job.

- **Look out for your own interests.** Other caregivers may provide emotional support, respite care may give a break, but still the caregiver continues to juggle several demanding roles each and every day. It is a monumental task, one for which formal services are lacking. So the caregiver must take on yet another role—caring for himself or herself. Try not to take on more than you can handle. Stop before you do something and ask, "Is this **really** necessary? Can someone else do it?" Don't sacrifice friends, hobbies or values. If you do, anger and resentment will surely follow. Always look for other options.

• **Some other ways to ease the burden.** Communicate. Tell other family members that you need help; let them know how they can pitch in, perhaps by performing specific caregiving duties or other household tasks. You may need to "level" with your care recipient and others about the importance of your job and your other interests.

If you are working, make sure that your supervisor understands your situation. Perhaps you can alter your working hours, if that would be helpful. Also, you might be able to arrange for occasional time off to take your older relative to the doctor, or to perform other caregiving duties.

Think about ways to enlist the older person's help. Can he or she take on any housekeeping responsibilities or help out with child care? Not only will these duties make your life easier, but they will make the older person feel needed, and improve his or her feelings of self-worth.

Because you are in a demanding, stressful situation, you must make a special effort to take care of your health—to exercise regularly, eat properly, get sufficient rest and maintain contact with the outside world. Section II of this book provides information on LifeSkills that can help you with your self-care needs.

Also, beware of negative coping strategies, such as reliance on caffeine, cigarettes, alcohol and other drugs; angry outbursts; or overeating. These do nothing to improve your situation and ultimately will be harmful to yourself and others. Section II, Chapter Three can help you replace these behaviors with positive, effective stress-management skills.

Following Through

Planning for another's long-term care involves experimentation. After you have investigated all possible solutions, it's time to select those that seem most appropriate and workable. You implement your plan and evaluate its effectiveness. If needs remain unmet or a new problem occurs, the problem-solving process is repeated.

The same thing should happen when you plan to take care of yourself. Once you have explored all of the avenues of assistance that are open to you, you need to develop your personal care plan. Try it out for several weeks, and then evaluate its effectiveness. You may find it helpful to complete the Caregiver's Emotional Checklist again, and compare your two sets of responses. If problem areas continue to exist, look for alternative solutions.

Caregiving is never an easy job, but it need not be overwhelming. As a caregiver, you must learn to care for yourself. You must maintain your independence and live as normal a life as possible.

Appendices

APPENDIX I

Personal Health Record

This Personal Health Record is designed to help individuals and families keep track of important health information—what happened in the past as well as what you need to plan for the future. It will make this information available not only to you, but to health professionals when needed.

Space is provided for you to record information on up to four family members.

Immunizations

If you have been immunized against tetanus and diphtheria, just give the date of immunization. But it is very important to know the date of your last tetanus booster, since you need a booster every 10 years. If you actually had the illness listed, put the date you were ill preceded by the letter "I" - for example: "I-1967."

Vaccine	Recommended Age	Initials ____	Initials ____	Initials ____	Initials ____
Tetanus and Diphtheria (Td)	14-16 years & every 10 years				

Drugs

List any drugs you take regularly. Give the dosage and how often you take the drug—for example: "Hydrochlorothiazide 50 mg. (milligrams) twice a day." If you do not know the dosage, it's time you found out.

	Name of Drug	Dosage	How Often
Name _____			
Name _____			
Name _____			
Name _____			

Drug Allergies

If you or any family members are allergic to any medications, list those medications here. Be sure to mention this information when drugs are prescribed.

Name _____	Name _____	Name _____	Name _____

Hospitalizations

Listing the hospital and its address as well as the date of hospitalization and problem will help in getting records if they are ever needed.

	Name	Name	Name	Name
Problem				
Date				
Hospital				
Address				
Problem				
Date				
Hospital				
Address				

Serious Illnesses

Giving the name of the attending physician and his or her telephone number will help in obtaining records if they are ever needed.

	Name	Name	Name	Name
Problem				
Date				
Doctor				
Phone				
Problem				
Date				
Doctor				
Phone				

X-Rays

Being able to locate past X-rays could save you from further exposure to X-ray radiation.

	Date of X-Ray	Type of X-Ray	Where X-Ray Can Be Found
Name _____			
Name _____			
Name _____			
Name _____			

Family History

Make note of any family history of the following diseases or conditions. Your family history is important to your physician, and you may not remember all of this information at the time he or she asks you.

	Name _____	Name _____	Name _____	Name _____
Cancer				
Heart Disease				
Diabetes				
Stroke				
High Blood Pressure				
Glaucoma/Cataracts				
Arthritis/Gout				
Hearing				
Cholesterol Record the Dates of Blood Cholesterol Tests and the Results Here	Date Reading	Date Reading	Date Reading	Date Reading
Record of the Dates of Yearly Blood Pressure Tests and the Actual Blood Pressure Readings Here	Date Reading Date Reading	Date Reading Date Reading	Date Reading Date Reading	Date Reading Date Reading
Women Should Record the Dates of Pap Smears Here	Date Date	Date Date	Date Date	Date Date
Women Should Record the Dates of Yearly Breast Examinations by a Physician Here	Date Date	Date Date	Date Date	Date Date
Record the Dates of Yearly Dental Examinations Here	Date Date	Date Date	Date Date	Date Date
Men Over Age 40 Should Record Digital Exam (Prostate) Recommended Once Every 3 Years	Date Date	Date Date	Date Date	Date Date
Those Over Age 50 Should Record Proctosigmoidoscopy Exams (Recommended Once Every 2 Yrs.)	Date Date	Date Date	Date Date	Date Date

Resources

Record important telephone numbers here. Make sure all family members know the location of this list, so they can refer to it as needed.

Physicians

Name	Telephone Number	Specialty

Poison control center _____

Hospitals _____

Ambulance _____

Fire department _____

Pharmacy _____

Dentist _____

Mental health specialists _____

Hotlines _____

Friend or neighbor who can help in an emergency _____

Taking Care of Your Parents

Overseeing the health care of their parents is a responsibility that all adults may one day face. Many have assumed this responsibility already. Because a parent may require your help suddenly, it is important to have some knowledge of your parents' health status. You can record needed information here.

	Doctor	Specialty	Phone
Name			
Name			
Name			
Name			

Drugs

List any drugs your parents take regularly. Give the dosage and how often they take the drug.

	Drug	Dosage	How Often
Name _____			
Name _____			
Name _____			
Name _____			

Drugs

List any drugs to which your parents are allergic.

Name _____	Name _____	Name _____	Name _____

Hospitalizations

Listing the hospital and its address, as well as the date of hospitalization and problem, will help in getting records if they are ever needed.

Name	Name	Name	Name
Problem			
Date			
Hospital			
Address			
Problem			
Date			
Hospital			
Address			

Illnesses and Injuries

List the name and telephone number of the attending physician. This will help in obtaining records if they are ever needed.

Name	Name	Name	Name
Problem			
Date			
Doctor			
Phone			
Problem			
Date			
Doctor			
Phone			

Dietary Recommendations

If a parent has been put on a restricted or modified diet by a physician, record the type of diet and the date it began here.

Name _____ Name _____ Name _____ Name _____

Diet _____

Date _____

Diet _____

Date _____

Diet _____

Date _____

Diet _____

Date _____

Important Numbers for Caregivers

Physicians Treating a Parent or Other Older Relative

Name	Telephone Number	Specialty

Area Agency on Aging _____

Friend or neighbor of the older person _____

Other Caregiving Resources:

Agency	Telephone Number

APPENDIX II

Toll-Free Numbers for Health Information

ALZHEIMER'S DISEASE

Alzheimer's Disease and Related Disorders Association
800/621-0379
800/572-6037 in Illinois

Offers information on publications about Alzheimer's disease and related disorders. Gives referrals to local chapters and support groups.

CANCER

AMC Cancer Information
800/525-3777

Provides current information on cancer's causes, prevention, methods of detection, diagnosis, rehabilitation and treatment. Also gives information on treatment facilities and counseling services. A service of AMC Cancer Research Center, Denver, CO.

Cancer Information Service (CIS)
800/422-6237
808/524-1234 in Oahu, HI (call collect from neighboring islands)

Answers cancer-related questions from the public, cancer patients and their families, and health professionals. CIS staff members neither diagnose cancer nor recommend treatment for individual cases. Spanish-speaking staff members are available for callers from the following areas: California, Florida, Georgia, Illinois, Northern New Jersey, New York City and Texas. A service of the National Cancer Institute, U.S. Department of Health and Human Services.

DIABETES

American Diabetes Association
800/232-3472
703/549-1500 in Virginia

Provides free printed materials, newsletter, health education information and support-group assistance information.

EYE CARE

American Council for the Blind
800/424-8666
202/393-3666 in Washington, DC

Offers information on blindness. Provides referrals to clinics, rehabilitation organizations, research centers and local chapters. Also publishes printed resource lists.

National Eye Care Project Hotline
800/222-EYES

Provides information for senior citizens on how to get a free eye examination. Eligible persons must be American citizens or legal residents who have not been to see an ophthalmologist in three years and who are in financial need.

Library of Congress National Library Services for the Blind and Physically Handicapped
800/424-8567
202/287-5100 in Washington, DC

Guides individuals incapacitated by short- or long-term illness to libraries that utilize the talking-book service. Also provides a listing of books and magazines in Braille.

National Rehabilitation Center
800/34-NARIC
301/588-9284 in Washington, DC

Rehabilitation information service and research library. Makes available information about assistive devices. Also disseminates information about other rehabilitation-related services.

HEALTH INFORMATION

ODPHP Health Information Center
800/336-4797
301/565-4167 in Washington, DC

Provides a central source of information and referral for health questions. Staff members neither diagnose nor recommend treatment for medical conditions. A service of the Office of Disease Prevention and Health Promotion, U.S. Department of Health and Human Services.

HEARING IMPAIRMENT

Federal Internal Revenue Service for TDD Users
800/428-4732
800/382-4059 in Indiana

Answers questions about the federal income tax, such as whether medical deductions are allowed for the cost of telecommunications devices for the deaf (TDDs), hearing aids, trained hearing-ear dogs and sending deaf children to special schools. Accepts orders for the free publication, "Tax Information for Handicapped and Disabled Individuals," and other free IRS publications.

Hearing Helpline
800/424-8576
703/642-0580

Provides information on hearing and the prevention of deafness. Information is mailed upon request. A service of the Better Hearing Institute.

National Hearing Aid Helpline
800/521-5247
313/478-2610 in Michigan

Provides information on hearing aids and distributes a directory of hearing-aid specialists certified by the National Hearing Aid Society.

HUNTINGTON'S DISEASE

Huntington's Disease Society of America
800/345-4372
212/242-1968 in New York

Gives information on Huntington's disease. Provides referrals to physicians and support groups. Answers questions on presymptomatic testing.

INSURANCE

American Council of Life Insurance
Health Insurance Association of America
800/635-1271
202/223-7780 in Washington, DC

Answers general questions and sends materials about life and health insurance. Does not handle complaints regarding insurance claims.

KIDNEY DISEASES

American Kidney Fund
800/638-8299
800/492-8361 in Maryland

Grants financial assistance to kidney patients who are unable to pay treatment-related costs. Also provides information on organ donations and kidney-related diseases.

LIVER DISEASES

American Liver Foundation
800/223-0179
201/857-2626 in New Jersey

Provides information on liver diseases, including fact sheets. Also makes physician referrals.

LUNG DISEASES

National Asthma Center
800/222-5864
303/398-1477 in Colorado

Answers questions about asthma, emphysema, chronic bronchitis, allergies, juvenile rheumatoid arthritis and other respiratory and immune-system disorders. Questions are answered by registered nurses or other health professionals. A service of the National Jewish Center for Immunology and Respiratory Medicine.

MEDICARE/MEDICAID

DHHS Inspector General's Hotline
800/368-5779
301/597-0724 in Maryland

Handles complaints regarding fraud, waste and abuse of such government funds as Medicare, Medicaid and Social Security. Assists people who have been billed for services.

ORGAN DONATION

The Living Bank
800/528-2971
713/528-2971 in Texas

Operates a registry and referral service for people wanting to commit their tissues, bones, vital organs or bodies to transplantation or research. Informs the public about organ transplants and donations.

PARKINSON'S DISEASE

National Parkinson Foundation
800/327-4545
800/433-7022 in Florida
305/547-6666 in the Miami area

Answers questions about Parkinson's disease and provides written information on request.

PLASTIC SURGERY

American Society of Plastic and
Reconstructive Surgeons
800/635-0635
312/856-1818 in Illinois

Provides referrals to board-certified plastic surgeons. Also offers pamphlets describing procedures and realistic results.

SAFETY

National Safety Council
800/621-7619

Provides information on safety. Posters, brochures and booklets on all aspects of safety and accident prevention are available.

SURGERY

National Second Surgical Opinion Program Hotline
800/638-6833
800/492-6603 in Maryland

Helps consumers locate specialists near them for a second opinion on non-emergency surgery. A service of the Health Care Financing Administration, U.S. Department of Health and Human Services.

URINARY INCONTINENCE

Simon Foundation
800/23-SIMON

Provides information on incontinence. Written materials, including a quarterly newsletter and other publications, are available to the public.

APPENDIX III

Support Groups for You and Your Parents

ELDERCARE

Children of Aging Parents
2761 Trenton Road
Levittown, PA 19056

This organization provides support and guidance to people caring for aged family members.

National Support Center for Families of the Aging
P.O. Box 245
Swarthmore, PA 19081

This network of support groups also provides referrals to agencies and resources.

ILLNESS AND SURGERY

The Alzheimer's Disease and Related Disorders Association
70 East Lake Street
Suite 600
Chicago, IL 60601

This organization provides assistance and support for the relatives and caregivers of people with Alzheimer's disease. A newsletter, group development guidelines and referrals are also provided.

Arthritis Foundation Support Groups
1314 Spring Street
Atlanta, GA 30309

In 72 chapters nationwide, people with arthritis, their families and friends receive education and support and participate in social activities. The organization publishes a quarterly newsletter.

The American Diabetes Association, Inc.
P.O. Box 25757
1660 Duke Street
Alexandria, VA 22313

More than 700 affiliates and chapters provide support and information to diabetics and their families.

Emphysema Anonymous
7976 Seminole Blvd.
Suite 6
Seminole, FL 33542

This organization provides support and education to people with emphysema and other lung disorders. A quarterly newsletter, "Battling the Breeze," is published.

Family Cancer Support Network
c/o Self-Help Center
1600 Dodge Avenue
Suite S-122
Evanston, IL 60201

The families of people with life-threatening illnesses receive support and learn to help themselves. A quarterly newsletter is published, and group development guidelines are available.

HEARTLIFE/AHP (Association of Heart Patients)
P.O. Box 54305
Atlanta, GA 30308

Heart patients and their families receive support and information. A monthly newsletter and a quarterly journal are published.

Make Today Count
P.O. Box 222
Osage Beach, MO 65065

Those who have faced a life-threatening illness share their experiences and receive support. A newsletter is published six times per year, and chapter development guidelines are available.

Mended Hearts
7320 Greenville Avenue
Dallas, TX 75231

People who have had heart surgery and their families constitute the membership of this organization's more than 150 chapters. A quarterly newsletter is published, and a chapter development guide is available.

National Association of Patients on Hemodialysis and Transplantation
211 East 43rd Street
New York, NY 10038

People who have had kidney transplants or who are on hemodialysis receive support and education, as do their families and friends.

National Shut-In Society
225 West 99th Street
New York, NY 10025

Organized in 1877, this society provides support, encouragement and opportunities for communication to people who are chronically ill or housebound. A bimonthly newsletter, "The Open Window," is published.

Stroke Clubs
American Heart Association
National Center
7320 Greenville Avenue
Dallas, TX 75231

Support, education and social activities are the benefits received by stroke victims and their families in this organization's more than 300 clubs nationwide.

United Ostomy Association
2001 W. Beverly Blvd.
Los Angeles, CA 90057-2491

Ostomy patients and their families share experiences and receive information and support. A quarterly publication and chapter development kit are available.

We Can Do!
P.O. Box 723
Arcadia, CA 91006

Cancer patients receive education and support through weekly group meetings and a telephone network. Chapter development guidelines are available.

HEARING IMPAIRMENTS

Consumers Organization for the Hearing Impaired
cb NAHSA
10801 Rockville Pike
Rockville, MD 20852

Hearing-impaired persons get support and assistance in adjusting to their situation. This organization promotes the use of professional services and audiologic devices.

SHHH: Self-Help for Hard of Hearing People, Inc.
7800 Wisconsin Avenue
Bethesda, MD 20814

This organization of the hearing impaired, their relatives and friends provides support, education, referrals and social activities. A bimonthly journal and chapter development guidelines are available.

GENERAL INFORMATION

National Self-Help Clearinghouse
City University of New York
Graduate Center
Room 620N
33 West 42nd Street
New York, NY 10036

The National Self-Help Clearinghouse can refer people to sources of information on specific types of support groups and regional clearinghouses. The organization also provides guidelines for starting your own self-help groups.

APPENDIX IV

Aging-Related Resources

American Association of Retired Persons
1909 K Street, N.W.
Washington, DC 20049

American Association of Homes for the Aging
1129 29th Street, N.W.
Washington, DC 20036

American Bar Association
Commission on Legal Problems of the Elderly
1800 M Street, N.W.
Washington, DC 20036

American Society on Aging
833 Market Street, Suite 512
San Francisco, CA 94103

Institute on Law and Rights of Older Adults
Brookdale Center on Aging at Hunter College
425 E. 25th Street
New York, NY 10107

National Council on the Aging
600 Maryland Avenue, S.W.
Washington, DC 20024

National Senior Citizens Law Center
2025 H Street, N.W.
Washington, DC 20036

Retired Senior Volunteer Program (RSVP)
ACTION
806 Connecticut Avenue, N.W.
Washington, DC 20525

National Council of Senior Citizens
925 15th Street, N.W.
Washington, DC 20005

Gray Panthers
311 S. Juniper Street, Suite 3601
Philadelphia, PA 19107

National Institute on Aging
9000 Rockville Pike
Bethesda, MD 20892

National Caucus and Center on Black Aged
1424 K Street, N.W.
Washington, DC 20005

OWL – Older Women's League
730 11th Street, N.W., Suite 300
Washington, DC 20001

United Seniors Consumer Cooperative
1334 G Street, N.W. #500
Washington, DC 20005

The Travelers Center on Aging
University of Connecticut
   Health Center
Farmington, CT 06032

APPENDIX V

State Units on Aging

Alabama
Commission on Aging
State Capitol
Montgomery, AL 36130
205/261-5743

Alaska
State Agency on Aging
Older Alaskans Commission
Pouch C, Mail Stop 0209
Juneau, AK 99811
907/465-3250

Arizona
Aging and Adult Administration
P.O. Box 6123
1400 West Washington St.
Phoenix, AZ 85005
602/255-4448

Arkansas
Arkansas State Office on Aging
Donaghey Building
Suite 1428
7th and Main Streets
Little Rock, AR 72201
501/371-2441

California
Department on Aging
Health and Welfare Agency
1020 19th St.
Sacramento, CA 95814
916/322-5290

Colorado
Aging and Adult Services Division
Department of Social Services
717 7th St., Box 181000
Denver, CO 80218-0899
303/294-5913

Connecticut
Department on Aging
175 Main St.
Hartford, CT 06106
203/566-7725

Delaware
Division on Aging
Department of Health and Social Services
1901 N. Dupont Highway
New Castle, DE 19720
302/421-6791

District of Columbia
District of Columbia
Office on Aging
1424 K Street, N.W.
Second Floor
Washington, DC 20005
202/724-5622

Florida
Program Office of Aging
Department of Health and Rehabilitation Services
1317 Winewood Blvd.
Tallahassee, FL 32301
904/488-8922

Georgia
Dept. of Human Resources
878 Peachtree St., N.W.
Room 632
Atlanta, GA 30309
404/894-5333

Hawaii
Executive Office on Aging
Office of the Governor
State of Hawaii
335 Merchant St., Rm. 241
Honolulu, HI 96813
808/548-2593

Idaho
Idaho Office on Aging
Statehouse - Room 114
Boise, ID 83720
208/334-3833

Illinois
Department on Aging
421 East Capitol Ave.
Springfield, IL 62706
217/785-3356

Indiana
Department on Aging and Community Services
115 North Penn Street
Suite 1350
Indianapolis, IN 46204
316/232-7006

Iowa
Commission on Aging
914 Grand Avenue
Jewett Building
Des Moines, IA 50319
515/281-5187

Kansas
Department on Aging
610 West 10th St.
Topeka, KS 66612
913/296-4986

Kentucky
Division for Aging Services
Bureau of Social Services
275 East Main St.
Frankfort, KY 40601
502/564-6930

Louisiana
Office of Elderly Affairs
P.O. Box 80374
Capitol Station
Baton Rouge, LA 70898
504/925-1700

Maine
Bureau of Maine's Elderly
Dept. of Human Services
State House, Station 11
Augusta, ME 04333
207/289-2561

Maryland
Office on Aging
State Office Bldg.
301 West Preston St.
Baltimore, MD 21201
301/225-1100

Massachusetts
Dept. of Elder Affairs
38 Chauncy Street
Boston, MA 02111
617/727-7751

Michigan
Office of Services to the Aging
300 East Michigan
P.O. Box 30026
Lansing, MI 48909
517/373-8230

Minnesota
Board on Aging
204 Metro Square Bldg.
7th and Robert Streets
St. Paul, MN 55101
612/296-2544

Mississippi
Council on Aging
301 West Pearl St.
Jackson, MS 39201
601/949-2070

Missouri
Office of Aging
Department of Social Services
Broadway State Office Building
P.O. Box 570
Jefferson City, MO 65101

Montana
Community Services Division
Department of Social and Rehabilitation Services
P.O. Box 4210
Helena, MT 59604
406/449-3865

Nebraska
Department of Aging
P.O. Box 85044
301 Centennial Mall South
Lincoln, NE 68509
402/471-2306

Nevada
Division of Aging Services
Department of Human Resources
505 East King Street
Room 101
Kinkead Building
Carson City, NV 89710
702/885-4210

New Hampshire
Council on Aging
105 London Road
Building 3
Concord, NH 03301
603/271-2751

New Jersey
Department of Community Affairs
P.O. Box 2768
363 West State Street
Trenton, NJ 08625
609/292-4833

New Mexico
State Agency on Aging
La Villa Rivera Building
224 East Palace Avenue
Santa Fe, NM 87501
505/827-7640

New York
Office for the Aging
Agency Building 2
Empire State Plaza
Albany, NY 12223
518/474-5731

North Carolina
Division on Aging
Department of Human Resources
708 Hillsborough St.
Raleigh, NC 27603
919/733-3983

North Dakota
State Agency on Aging
Department of Human Services
State Capitol Building
Bismarck, ND 58505
701/224-2577

Ohio
Commission on Aging
50 West Broad Street
Columbus, OH 43125
614/466-5500

Oklahoma
Special Unit on Aging
Department of Human Services
P.O. Box 25352
Oklahoma City, OK 73125
405/521-2281

Oregon
Senior Services Division
Human Resources Department
Room 313
Public Services Bldg.
Salem, OR 97301
503/378-4728

Pennsylvania
Department of Aging
231 State Street
Harrisburg, PA 17101
717/783-1550

Rhode Island
Department of Elderly Affairs
79 Washington Street
Providence, RI 02903
401/277-2858

South Carolina
Commission on Aging
915 Main Street
Columbia, SC 29201
803/758-2576

South Dakota
Office of Adult Services and Aging
Division of Human Development
Richard F. Dreip Bldg.
700 N. Illinois Street
Pierre, SD 57501
605/773-3656

Tennessee
Commission on Aging
703 Tennessee Building
535 Church Street
Nashville, TN 37219
615/741-2056

Texas
Department of Aging
P.O. Box 12786
Capitol Station
Austin, TX 78711
512/475-2717

Utah
Division of Aging Services
150 West North Temple
Room 326
Salt Lake City, UT 84103
801/533-6422

Vermont
Office on the Aging
103 Main Street
Waterbury, VT 05676
802/241-2400

Virginia
Office on Aging
101 North 14th Street
James Monroe Building
18th Floor
Richmond, VA 23219
804/225-2271

Washington
Bureau of Aging and Adult Services
Department of Social and Health Services
OB-43G
Olympia, WA 98504
206/753-2502

West Virginia
Commission on Aging
State Capitol
Charleston, WV 25305
304/348-3317

Wisconsin
Department of Health
and Social Services
1 West Wilson Street
Room 686
Madison, WI 53703
608/266-2536

Wyoming
Commission on Aging
Hathaway Building
Room 139
Cheyenne, WY 82002
307/777-7986

APPENDIX VI

Living Will

[SAMPLE]*
DECLARATION

Declaration made this _____ day of
_____, 198 __ .

I, _____, being of
sound mind, willfully and voluntarily make known
my desires that my dying shall not be artificially prolonged under the circumstances set forth below, and
do declare:

If, at any time, I should have an incurable injury,
disease, or illness certified to be a terminal condition
by two (2) physicians who have personally examined
me, one of whom shall be my attending physician,
and the physicians have determined that my death
will occur whether or not life-sustaining procedures
would serve only to artificially prolong the dying
process, I direct that such procedures be withheld or
withdrawn and that I be permitted to die naturally
with only the administration of medication or the performance of any medical procedure deemed necessary
to provide me with comfort, care or to alleviate pain.

In the absence of my ability to give directions regarding the use of such life-sustaining procedures, it
is my intention that this declaration shall be honored
by my family and physician(s) as the final expression
of my legal right to refuse medical or surgical treatment and accept the consequences from such refusal.

I understand the full import of this declaration and I
am emotionally and mentally competent to make this
declaration.

Signed _____

Address _____

_____

I believe the declarant to be of sound mind. I did not
sign the declarant's signature above for or at the direction of the declarant. I am at least 18 years of age and
am not related to the declarant by blood or marriage.

I am not entitled to any portion of the estate of the
declarant according to the laws of intestate succession
of the _____ or under any will of the
declarant or codicil thereto, or directly financially responsible for the declarant's medical care. I am not the
declarant's attending physician, an employee of the
attending physician, or an employee of the health
facility in which the declarant is a patient.

Witness _____

Address _____

_____

Witness _____

Address _____

_____

ss.:

Before me, the undersigned authority, on this
_____ day of _____, 19 __, personally appeared _____
and _____ known to me
to be the declarant and the witness, respectively,
whose names are signed to the foregoing instrument,
and who, in the presence of each other, did subscribe
their names to the attached Declaration (Living Will)
on this date and that said declarant at the time of
execution of said Declaration was over the age of
eighteen (18) years and of sound mind.

(SEAL)

My commission expires:

_____

_____

Notary Public

* Check requirements of individual state statute.
Source: President's Commission for the Study of Ethical
Problems in Medicine and Biobehavioral Research, "Deciding To Forego Life Sustaining Treatment," U.S. Government Printing Office, pages 314-315.

APPENDIX VII

Durable Power of Attorney for Health Care

[SAMPLE]*

I, _____ hereby appoint:

_____
name

_____
home address

_____

_____
home telephone number

_____
work telephone number

as my agent to make health care decisions for me if and when I am unable to make my own health care decisions. This gives my agent the power to consent to giving, withholding or stopping any health care, treatment, service, or diagnostic procedure. My agent also has the authority to talk with health care personnel, get information, and sign forms necessary to carry out those decisions.

If the person named as my agent is not available or is unable to act as my agent then I appoint the following person(s) to serve in the order listed below:

1. _____
    name

_____
home address

_____

_____
home telephone number

_____
work telephone number

*Check requirements of individual state statute.
Source: *A Matter of Choice: Planning Ahead for Health Care Decisions* distributed by American Association for Retired Persons.

2. _____
    name

_____
home address

_____

_____
home telephone

_____
work telephone

By this document I intend to create a power of attorney for health care which shall take effect upon my incapacity to make my own health care decisions and shall continue during that incapacity.

My agent shall make health care decisions as I direct below or as I make known to him or her in some other way.

(a) STATEMENT OF DESIRES CONCERNING LIFE-PROLONGING CARE, TREATMENT, SERVICES, AND PROCEDURES:

_____

_____

_____

_____

_____

(b) SPECIAL PROVISIONS AND LIMITATIONS:

_____

_____

_____

_____

BY SIGNING HERE I INDICATE THAT I UNDERSTAND THE PURPOSE AND EFFECT OF THIS DOCUMENT.

I sign my name to this form on _____ .
                                (date)

My current home address: _____

_____

_____

_____
(you sign here)

WITNESSES

I declare that the person who signed or acknowledged this document is personally known to me, that he/she signed or acknowledged this durable power of attorney in my presence, and that he/she appears to be of sound mind and under no duress, fraud, or undue influence. I am not the person appointed as agent by this document, nor am I the patient's health care provider, or an employee of the patient's health care provider.

First Witness

Signature: _____

Home Address: _____

Print Name: _____

Date: _____

Second Witness

Signature: _____

Home Address: _____

Print Name: _____

Date: _____

(AT LEAST ONE OF THE ABOVE WITNESSES MUST ALSO SIGN THE FOLLOWING DECLARATION.)

I further declare that I am not related to the patient by blood, marriage, or adoption, and, to the best of my knowledge, I am not entitled to any part of his/her estate under a will now existing or by operation of law.

Signature: _____

Signature: _____

APPENDIX VIII

Bibliography

Aging

Averyt, Anne C. **Successful Aging. A Sourcebook for Older People and Their Families**. New York: Ballantine Books, 1987.

Butler, Robert N. **Why Survive? Being Old in America.** New York: Harper and Row, 1985.

Downs, Hugh and Richard Roll. **The Best Years Book**. New York: Dell Publishing Co., Inc., 1982.

Dychtwald, Ken. **Wellness and Health Promotion for the Elderly.** Rockville, MD: Aspen Publications, 1986.

Dychtwald, Ken. **The Age Wave.** Los Angeles: Jeremy P. Tarcher, Inc., 1989.

Fries, J.F. and L.M. Crapo. **Vitality and Aging**. San Francisco: W.H. Freeman, 1981.

Maddox, George L. **The Encyclopedia of Aging.** New York: Springer Publishing Company, 1987.

Pelletier, Kenneth. **Longevity. Fulfilling Our Biological Potential.** New York: Delacorte Press/Seymour Lawrence, 1981.

The Travelers Companies. **America's Aging Workforce. A Monograph of Proceedings From a Leadership Symposium**. Hartford, CT: The Travelers National Accounts Group, 1986.

LifeSkills: Exercise, Nutrition, Stress Management, etc.

Alpert, Joseph. **The Heart Attack Handbook**. Boston: Little, Brown and Company, 1984.

Benson, H. and M. Lipper. **The Relaxation Response.** New York: Avon Books, 1976.

Bolles, Richard N. **The Three Boxes of Life. An Introduction to Life/Work Planning.** Berkeley, CA: Ten Speed Press, 1981.

Borysenko, Joan. **Minding the Body, Mending the Mind.** Reading, MA: Addison-Wesley Publishing Company, 1987.

Brody, Jane. **Jane Brody's Nutrition Book**. New York: New York Times/Bantam Books, 1982.

Brown, Barbara. **New Mind, New Body**. New York: McGraw-Hill, 1976.

Cooper, Kenneth H. **The New Aerobics.** New York: M. Evans and Company, 1970.

Cooper, Kenneth H. **The Aerobics Way.** New York: M. Evans and Company, 1977.

Dishmen, Rod K. **Exercise Adherence: Its Impact on Public Health.** Champaign, IL: Human Kinetics Books, 1988.

Eliot, Robert and Dennis Breo. **Is It Worth Dying For?** New York: Bantam Books, 1984.

Ferguson, Tom. **The Smoker's Book of Health.** New York: G.P. Putnam's Sons, 1987.

Friedman, Meyer and Ray Rosenman. **Type A Behavior and Your Heart**. New York: Knopf, 1974.

Hipp, Earl. **Fighting Invisible Tigers. A Student Guide to Life In "The Jungle."** Minneapolis: Free Spirit Publishing Co., 1985.

Klein, Robert. **The Money Book of Money. Your Personal Financial Planner**. Boston: Little, Brown and Company, 1987.

Loeb, Marshall. **Marshall Loeb's 1987 Money Guide**. Boston: Little, Brown and Company, 1987.

Mackensie, R. Alec. **The Time Trap. How to Get More Done in Less Time.** New York: McGraw-Hill Book Company, 1972.

Office of Disease Prevention and Health Promotion. **Disease Prevention/Health Promotion. The Facts**. Palo Alto, CA: Dell Publishing Company, 1988.

Ostrander, Sheila and Lynn Schroeder. **Super-Learning.** New York: Dell Publishing Co., 1979.

Pelletier, Kenneth R. **Mind as Healer, Mind as Slayer. A Holistic Approach to Preventing Stress Disorders.** New York: Dell Publishing, 1977.

Porcino, Jane. **Growing Older, Getting Better. A Handbook for Women in the Second Half of Life.** Reading, MA: Addison-Wesley Publishing Company, 1983.

Selye, Hans. **The Stress of Life**. New York: McGraw-Hill, 1976.

Sheehan, George. **Running and Being. The Total Experience**. New York: Warner Books, 1978.

Smith, Everett L. **Exercise and Aging: The Scientific Basis.** Hillside, NJ: Enslow Publishers, 1981.

Stroebel, Charles F. **QR. The Quieting Reflex.** New York: Berkley Books, 1982.

Sweetgall, Robert. **Rockport's Fitness Walking.** New York: Perigree Books, 1985.

Vickery, Donald M. **Taking Part. The Consumer's Guide to the Hospital.** Reston, VA: Center for Corporate Health Promotion, 1986.

Vickery, Donald M. **LifePlan For Your Health.** Reston, VA: Vicktor, Inc., 1984.

Vickery, Donald M. and James F. Fries. **Take Care of Yourself. The Consumer's Guide to Medical Care.** Reading, MA: Addison-Wesley Publishing Company, 1986.

Weil, Andrew and Winifred Rosen. **Chocolate to Morphine. Understanding Mind-Active Drugs.** Boston: Houghton Mifflin Company, 1982.

Winston, Stephanie. **Getting Organized.** New York: Warner Books, 1978.

Chronic Ailments

Bennett, W.I., S.E. Goldfinger and T.G. Johnson. **Your Good Health. How to Stay Well, and What To Do When You're Not.** Cambridge, MA: Harvard University Press, 1987.

Bernheim, Kayla F., et al. **The Caring Family. Living with Chronic Mental Illness.** New York: Random House, 1982.

Fries, James F. **Arthritis. A Comprehensive Guide.** Reading, MA: Addison-Wesley Publishing Company, 1979.

Holleb, Arthur I. **The American Cancer Society Cancer Book.** Garden City, NY: Doubleday & Company, 1986.

Mace, Nancy L. and Peter V. Rabins. **The 36-Hour Day.** Baltimore: John Hopkins University Press, 1982.

Morra, Marion and Eve Potts. **Choices.** New York: Avon Books, 1987.

National Diabetes Clearinghouse. **Non-Insulin Dependent Diabetes.** Clearinghouse, Box NDIC, Bethesda, MD 20892.

National Institute of Mental Health. **Helpful Facts About Depressive Disorders.** 5600 Fishers Lane, Rockville, MD 20857.

National Society to Prevent Blindness. **The Aging Eye: Facts on Eye Care for Older Persons.** 500 E. Remington Road, Schaumberg, IL 60173.

National Institute of Neurological and Communicative Disorders and Stroke. **Hearing Loss: Hope Through Research.** Bethesda, MD 20892.

Powell, Lenore S. and Katie Courtice. **Alzheimer's: A Guide for Families.** Reading, MA: Addison-Wesley Publishing Company, 1982.

Public Citizens Health Research Group. **Cataracts: A Consumer's Guide to Choosing the Best Treatment.** 2000 P Street N.W., Suite 708, Washington, DC 20036.

Long-Term Care

Horne, Jo. **Caregiving: Helping an Aging Loved One.** Mt. Prospect, IL: AARP Books/Scott, Foresman & Co., 1985.

MacLean, Helene. **Caring for Your Parents. A Sourcebook of Options and Solutions for Both Generations.** Garden City, NY: Doubleday & Company, Inc., 1987.

Portnow, Jay and Martha Houtmann. **Home Care for the Elderly. A Complete Guide.** New York: McGraw-Hill Book Company, 1987.

Silverstone, Barbara and Helen Kandel Hyman. **You and Your Aging Parent. The Modern Family's Guide to Emotional, Physical, and Financial Problems.** New York: Pantheon Books, 1982.

Tomb, David A. **Growing Old: A Handbook for You and Your Aging Parents.** New York: Viking Penguin Inc., 1984.

The following are relevant publications of the American Association of Retired Persons. Write: AARP Books, Scott, Foresman and Company, 1865 Miner Street, Des Plaines, IL, 60016. Add $1.75 per total order (not per book) for shipping and handling.

Caregiving. $13.95 (AARP members $9.95)

Essential Guide to Wills, Estates, Trusts and Death Taxes. $12.95 (AARP members $9.45)

It's Your Choice: A Practical Guide to Planning a Funeral. $4.95 (AARP members $3.00)

Planning Your Retirement Housing. $8.95 (AARP members $6.50)

Survival Handbook for Widows. $5.95 (AARP members $4.35)

The Myth of Senility. $14.95 (AARP members $10.85)

The Gadget Book. $10.95 (AARP members $7.95)

Free AARP Resources:

Title	Order Number
To Serve, Not to Be Served	D12028
Join an AARP Chapter	C383
On Being Alone	D150
Housing Options for Older Americans	D12063
Your Home Your Choice	D12143
The Right Place at the Right Time	D12381
A Handbook About Care in the Home	D955
Healthy Questions	D12194
Eating for Your Health	D12164
Information on Medicare and Health Insurance	C38
Miles Away and Still Caring	D12748
Coping and Caring	D12441

To order free AARP resources, send a request listing the title and order number to: AARP Fulfillment Section, 1909 K Street, N.W., Washington, DC 20049.

Index

About the Author

George J. Pfeiffer is a nationally recognized authority on worksite health promotion and author of numerous articles on health and wellness. His works regularly appear in national professional and lay journals. Pfeiffer has been cited in the nation's most respected magazines and newspapers: *Fortune*, *Business Week*, *The New York Times*, and *USA Today*.

An accomplished speaker, Pfeiffer has conducted more than 300 workshops, seminars, and keynotes for such national and international organizations as the Washinton Business Group on Health, the U.S. Department of Energy, the World Health Organization, and the American College of Sports Medicine.

Pfeiffer has served as consultant to the U.S. Department of Health and Human Services, the National Institutes of Health, the State Health Department of Indiana, the University of North Carolina at Ashville, the U.S. Sports Academy, the National YMCA, the American Heart Association, and the American Association for Health, Physical Education, Recreation and Dance. Such Fortune 500 companies as Xerox, General Dynamics, The Travelers Companies and Honeywell have also called on Pfeiffer's expertise and experience of more than 15 years.

He is a trustee and former president of the Association for Fitness in Business, a membership organization of more than 3,000 corporate fitness and health promotion experts. He is also a member of the National Fitness Leaders Association and, in 1984, received the Healthy American Fitness Award presented by the President's Council on Physical Fitness and Sports and the U.S. Jaycees.

A former adjunct assistant professor at the State University of New York at Buffalo, Pfeiffer serves on numerous editorial advisory boards including those of the *American Journal of Health Promotion*, *Fitness and Business*, *Employee Health and Fitness*, and *Corporate Fitness*.

A visionary and advocate of life planning, Pfeiffer is vice president of the Center For Corporate Health Promotion in Reston, Virginia, where he directs product development and program evaluation.

HELP US IMPROVE TAKING CARE OF TODAY AND TOMORROW

*Receive a Chance to Win a FREE Medical Self-Care Library
Valued at Over $100*

The Center for Corporate Health Promotion, publisher of this book, continually strives to improve its products. Your input is essential. Your opinion can help us better meet your needs and interests.

Please help us by completing and returning the following survey. In appreciation, you will receive a chance to win a medical self-care library worth over $100.

All responses will be kept confidential, but remember to include your name and address.

Winners will be selected via a random drawing from every 1,000 responses received; one prize will be awarded per drawing. The first drawing will not be held until 1,000 responses have been received. Entrants are eligible for only one random drawing. Odds of winning: 1 in 1,000. Winners will be notified by mail. This promotion will continue from January 1, 1990, to December 31, 1991. Void where prohibited by law.

How much of the book *Taking Care of Today and Tomorrow* have you read?

_____ All of it (100%)
_____ Most of it (65%-99%)
_____ Some of it (30%-64%)
_____ Little of it (1%-29%)
_____ None of it (0%)

Which of the following self-tests or planning areas have you completed?

_____ What's Your Aging I.Q.?
_____ LifeSkills Inventory
_____ What's Your Stress Style?
_____ What Are the Changes in Your Life?
_____ Net Worth Worksheet
_____ Budget Worksheet
_____ Do You Have a Substance Abuse Problem?
_____ Developing a Self-Management Plan

For each question or statement, please mark the number on the scale that is closest to your opinion. If you cannot answer the question (if you don't know the answer or the question does not apply to you) mark the NA found to the right of the scale. Note: Zero is a neutral response indicating that you have no opinion or there was no effect.

1. How understandable is *Taking Care of Today and Tomorrow?*

Very understandable	No opinion			Very confusing			
3	2	1	0	−1	−2	−3	NA

2. How has *Taking Care of Today and Tomorrow* changed your understanding of lifestyle and its role in healthy aging?

Increased understanding	No effect			Increased confusion			
3	2	1	0	−1	−2	−3	NA

3. How has *Taking Care of Today and Tomorrow* changed your health-related skills (knowing how to plan an exercise or diet program, how to plan for long-term care, etc.)?

Increased skills	No effect			Decreased skills			
3	2	1	0	−1	−2	−3	NA

4. How has *Taking Care of Today and Tomorrow* changed your practice of healthy behavior (staying active, eating well, managing stress, etc.)?

Increased behavior	No effect			Decreased behavior			
3	2	1	0	−1	−2	−3	NA

5. How has *Taking Care of Today and Tomorrow* changed your understanding of the common chronic ailments associated with adulthood?

Increased understanding	No effect			Increased confusion			
3	2	1	0	−1	−2	−3	NA

6. How has *Taking Care of Today and Tomorrow* affected your understanding of when to seek medical screening tests or services (blood pressure tests, Pap test, etc.)?

Increased understanding	No effect			Increased confusion			
3	2	1	0	−1	−2	−3	NA

7. How has *Taking Care of Today and Tomorrow* changed your understanding of long-term care?

Increased understanding	No effect			Increased confusion			
3	2	1	0	−1	−2	−3	NA

8. How has *Taking Care of Today and Tomorrow* affected your understanding of how to seek financial support for long-term care?

Increased understanding	No effect			Decreased understanding			
3	2	1	0	−1	−2	−3	NA

9. How has *Taking Care of Today and Tomorrow* changed your understanding of caregiving resources?

Increased understanding	No effect			Increased confusion			
3	2	1	0	−1	−2	−3	NA

10. About how many times have you referred to *Taking Care of Today and Tomorrow* for information on community resources for caregiving assistance?

0	1	2	3	4	5	6+	NA

11. About how many times have you referred to *Taking Care of Today and Tomorrow* for information on public financing for caregiving services?

  0   1   2   3   4   5   6+   NA

12. About how many times have you referred to *Taking Care of Today and Tomorrow* for information on private insurance coverage for caregiving services?

  0   1   2   3   4   5   6+   NA

13. How has *Taking Care of Today and Tomorrow* affected the level of stress you experience from caregiving responsibilities?

Decreased stress	No effect			Increased stress			
3	2	1	0	−1	−2	−3	NA

14. How has *Taking Care of Today and Tomorrow* affected your absence from work due to caregiving-related responsibilities?

Decreased absence	No effect			Increased absence			
3	2	1	0	−1	−2	−3	NA

15. How has *Taking Care of Today and Tomorrow* affected your absence from work due to stress and lifestyle-related illnesses?

Decreased absence	No effect			Increased absence			
3	2	1	0	−1	−2	−3	NA

16. How has *Taking Care of Today and Tomorrow* affected your health and/or the health of your family?

Increased health	No effect			Decreased health			
3	2	1	0	−1	−2	−3	NA

17. How do you rate *Taking Care of Today and Tomorrow* as a source of advice on lifestyle?

Very valuable	No opinion			Worthless			
3	2	1	0	−1	−2	−3	NA

18. How do you rate *Taking Care of Today and Tomorrow* as a source of advice on the prevention, treatment and prognosis of common chronic ailments?

Very valuable	No opinion			Worthless			
3	2	1	0	−1	−2	−3	NA

19. How do you rate *Taking Care of Today and Tomorrow* as a source of advice on long-term care issues and options?

Very valuable	No opinion			Worthless			
3	2	1	0	−1	−2	−3	NA

20. How do you rate *Taking Care of Today and Tomorrow* as an employee health care benefit?

Very valuable	No opinion			Worthless			
3	2	1	0	−1	−2	−3	NA

21. How has *Taking Care of Today and Tomorrow* affected your opinion of your employer regarding its concern for the well-being of employees and their families?

Improved opinion	No opinion			Decreased opinion			
3	2	1	0	−1	−2	−3	NA

22. Your employer should continue to provide other self-care or health promotion products or services.

Strongly agree	No opinion			Strongly Disagree			
3	2	1	0	−1	−2	−3	NA

Demographics

Age:
____ ◄20
____ 20-29
____ 30-39
____ 40-49
____ 50-59
____ ►60

Gender:
____ Male
____ Female

Race:
____ Asian
____ Black
____ Caucasian
____ Hispanic
____ American Indian
____ Polynesian
____ Other

Education:
____ Some high school/vocational school or less
____ High school/vocational school graduate
____ Some college
____ College graduate (4-year degree)
____ Some graduate course work
____ Graduate/professional degree

Job Function:
____ Clerical/secretarial
____ Computer specialist (programmer, analyst, etc.)
____ Foreman/supervisor
____ Laborer
____ Manager/administrator
____ Production/assembly line
____ Professional
____ Sales
____ Skilled tradesman/technician
____ Other

Household Status:
Including yourself, how many people reside in your household?

1   2   3   4   5   6   7   8+

Are you or is someone in your household the primary caregiver for an older relative/loved one? (Caregiving is defined as providing care for a relative or friend aged 55 or older, in need of your time or help due to illness or other limitation.)

____ yes   ____ no

Will you or will someone in your household be responsible for the care of an elderly individual in the near future?

____ yes   ____ no

Does the older relative or loved one for whom you or another currently or will provide care reside in your household? (Caregiving is defined as providing care for a relative or friend aged 55 or older, in need of your time or help due to illness or other limitation.)

____ yes   ____ no

Name: _____

Address: _____

_____

Telephone: _____
          (optional)

Mail your completed surveys (facsimiles accepted, no purchase necessary) to:

TCTT Research

The Center For Corporate Health Promotion

1850 Centennial Park Drive

Suite 520

Reston, Virginia 22091